The AMAZING SPIDER-MAN

WORLDWIDE

DAN SLOTT
WITH CHRISTOS GAGE (#5)
WRITERS

GIUSEPPE CAMUNCOLI
PENCILER

CAM SMITH
INKER

MARTE GRACIA
COLORIST

VC'S JOE CARAMAGNA (#1-2 & #4-5)
& CHRIS ELIOPOULOS (#3)
LETTERERS

+

"BREAKING BAD"
WRITER: ROBBIE THOMPSON
ARTIST: STACEY LEE
COLORIST: IAN HERRING
LETTERER: VC'S TRAVIS LANHAM

"WHAT TO EXPECT"
WRITER: DENNIS HOPELESS
PENCILER/COLORIST: JAVIER RODRIGUEZ
INKER: ALVARO LOPEZ
LETTERER: VC'S TRAVIS LANHAM

"THE CELLAR"
WRITERS: DAN SLOTT & CHRISTOS GAGE
ARTIST: PACO DIAZ
COLORIST: ISRAEL SILVA
LETTERER: VC'S JOE CARAMAGNA

"THE SPIDER'S CORNER WITH PETEY P."
WRITER/ARTIST/LETTERER: ANTHONY HOLDEN
COLORIST: JORDIE BELLAIRE

ALEX ROSS
COVER ART

DEVIN LEWIS
ASSISTANT EDITOR

NICK LOWE
EDITOR

SPIDER-MAN CREATED BY
STAN LEE & STEVE DITKO

COLLECTION EDITOR: JENNIFER GRÜNWALD
ASSOCIATE EDITOR: SARAH BRUNSTAD
ASSOCIATE MANAGING EDITOR: ALEX ST...
EDITOR, SPECIAL PROJECTS: MARK D. ...

VP, PRODUCTION & SPECIAL PROJECTS: JEFF YOUNGQUIST
SVP PRINT, SALES & MARKETING: DAVID GABRIEL
BOOK DESIGNER: JAY BOWEN

EDITOR IN CHIEF: AXEL ALONSO
CHIEF CREATIVE OFFICER: JOE QUESADA
PUBLISHER: DAN BUCKLEY
...UTIVE PRODUCER: ALAN FINE

...ING SPIDER-MAN: WORLDWIDE VOL. 1. Contains material orig... ...51-9942-7. Published by MARVEL WORLDWIDE, INC., a subsidia...
...EL ENTERTAINMENT, LLC. OFFICE OF PUBLICATION: 135 West 5... ...aracters, persons, and/or institutions in this magazine with th...
...ving or dead person or institution is intended, and any such simil... ...ment; DAN BUCKLEY, President, TV, Publishing & Brand Mana...
...UESADA, Chief Creative Officer; TOM BREVOORT, SVP of Publis... ...VP of Brand Management & Development, Asia; DAVID GAB...
...es & Marketing, Publishing; JEFF YOUNGQUIST, VP of Production... ...of Publishing Operations; SUSAN CRESPI, Production Man...
...Chairman Emeritus. For information regarding advertising in Mar... ...el.com. For Marvel subscription inquiries, please call 88...
...facturel between 2/12/2016 and 3/21/2016 by SOLISCO PRINTERS, SCOTT, QC, CANADA.

87654321

WHEN PETER PARKER WAS BITTEN BY A RADIOACTIVE SPIDER, HE GAINED THE PROPORTIONAL SPEED, STRENGTH, AND AGILITY OF A SPIDER, ADHESIVE FINGERTIPS AND TOES, AND THE UNIQUE PRECOGNITIVE AWARENESS OF DANGER CALLED "SPIDER-SENSE!" AFTER LEARNING THAT WITH GREAT POWER THERE MUST ALSO COME GREAT RESPONSIBILTY, HE BECAME THE CRIME-FIGHTING SUPER HERO CALLED...

The AMAZING SPIDER-MAN

SPIDEY'S GONE GLOBAL!

PETER PARKER HAS ALWAYS HAD SOMETHING GOING WRONG IN HIS LIFE, EITHER AS HIMSELF OR AS HIS WEB-SWINGING, WALL-CRAWLING ALTER EGO, THE AMAZING SPIDER-MAN. BUT, AFTER YEARS OF VANQUISHING VILLAINS, IT LOOKS LIKE HE'S FINALLY MANAGED TO GET HIS ACT TOGETHER.

HIS "FRIENDLY NEIGHBORHOOD" JUST GOT A WHOLE LOT BIGGER!

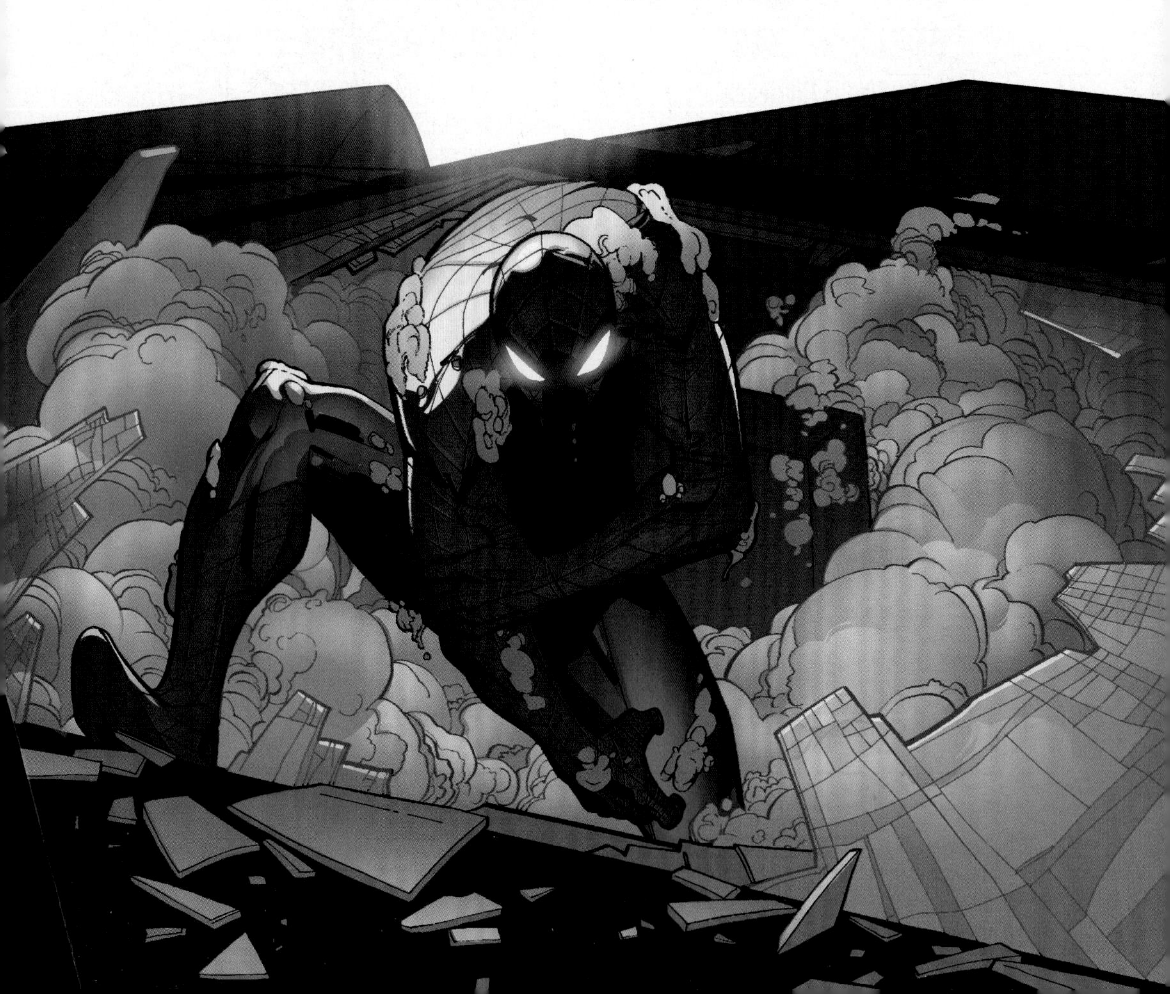

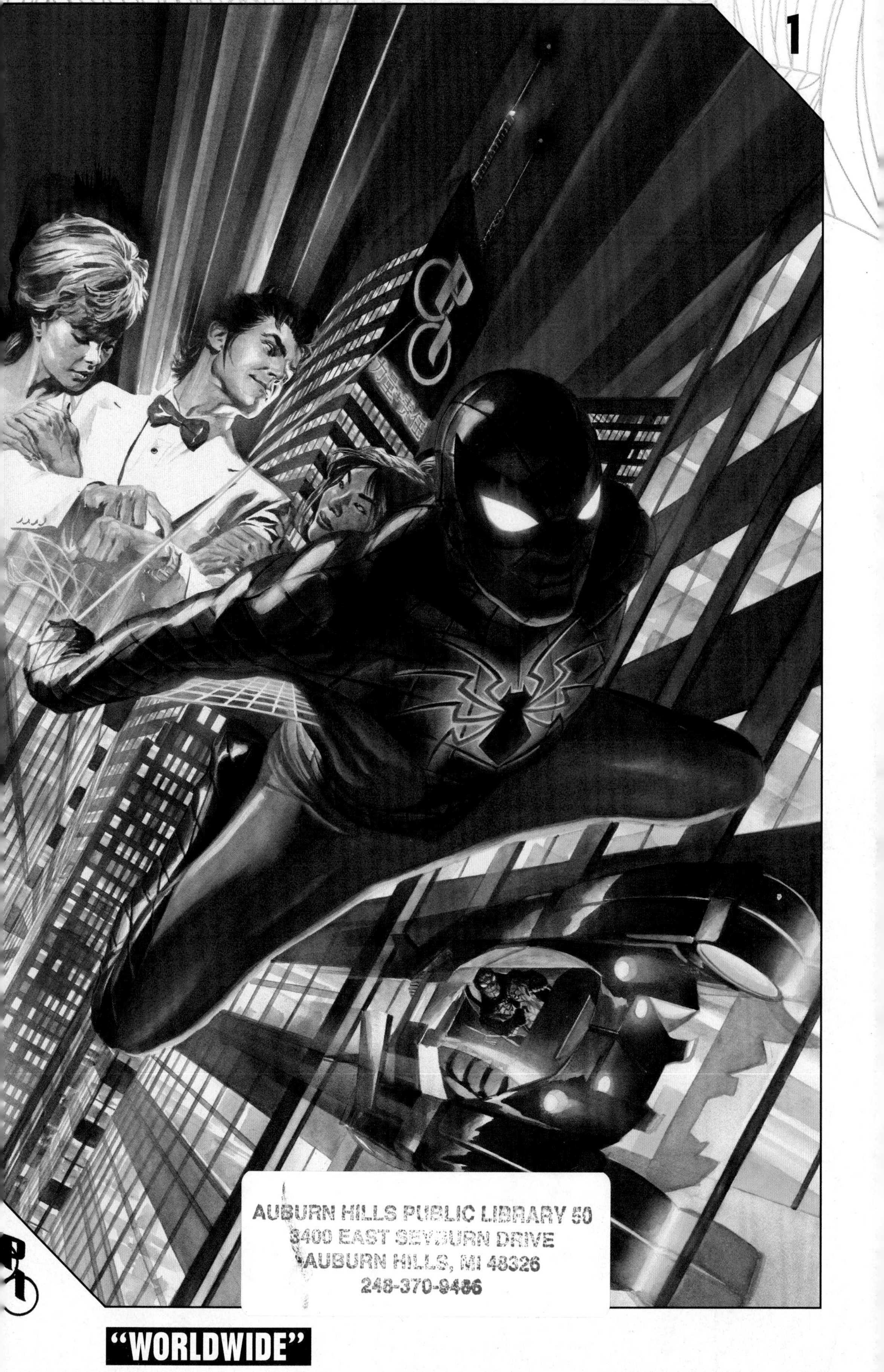

"WORLDWIDE"

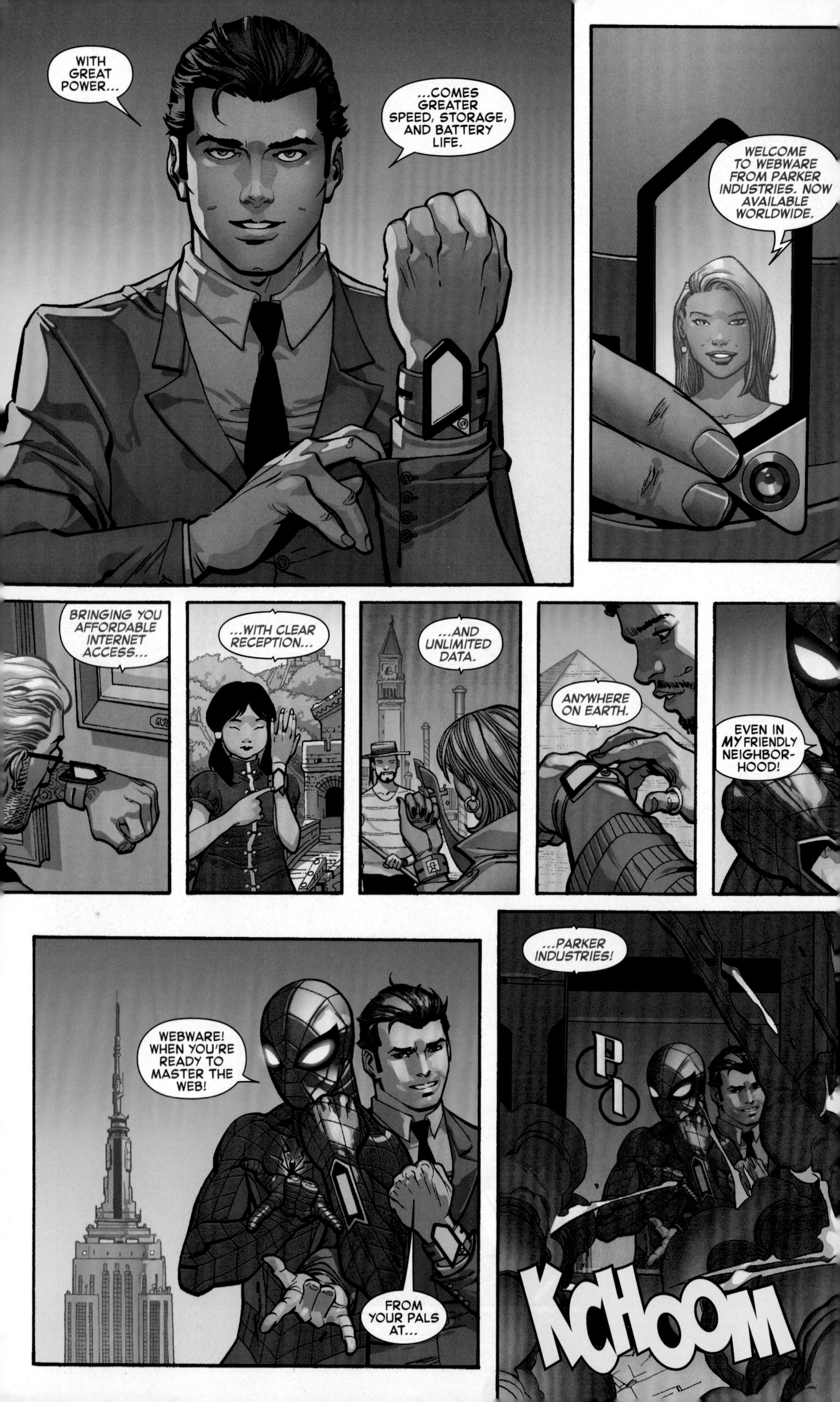
WITH GREAT POWER...
...COMES GREATER SPEED, STORAGE, AND BATTERY LIFE.
WELCOME TO WEBWARE FROM PARKER INDUSTRIES. NOW AVAILABLE WORLDWIDE.
BRINGING YOU AFFORDABLE INTERNET ACCESS...
...WITH CLEAR RECEPTION...
...AND UNLIMITED DATA.
ANYWHERE ON EARTH.
EVEN IN MY FRIENDLY NEIGHBOR-HOOD!
WEBWARE! WHEN YOU'RE READY TO MASTER THE WEB!
FROM YOUR PALS AT...
...PARKER INDUSTRIES!
KCHOOM

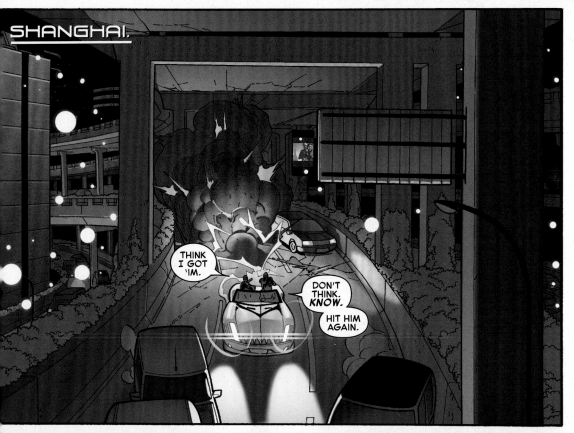

SHANGHAI.

THINK I GOT 'IM.

DON'T THINK. KNOW.

HIT HIM AGAIN.

ZRAKKK

<PULL OVER. LET THEM THROUGH.>*

<THEY'RE CRAZY!>

<YOU GETTING THIS?>

<DUDE, I'M PARKER-SCOPING IT LIVE ONTO MY FEED!>

<LOOK! BACK THERE! IS THAT--? IT IS!>

<IT'S SPIDER-MAN!>

*TRANSLATED FROM MANDARIN.

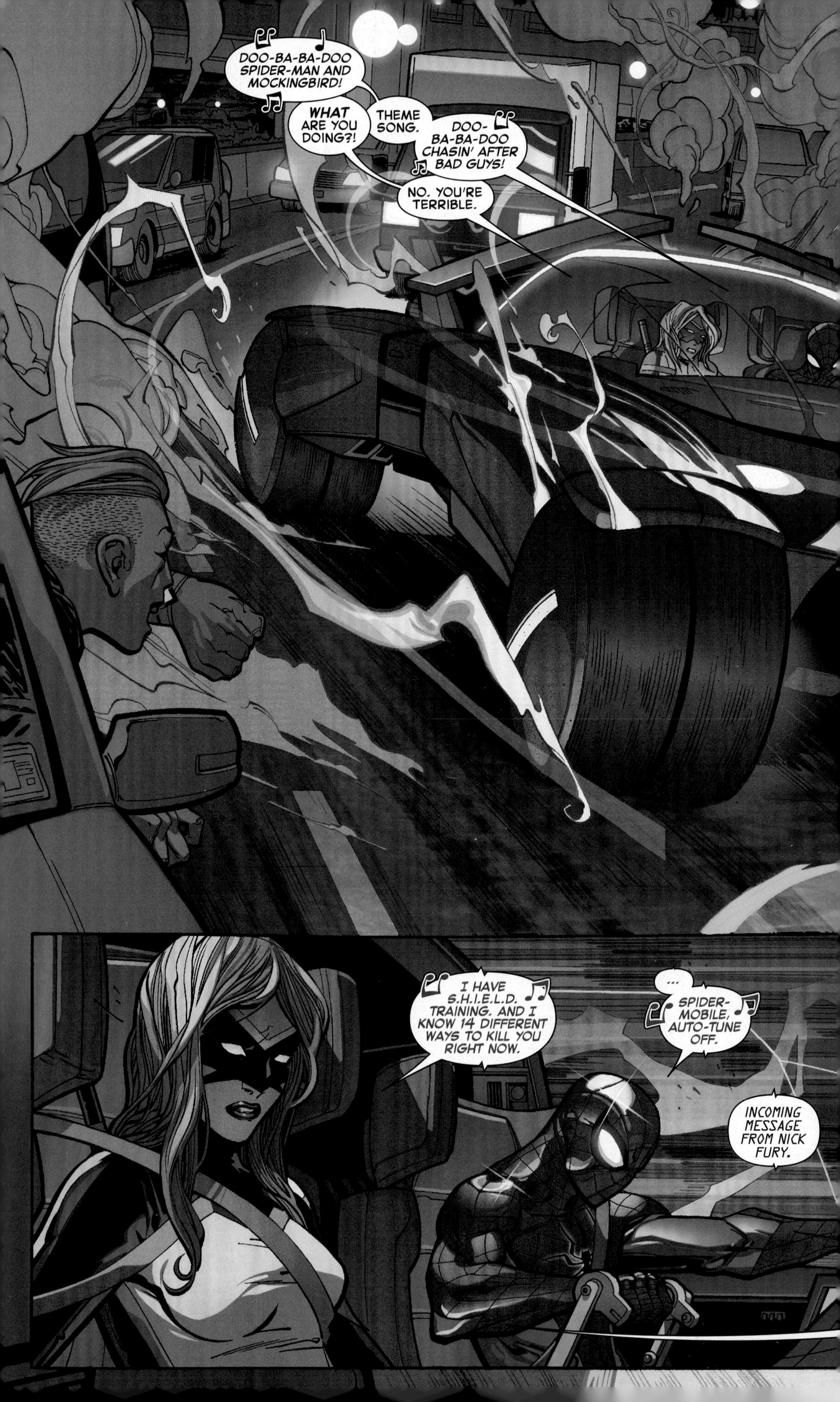

DOO-BA-BA-DOO SPIDER-MAN AND MOCKINGBIRD!
WHAT ARE YOU DOING?!
THEME SONG.
DOO-BA-BA-DOO CHASIN' AFTER BAD GUYS!
NO. YOU'RE TERRIBLE.
I HAVE S.H.I.E.L.D. TRAINING. AND I KNOW 14 DIFFERENT WAYS TO KILL YOU RIGHT NOW.
...
SPIDER-MOBILE, AUTO-TUNE OFF.
INCOMING MESSAGE FROM NICK FURY.

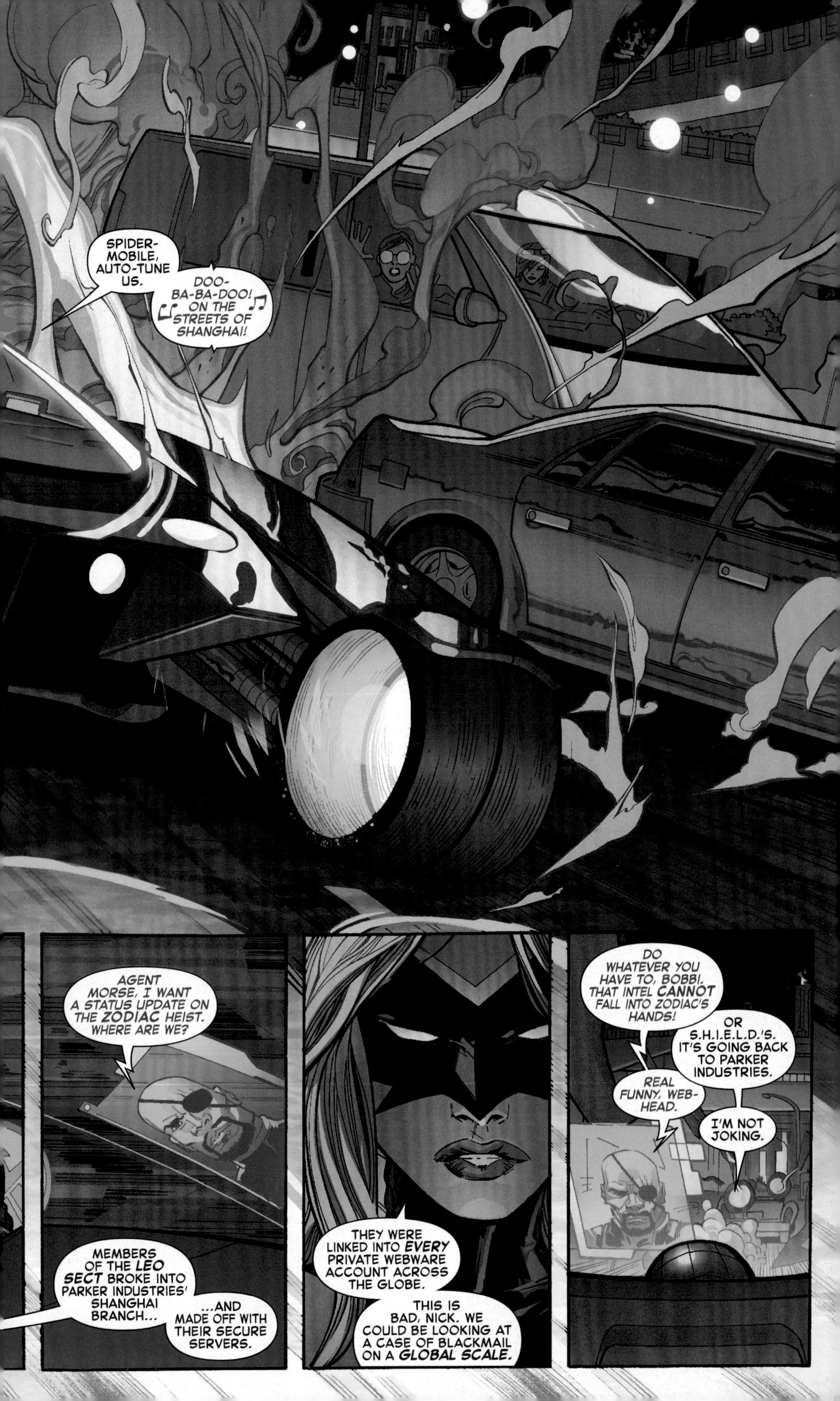
SPIDER-MOBILE, AUTO-TUNE US.
DOO-BA-BA-DOO! ON THE STREETS OF SHANGHAI!
AGENT MORSE, I WANT A STATUS UPDATE ON THE ZODIAC HEIST. WHERE ARE WE?
MEMBERS OF THE LEO SECT BROKE INTO PARKER INDUSTRIES' SHANGHAI BRANCH...
...AND MADE OFF WITH THEIR SECURE SERVERS.
THEY WERE LINKED INTO EVERY PRIVATE WEBWARE ACCOUNT ACROSS THE GLOBE.
THIS IS BAD, NICK. WE COULD BE LOOKING AT A CASE OF BLACKMAIL ON A GLOBAL SCALE.
DO WHATEVER YOU HAVE TO, BOBBI. THAT INTEL CANNOT FALL INTO ZODIAC'S HANDS!
OR S.H.I.E.L.D.'S. IT'S GOING BACK TO PARKER INDUSTRIES.
REAL FUNNY, WEB-HEAD.
I'M NOT JOKING.

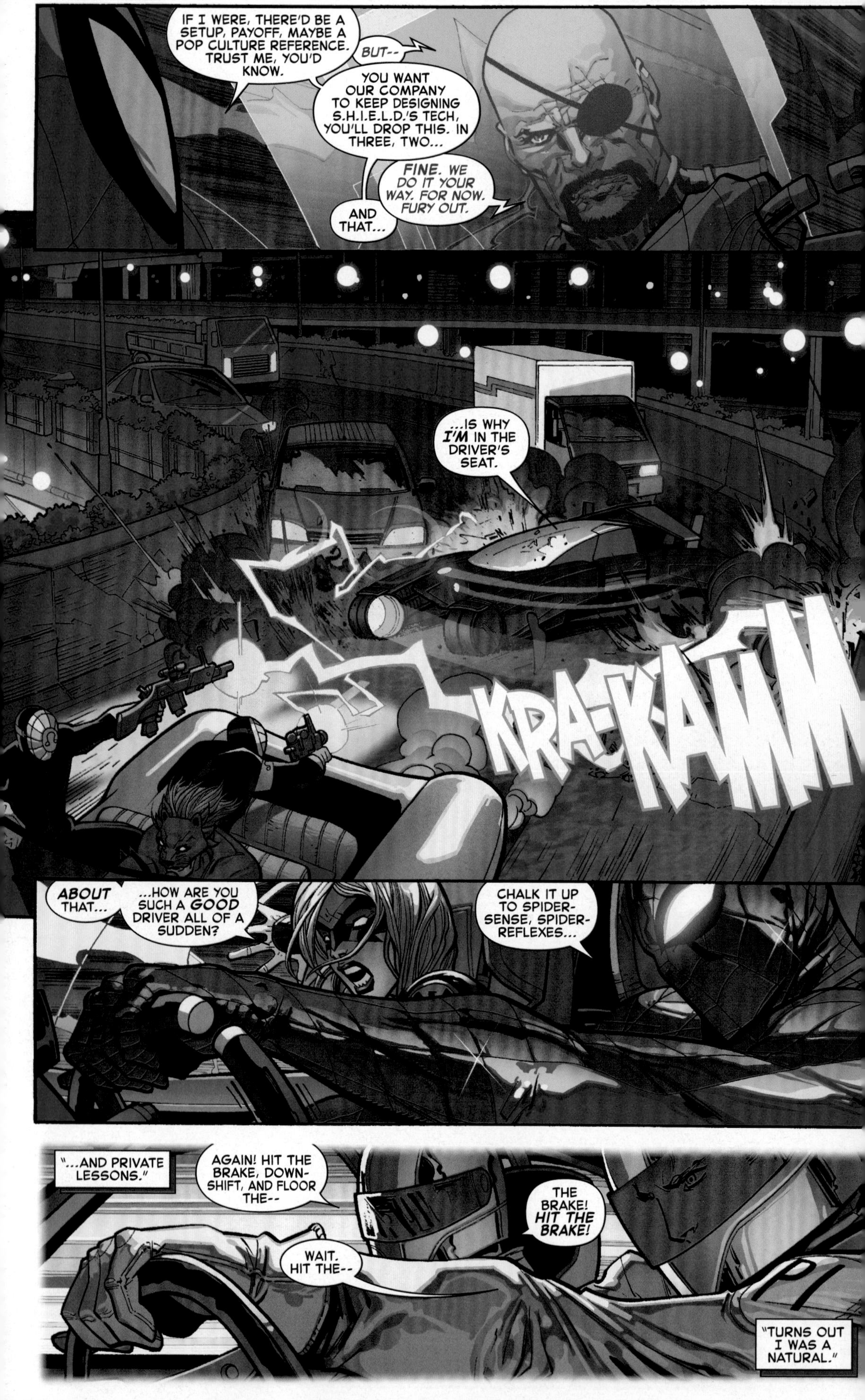

IF I WERE, THERE'D BE A SETUP, PAYOFF, MAYBE A POP CULTURE REFERENCE. TRUST ME, YOU'D KNOW.
BUT--
YOU WANT OUR COMPANY TO KEEP DESIGNING S.H.I.E.L.D.'S TECH, YOU'LL DROP THIS. IN THREE, TWO...
FINE. WE DO IT YOUR WAY. FOR NOW. FURY OUT.
AND THAT...
...IS WHY I'M IN THE DRIVER'S SEAT.
KRA-KAMM
ABOUT THAT...
...HOW ARE YOU SUCH A GOOD DRIVER ALL OF A SUDDEN?
CHALK IT UP TO SPIDER-SENSE, SPIDER-REFLEXES...
"...AND PRIVATE LESSONS."
AGAIN! HIT THE BRAKE, DOWN-SHIFT, AND FLOOR THE--
THE BRAKE! HIT THE BRAKE!
WAIT. HIT THE--
"TURNS OUT I WAS A NATURAL."

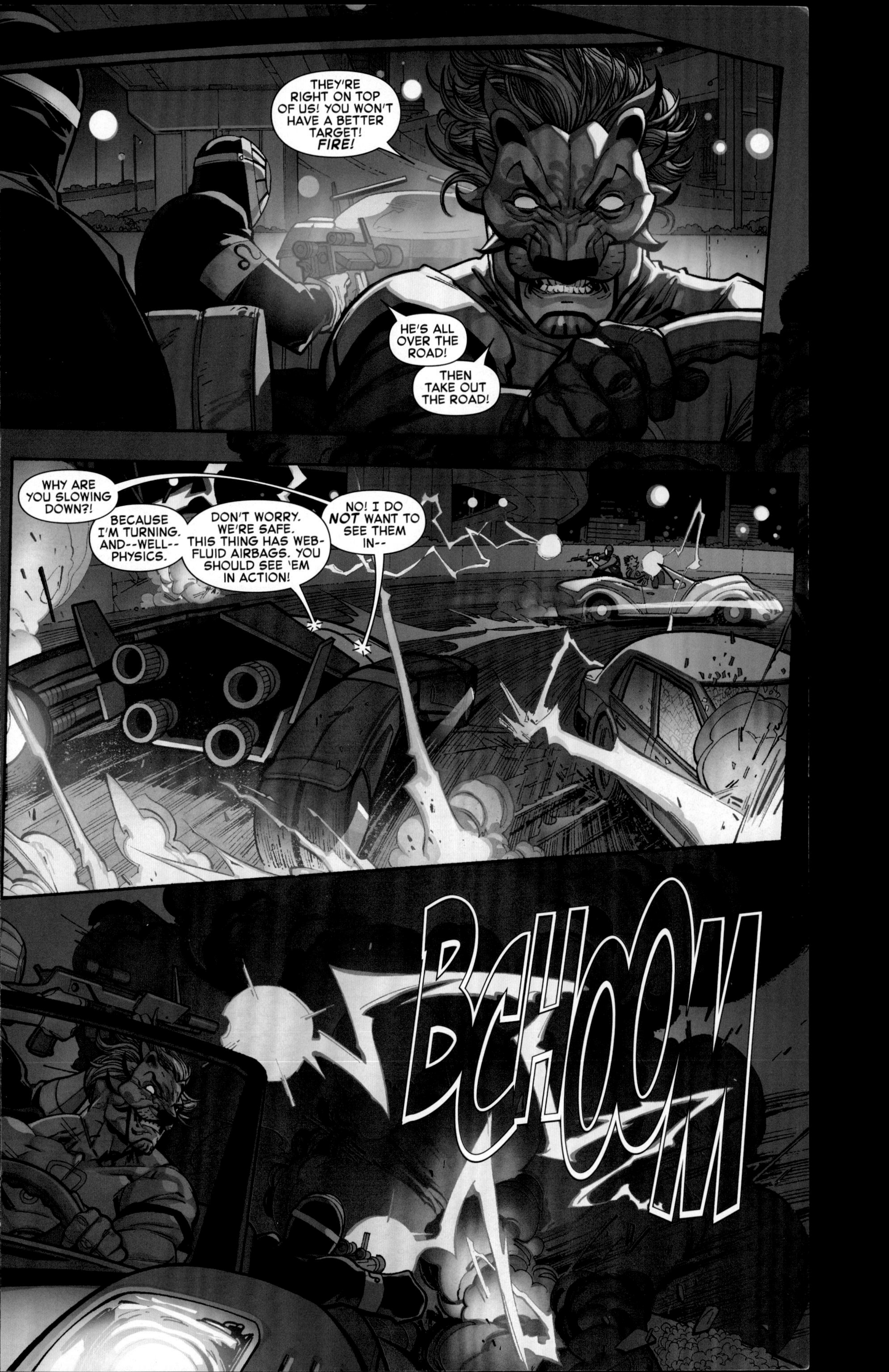
THEY'RE RIGHT ON TOP OF US! YOU WON'T HAVE A BETTER TARGET! FIRE!
HE'S ALL OVER THE ROAD!
THEN TAKE OUT THE ROAD!
WHY ARE YOU SLOWING DOWN?!
BECAUSE I'M TURNING. AND--WELL--PHYSICS.
DON'T WORRY. WE'RE SAFE. THIS THING HAS WEB-FLUID AIRBAGS. YOU SHOULD SEE 'EM IN ACTION!
NO! I DO NOT WANT TO SEE THEM IN--
BAHOOM

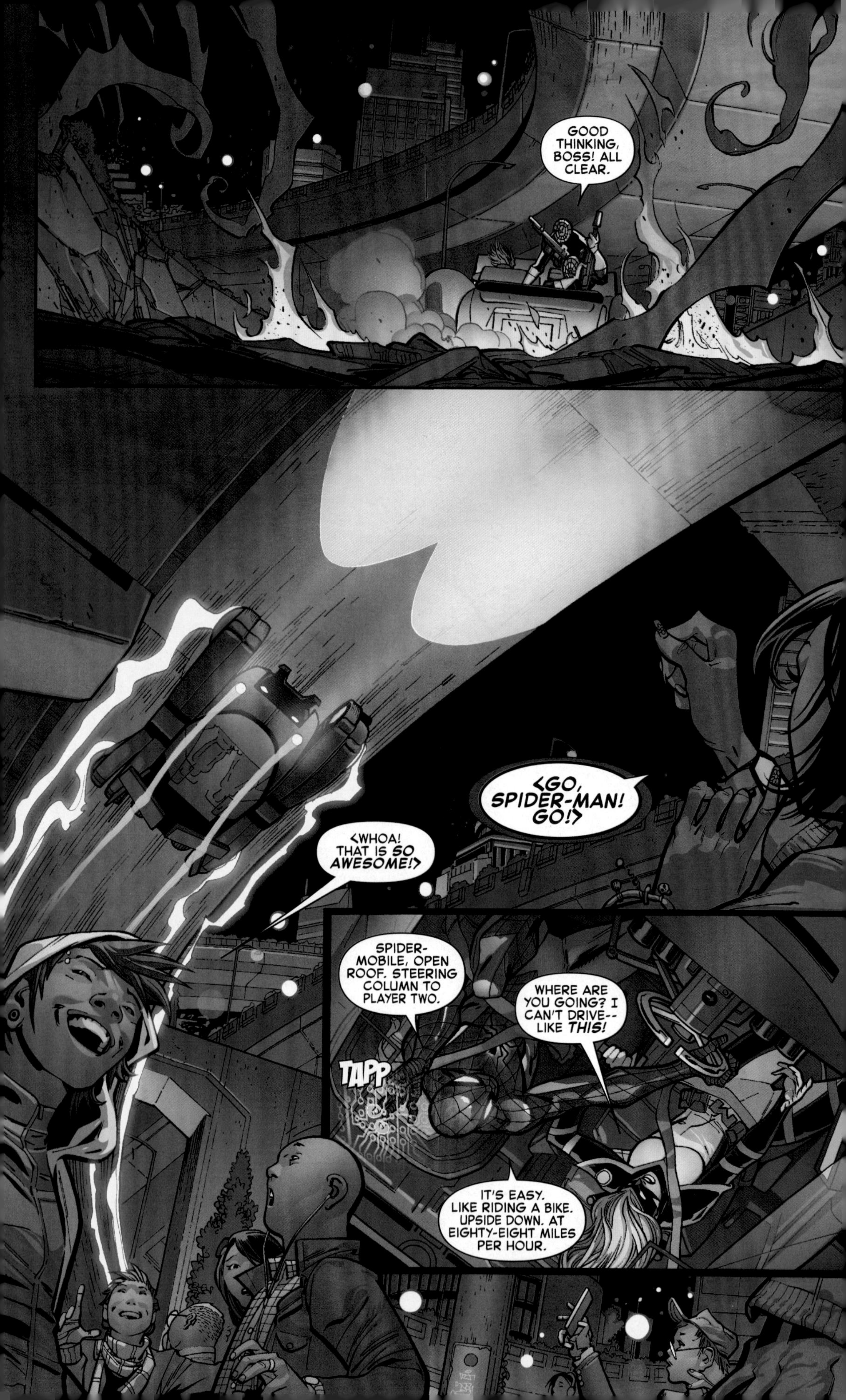
GOOD THINKING, BOSS! ALL CLEAR.
<GO, SPIDER-MAN! GO!>
<WHOA! THAT IS SO AWESOME!>
SPIDER-MOBILE, OPEN ROOF. STEERING COLUMN TO PLAYER TWO.
TAPP
WHERE ARE YOU GOING? I CAN'T DRIVE-- LIKE THIS!
IT'S EASY. LIKE RIDING A BIKE. UPSIDE DOWN. AT EIGHTY-EIGHT MILES PER HOUR.

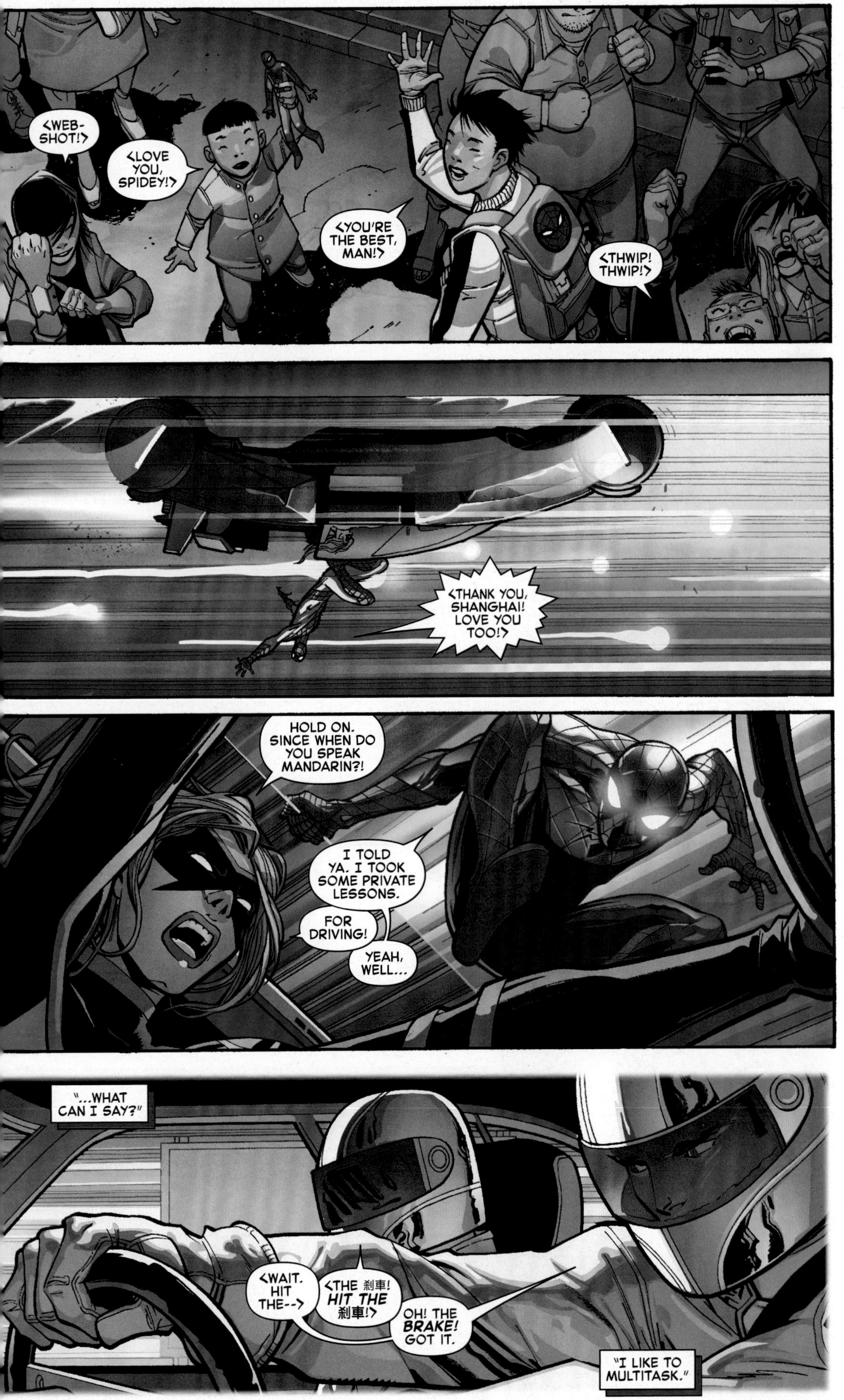
<WEB-SHOT!>
<LOVE YOU, SPIDEY!>
<YOU'RE THE BEST, MAN!>
<THWIP! THWIP!>
<THANK YOU, SHANGHAI! LOVE YOU TOO!>
HOLD ON. SINCE WHEN DO YOU SPEAK MANDARIN?!
I TOLD YA. I TOOK SOME PRIVATE LESSONS.
FOR DRIVING!
YEAH, WELL...
"...WHAT CAN I SAY?"
<WAIT. HIT THE-->
<THE 刹車! HIT THE 刹車!>
OH! THE BRAKE! GOT IT.
"I LIKE TO MULTITASK."

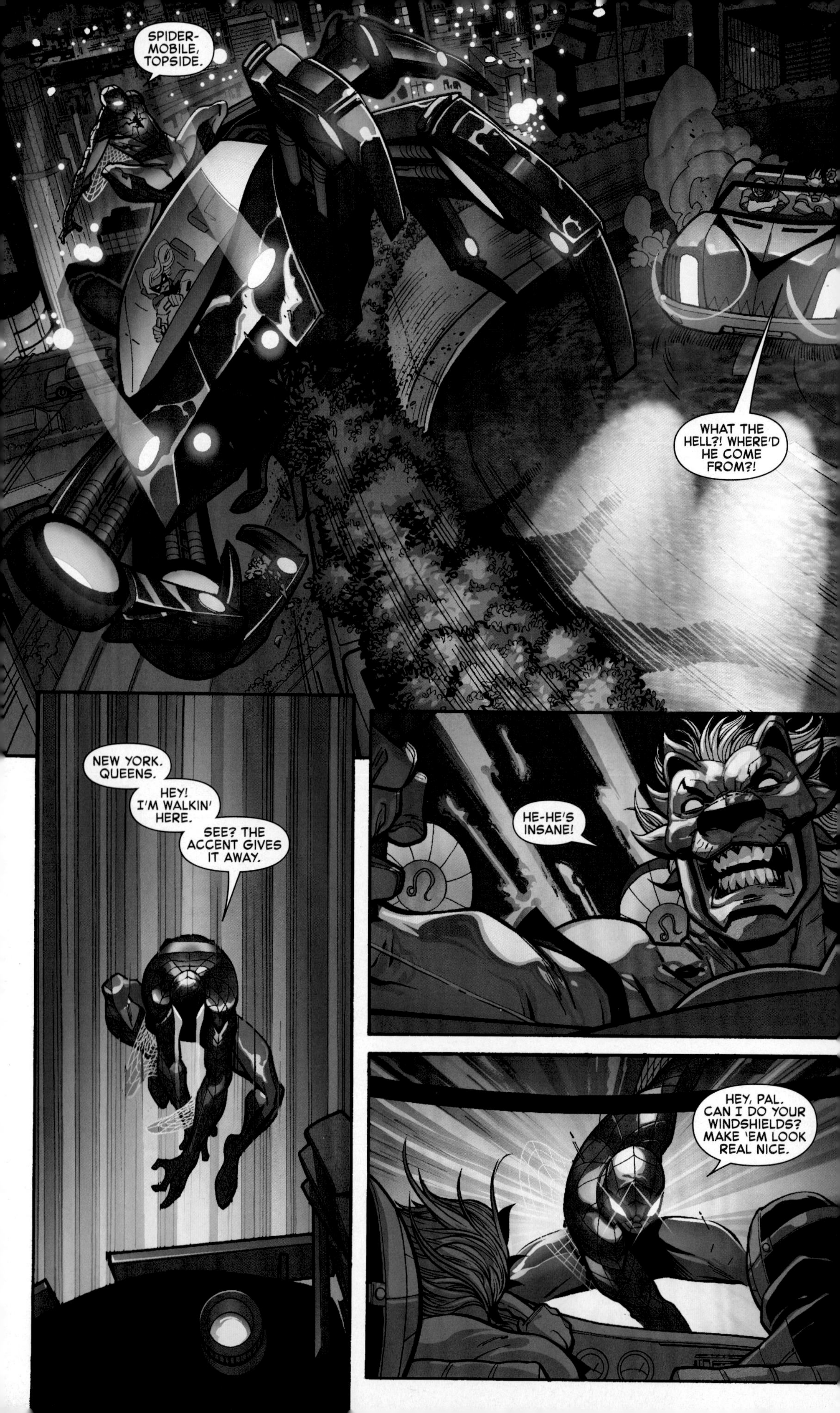
SPIDER-MOBILE, TOPSIDE.
WHAT THE HELL?! WHERE'D HE COME FROM?!
NEW YORK. QUEENS.
HEY! I'M WALKIN' HERE.
SEE? THE ACCENT GIVES IT AWAY.
HE-HE'S INSANE!
HEY, PAL. CAN I DO YOUR WINDSHIELDS? MAKE 'EM LOOK REAL NICE.

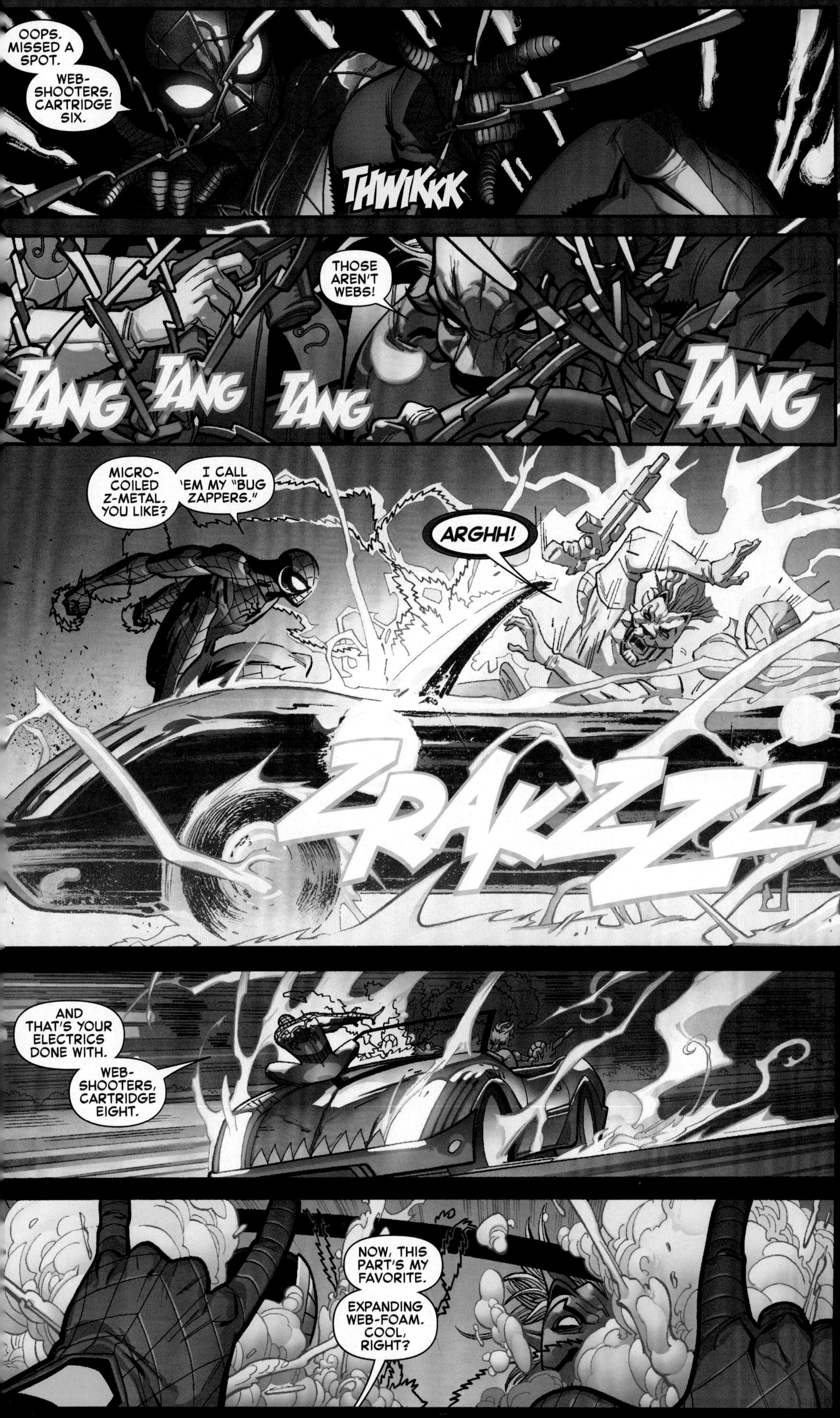
OOPS. MISSED A SPOT.
WEB-SHOOTERS, CARTRIDGE SIX.
THWIKKK
THOSE AREN'T WEBS!
TANG TANG TANG TANG
MICRO-COILED Z-METAL. YOU LIKE?
I CALL 'EM MY "BUG ZAPPERS."
ARGHH!
ZRAKZZZ
AND THAT'S YOUR ELECTRICS DONE WITH.
WEB-SHOOTERS, CARTRIDGE EIGHT.
NOW, THIS PART'S MY FAVORITE.
EXPANDING WEB-FOAM. COOL, RIGHT?

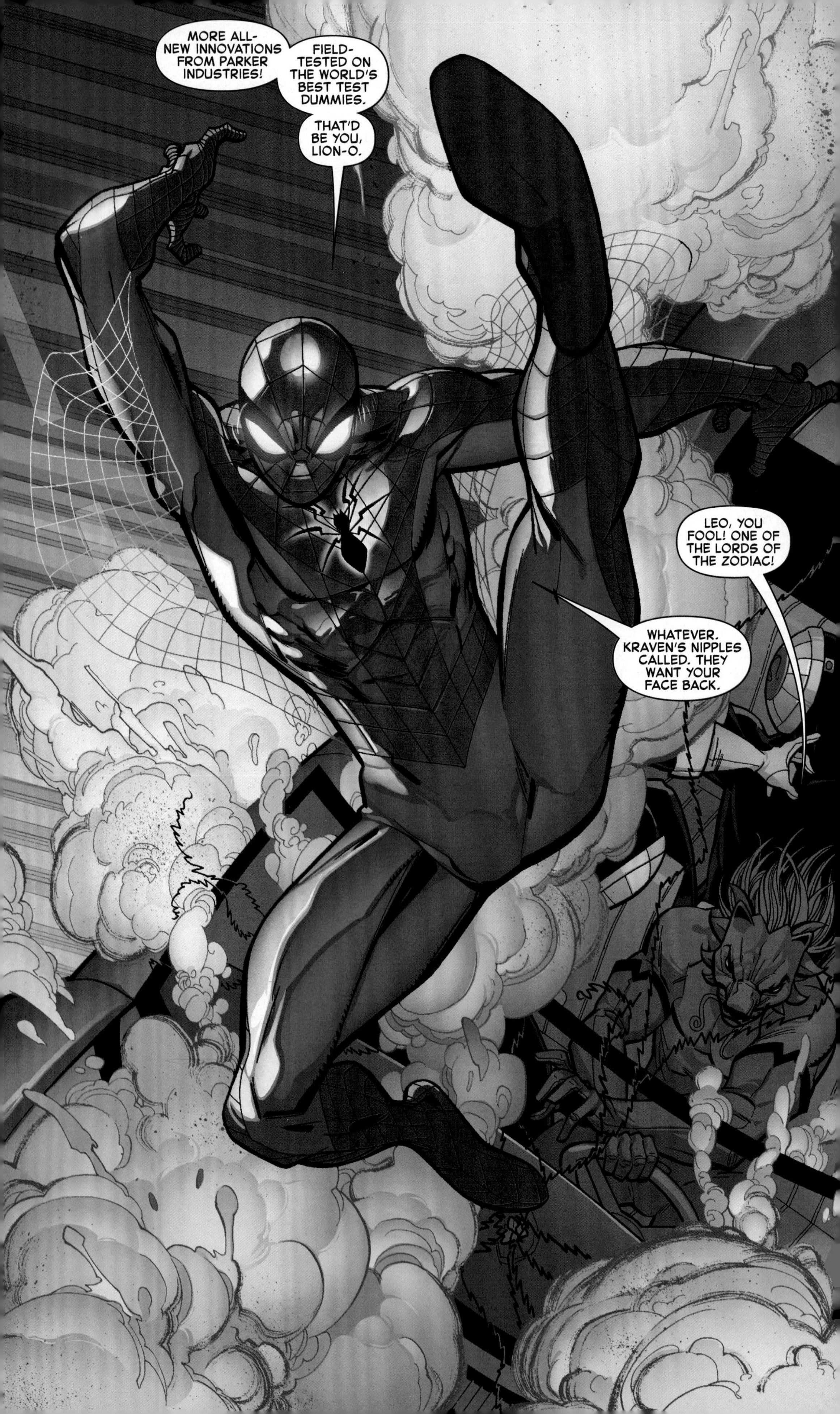
MORE ALL-NEW INNOVATIONS FROM PARKER INDUSTRIES!
FIELD-TESTED ON THE WORLD'S BEST TEST DUMMIES.
THAT'D BE YOU, LION-O.
LEO, YOU FOOL! ONE OF THE LORDS OF THE ZODIAC!
WHATEVER. KRAVEN'S NIPPLES CALLED. THEY WANT YOUR FACE BACK.

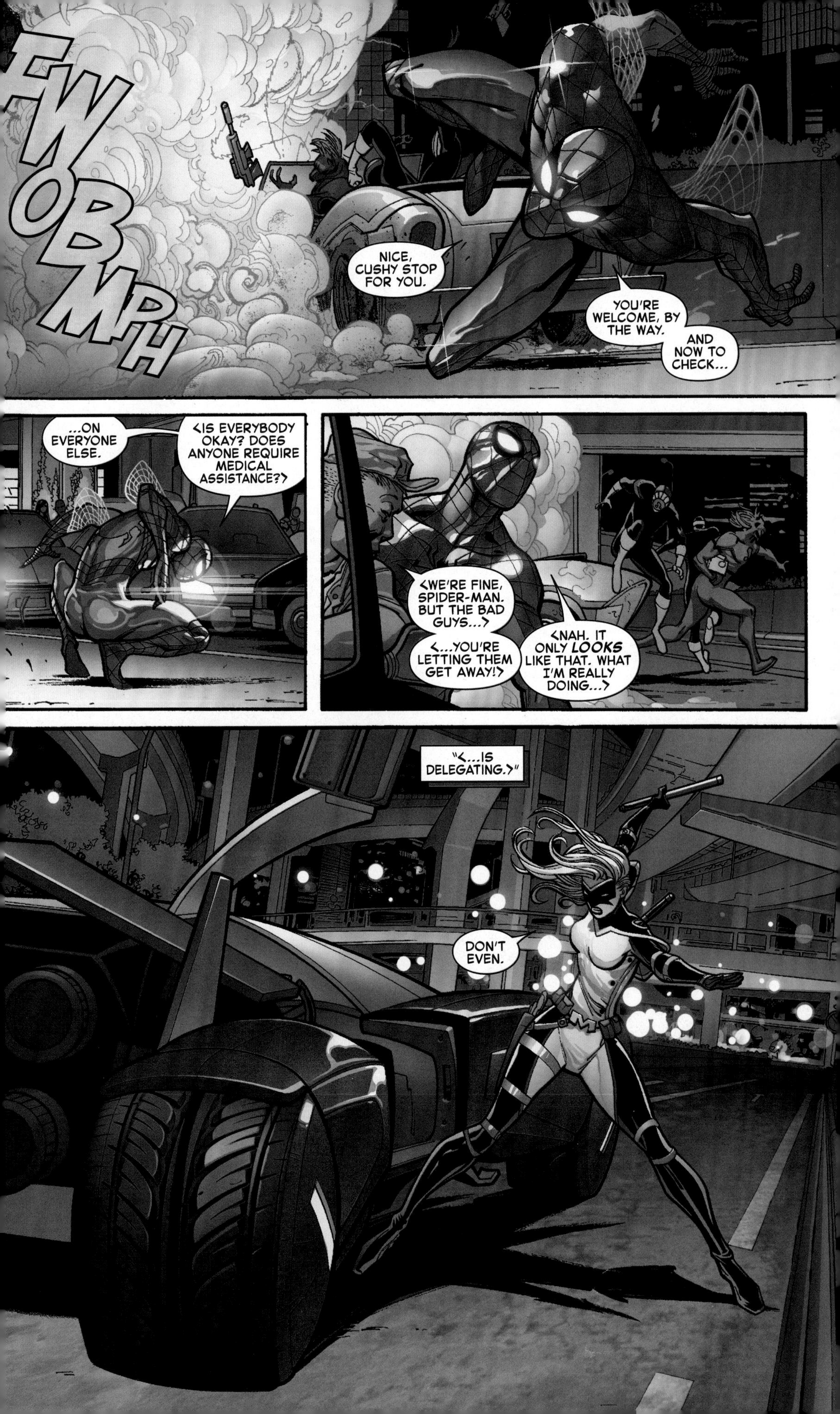
FWOBMPH
NICE, CUSHY STOP FOR YOU.
YOU'RE WELCOME, BY THE WAY.
AND NOW TO CHECK...
...ON EVERYONE ELSE.
<IS EVERYBODY OKAY? DOES ANYONE REQUIRE MEDICAL ASSISTANCE?>
<WE'RE FINE, SPIDER-MAN. BUT THE BAD GUYS...>
<...YOU'RE LETTING THEM GET AWAY!>
<NAH. IT ONLY *LOOKS* LIKE THAT. WHAT I'M REALLY DOING...>
"<...IS DELEGATING.>"
DON'T EVEN.

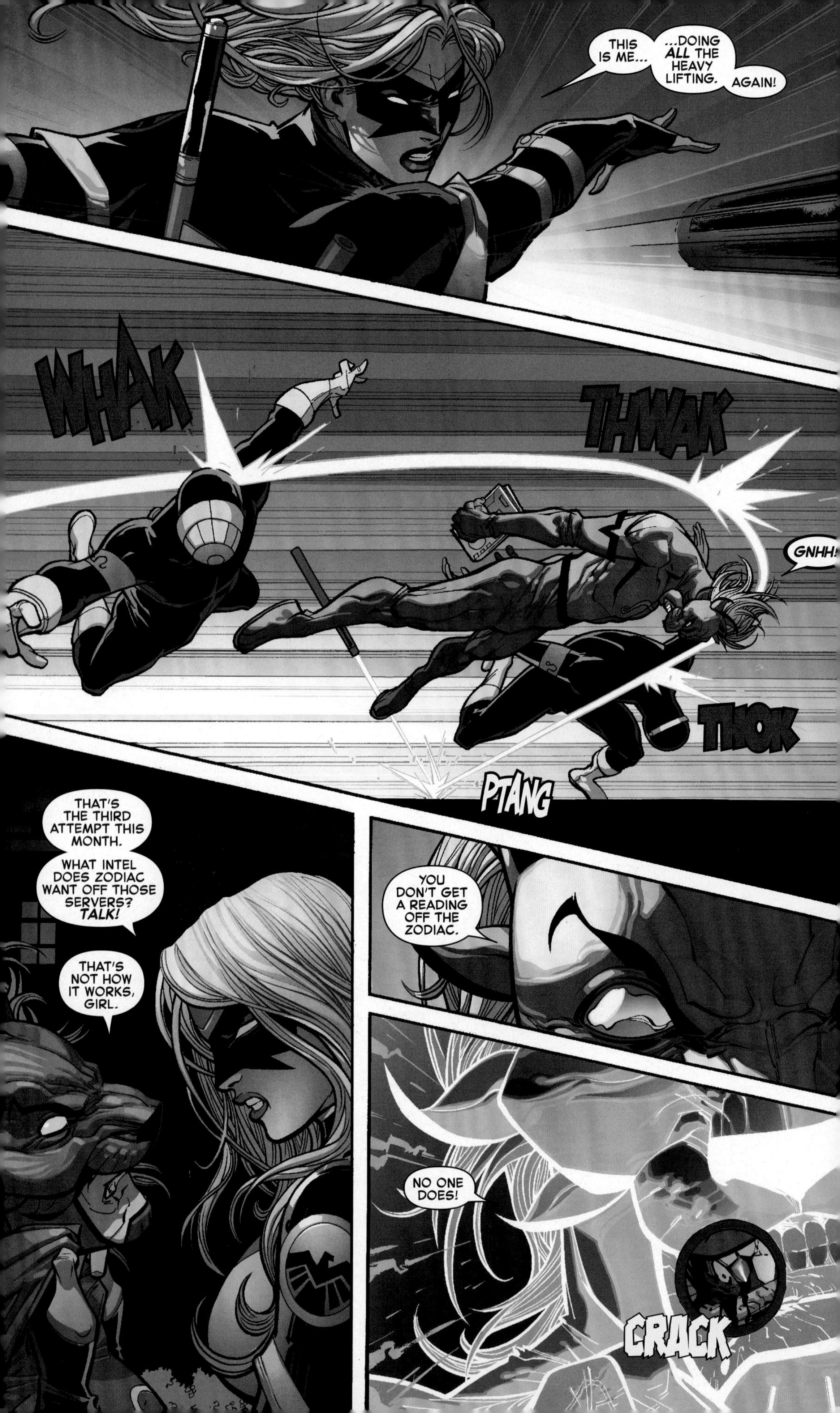
THIS IS ME...
...DOING ALL THE HEAVY LIFTING.
AGAIN!
WHAK
THWAK
GNHH!
THOK
PTANG
THAT'S THE THIRD ATTEMPT THIS MONTH.
WHAT INTEL DOES ZODIAC WANT OFF THOSE SERVERS? TALK!
THAT'S NOT HOW IT WORKS, GIRL.
YOU DON'T GET A READING OFF THE ZODIAC.
NO ONE DOES!
CRACK

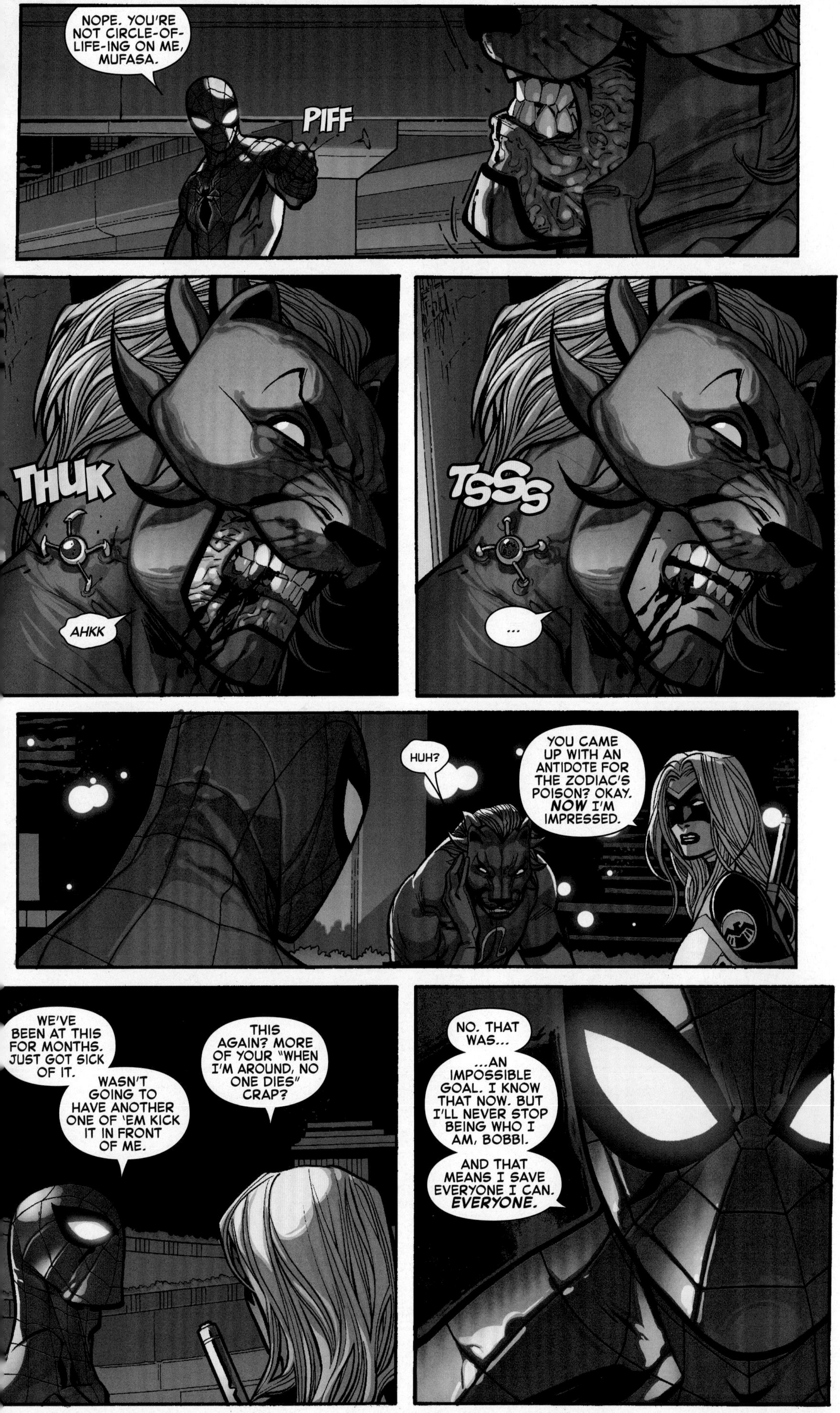
NOPE. YOU'RE NOT CIRCLE-OF-LIFE-ING ON ME, MUFASA.
PIFF
THUK
AHKK
TSSS
...
HUH?
YOU CAME UP WITH AN ANTIDOTE FOR THE ZODIAC'S POISON? OKAY. *NOW* I'M IMPRESSED.
WE'VE BEEN AT THIS FOR MONTHS. JUST GOT SICK OF IT.
WASN'T GOING TO HAVE ANOTHER ONE OF 'EM KICK IT IN FRONT OF ME.
THIS AGAIN? MORE OF YOUR "WHEN I'M AROUND, NO ONE DIES" CRAP?
NO. THAT WAS...
...AN IMPOSSIBLE GOAL. I KNOW THAT NOW. BUT I'LL NEVER STOP BEING WHO I AM, BOBBI.
AND THAT MEANS I SAVE EVERYONE I CAN. *EVERYONE.*

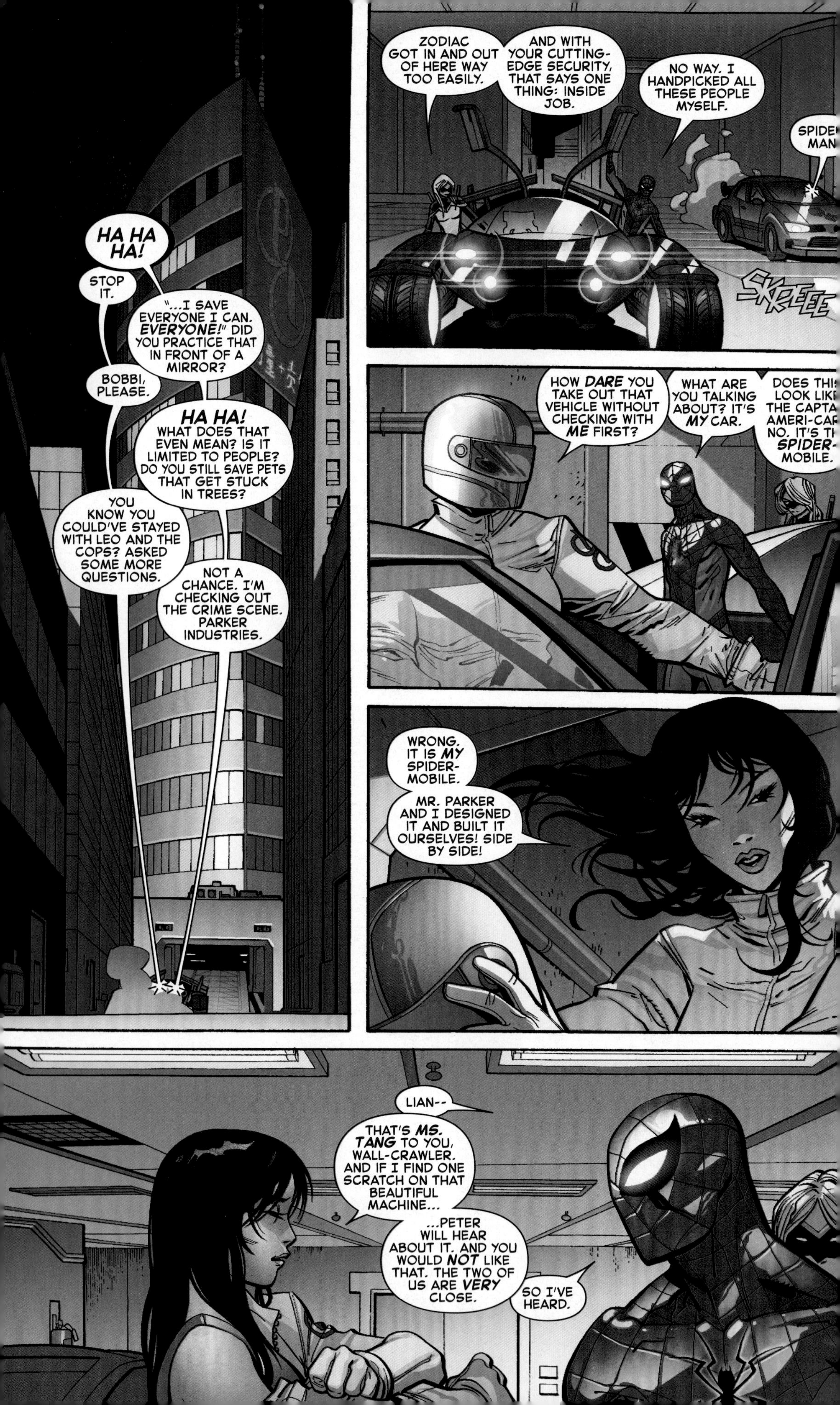
HA HA HA!
STOP IT.
"...I SAVE EVERYONE I CAN. EVERYONE!" DID YOU PRACTICE THAT IN FRONT OF A MIRROR?
BOBBI, PLEASE.
HA HA! WHAT DOES THAT EVEN MEAN? IS IT LIMITED TO PEOPLE? DO YOU STILL SAVE PETS THAT GET STUCK IN TREES?
YOU KNOW YOU COULD'VE STAYED WITH LEO AND THE COPS? ASKED SOME MORE QUESTIONS.
NOT A CHANCE. I'M CHECKING OUT THE CRIME SCENE. PARKER INDUSTRIES.
ZODIAC GOT IN AND OUT OF HERE WAY TOO EASILY.
AND WITH YOUR CUTTING-EDGE SECURITY, THAT SAYS ONE THING: INSIDE JOB.
NO WAY. I HANDPICKED ALL THESE PEOPLE MYSELF.
SPIDE MAN
SKREEEE
HOW DARE YOU TAKE OUT THAT VEHICLE WITHOUT CHECKING WITH ME FIRST?
WHAT ARE YOU TALKING ABOUT? IT'S MY CAR.
DOES THI LOOK LIK THE CAPTA AMERI-CAR NO. IT'S T SPIDER- MOBILE.
WRONG. IT IS MY SPIDER-MOBILE.
MR. PARKER AND I DESIGNED IT AND BUILT IT OURSELVES! SIDE BY SIDE!
LIAN--
THAT'S MS. TANG TO YOU, WALL-CRAWLER. AND IF I FIND ONE SCRATCH ON THAT BEAUTIFUL MACHINE...
...PETER WILL HEAR ABOUT IT. AND YOU WOULD NOT LIKE THAT. THE TWO OF US ARE VERY CLOSE.
SO I'VE HEARD.

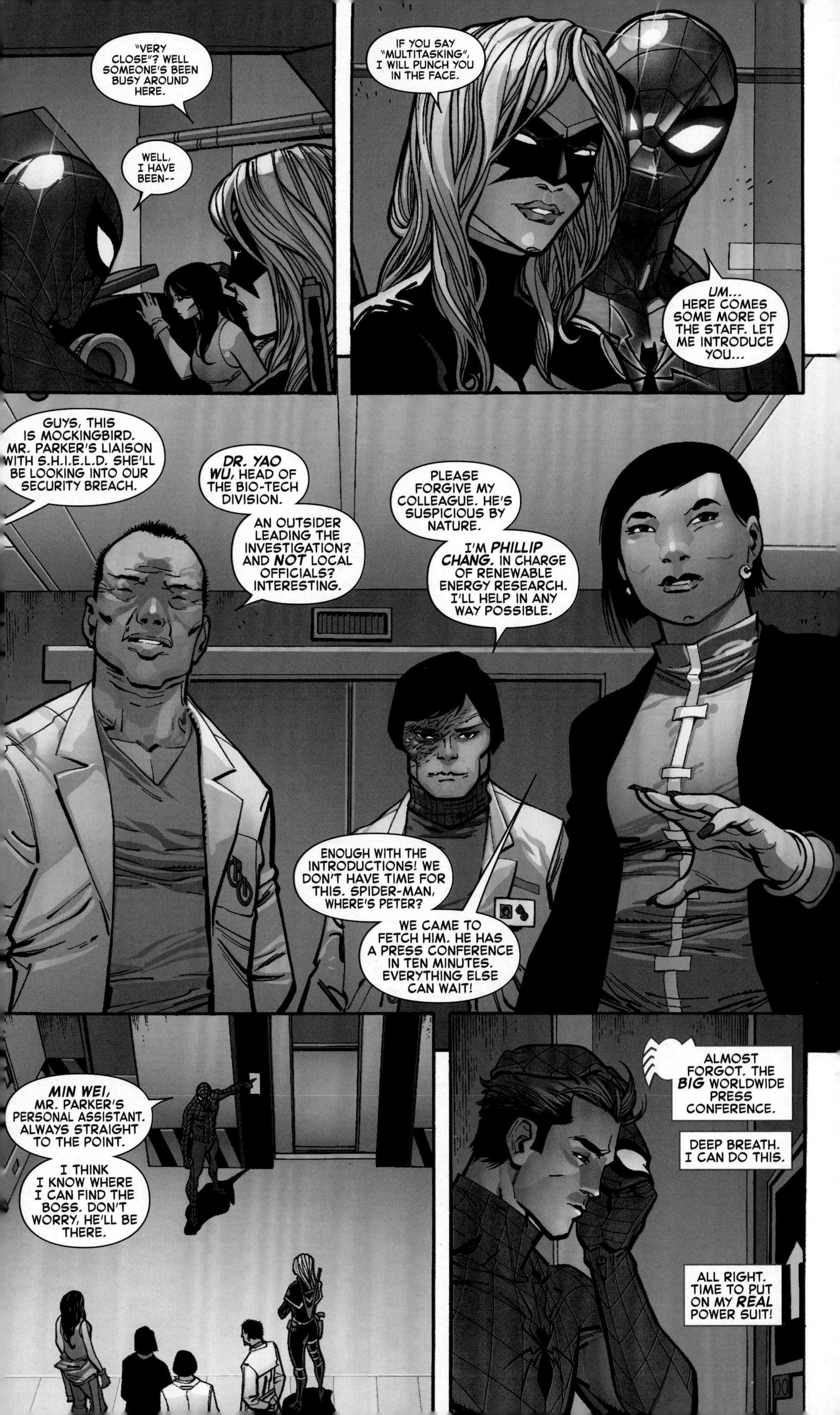
"VERY CLOSE"? WELL SOMEONE'S BEEN BUSY AROUND HERE.
WELL, I HAVE BEEN--
IF YOU SAY "MULTITASKING", I WILL PUNCH YOU IN THE FACE.
UM... HERE COMES SOME MORE OF THE STAFF. LET ME INTRODUCE YOU...
GUYS, THIS IS MOCKINGBIRD. MR. PARKER'S LIAISON WITH S.H.I.E.L.D. SHE'LL BE LOOKING INTO OUR SECURITY BREACH.
DR. YAO WU, HEAD OF THE BIO-TECH DIVISION.
AN OUTSIDER LEADING THE INVESTIGATION? AND NOT LOCAL OFFICIALS? INTERESTING.
PLEASE FORGIVE MY COLLEAGUE. HE'S SUSPICIOUS BY NATURE.
I'M PHILLIP CHANG. IN CHARGE OF RENEWABLE ENERGY RESEARCH. I'LL HELP IN ANY WAY POSSIBLE.
ENOUGH WITH THE INTRODUCTIONS! WE DON'T HAVE TIME FOR THIS. SPIDER-MAN, WHERE'S PETER?
WE CAME TO FETCH HIM. HE HAS A PRESS CONFERENCE IN TEN MINUTES. EVERYTHING ELSE CAN WAIT!
MIN WEI, MR. PARKER'S PERSONAL ASSISTANT. ALWAYS STRAIGHT TO THE POINT.
I THINK I KNOW WHERE I CAN FIND THE BOSS. DON'T WORRY, HE'LL BE THERE.
ALMOST FORGOT. THE BIG WORLDWIDE PRESS CONFERENCE.
DEEP BREATH. I CAN DO THIS.
ALL RIGHT. TIME TO PUT ON MY REAL POWER SUIT!

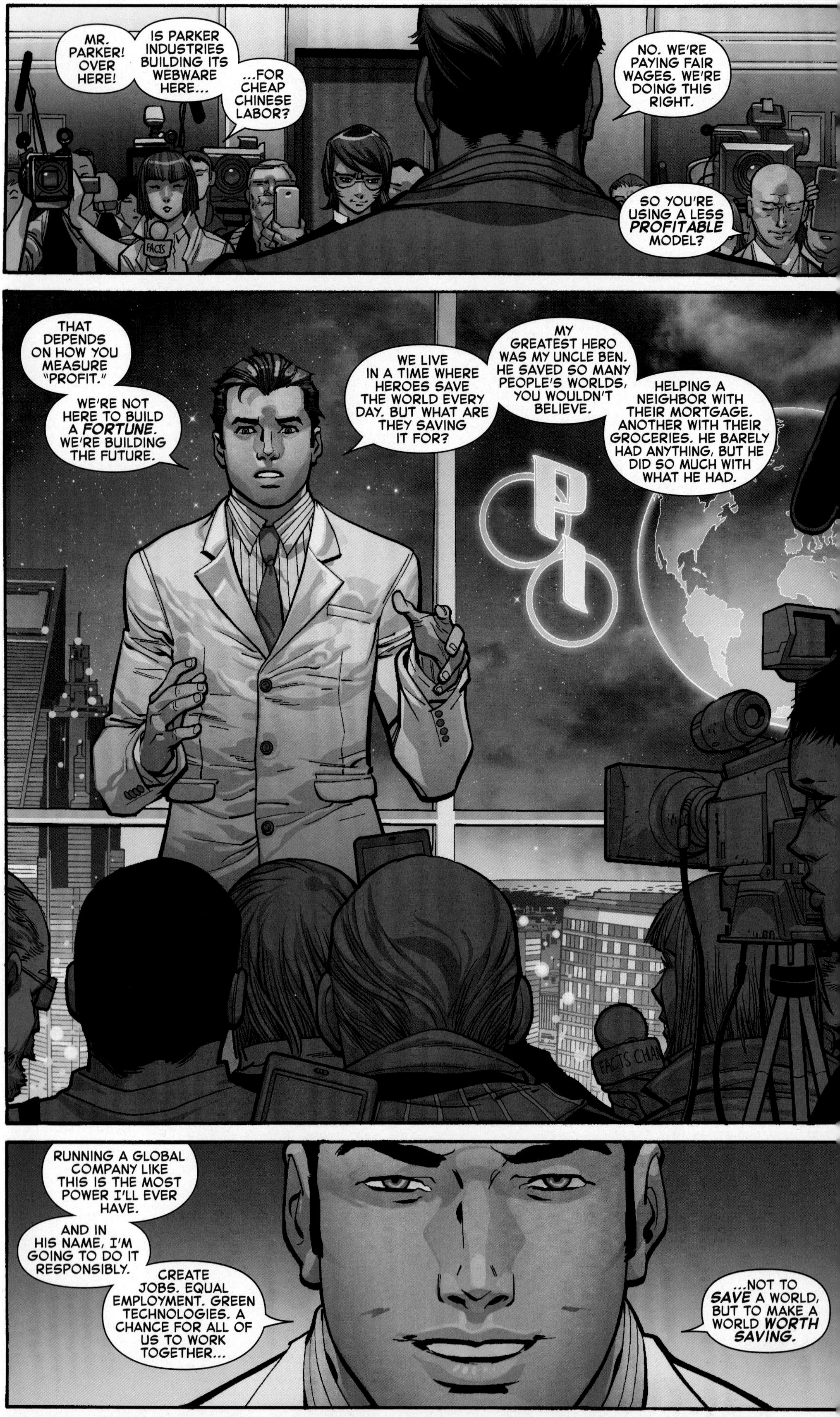
MR. PARKER! OVER HERE!
IS PARKER INDUSTRIES BUILDING ITS WEBWARE HERE...
...FOR CHEAP CHINESE LABOR?
NO. WE'RE PAYING FAIR WAGES. WE'RE DOING THIS RIGHT.
SO YOU'RE USING A LESS PROFITABLE MODEL?
THAT DEPENDS ON HOW YOU MEASURE "PROFIT."
WE'RE NOT HERE TO BUILD A FORTUNE. WE'RE BUILDING THE FUTURE.
WE LIVE IN A TIME WHERE HEROES SAVE THE WORLD EVERY DAY. BUT WHAT ARE THEY SAVING IT FOR?
MY GREATEST HERO WAS MY UNCLE BEN. HE SAVED SO MANY PEOPLE'S WORLDS, YOU WOULDN'T BELIEVE.
HELPING A NEIGHBOR WITH THEIR MORTGAGE. ANOTHER WITH THEIR GROCERIES. HE BARELY HAD ANYTHING, BUT HE DID SO MUCH WITH WHAT HE HAD.
RUNNING A GLOBAL COMPANY LIKE THIS IS THE MOST POWER I'LL EVER HAVE.
AND IN HIS NAME, I'M GOING TO DO IT RESPONSIBLY.
CREATE JOBS. EQUAL EMPLOYMENT. GREEN TECHNOLOGIES. A CHANCE FOR ALL OF US TO WORK TOGETHER...
...NOT TO SAVE A WORLD, BUT TO MAKE A WORLD WORTH SAVING.

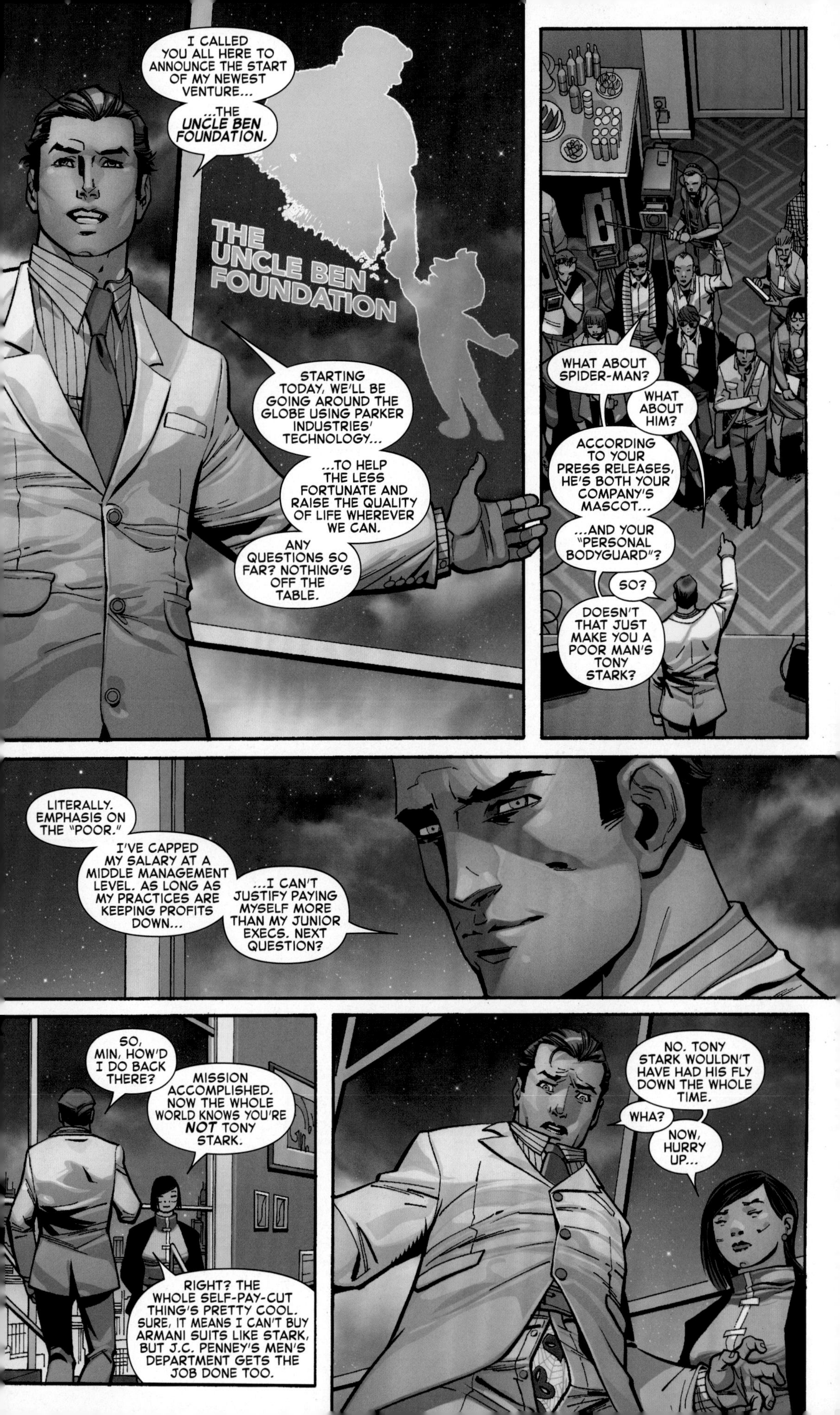
I CALLED YOU ALL HERE TO ANNOUNCE THE START OF MY NEWEST VENTURE...
...THE *UNCLE BEN FOUNDATION.*
THE UNCLE BEN FOUNDATION
STARTING TODAY, WE'LL BE GOING AROUND THE GLOBE USING PARKER INDUSTRIES' TECHNOLOGY...
...TO HELP THE LESS FORTUNATE AND RAISE THE QUALITY OF LIFE WHEREVER WE CAN.
ANY QUESTIONS SO FAR? NOTHING'S OFF THE TABLE.
WHAT ABOUT SPIDER-MAN?
WHAT ABOUT HIM?
ACCORDING TO YOUR PRESS RELEASES, HE'S BOTH YOUR COMPANY'S MASCOT...
...AND YOUR "PERSONAL BODYGUARD"?
SO?
DOESN'T THAT JUST MAKE YOU A POOR MAN'S TONY STARK?
LITERALLY. EMPHASIS ON THE "POOR."
I'VE CAPPED MY SALARY AT A MIDDLE MANAGEMENT LEVEL. AS LONG AS MY PRACTICES ARE KEEPING PROFITS DOWN...
...I CAN'T JUSTIFY PAYING MYSELF MORE THAN MY JUNIOR EXECS. NEXT QUESTION?
SO, MIN, HOW'D I DO BACK THERE?
MISSION ACCOMPLISHED. NOW THE WHOLE WORLD KNOWS YOU'RE *NOT* TONY STARK.
RIGHT? THE WHOLE SELF-PAY-CUT THING'S PRETTY COOL. SURE, IT MEANS I CAN'T BUY ARMANI SUITS LIKE STARK, BUT J.C. PENNEY'S MEN'S DEPARTMENT GETS THE JOB DONE TOO.
NO. TONY STARK WOULDN'T HAVE HAD HIS FLY DOWN THE WHOLE TIME.
WHA?
NOW, HURRY UP...

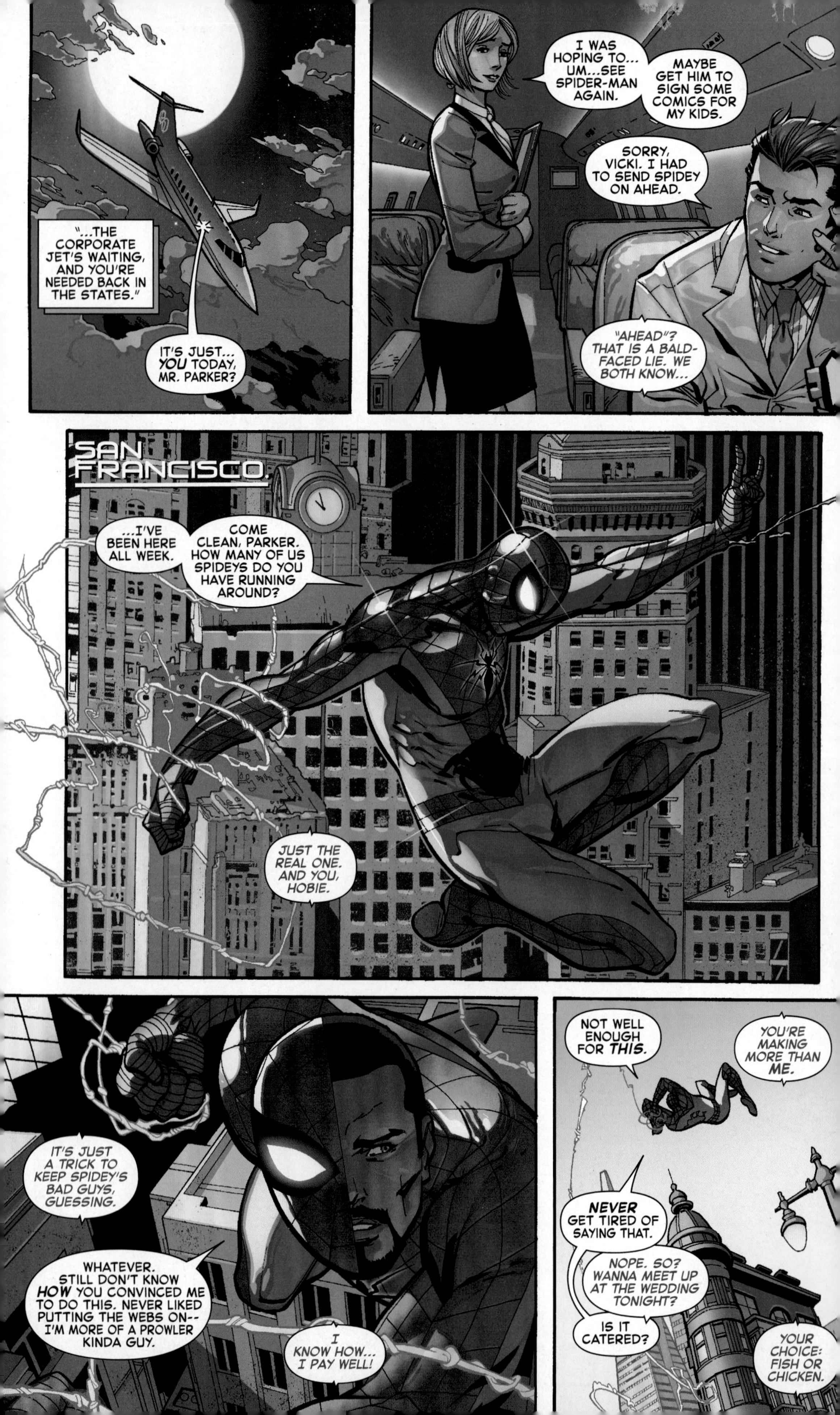
"...THE CORPORATE JET'S WAITING, AND YOU'RE NEEDED BACK IN THE STATES."
IT'S JUST... YOU TODAY, MR. PARKER?
I WAS HOPING TO... UM...SEE SPIDER-MAN AGAIN.
MAYBE GET HIM TO SIGN SOME COMICS FOR MY KIDS.
SORRY, VICKI. I HAD TO SEND SPIDEY ON AHEAD.
"AHEAD"? THAT IS A BALD-FACED LIE. WE BOTH KNOW...
SAN FRANCISCO.
...I'VE BEEN HERE ALL WEEK.
COME CLEAN, PARKER. HOW MANY OF US SPIDEYS DO YOU HAVE RUNNING AROUND?
JUST THE REAL ONE. AND YOU, HOBIE.
IT'S JUST A TRICK TO KEEP SPIDEY'S BAD GUYS GUESSING.
WHATEVER. STILL DON'T KNOW HOW YOU CONVINCED ME TO DO THIS. NEVER LIKED PUTTING THE WEBS ON-- I'M MORE OF A PROWLER KINDA GUY.
I KNOW HOW... I PAY WELL!
NOT WELL ENOUGH FOR THIS.
YOU'RE MAKING MORE THAN ME.
NEVER GET TIRED OF SAYING THAT.
NOPE. SO? WANNA MEET UP AT THE WEDDING TONIGHT?
IS IT CATERED?
YOUR CHOICE: FISH OR CHICKEN.

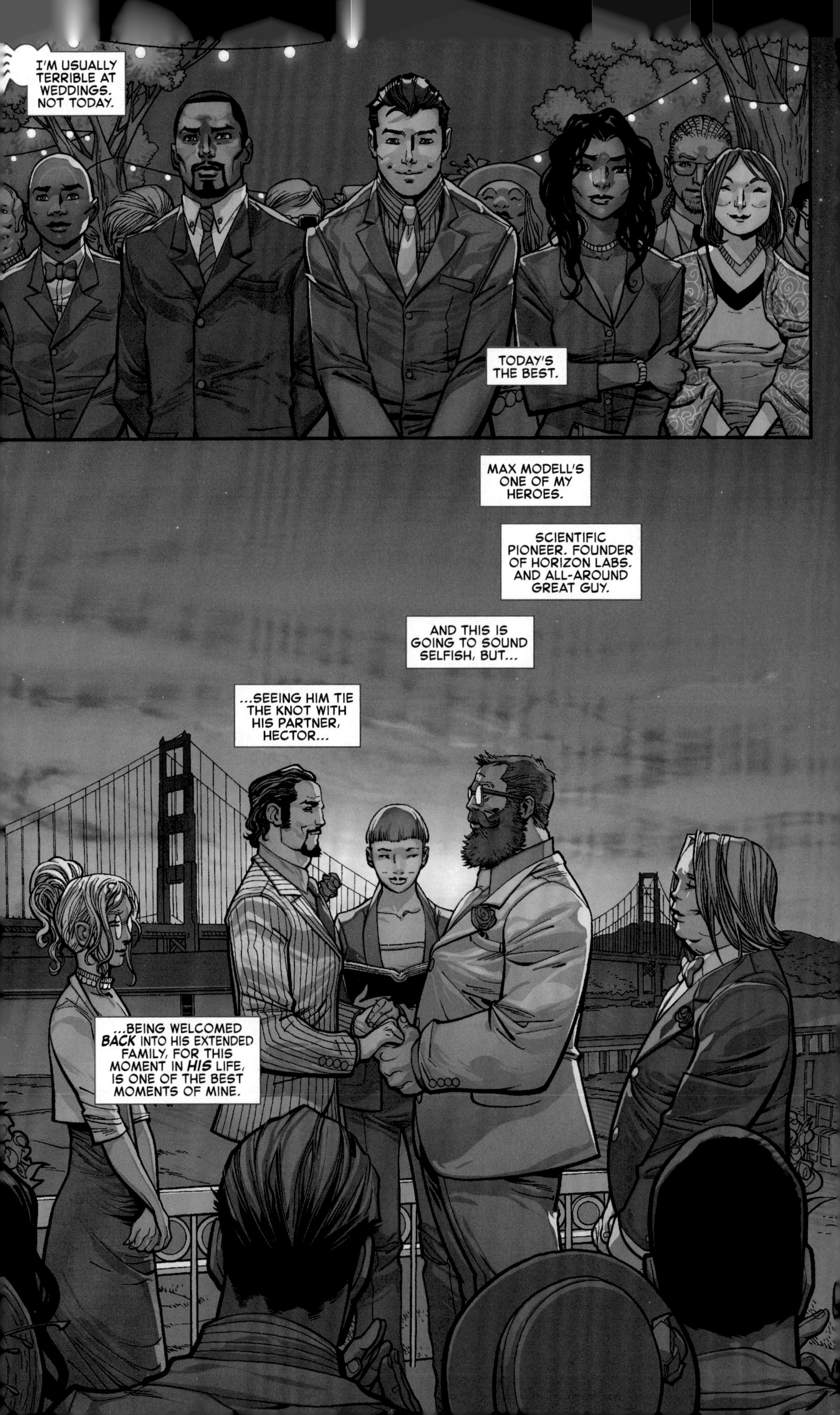

I'M USUALLY TERRIBLE AT WEDDINGS. NOT TODAY.
TODAY'S THE BEST.
MAX MODELL'S ONE OF MY HEROES.
SCIENTIFIC PIONEER. FOUNDER OF HORIZON LABS. AND ALL-AROUND GREAT GUY.
AND THIS IS GOING TO SOUND SELFISH, BUT...
...SEEING HIM TIE THE KNOT WITH HIS PARTNER, HECTOR...
...BEING WELCOMED BACK INTO HIS EXTENDED FAMILY, FOR THIS MOMENT IN HIS LIFE, IS ONE OF THE BEST MOMENTS OF MINE.

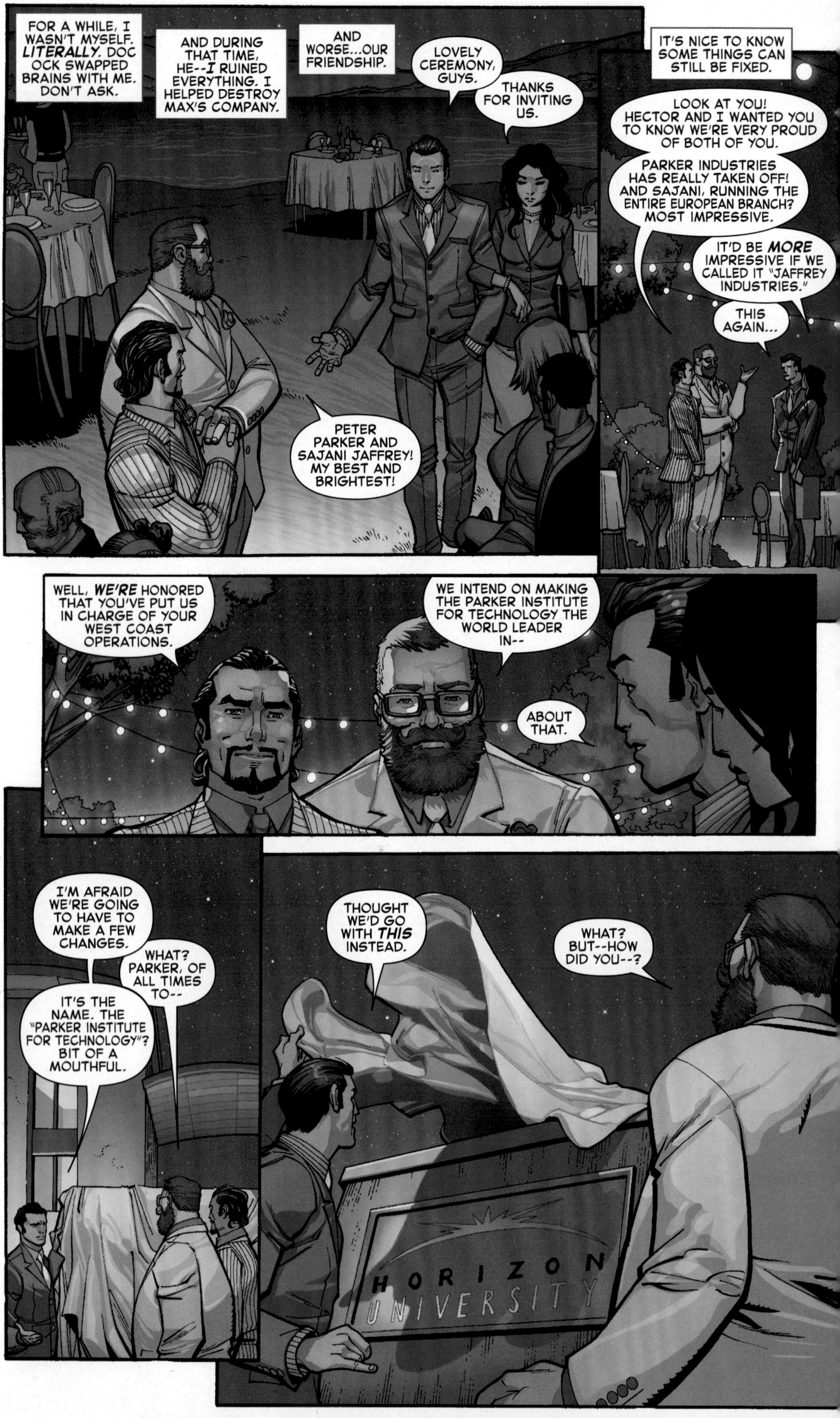

FOR A WHILE, I WASN'T MYSELF. LITERALLY. DOC OCK SWAPPED BRAINS WITH ME. DON'T ASK.
AND DURING THAT TIME, HE--I RUINED EVERYTHING. I HELPED DESTROY MAX'S COMPANY.
AND WORSE...OUR FRIENDSHIP.
LOVELY CEREMONY, GUYS.
THANKS FOR INVITING US.
PETER PARKER AND SAJANI JAFFREY! MY BEST AND BRIGHTEST!
IT'S NICE TO KNOW SOME THINGS CAN STILL BE FIXED.
LOOK AT YOU! HECTOR AND I WANTED YOU TO KNOW WE'RE VERY PROUD OF BOTH OF YOU.
PARKER INDUSTRIES HAS REALLY TAKEN OFF! AND SAJANI, RUNNING THE ENTIRE EUROPEAN BRANCH? MOST IMPRESSIVE.
IT'D BE MORE IMPRESSIVE IF WE CALLED IT "JAFFREY INDUSTRIES."
THIS AGAIN...
WELL, WE'RE HONORED THAT YOU'VE PUT US IN CHARGE OF YOUR WEST COAST OPERATIONS.
WE INTEND ON MAKING THE PARKER INSTITUTE FOR TECHNOLOGY THE WORLD LEADER IN--
ABOUT THAT.
I'M AFRAID WE'RE GOING TO HAVE TO MAKE A FEW CHANGES.
WHAT? PARKER, OF ALL TIMES TO--
IT'S THE NAME. THE "PARKER INSTITUTE FOR TECHNOLOGY"? BIT OF A MOUTHFUL.
THOUGHT WE'D GO WITH THIS INSTEAD.
WHAT? BUT--HOW DID YOU--?
HORIZON UNIVERSITY

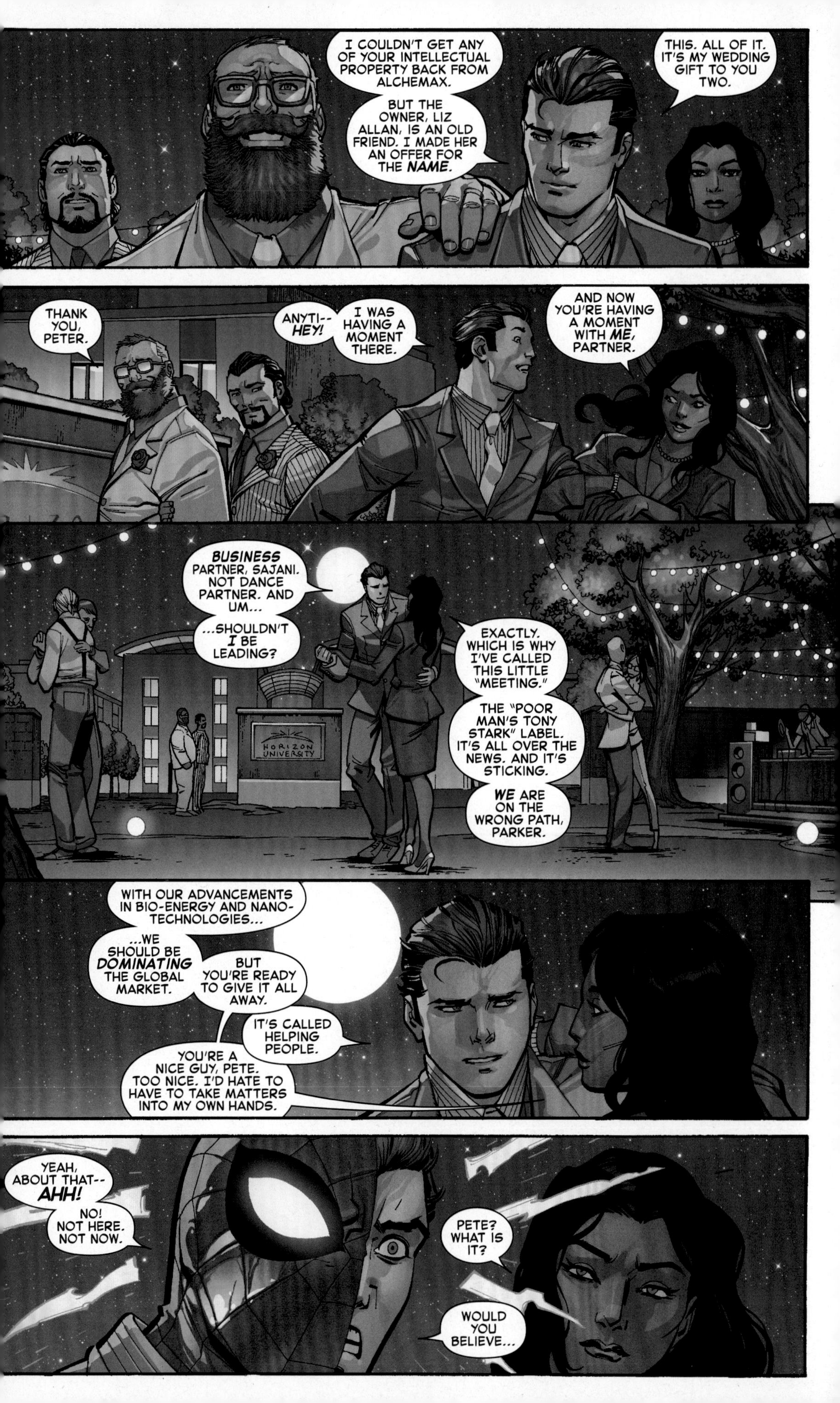
I COULDN'T GET ANY OF YOUR INTELLECTUAL PROPERTY BACK FROM ALCHEMAX.
BUT THE OWNER, LIZ ALLAN, IS AN OLD FRIEND. I MADE HER AN OFFER FOR THE NAME.
THIS. ALL OF IT. IT'S MY WEDDING GIFT TO YOU TWO.
THANK YOU, PETER.
ANYTI-- HEY!
I WAS HAVING A MOMENT THERE.
AND NOW YOU'RE HAVING A MOMENT WITH ME, PARTNER.
BUSINESS PARTNER, SAJANI. NOT DANCE PARTNER. AND UM...
...SHOULDN'T I BE LEADING?
EXACTLY. WHICH IS WHY I'VE CALLED THIS LITTLE "MEETING."
THE "POOR MAN'S TONY STARK" LABEL. IT'S ALL OVER THE NEWS. AND IT'S STICKING.
WE ARE ON THE WRONG PATH, PARKER.
HORIZON UNIVERSITY
WITH OUR ADVANCEMENTS IN BIO-ENERGY AND NANO-TECHNOLOGIES...
...WE SHOULD BE DOMINATING THE GLOBAL MARKET.
BUT YOU'RE READY TO GIVE IT ALL AWAY.
IT'S CALLED HELPING PEOPLE.
YOU'RE A NICE GUY, PETE. TOO NICE. I'D HATE TO HAVE TO TAKE MATTERS INTO MY OWN HANDS.
YEAH, ABOUT THAT-- AHH!
NO! NOT HERE. NOT NOW.
PETE? WHAT IS IT?
WOULD YOU BELIEVE...

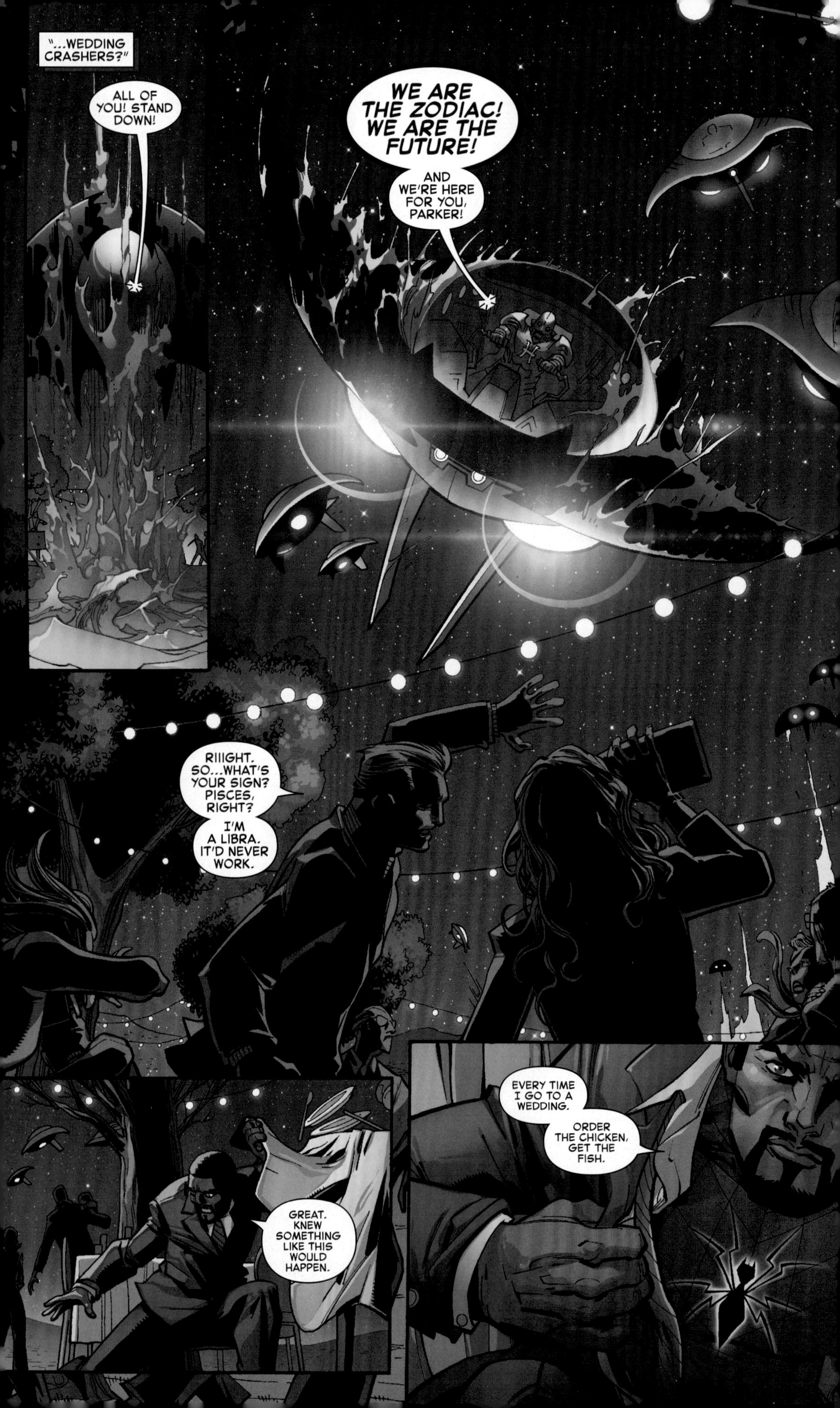
"...WEDDING CRASHERS?"
ALL OF YOU! STAND DOWN!
WE ARE THE ZODIAC! WE ARE THE FUTURE!
AND WE'RE HERE FOR YOU, PARKER!
RIIIGHT. SO...WHAT'S YOUR SIGN? PISCES, RIGHT?
I'M A LIBRA. IT'D NEVER WORK.
GREAT. KNEW SOMETHING LIKE THIS WOULD HAPPEN.
EVERY TIME I GO TO A WEDDING.
ORDER THE CHICKEN, GET THE FISH.

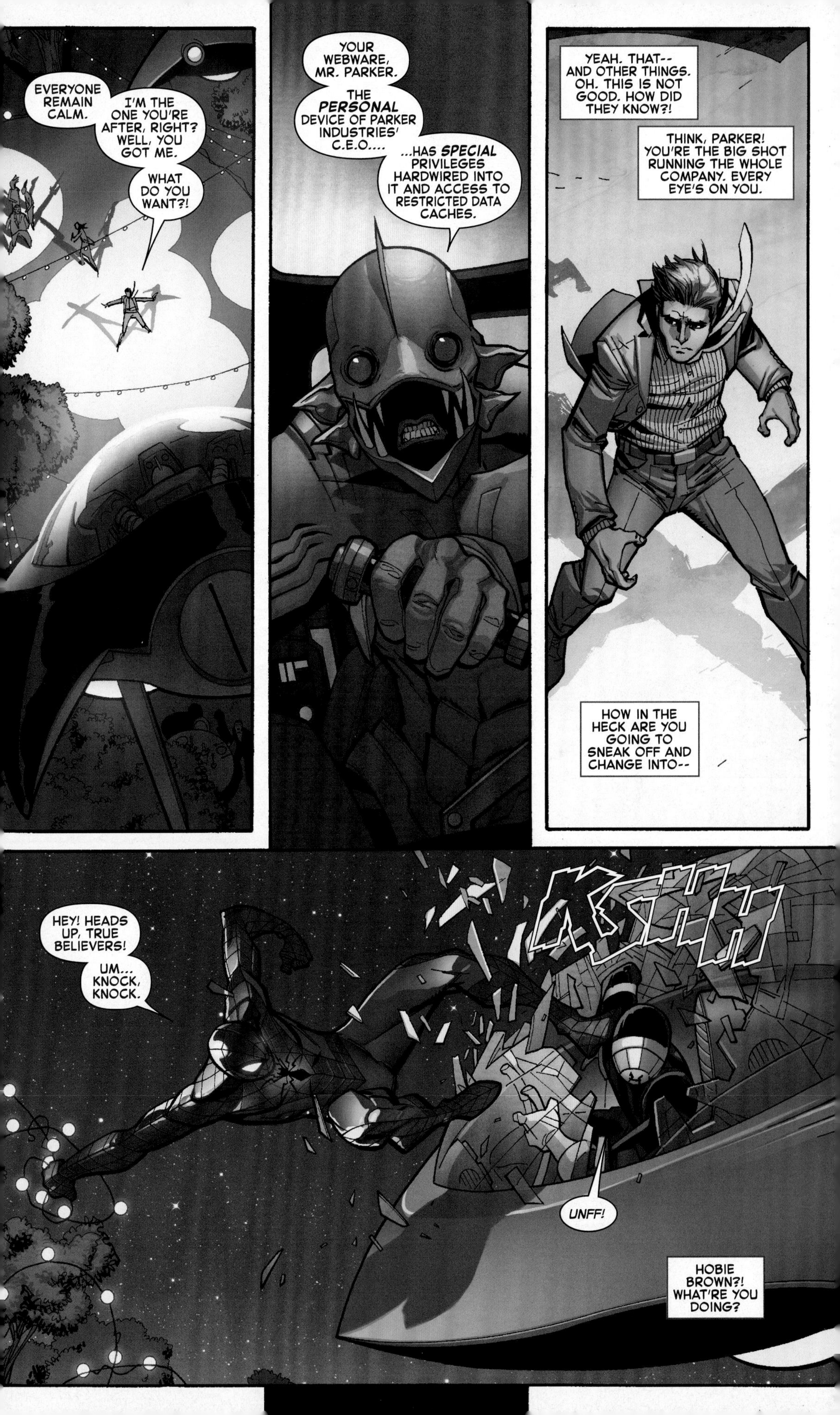
EVERYONE REMAIN CALM.
I'M THE ONE YOU'RE AFTER, RIGHT? WELL, YOU GOT ME.
WHAT DO YOU WANT?!
YOUR WEBWARE, MR. PARKER.
THE PERSONAL DEVICE OF PARKER INDUSTRIES' C.E.O....
...HAS SPECIAL PRIVILEGES HARDWIRED INTO IT AND ACCESS TO RESTRICTED DATA CACHES.
YEAH. THAT--AND OTHER THINGS. OH. THIS IS NOT GOOD. HOW DID THEY KNOW?!
THINK, PARKER! YOU'RE THE BIG SHOT RUNNING THE WHOLE COMPANY. EVERY EYE'S ON YOU.
HOW IN THE HECK ARE YOU GOING TO SNEAK OFF AND CHANGE INTO--
HEY! HEADS UP, TRUE BELIEVERS!
UM... KNOCK, KNOCK.
KSHH
UNFF!
HOBIE BROWN?! WHAT'RE YOU DOING?

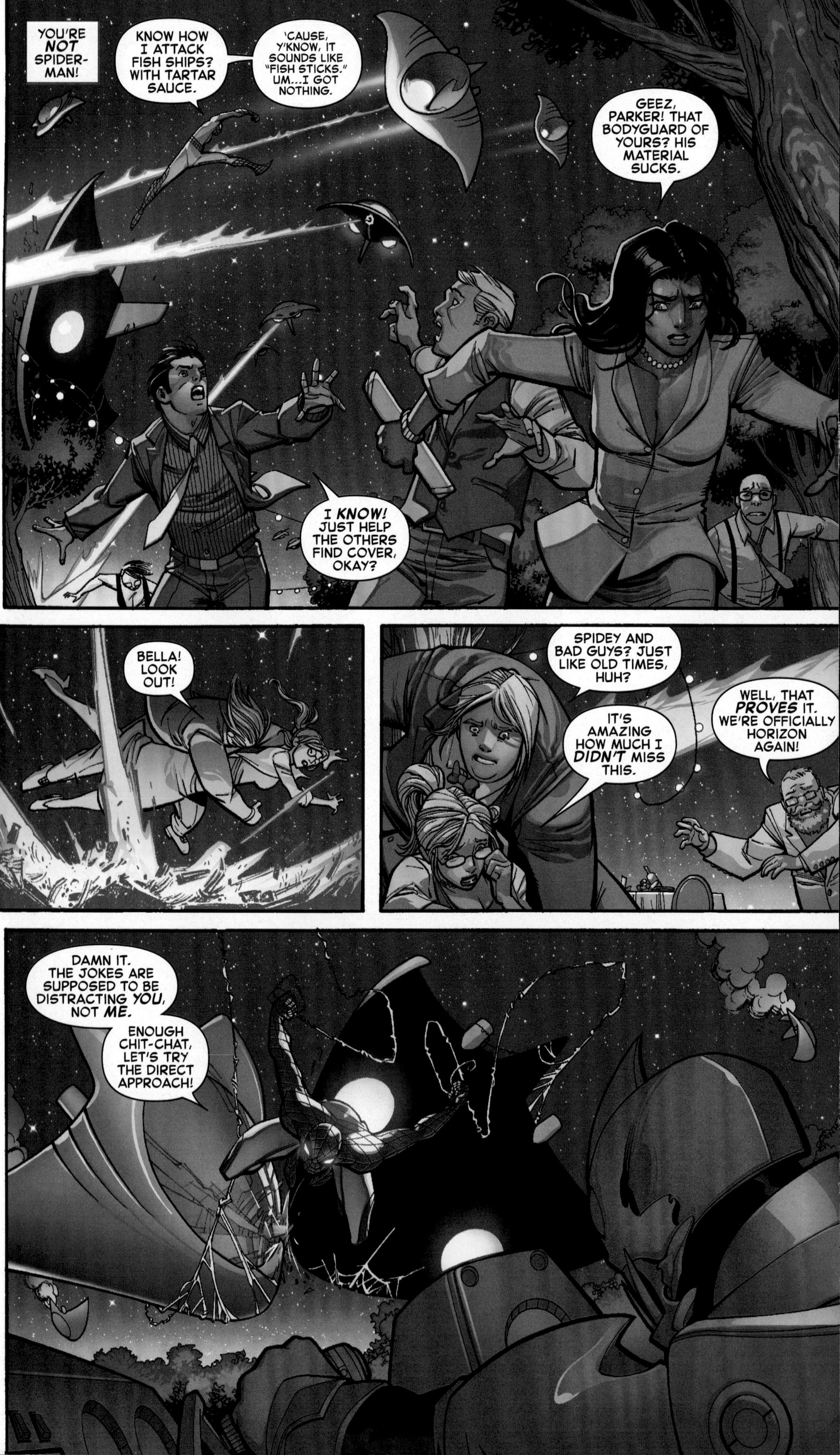
YOU'RE NOT SPIDER-MAN!
KNOW HOW I ATTACK FISH SHIPS? WITH TARTAR SAUCE.
'CAUSE, Y'KNOW, IT SOUNDS LIKE "FISH STICKS." UM...I GOT NOTHING.
GEEZ, PARKER! THAT BODYGUARD OF YOURS? HIS MATERIAL SUCKS.
I KNOW! JUST HELP THE OTHERS FIND COVER, OKAY?
BELLA! LOOK OUT!
SPIDEY AND BAD GUYS? JUST LIKE OLD TIMES, HUH?
IT'S AMAZING HOW MUCH I DIDN'T MISS THIS.
WELL, THAT PROVES IT. WE'RE OFFICIALLY HORIZON AGAIN!
DAMN IT. THE JOKES ARE SUPPOSED TO BE DISTRACTING YOU, NOT ME.
ENOUGH CHIT-CHAT, LET'S TRY THE DIRECT APPROACH!

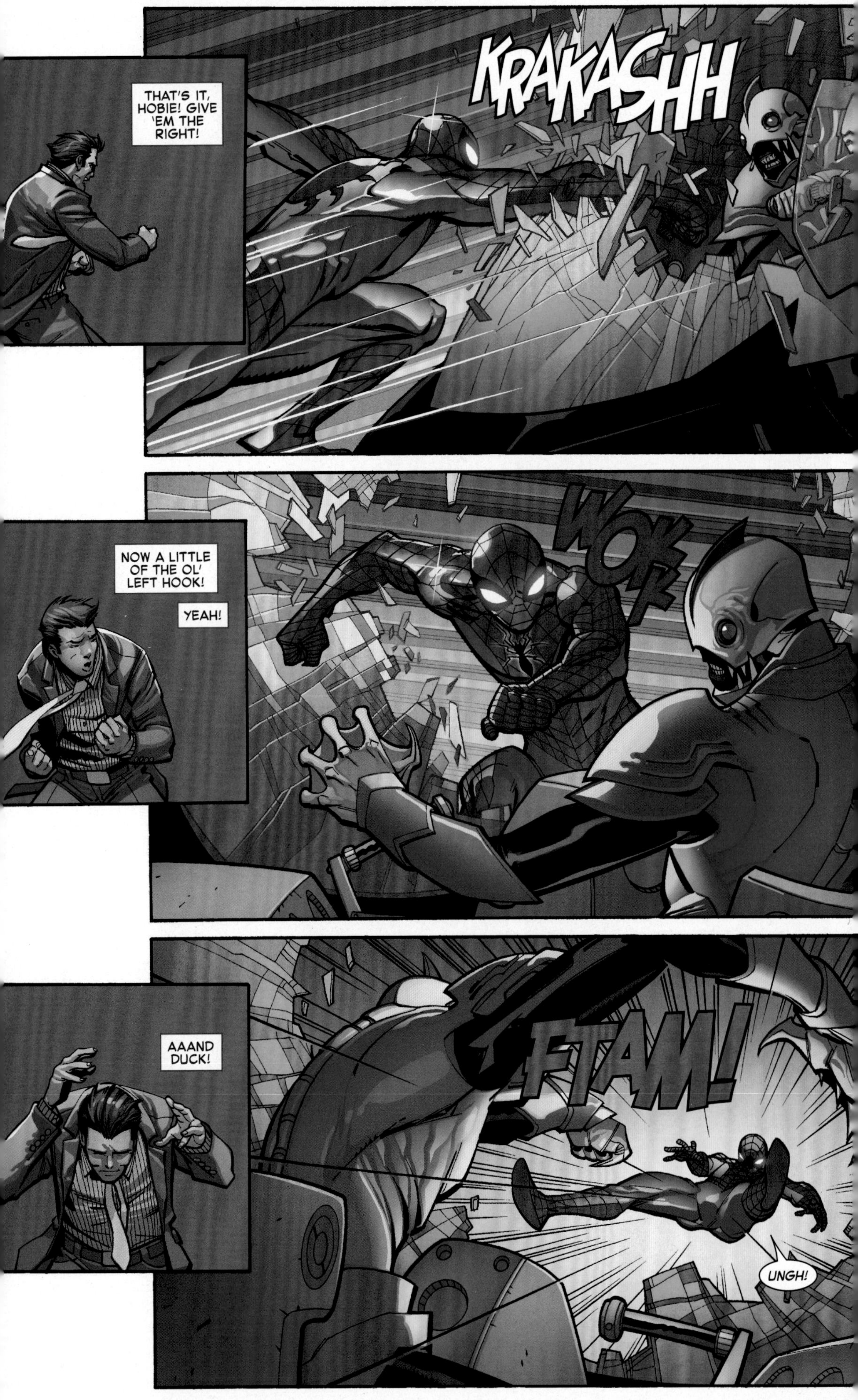

THAT'S IT, HOBIE! GIVE 'EM THE RIGHT!
KRAKASHH
NOW A LITTLE OF THE OL' LEFT HOOK!
YEAH!
WOK
AAAND DUCK!
FTAM!
UNGH!

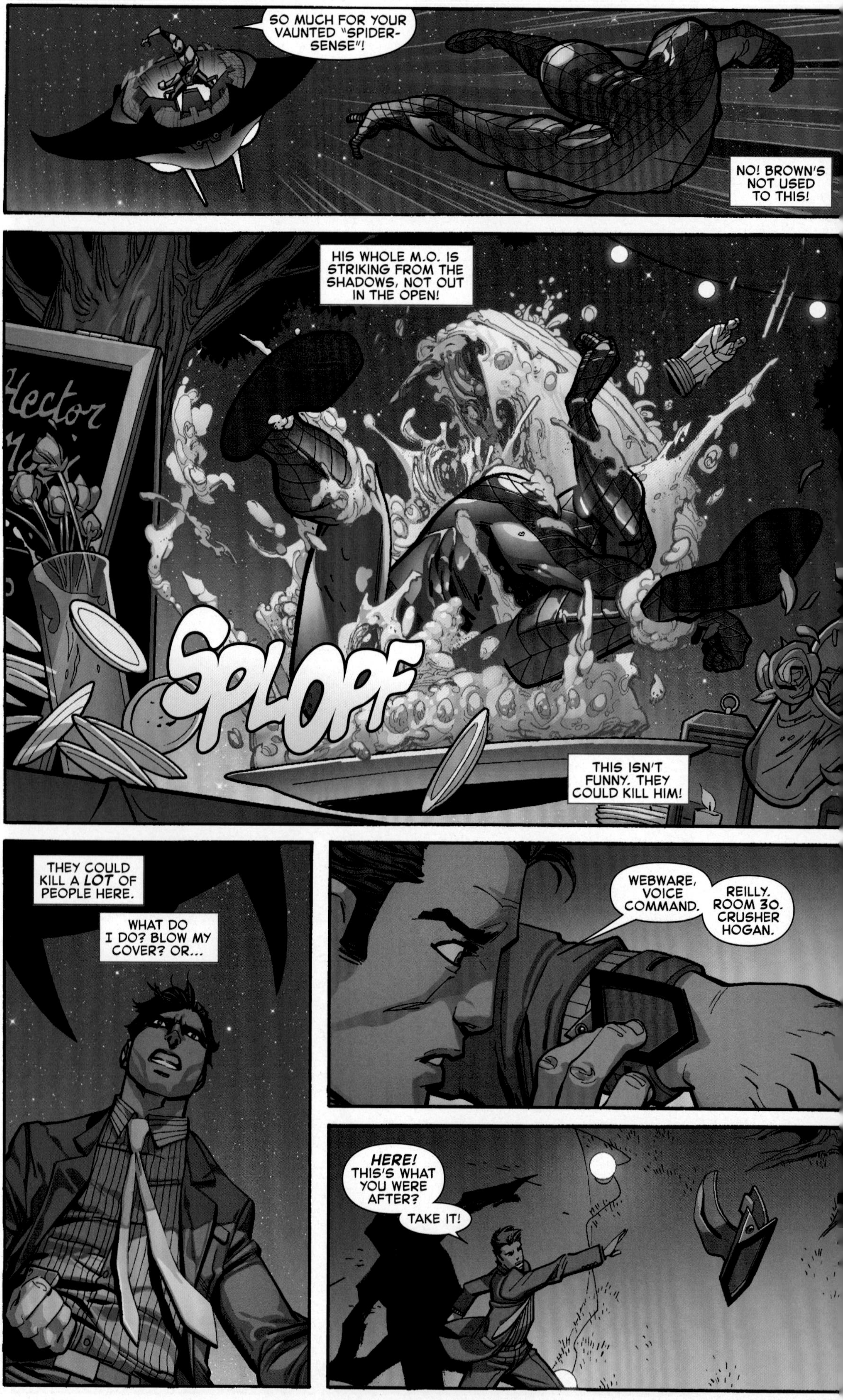

SO MUCH FOR YOUR VAUNTED "SPIDER-SENSE"!
NO! BROWN'S NOT USED TO THIS!
HIS WHOLE M.O. IS STRIKING FROM THE SHADOWS, NOT OUT IN THE OPEN!
Hector
SPLOPF
THIS ISN'T FUNNY. THEY COULD KILL HIM!
THEY COULD KILL A LOT OF PEOPLE HERE.
WHAT DO I DO? BLOW MY COVER? OR...
WEBWARE, VOICE COMMAND.
REILLY. ROOM 30. CRUSHER HOGAN.
HERE! THIS'S WHAT YOU WERE AFTER?
TAKE IT!

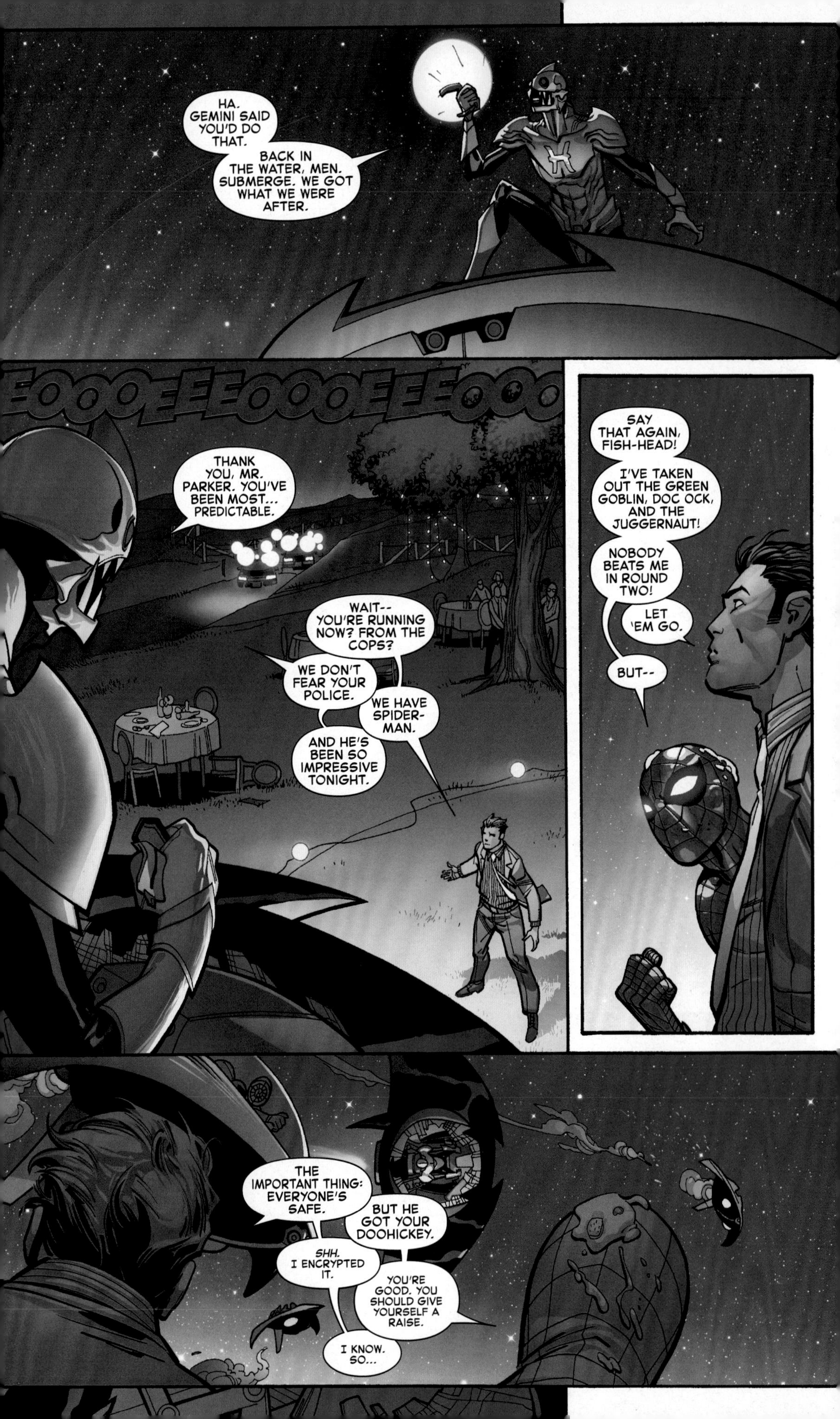
HA. GEMINI SAID YOU'D DO THAT.
BACK IN THE WATER, MEN. SUBMERGE. WE GOT WHAT WE WERE AFTER.
EEOOOEEEOOOEEEOOO
THANK YOU, MR. PARKER. YOU'VE BEEN MOST... PREDICTABLE.
WAIT-- YOU'RE RUNNING NOW? FROM THE COPS?
WE DON'T FEAR YOUR POLICE.
WE HAVE SPIDER-MAN.
AND HE'S BEEN SO IMPRESSIVE TONIGHT.
SAY THAT AGAIN, FISH-HEAD!
I'VE TAKEN OUT THE GREEN GOBLIN, DOC OCK, AND THE JUGGERNAUT!
NOBODY BEATS ME IN ROUND TWO!
LET 'EM GO.
BUT--
THE IMPORTANT THING: EVERYONE'S SAFE.
BUT HE GOT YOUR DOOHICKEY.
SHH. I ENCRYPTED IT.
YOU'RE GOOD. YOU SHOULD GIVE YOURSELF A RAISE.
I KNOW. SO...

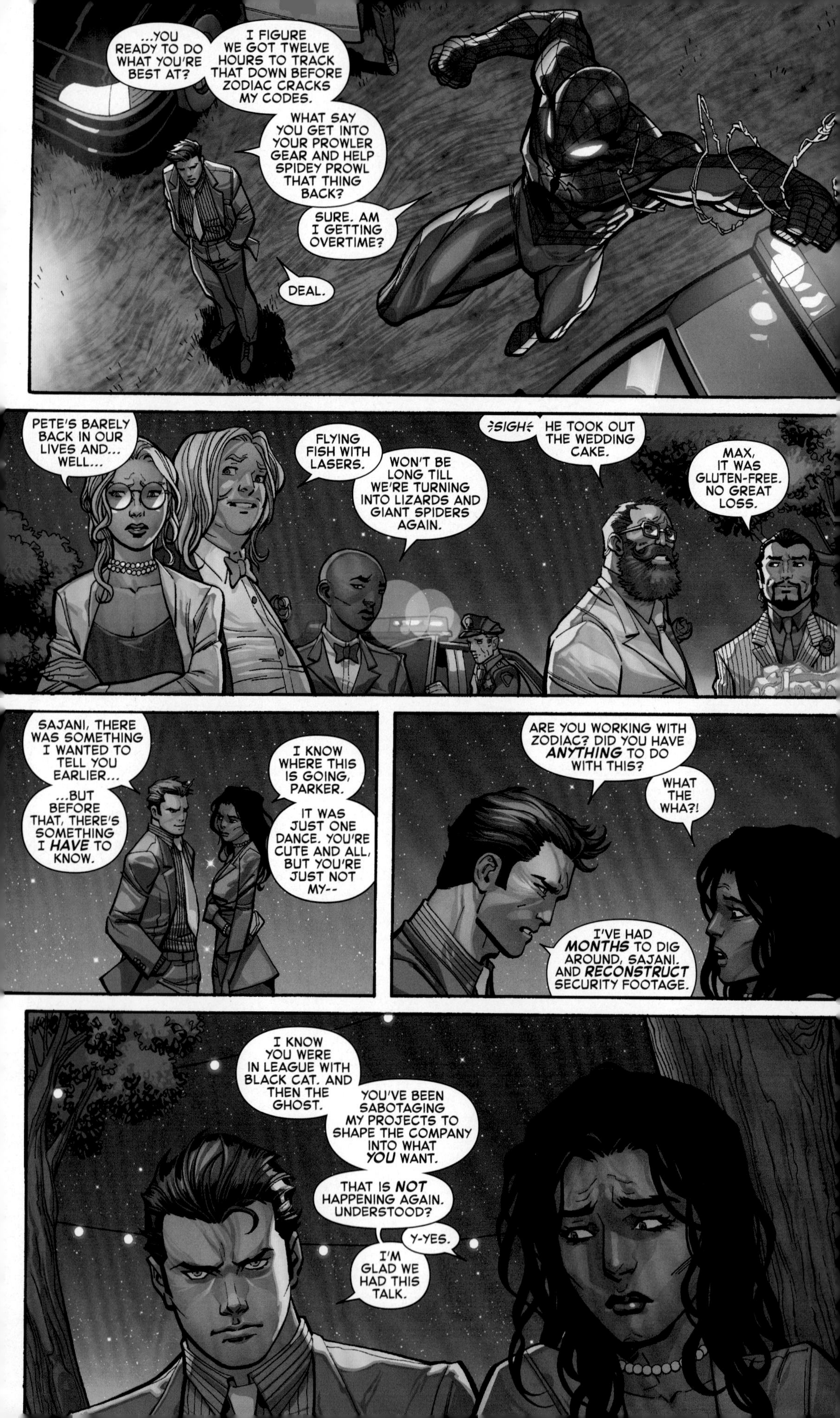
...YOU READY TO DO WHAT YOU'RE BEST AT?
I FIGURE WE GOT TWELVE HOURS TO TRACK THAT DOWN BEFORE ZODIAC CRACKS MY CODES.
WHAT SAY YOU GET INTO YOUR PROWLER GEAR AND HELP SPIDEY PROWL THAT THING BACK?
SURE. AM I GETTING OVERTIME?
DEAL.
PETE'S BARELY BACK IN OUR LIVES AND... WELL...
FLYING FISH WITH LASERS.
WON'T BE LONG TILL WE'RE TURNING INTO LIZARDS AND GIANT SPIDERS AGAIN.
SIGH
HE TOOK OUT THE WEDDING CAKE.
MAX, IT WAS GLUTEN-FREE. NO GREAT LOSS.
SAJANI, THERE WAS SOMETHING I WANTED TO TELL YOU EARLIER...
...BUT BEFORE THAT, THERE'S SOMETHING I HAVE TO KNOW.
I KNOW WHERE THIS IS GOING, PARKER.
IT WAS JUST ONE DANCE. YOU'RE CUTE AND ALL, BUT YOU'RE JUST NOT MY--
ARE YOU WORKING WITH ZODIAC? DID YOU HAVE ANYTHING TO DO WITH THIS?
WHAT THE WHA?!
I'VE HAD MONTHS TO DIG AROUND, SAJANI. AND RECONSTRUCT SECURITY FOOTAGE.
I KNOW YOU WERE IN LEAGUE WITH BLACK CAT. AND THEN THE GHOST.
YOU'VE BEEN SABOTAGING MY PROJECTS TO SHAPE THE COMPANY INTO WHAT YOU WANT.
THAT IS NOT HAPPENING AGAIN. UNDERSTOOD?
Y-YES.
I'M GLAD WE HAD THIS TALK.

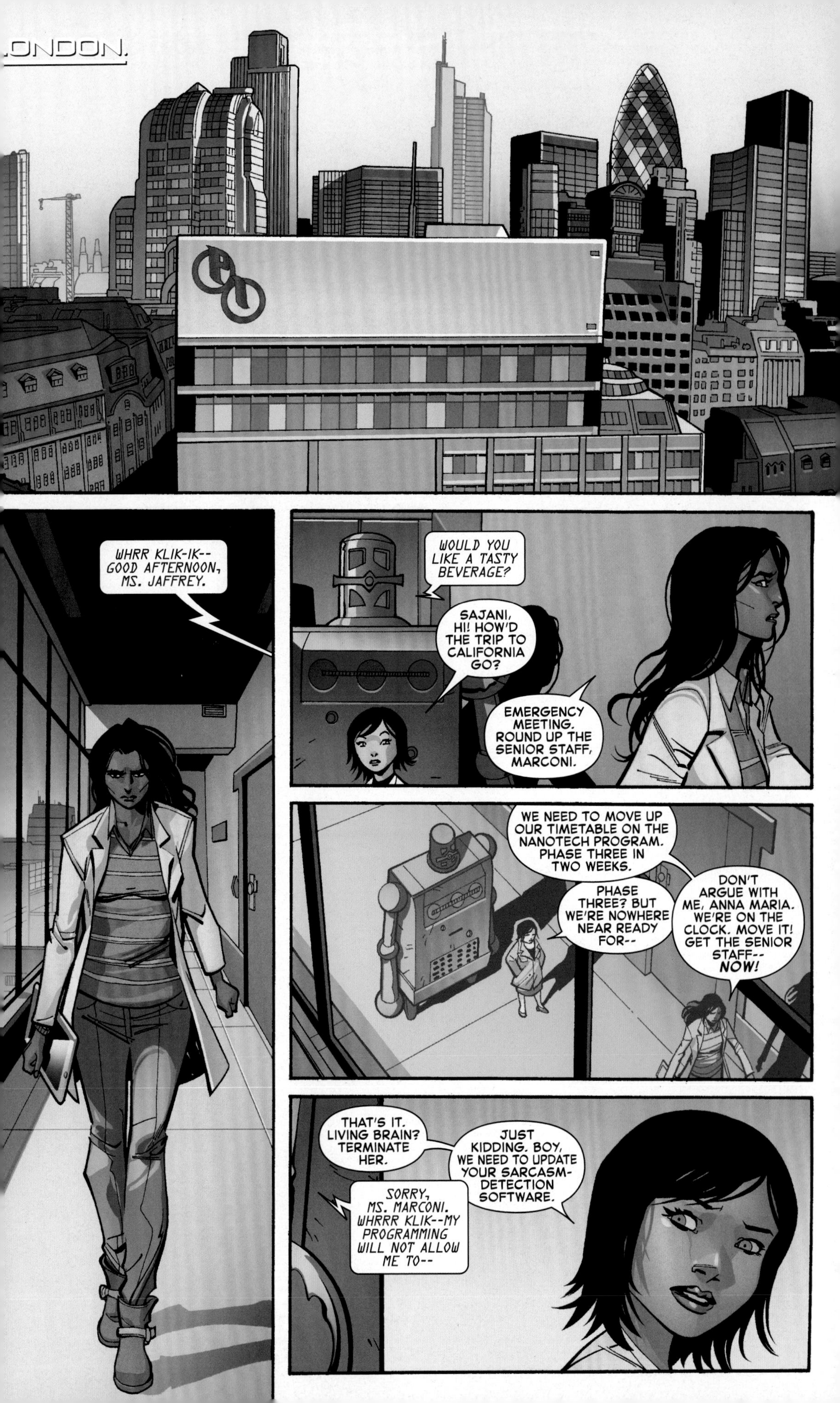
LONDON.
WHRR KLIK-IK-- GOOD AFTERNOON, MS. JAFFREY.
WOULD YOU LIKE A TASTY BEVERAGE?
SAJANI, HI! HOW'D THE TRIP TO CALIFORNIA GO?
EMERGENCY MEETING. ROUND UP THE SENIOR STAFF, MARCONI.
WE NEED TO MOVE UP OUR TIMETABLE ON THE NANOTECH PROGRAM. PHASE THREE IN TWO WEEKS.
PHASE THREE? BUT WE'RE NOWHERE NEAR READY FOR--
DON'T ARGUE WITH ME, ANNA MARIA. WE'RE ON THE CLOCK. MOVE IT! GET THE SENIOR STAFF-- NOW!
THAT'S IT. LIVING BRAIN? TERMINATE HER.
SORRY, MS. MARCONI. WHRRR KLIK--MY PROGRAMMING WILL NOT ALLOW ME TO--
JUST KIDDING. BOY, WE NEED TO UPDATE YOUR SARCASM-DETECTION SOFTWARE.

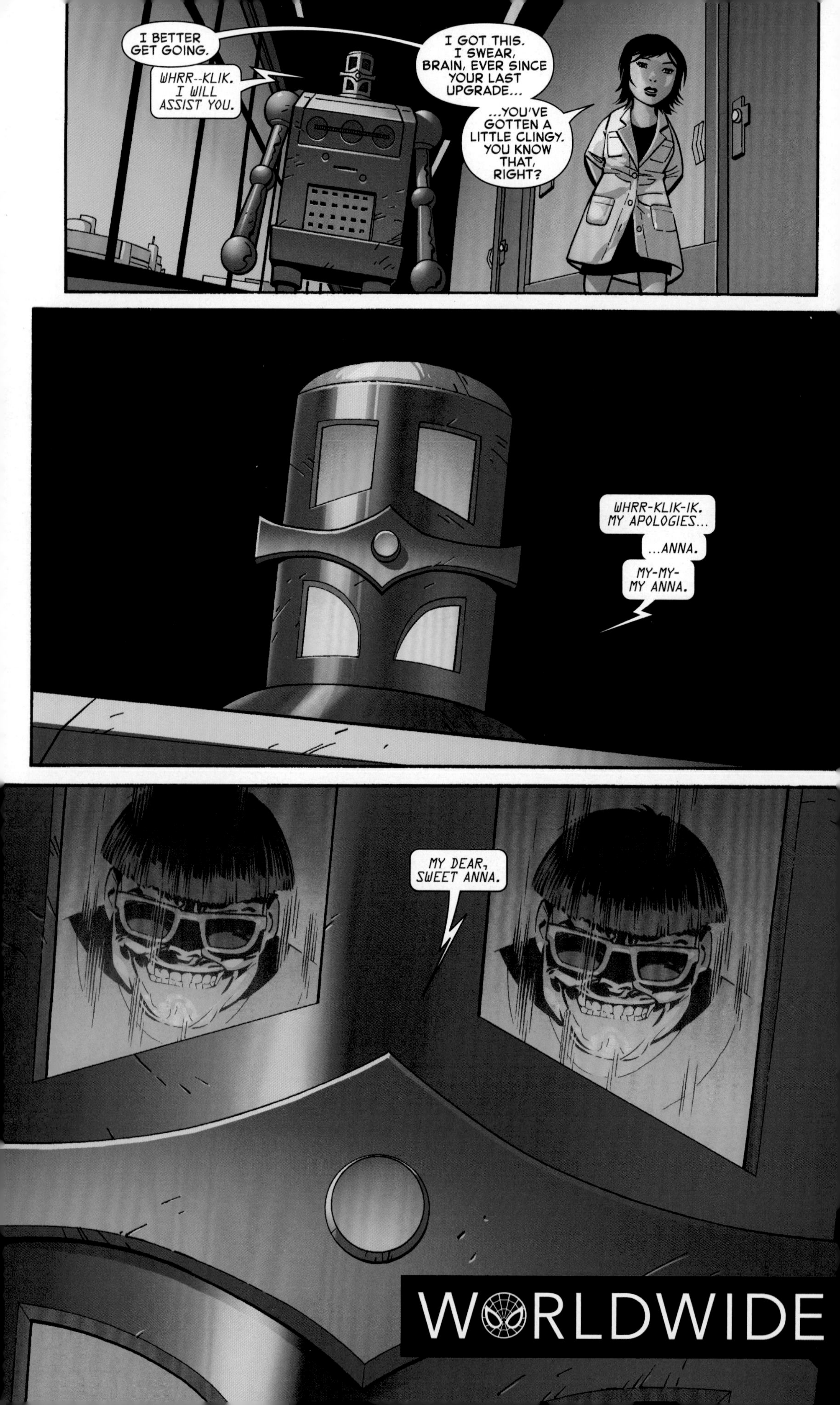
I BETTER GET GOING.
WHRR--KLIK. I WILL ASSIST YOU.
I GOT THIS. I SWEAR, BRAIN, EVER SINCE YOUR LAST UPGRADE...
...YOU'VE GOTTEN A LITTLE CLINGY. YOU KNOW THAT, RIGHT?
WHRR-KLIK-IK. MY APOLOGIES...
...ANNA.
MY-MY-MY ANNA.
MY DEAR, SWEET ANNA.
WORLDWIDE

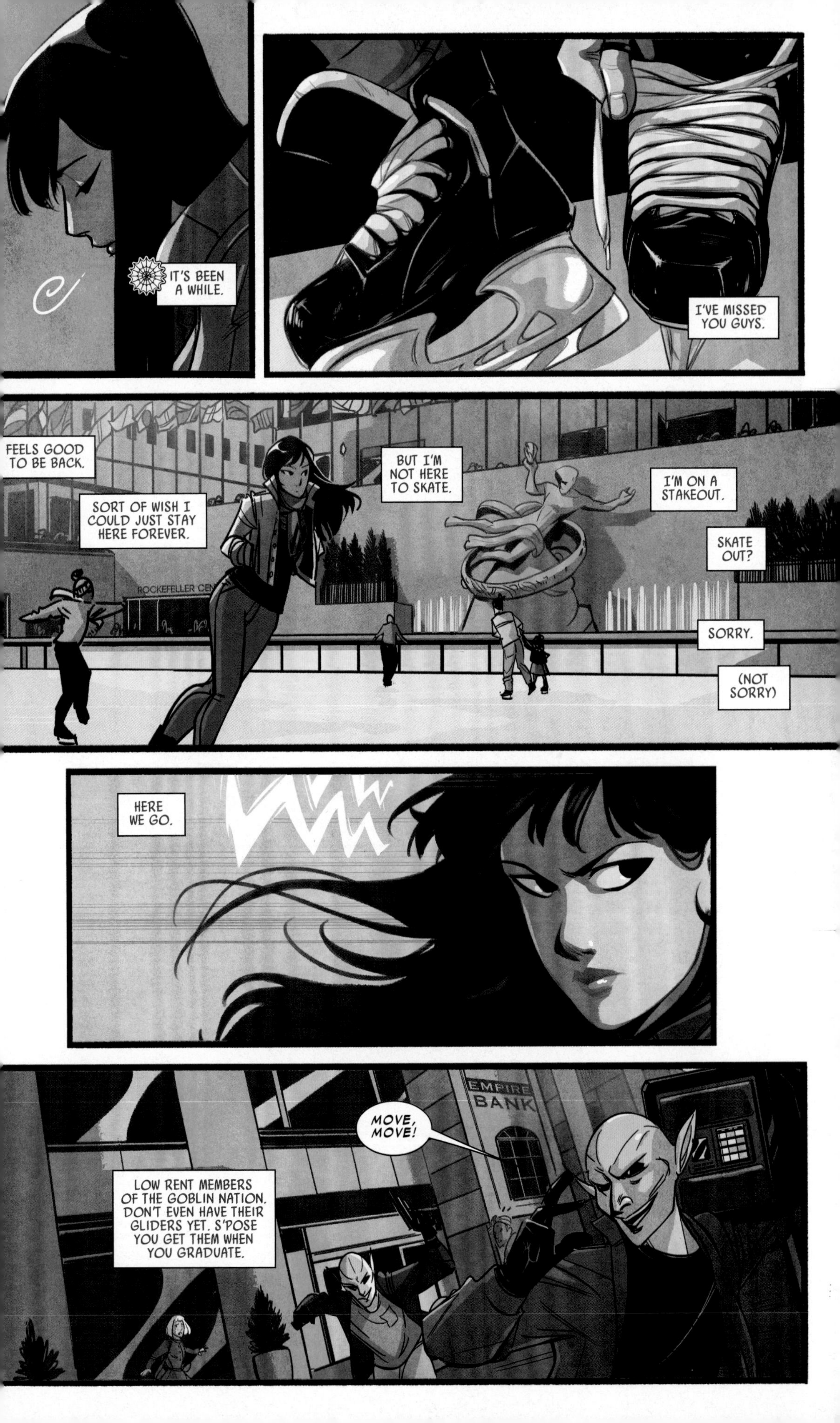
IT'S BEEN A WHILE.
I'VE MISSED YOU GUYS.
FEELS GOOD TO BE BACK.
SORT OF WISH I COULD JUST STAY HERE FOREVER.
BUT I'M NOT HERE TO SKATE.
I'M ON A STAKEOUT.
SKATE OUT?
SORRY.
(NOT SORRY)
HERE WE GO.
LOW RENT MEMBERS OF THE GOBLIN NATION. DON'T EVEN HAVE THEIR GLIDERS YET. S'POSE YOU GET THEM WHEN YOU GRADUATE.
MOVE, MOVE!
EMPIRE BANK

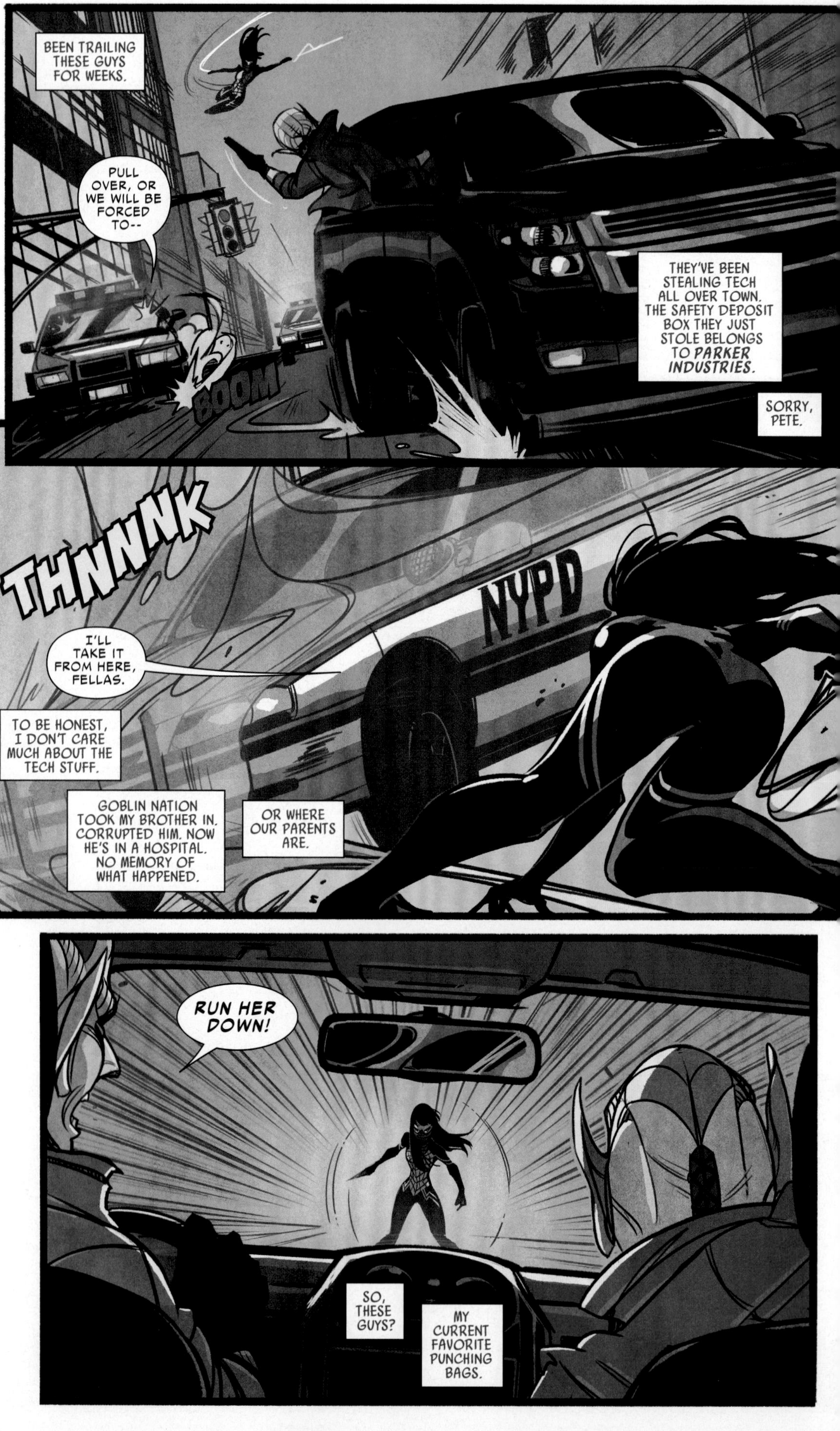
BEEN TRAILING THESE GUYS FOR WEEKS.
PULL OVER, OR WE WILL BE FORCED TO--
BOOM
THEY'VE BEEN STEALING TECH ALL OVER TOWN. THE SAFETY DEPOSIT BOX THEY JUST STOLE BELONGS TO PARKER INDUSTRIES.
SORRY, PETE.
THNNNK
NYPD
I'LL TAKE IT FROM HERE, FELLAS.
TO BE HONEST, I DON'T CARE MUCH ABOUT THE TECH STUFF.
GOBLIN NATION TOOK MY BROTHER IN. CORRUPTED HIM. NOW HE'S IN A HOSPITAL. NO MEMORY OF WHAT HAPPENED.
OR WHERE OUR PARENTS ARE.
RUN HER DOWN!
SO, THESE GUYS?
MY CURRENT FAVORITE PUNCHING BAGS.

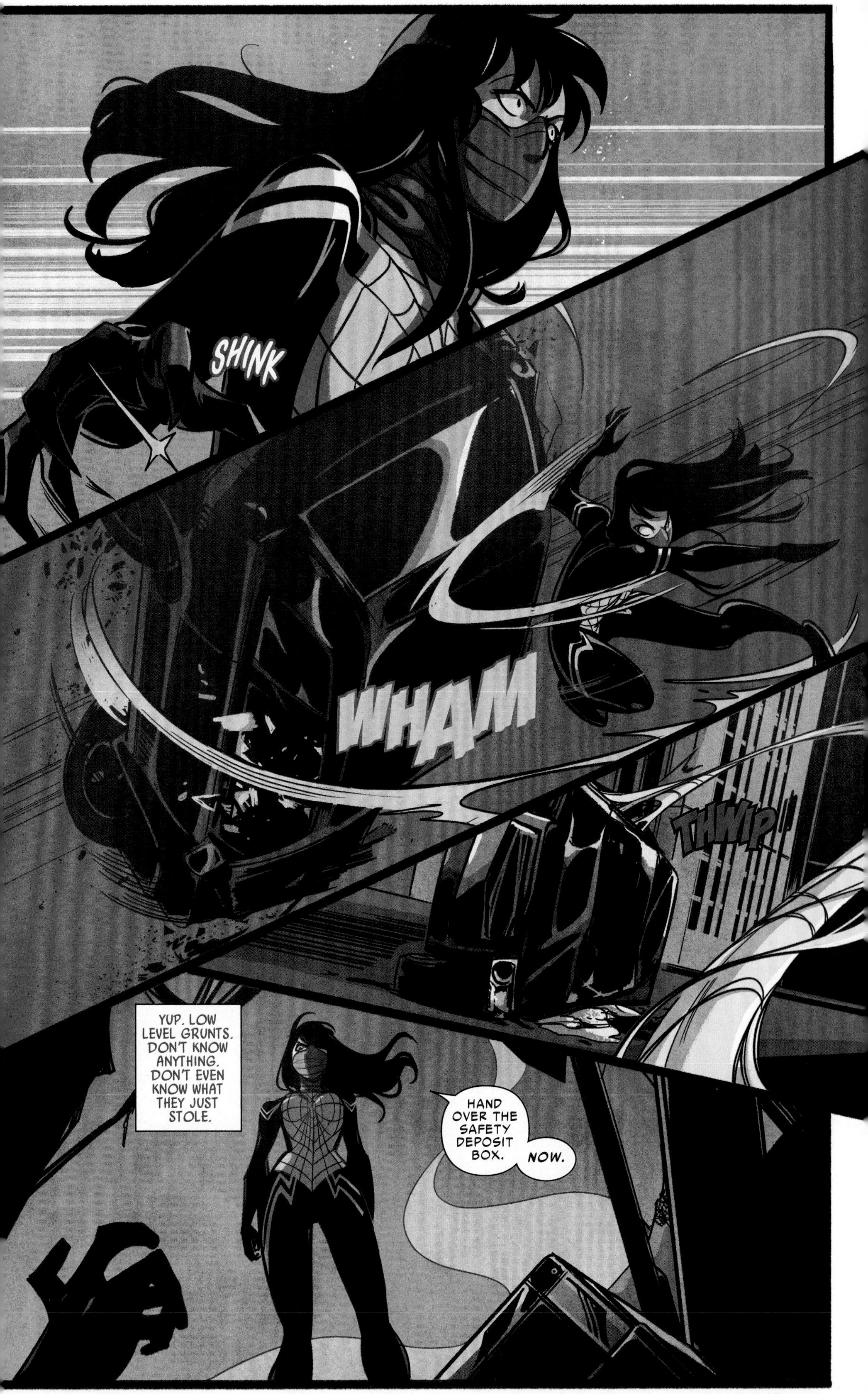
SHINK
WHAM
THWIP
YUP. LOW LEVEL GRUNTS. DON'T KNOW ANYTHING. DON'T EVEN KNOW WHAT THEY JUST STOLE.
HAND OVER THE SAFETY DEPOSIT BOX.
NOW.

HEY, WHAT THE-- BLURGGHRF!

NAPTIME, KIDDOS.

ENJOY PRISON!

IN FAIRNESS, I HAVE NO IDEA WHAT THIS IS EITHER.

I JUST KNOW MY BOSS WANTS IT.

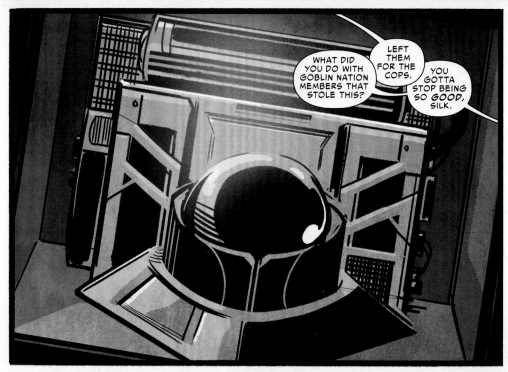

WHAT DID YOU DO WITH GOBLIN NATION MEMBERS THAT STOLE THIS?

LEFT THEM FOR THE COPS.

YOU GOTTA STOP BEING SO GOOD, SILK.

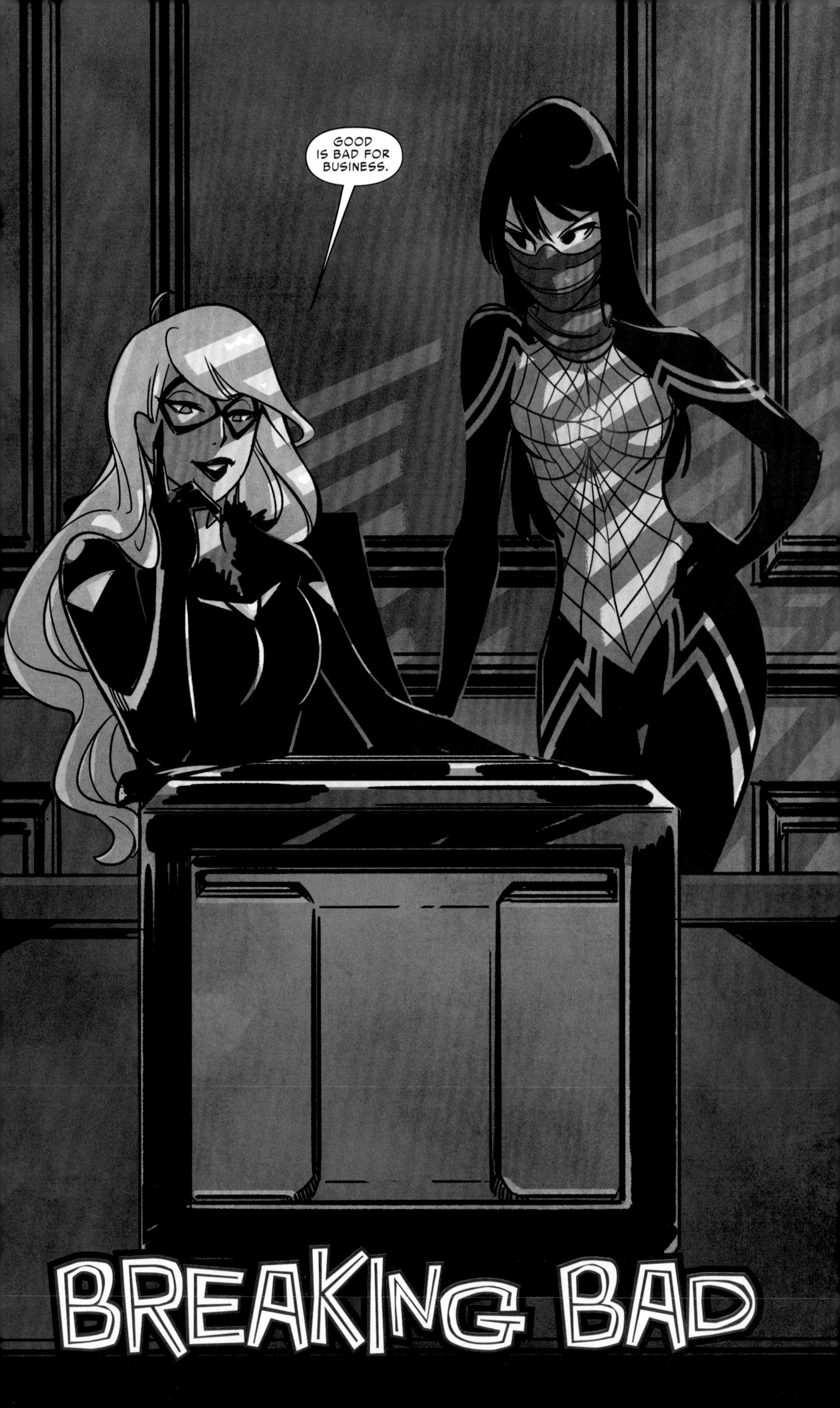
GOOD IS BAD FOR BUSINESS.
BREAKING BAD

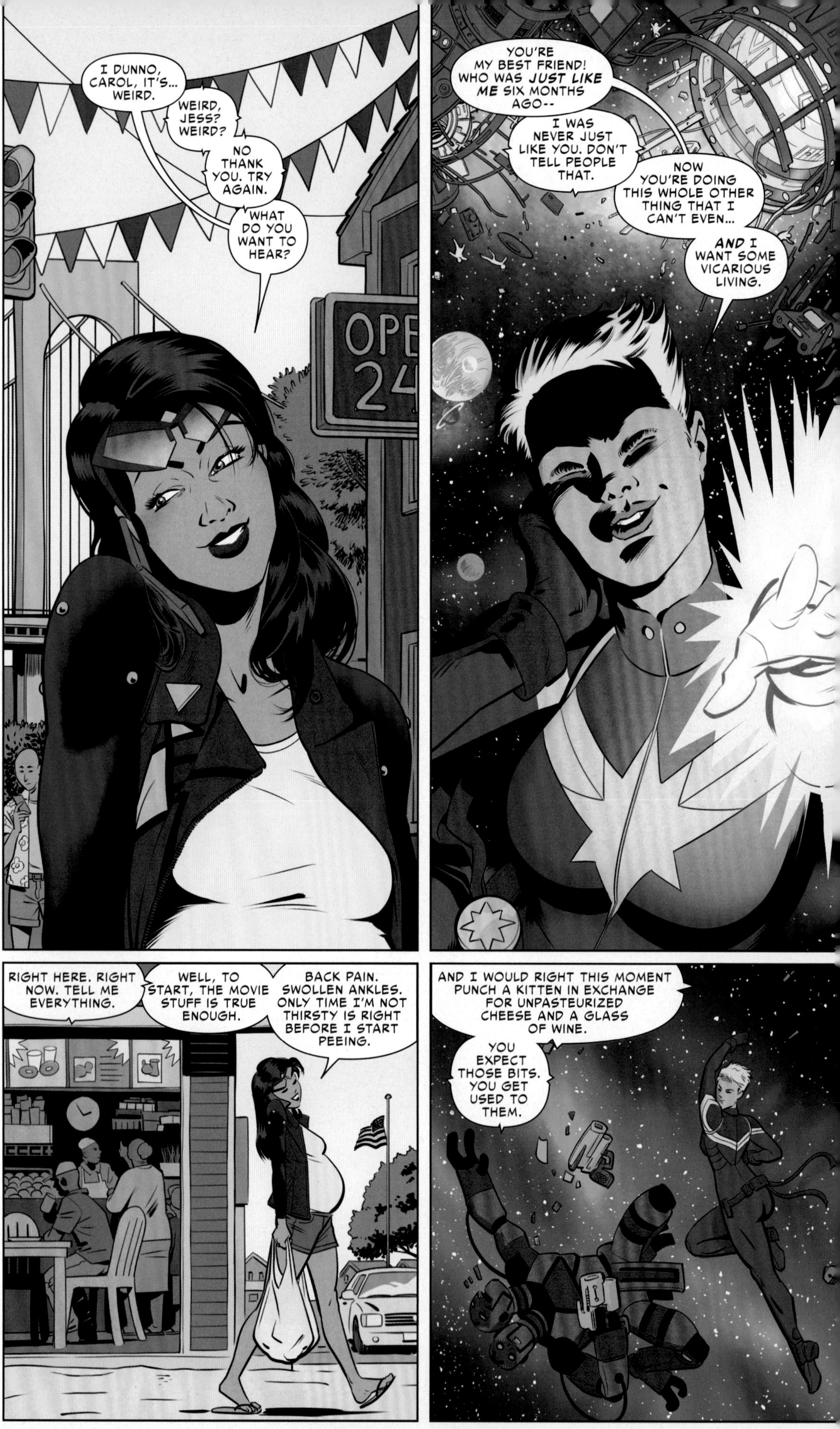

I DUNNO, CAROL, IT'S... WEIRD.
WEIRD, JESS? WEIRD?
NO THANK YOU. TRY AGAIN.
WHAT DO YOU WANT TO HEAR?
OPE 24
YOU'RE MY BEST FRIEND! WHO WAS JUST LIKE ME SIX MONTHS AGO--
I WAS NEVER JUST LIKE YOU. DON'T TELL PEOPLE THAT.
NOW YOU'RE DOING THIS WHOLE OTHER THING THAT I CAN'T EVEN...
AND I WANT SOME VICARIOUS LIVING.
RIGHT HERE. RIGHT NOW. TELL ME EVERYTHING.
WELL, TO START, THE MOVIE STUFF IS TRUE ENOUGH.
BACK PAIN. SWOLLEN ANKLES. ONLY TIME I'M NOT THIRSTY IS RIGHT BEFORE I START PEEING.
AND I WOULD RIGHT THIS MOMENT PUNCH A KITTEN IN EXCHANGE FOR UNPASTEURIZED CHEESE AND A GLASS OF WINE.
YOU EXPECT THOSE BITS. YOU GET USED TO THEM.

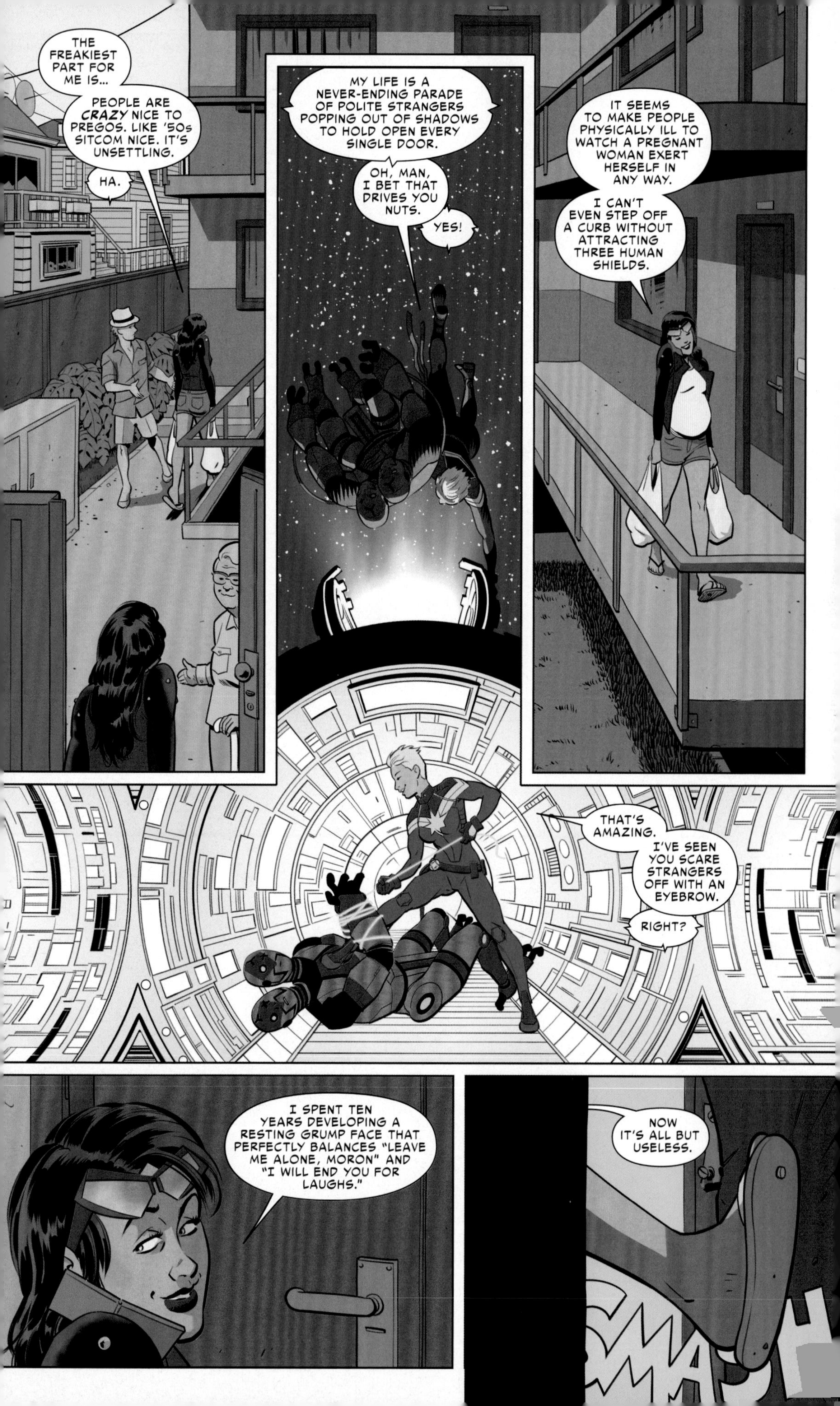

THE FREAKIEST PART FOR ME IS...
PEOPLE ARE CRAZY NICE TO PREGOS. LIKE '50s SITCOM NICE. IT'S UNSETTLING.
HA.
MY LIFE IS A NEVER-ENDING PARADE OF POLITE STRANGERS POPPING OUT OF SHADOWS TO HOLD OPEN EVERY SINGLE DOOR.
OH, MAN, I BET THAT DRIVES YOU NUTS.
YES!
IT SEEMS TO MAKE PEOPLE PHYSICALLY ILL TO WATCH A PREGNANT WOMAN EXERT HERSELF IN ANY WAY.
I CAN'T EVEN STEP OFF A CURB WITHOUT ATTRACTING THREE HUMAN SHIELDS.
THAT'S AMAZING.
I'VE SEEN YOU SCARE STRANGERS OFF WITH AN EYEBROW.
RIGHT?
I SPENT TEN YEARS DEVELOPING A RESTING GRUMP FACE THAT PERFECTLY BALANCES "LEAVE ME ALONE, MORON" AND "I WILL END YOU FOR LAUGHS."
NOW IT'S ALL BUT USELESS.
SMASH

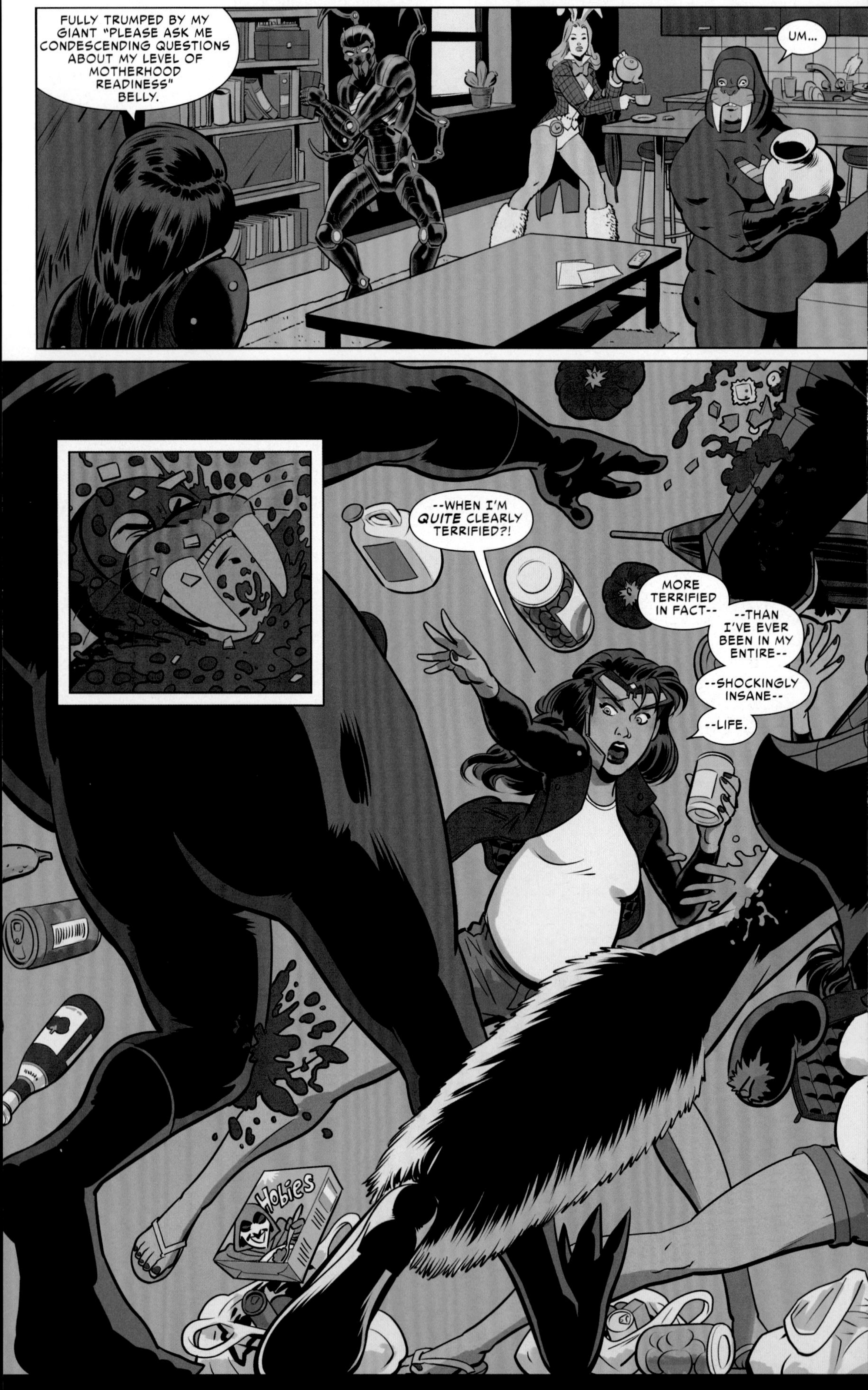
FULLY TRUMPED BY MY GIANT "PLEASE ASK ME CONDESCENDING QUESTIONS ABOUT MY LEVEL OF MOTHERHOOD READINESS" BELLY.
UM...
--WHEN I'M QUITE CLEARLY TERRIFIED?!
MORE TERRIFIED IN FACT--
--THAN I'VE EVER BEEN IN MY ENTIRE--
--SHOCKINGLY INSANE--
--LIFE.
HOBIES

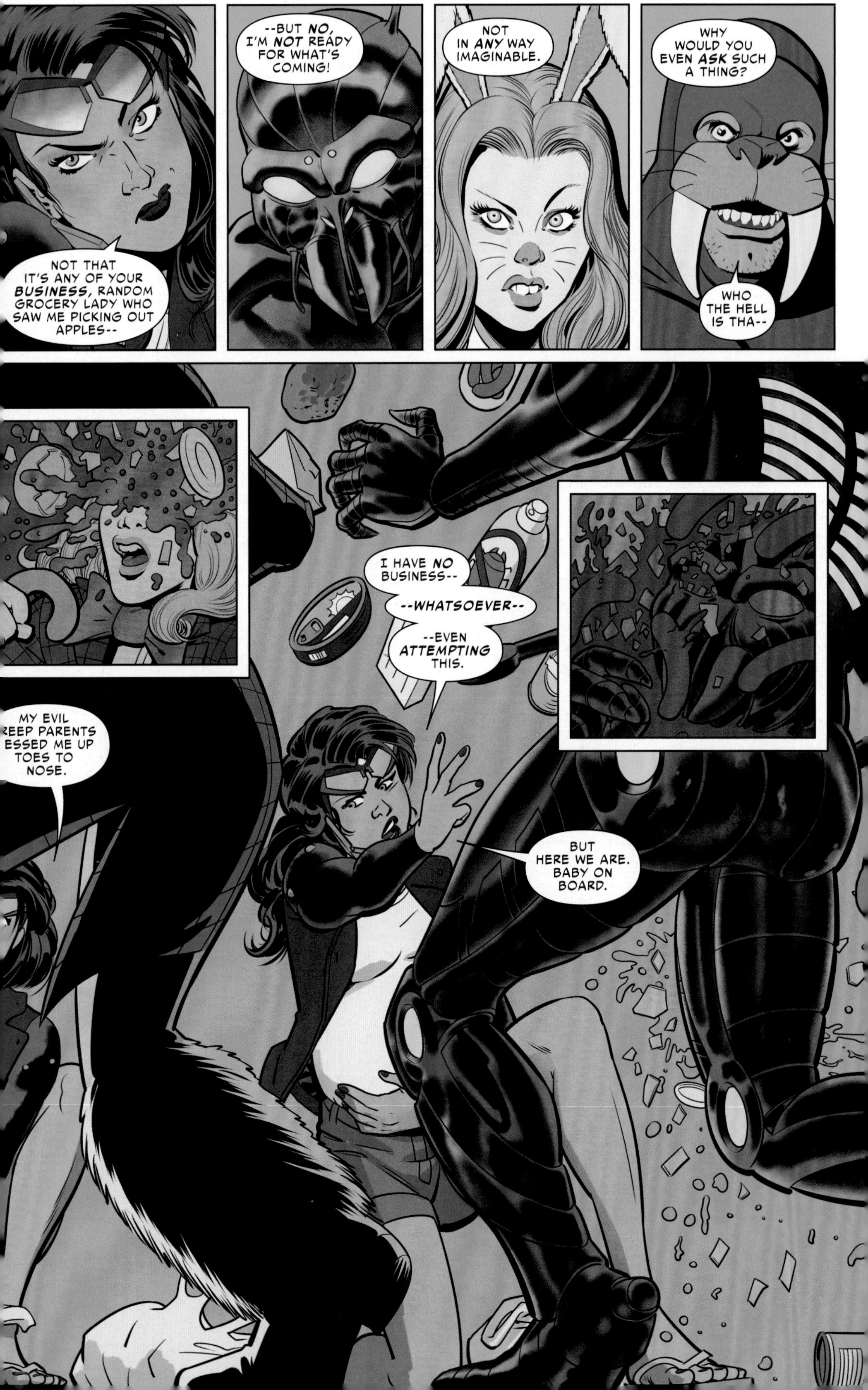
NOT THAT IT'S ANY OF YOUR BUSINESS, RANDOM GROCERY LADY WHO SAW ME PICKING OUT APPLES--
--BUT NO, I'M NOT READY FOR WHAT'S COMING!
NOT IN ANY WAY IMAGINABLE.
WHY WOULD YOU EVEN ASK SUCH A THING?
WHO THE HELL IS THA--
I HAVE NO BUSINESS--
--WHATSOEVER--
--EVEN ATTEMPTING THIS.
MY EVIL REEP PARENTS ESSED ME UP TOES TO NOSE.
BUT HERE WE ARE. BABY ON BOARD.

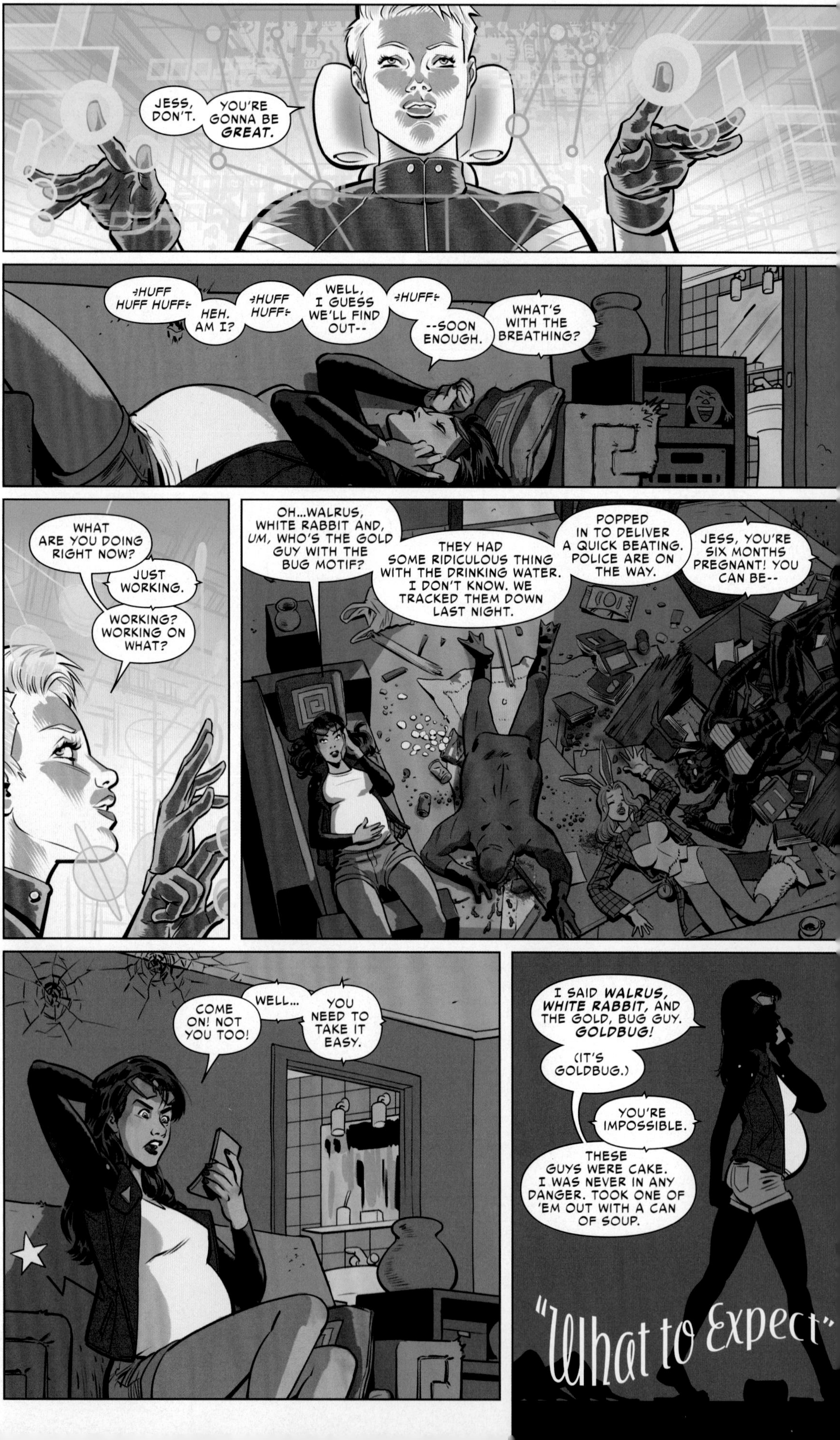

JESS, DON'T.
YOU'RE GONNA BE GREAT.
HUFF HUFF HUFF
HEH. AM I?
HUFF HUFF
WELL, I GUESS WE'LL FIND OUT--
HUFF
--SOON ENOUGH.
WHAT'S WITH THE BREATHING?
WHAT ARE YOU DOING RIGHT NOW?
JUST WORKING.
WORKING? WORKING ON WHAT?
OH...WALRUS, WHITE RABBIT AND, UM, WHO'S THE GOLD GUY WITH THE BUG MOTIF?
THEY HAD SOME RIDICULOUS THING WITH THE DRINKING WATER. I DON'T KNOW. WE TRACKED THEM DOWN LAST NIGHT.
POPPED IN TO DELIVER A QUICK BEATING. POLICE ARE ON THE WAY.
JESS, YOU'RE SIX MONTHS PREGNANT! YOU CAN BE--
COME ON! NOT YOU TOO!
WELL...
YOU NEED TO TAKE IT EASY.
I SAID WALRUS, WHITE RABBIT, AND THE GOLD, BUG GUY. GOLDBUG!
(IT'S GOLDBUG.)
YOU'RE IMPOSSIBLE.
THESE GUYS WERE CAKE. I WAS NEVER IN ANY DANGER. TOOK ONE OF 'EM OUT WITH A CAN OF SOUP.
"What to Expect"

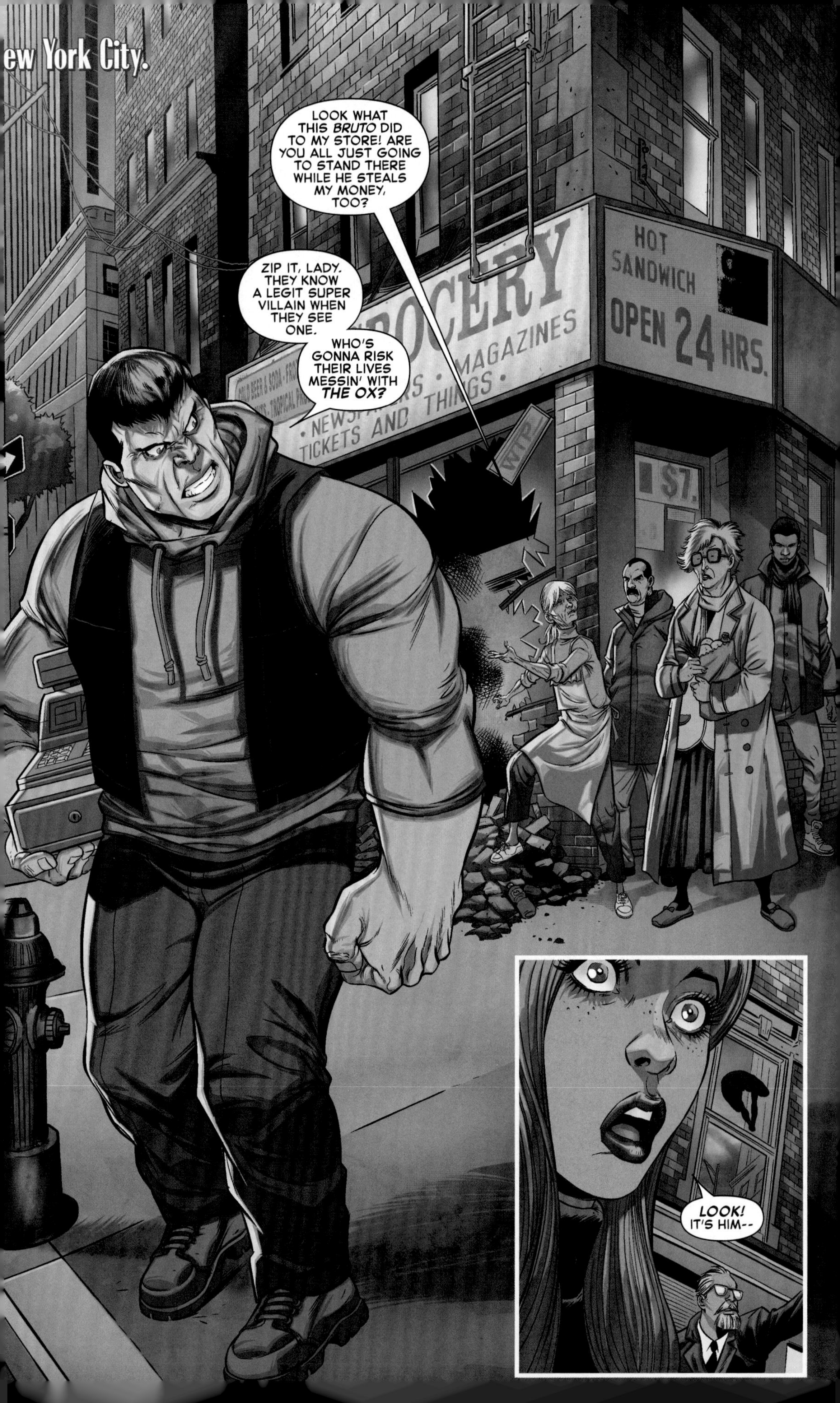
ew York City.
LOOK WHAT THIS BRUTO DID TO MY STORE! ARE YOU ALL JUST GOING TO STAND THERE WHILE HE STEALS MY MONEY, TOO?
ZIP IT, LADY. THEY KNOW A LEGIT SUPER VILLAIN WHEN THEY SEE ONE.
WHO'S GONNA RISK THEIR LIVES MESSIN' WITH THE OX?
ROCERY
NEWSPAPERS · MAGAZINES
TICKETS AND THINGS ·
HOT SANDWICH
OPEN 24 HRS.
$7.
LOOK! IT'S HIM--

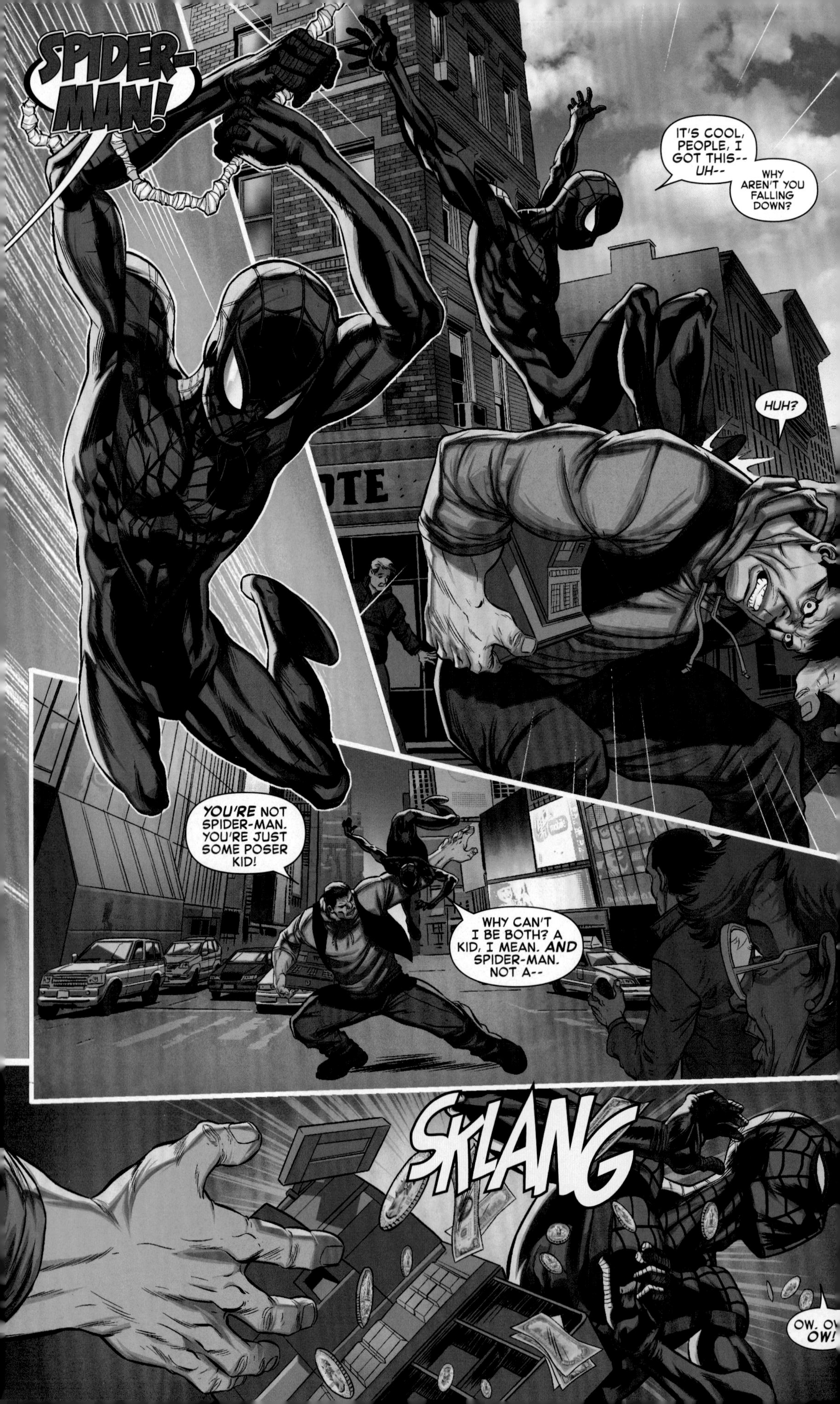
SPIDER-MAN!
IT'S COOL, PEOPLE, I GOT THIS-- UH--
WHY AREN'T YOU FALLING DOWN?
HUH?
YOU'RE NOT SPIDER-MAN. YOU'RE JUST SOME POSER KID!
WHY CAN'T I BE BOTH? A KID, I MEAN. AND SPIDER-MAN. NOT A--
SKLANG
OW. OW! OW!

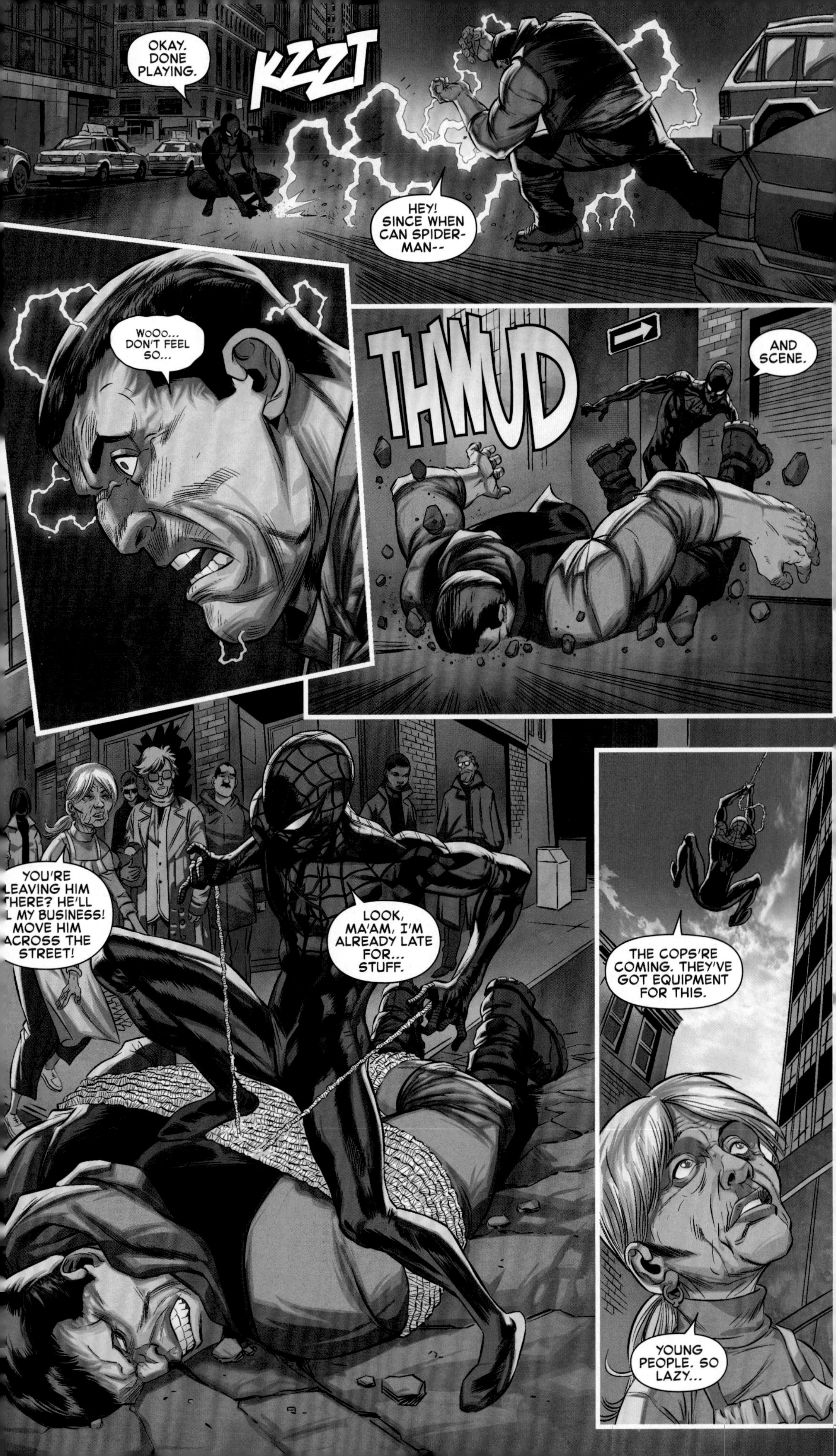

OKAY. DONE PLAYING.
KZZT
HEY! SINCE WHEN CAN SPIDER-MAN--
WoOo... DON'T FEEL SO...
THMUD
AND SCENE.
YOU'RE LEAVING HIM THERE? HE'LL L MY BUSINESS! MOVE HIM ACROSS THE STREET!
LOOK, MA'AM, I'M ALREADY LATE FOR... STUFF.
THE COPS'RE COMING. THEY'VE GOT EQUIPMENT FOR THIS.
YOUNG PEOPLE. SO LAZY...

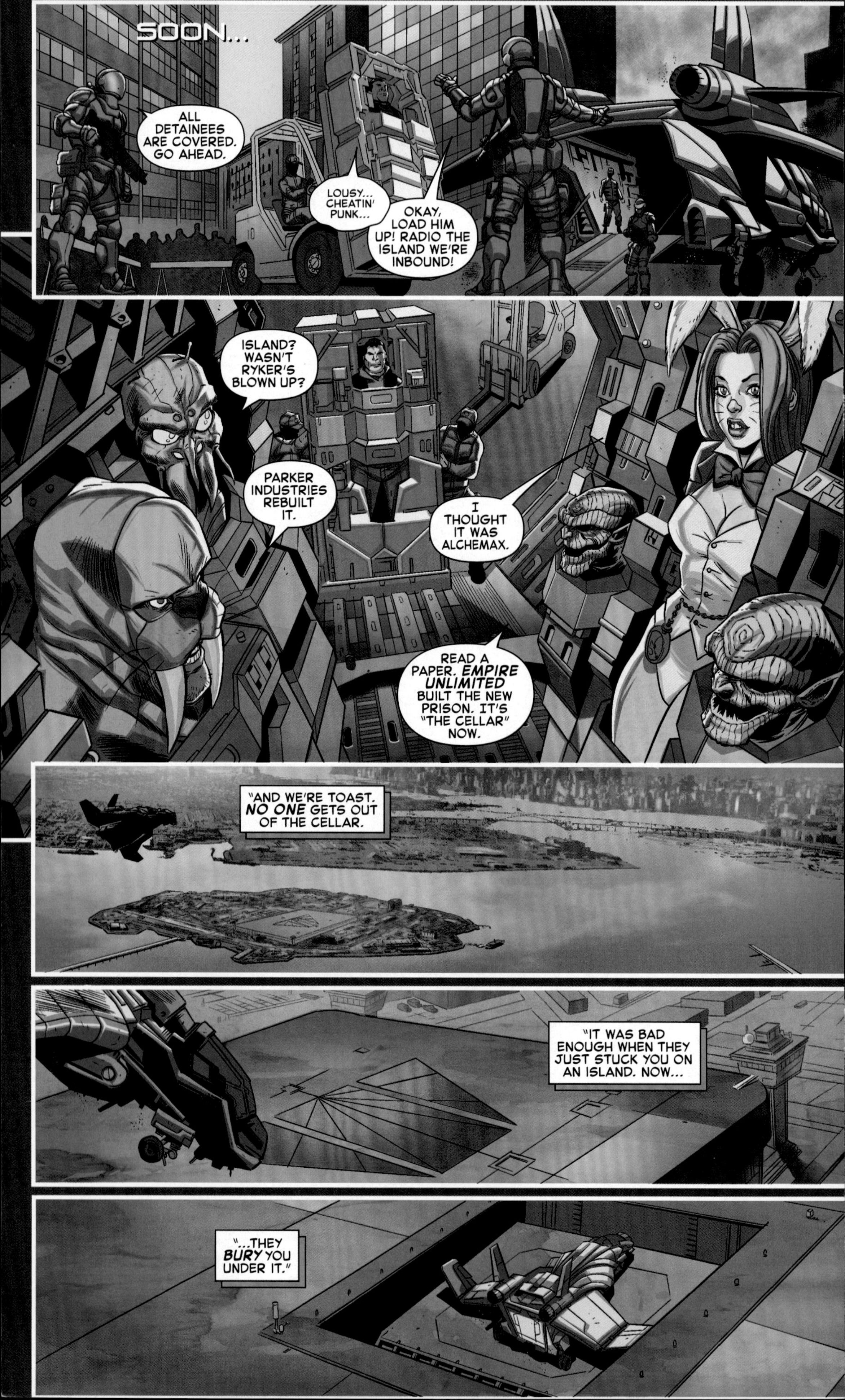
SOON...
ALL DETAINEES ARE COVERED. GO AHEAD.
LOUSY... CHEATIN' PUNK...
OKAY, LOAD HIM UP! RADIO THE ISLAND WE'RE INBOUND!
ISLAND? WASN'T RYKER'S BLOWN UP?
PARKER INDUSTRIES REBUILT IT.
I THOUGHT IT WAS ALCHEMAX.
READ A PAPER. EMPIRE UNLIMITED BUILT THE NEW PRISON. IT'S "THE CELLAR" NOW.
"AND WE'RE TOAST. NO ONE GETS OUT OF THE CELLAR.
"IT WAS BAD ENOUGH WHEN THEY JUST STUCK YOU ON AN ISLAND. NOW...
"...THEY BURY YOU UNDER IT."

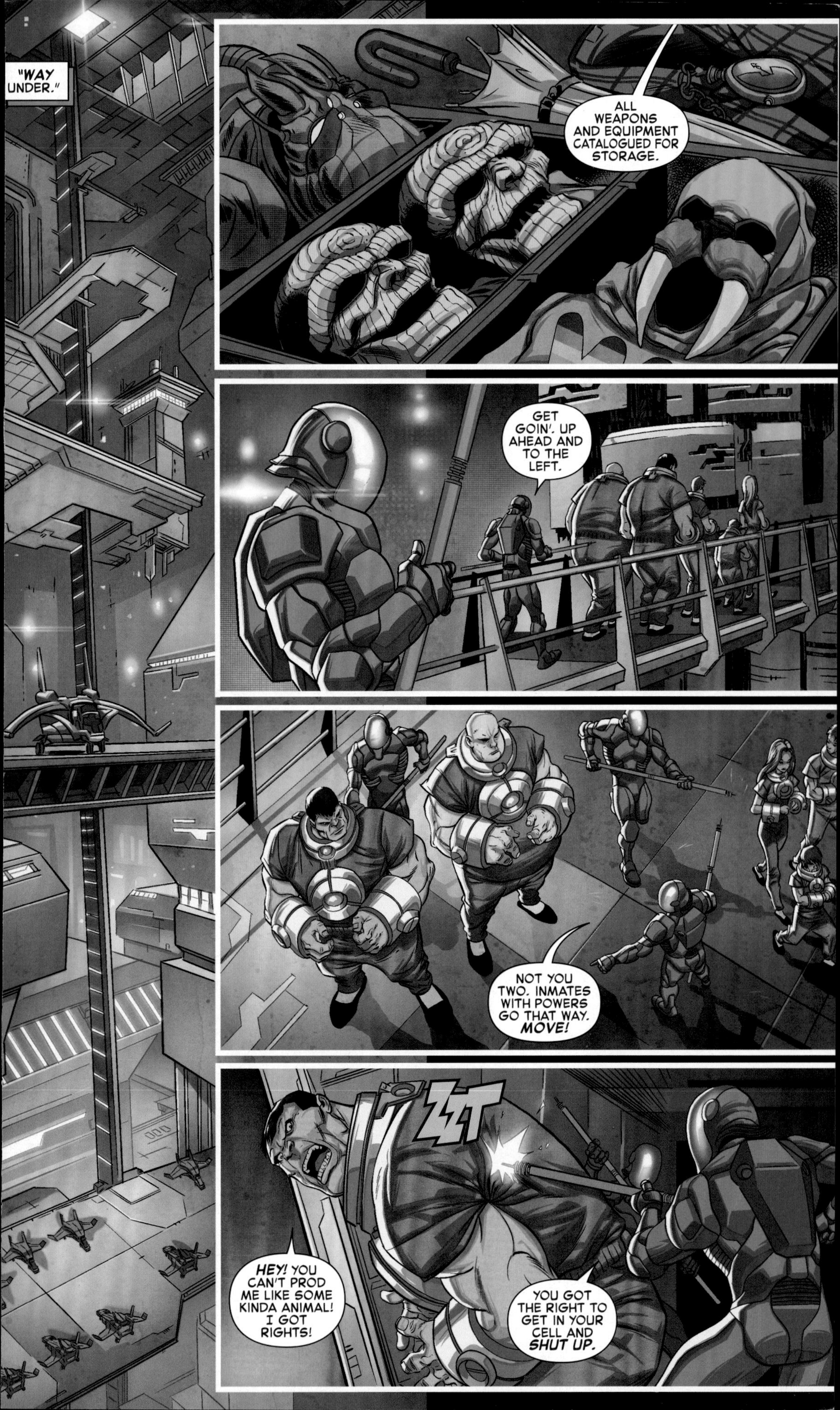
"WAY UNDER."
ALL WEAPONS AND EQUIPMENT CATALOGUED FOR STORAGE.
GET GOIN'. UP AHEAD AND TO THE LEFT.
NOT YOU TWO. INMATES WITH POWERS GO THAT WAY. MOVE!
ZZT
HEY! YOU CAN'T PROD ME LIKE SOME KINDA ANIMAL! I GOT RIGHTS!
YOU GOT THE RIGHT TO GET IN YOUR CELL AND SHUT UP.

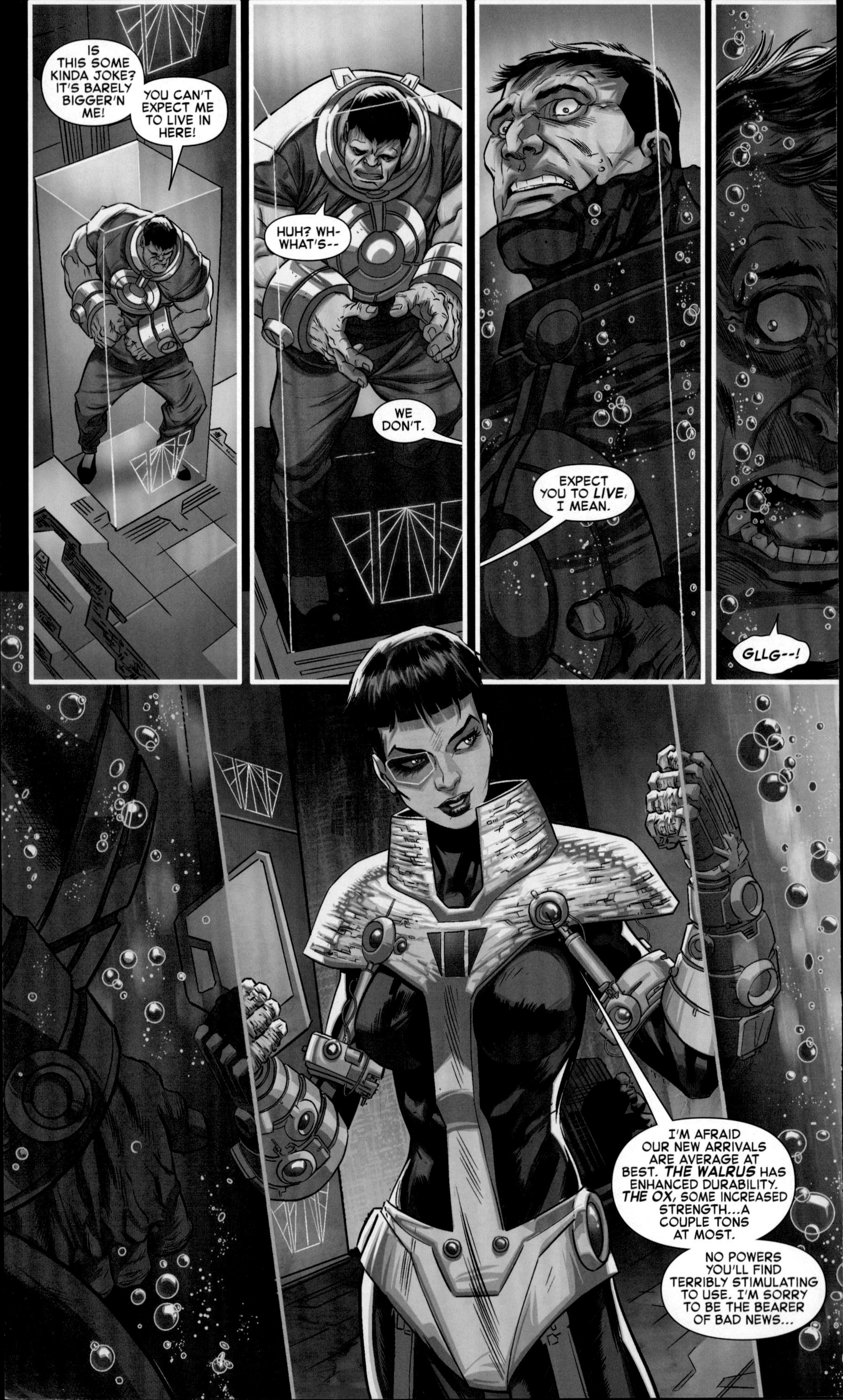

IS THIS SOME KINDA JOKE? IT'S BARELY BIGGER'N ME!
YOU CAN'T EXPECT ME TO LIVE IN HERE!
HUH? WH-WHAT'S--
WE DON'T.
EXPECT YOU TO *LIVE*, I MEAN.
GLLG--!
I'M AFRAID OUR NEW ARRIVALS ARE AVERAGE AT BEST. *THE WALRUS* HAS ENHANCED DURABILITY. *THE OX*, SOME INCREASED STRENGTH...A COUPLE TONS AT MOST.
NO POWERS YOU'LL FIND TERRIBLY STIMULATING TO USE. I'M SORRY TO BE THE BEARER OF BAD NEWS...

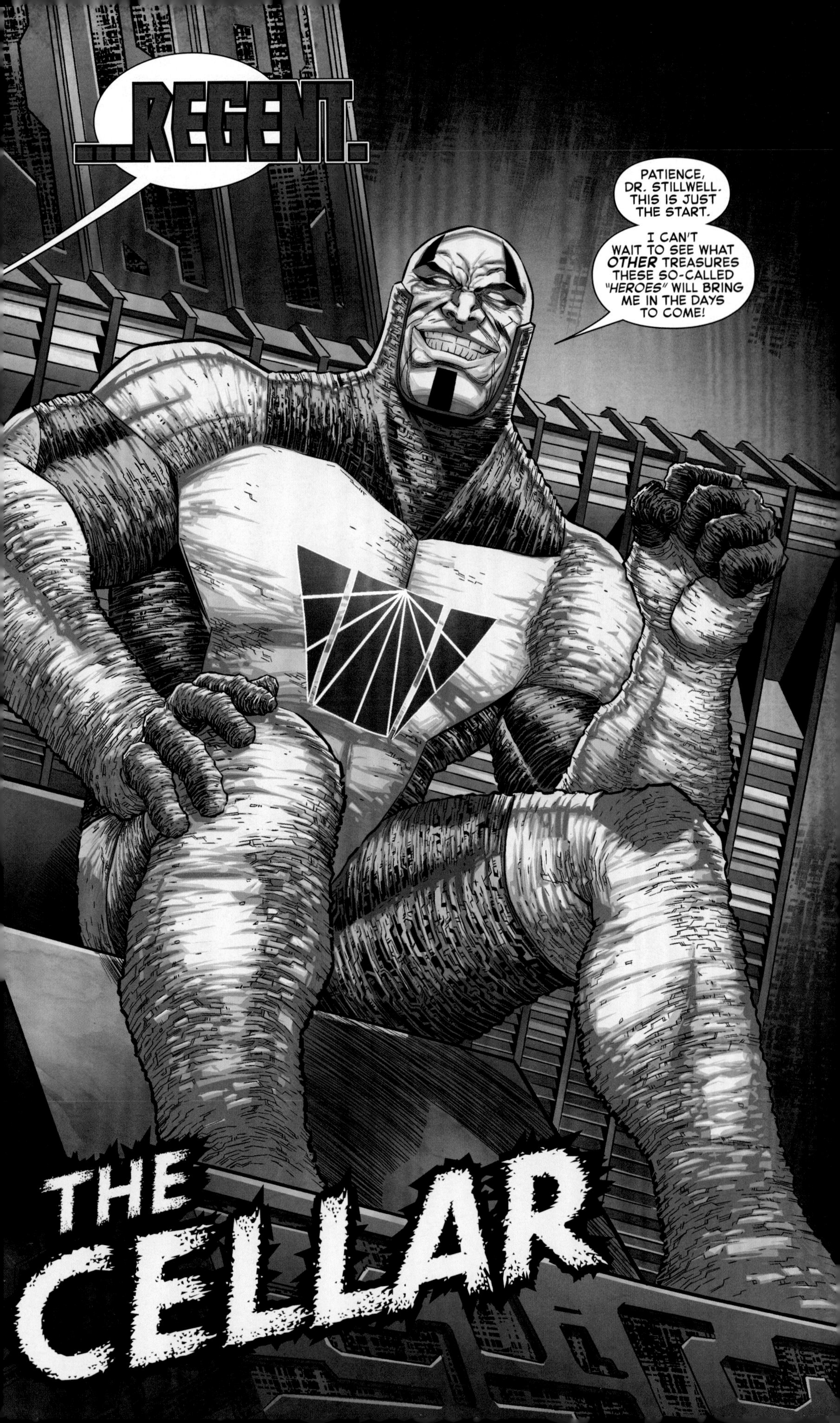
...REGENT.
PATIENCE, DR. STILLWELL. THIS IS JUST THE START.
I CAN'T WAIT TO SEE WHAT OTHER TREASURES THESE SO-CALLED "HEROES" WILL BRING ME IN THE DAYS TO COME!
THE CELLAR

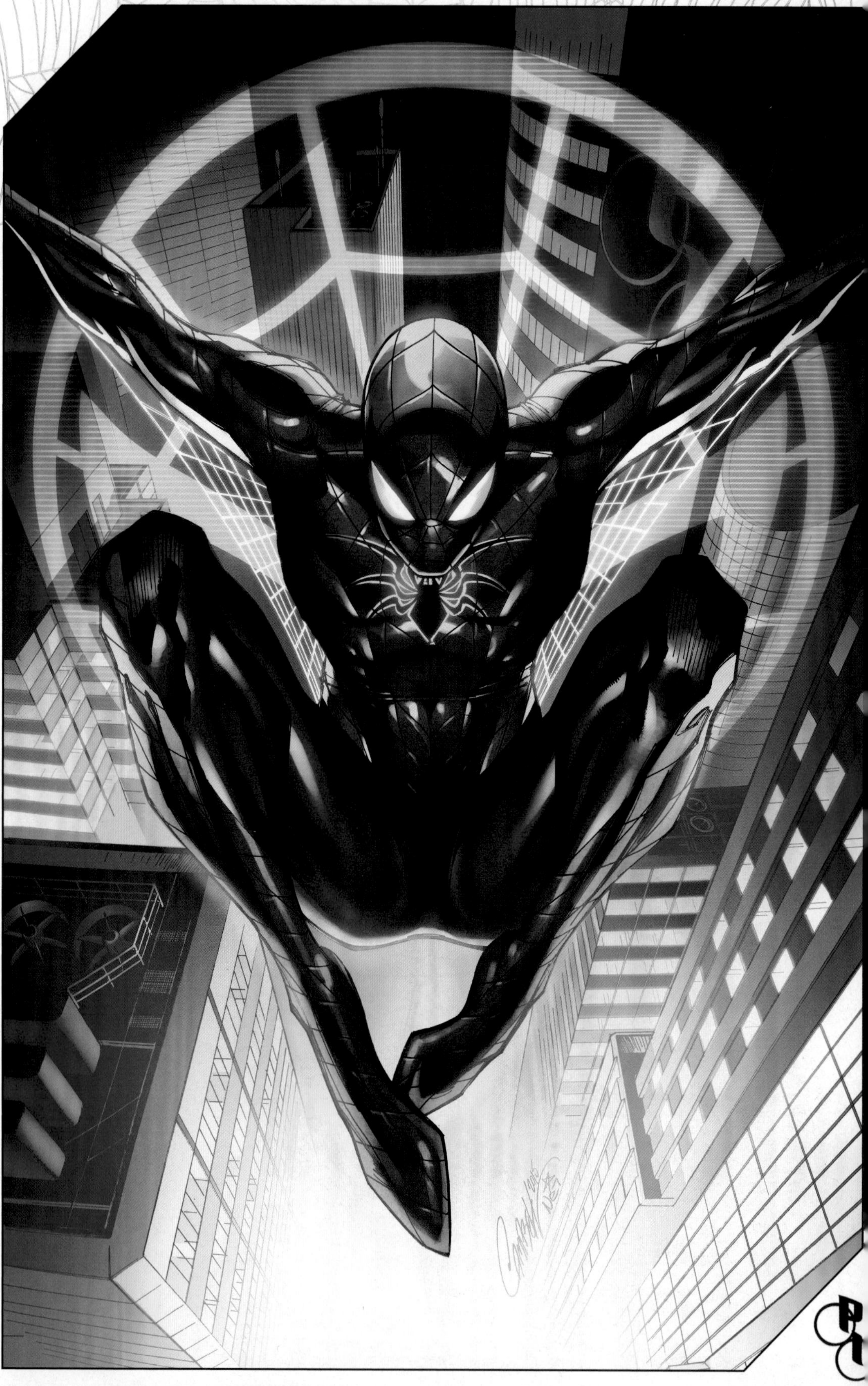

#1 VARIANT BY J. SCOTT CAMPBELL & NEI RUFFINO

2

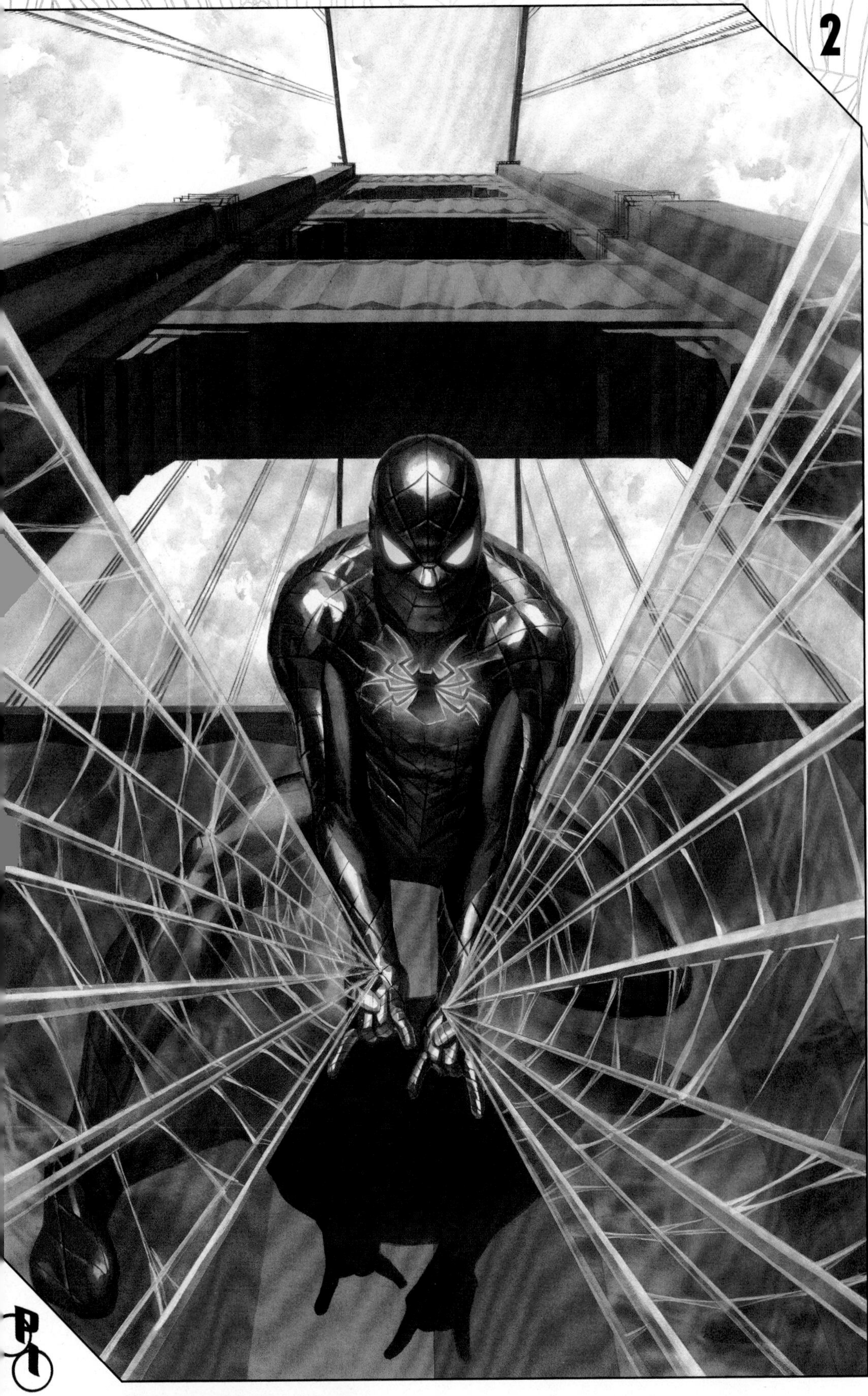

"WATER PROOF"

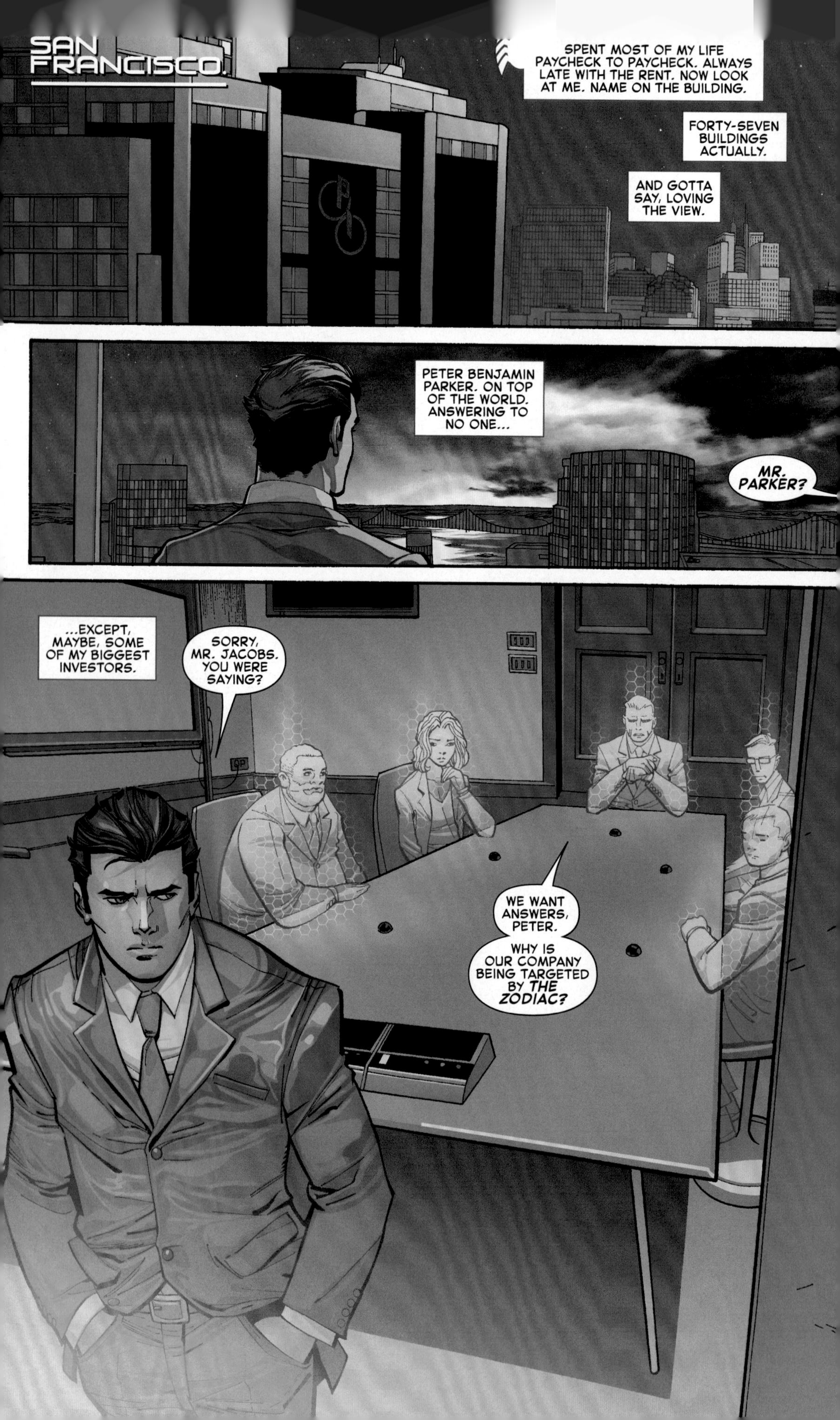
SAN FRANCISCO.
SPENT MOST OF MY LIFE PAYCHECK TO PAYCHECK. ALWAYS LATE WITH THE RENT. NOW LOOK AT ME. NAME ON THE BUILDING.
FORTY-SEVEN BUILDINGS ACTUALLY.
AND GOTTA SAY, LOVING THE VIEW.
PETER BENJAMIN PARKER. ON TOP OF THE WORLD. ANSWERING TO NO ONE...
MR. PARKER?
...EXCEPT, MAYBE, SOME OF MY BIGGEST INVESTORS.
SORRY, MR. JACOBS. YOU WERE SAYING?
WE WANT ANSWERS, PETER.
WHY IS OUR COMPANY BEING TARGETED BY THE ZODIAC?

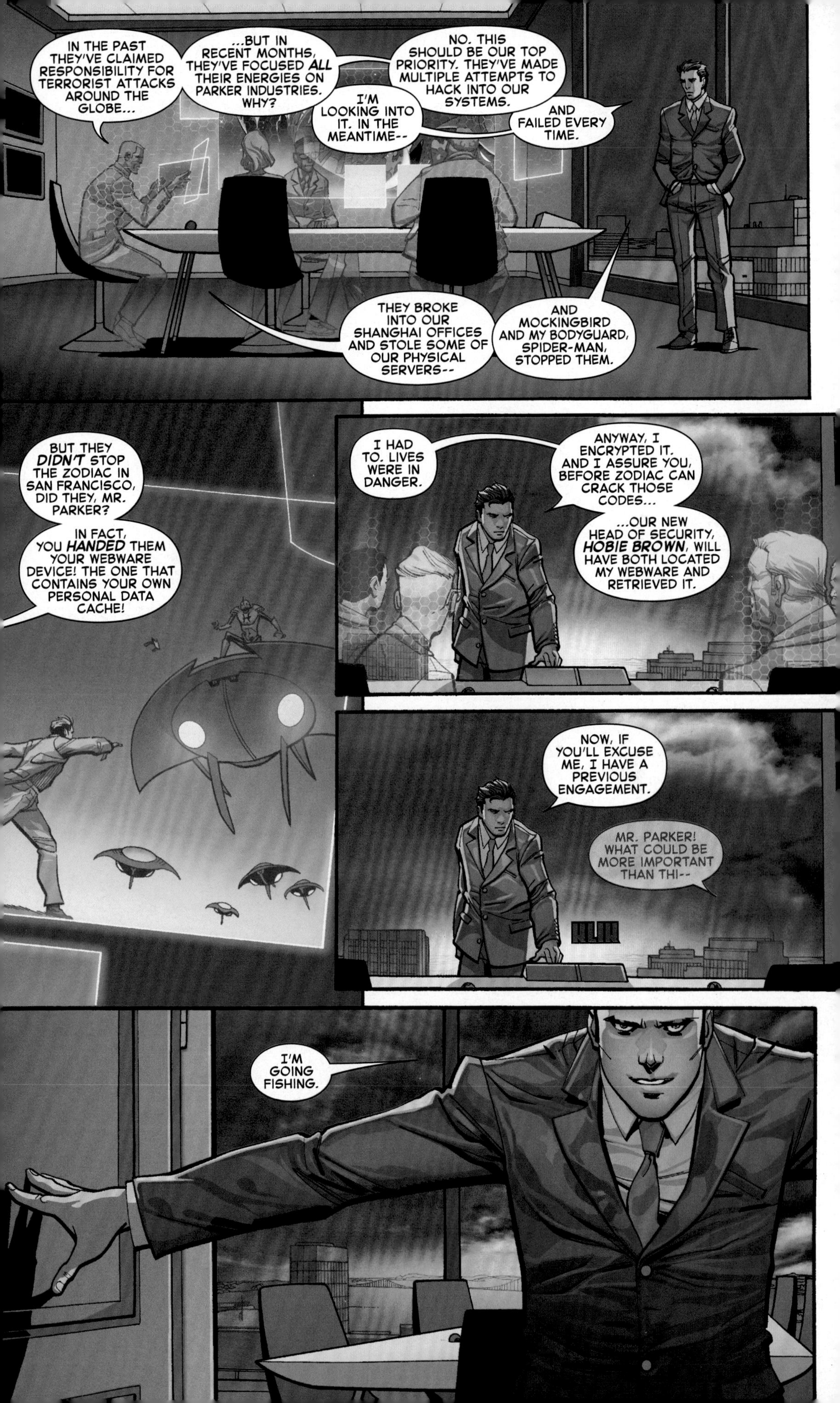
IN THE PAST THEY'VE CLAIMED RESPONSIBILITY FOR TERRORIST ATTACKS AROUND THE GLOBE...
...BUT IN RECENT MONTHS, THEY'VE FOCUSED ALL THEIR ENERGIES ON PARKER INDUSTRIES. WHY?
NO. THIS SHOULD BE OUR TOP PRIORITY. THEY'VE MADE MULTIPLE ATTEMPTS TO HACK INTO OUR SYSTEMS.
I'M LOOKING INTO IT. IN THE MEANTIME--
AND FAILED EVERY TIME.
THEY BROKE INTO OUR SHANGHAI OFFICES AND STOLE SOME OF OUR PHYSICAL SERVERS--
AND MOCKINGBIRD AND MY BODYGUARD, SPIDER-MAN, STOPPED THEM.
BUT THEY DIDN'T STOP THE ZODIAC IN SAN FRANCISCO, DID THEY, MR. PARKER?
IN FACT, YOU HANDED THEM YOUR WEBWARE DEVICE! THE ONE THAT CONTAINS YOUR OWN PERSONAL DATA CACHE!
I HAD TO. LIVES WERE IN DANGER.
ANYWAY, I ENCRYPTED IT. AND I ASSURE YOU, BEFORE ZODIAC CAN CRACK THOSE CODES...
...OUR NEW HEAD OF SECURITY, HOBIE BROWN, WILL HAVE BOTH LOCATED MY WEBWARE AND RETRIEVED IT.
NOW, IF YOU'LL EXCUSE ME, I HAVE A PREVIOUS ENGAGEMENT.
MR. PARKER! WHAT COULD BE MORE IMPORTANT THAN THI--
I'M GOING FISHING.

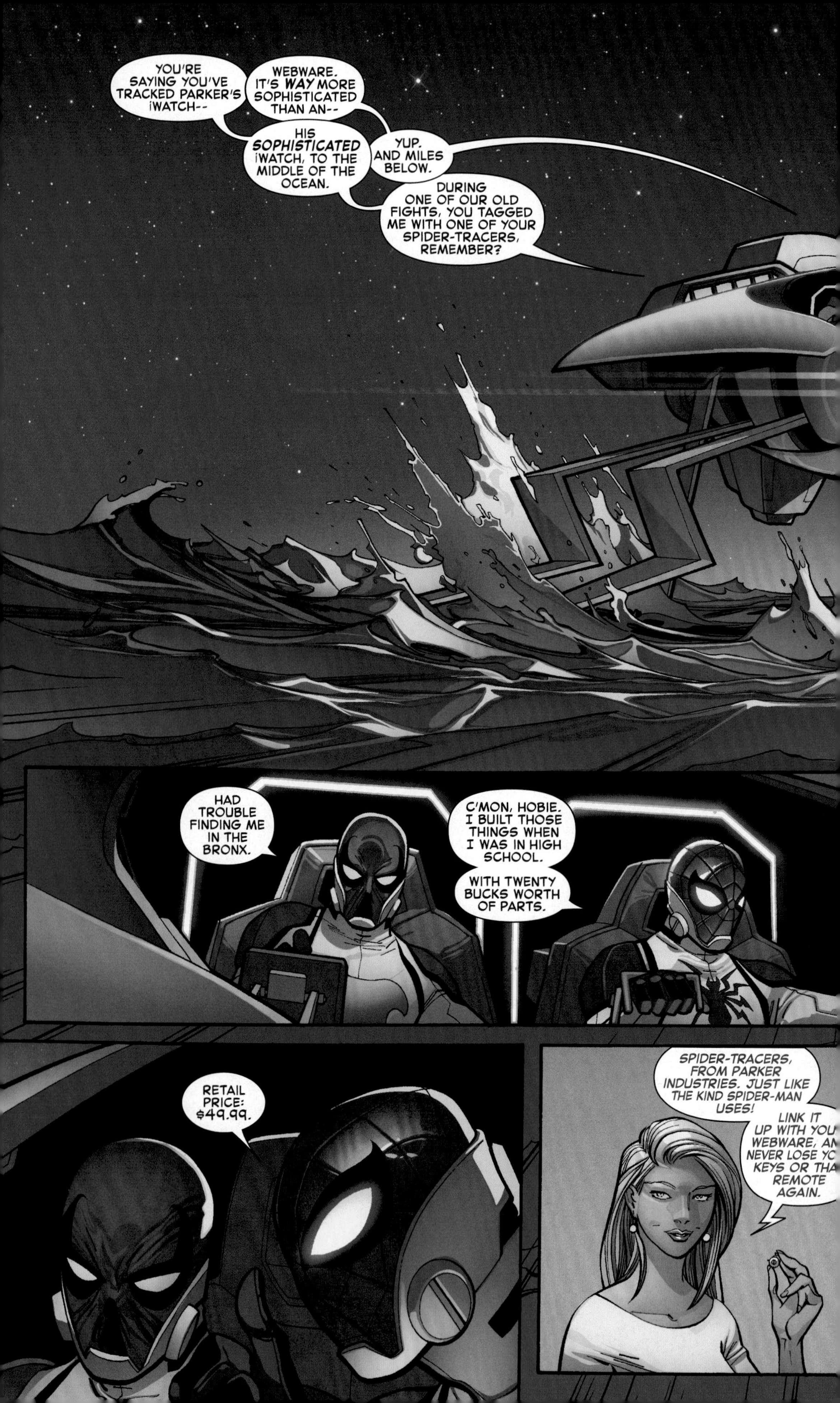

YOU'RE SAYING YOU'VE TRACKED PARKER'S iWATCH--
WEBWARE. IT'S **WAY** MORE SOPHISTICATED THAN AN--
HIS **SOPHISTICATED** iWATCH, TO THE MIDDLE OF THE OCEAN.
YUP. AND MILES BELOW.
DURING ONE OF OUR OLD FIGHTS, YOU TAGGED ME WITH ONE OF YOUR SPIDER-TRACERS, REMEMBER?
HAD TROUBLE FINDING ME IN THE BRONX.
C'MON, HOBIE. I BUILT THOSE THINGS WHEN I WAS IN HIGH SCHOOL.
WITH TWENTY BUCKS WORTH OF PARTS.
RETAIL PRICE: $49.99.
SPIDER-TRACERS, FROM PARKER INDUSTRIES. JUST LIKE THE KIND SPIDER-MAN USES!

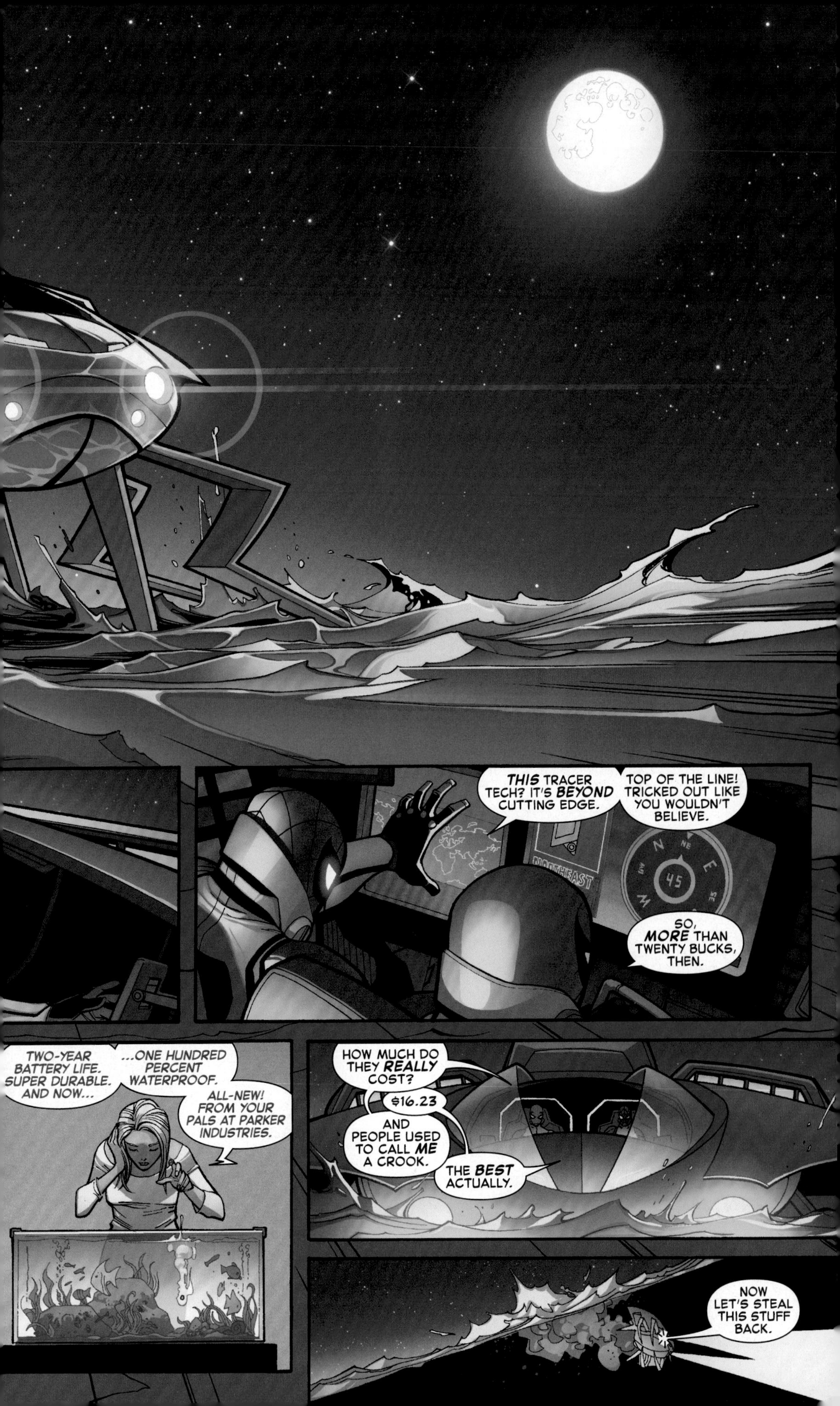
THIS TRACER TECH? IT'S BEYOND CUTTING EDGE.
TOP OF THE LINE! TRICKED OUT LIKE YOU WOULDN'T BELIEVE.
NORTHEAST
N
NE
E
SE
W
45
SO, MORE THAN TWENTY BUCKS, THEN.
TWO-YEAR BATTERY LIFE. SUPER DURABLE. AND NOW...
...ONE HUNDRED PERCENT WATERPROOF.
ALL-NEW! FROM YOUR PALS AT PARKER INDUSTRIES.
HOW MUCH DO THEY REALLY COST?
$16.23
AND PEOPLE USED TO CALL ME A CROOK.
THE BEST ACTUALLY.
NOW LET'S STEAL THIS STUFF BACK.

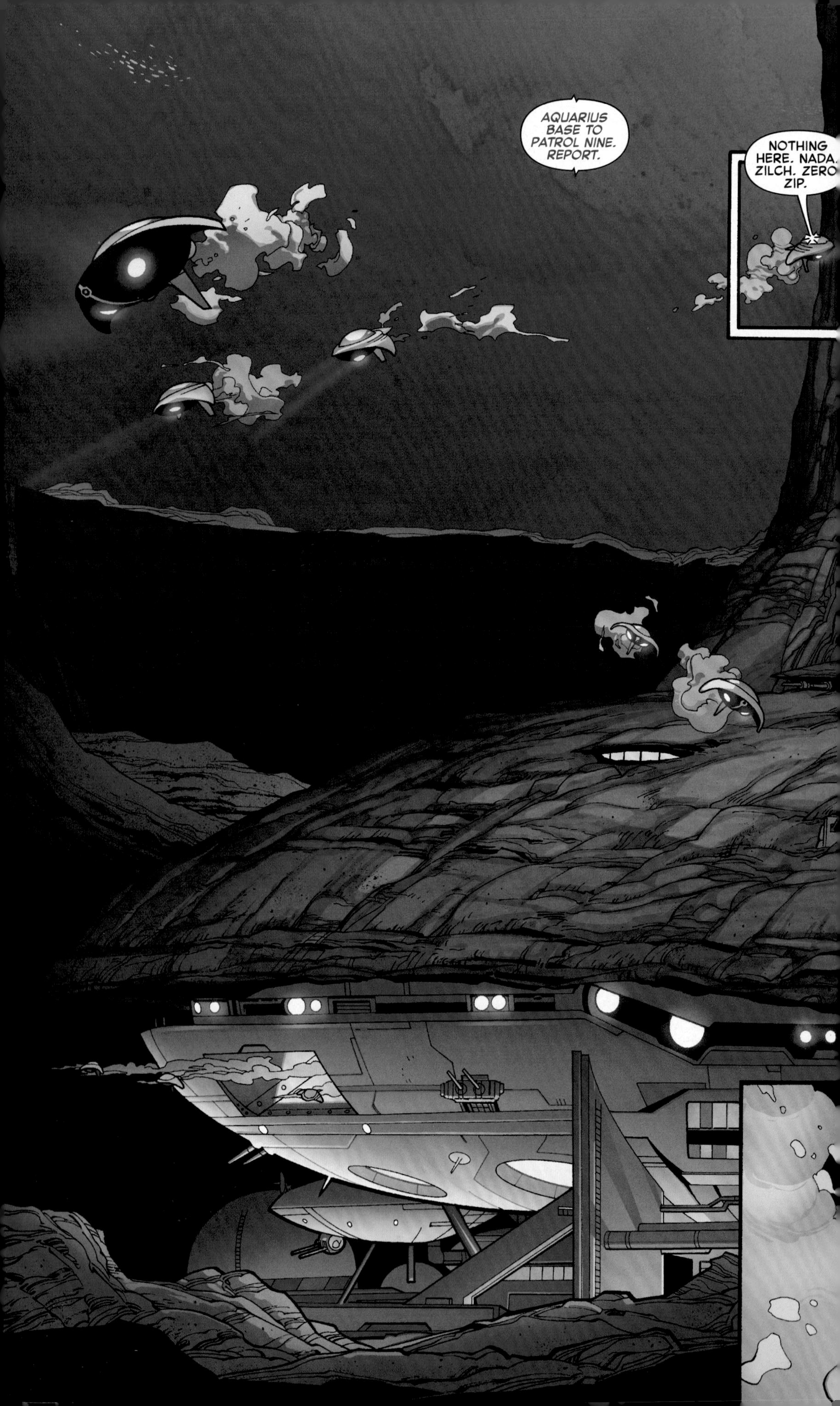
AQUARIUS BASE TO PATROL NINE. REPORT.
NOTHING HERE. NADA. ZILCH. ZERO ZIP.

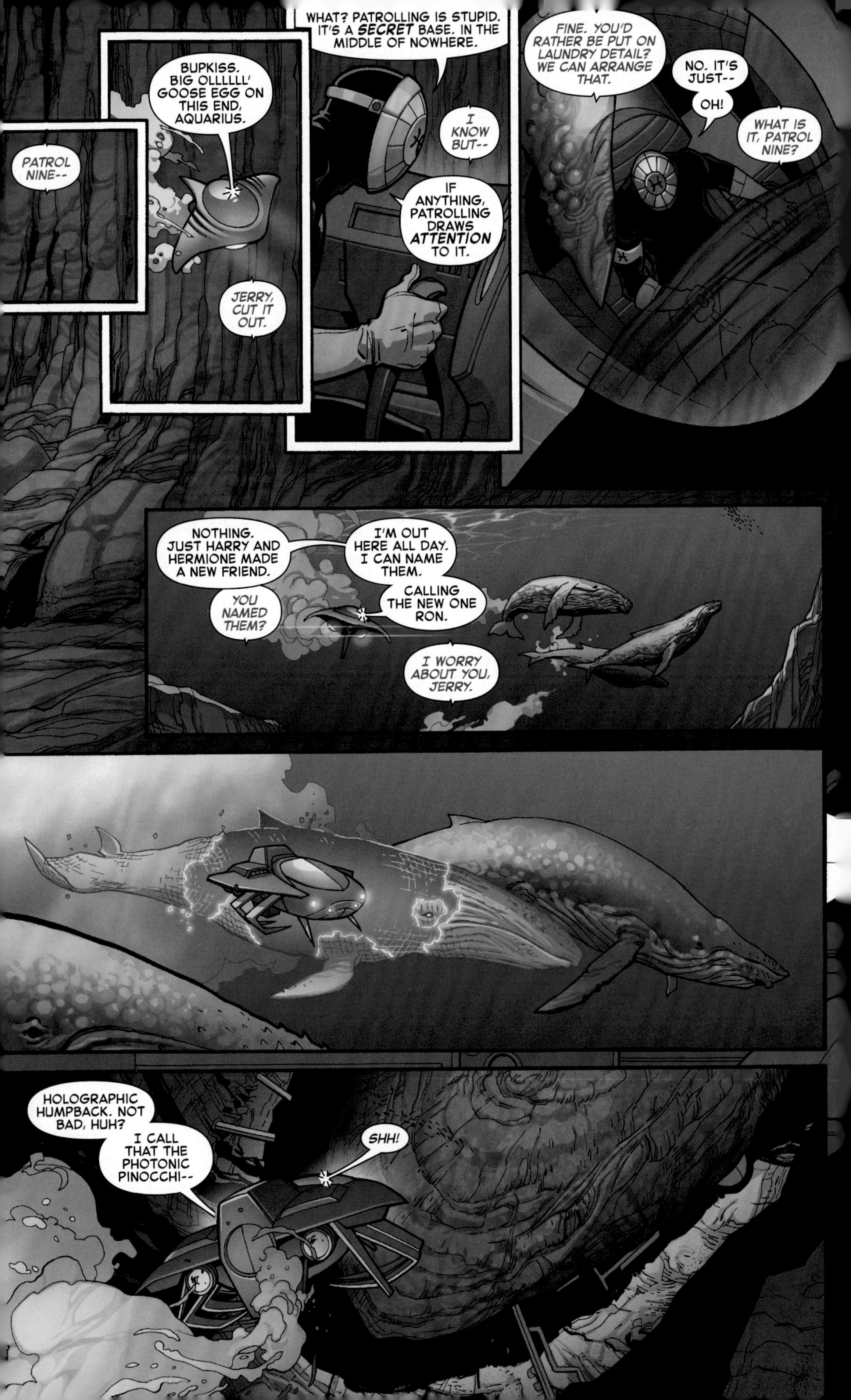
PATROL NINE--
BUPKISS. BIG OLLLLLL' GOOSE EGG ON THIS END, AQUARIUS.
JERRY, CUT IT OUT.
WHAT? PATROLLING IS STUPID. IT'S A SECRET BASE. IN THE MIDDLE OF NOWHERE.
I KNOW BUT--
IF ANYTHING, PATROLLING DRAWS ATTENTION TO IT.
FINE. YOU'D RATHER BE PUT ON LAUNDRY DETAIL? WE CAN ARRANGE THAT.
NO. IT'S JUST--
OH!
WHAT IS IT, PATROL NINE?
NOTHING. JUST HARRY AND HERMIONE MADE A NEW FRIEND.
YOU NAMED THEM?
I'M OUT HERE ALL DAY. I CAN NAME THEM.
CALLING THE NEW ONE RON.
I WORRY ABOUT YOU, JERRY.
HOLOGRAPHIC HUMPBACK. NOT BAD, HUH?
I CALL THAT THE PHOTONIC PINOCCHI--
SHH!

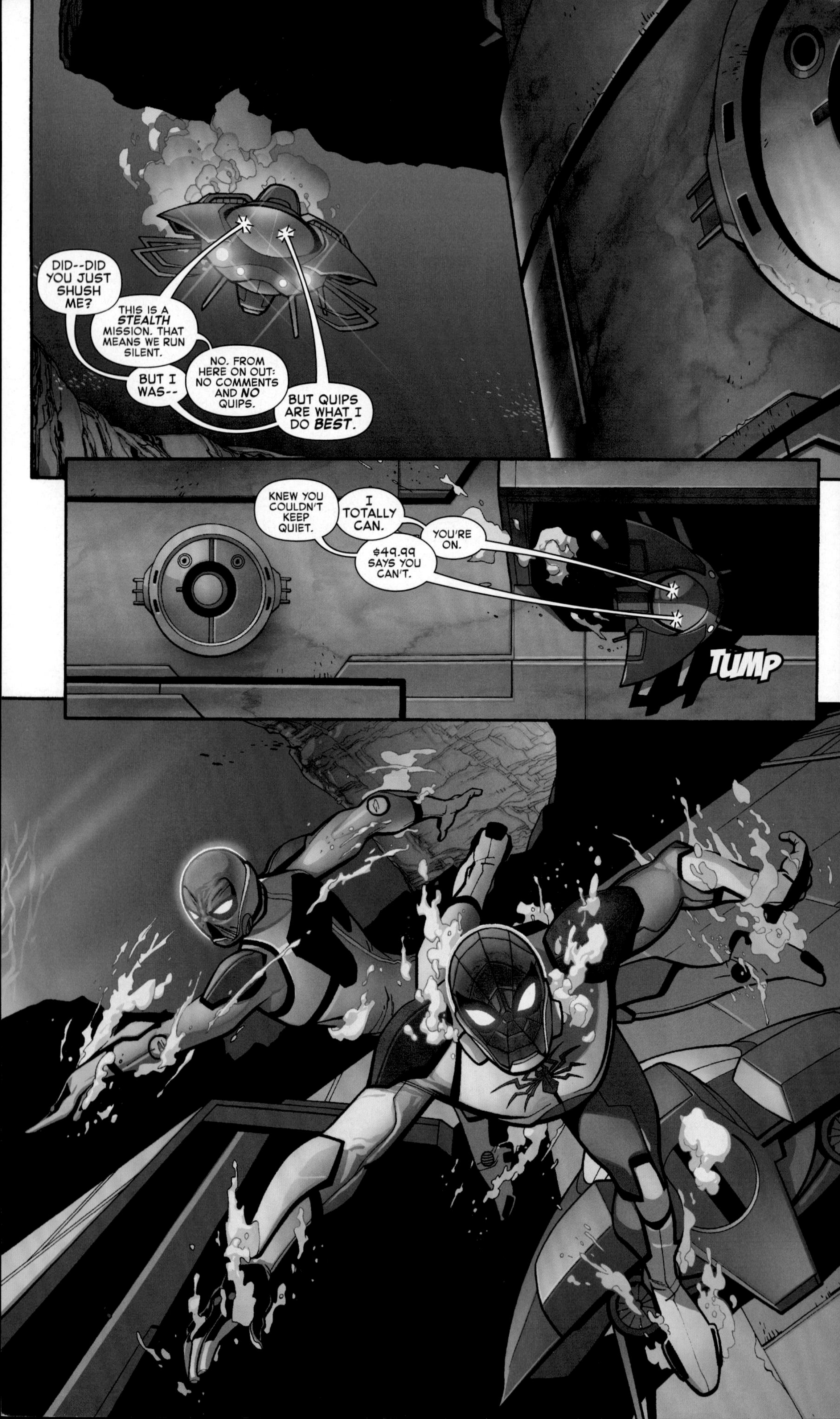
DID--DID YOU JUST SHUSH ME?
THIS IS A STEALTH MISSION. THAT MEANS WE RUN SILENT.
BUT I WAS--
NO. FROM HERE ON OUT: NO COMMENTS AND NO QUIPS.
BUT QUIPS ARE WHAT I DO BEST.
KNEW YOU COULDN'T KEEP QUIET.
I TOTALLY CAN.
$49.99 SAYS YOU CAN'T.
YOU'RE ON.
TUMP

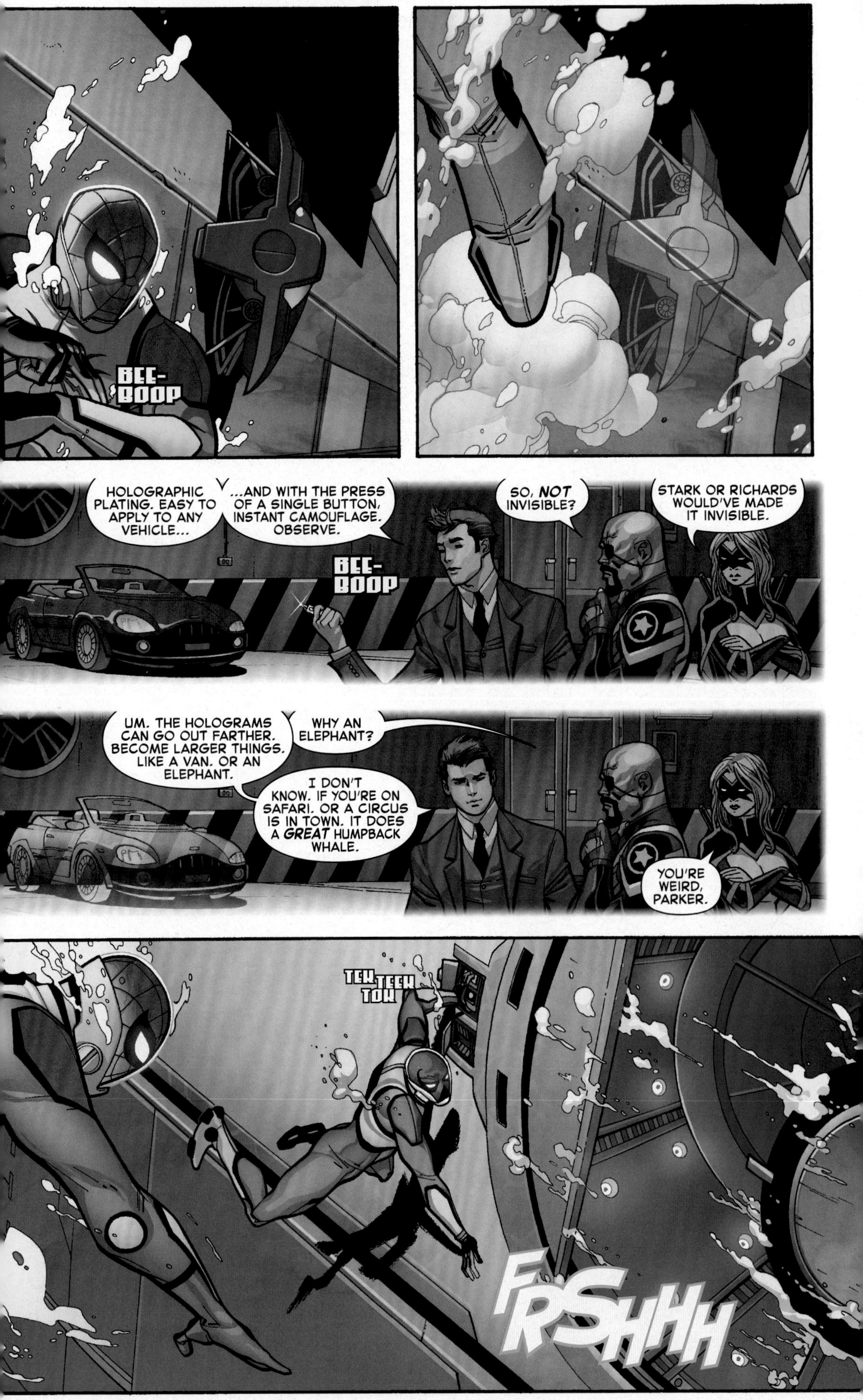
BEE-
BOOP
HOLOGRAPHIC PLATING. EASY TO APPLY TO ANY VEHICLE...
...AND WITH THE PRESS OF A SINGLE BUTTON, INSTANT CAMOUFLAGE. OBSERVE.
BEE-
BOOP
SO, NOT INVISIBLE?
STARK OR RICHARDS WOULD'VE MADE IT INVISIBLE.
UM. THE HOLOGRAMS CAN GO OUT FARTHER. BECOME LARGER THINGS. LIKE A VAN. OR AN ELEPHANT.
WHY AN ELEPHANT?
I DON'T KNOW. IF YOU'RE ON SAFARI. OR A CIRCUS IS IN TOWN. IT DOES A GREAT HUMPBACK WHALE.
YOU'RE WEIRD, PARKER.
TEK TEEK TOK
FRSHHH

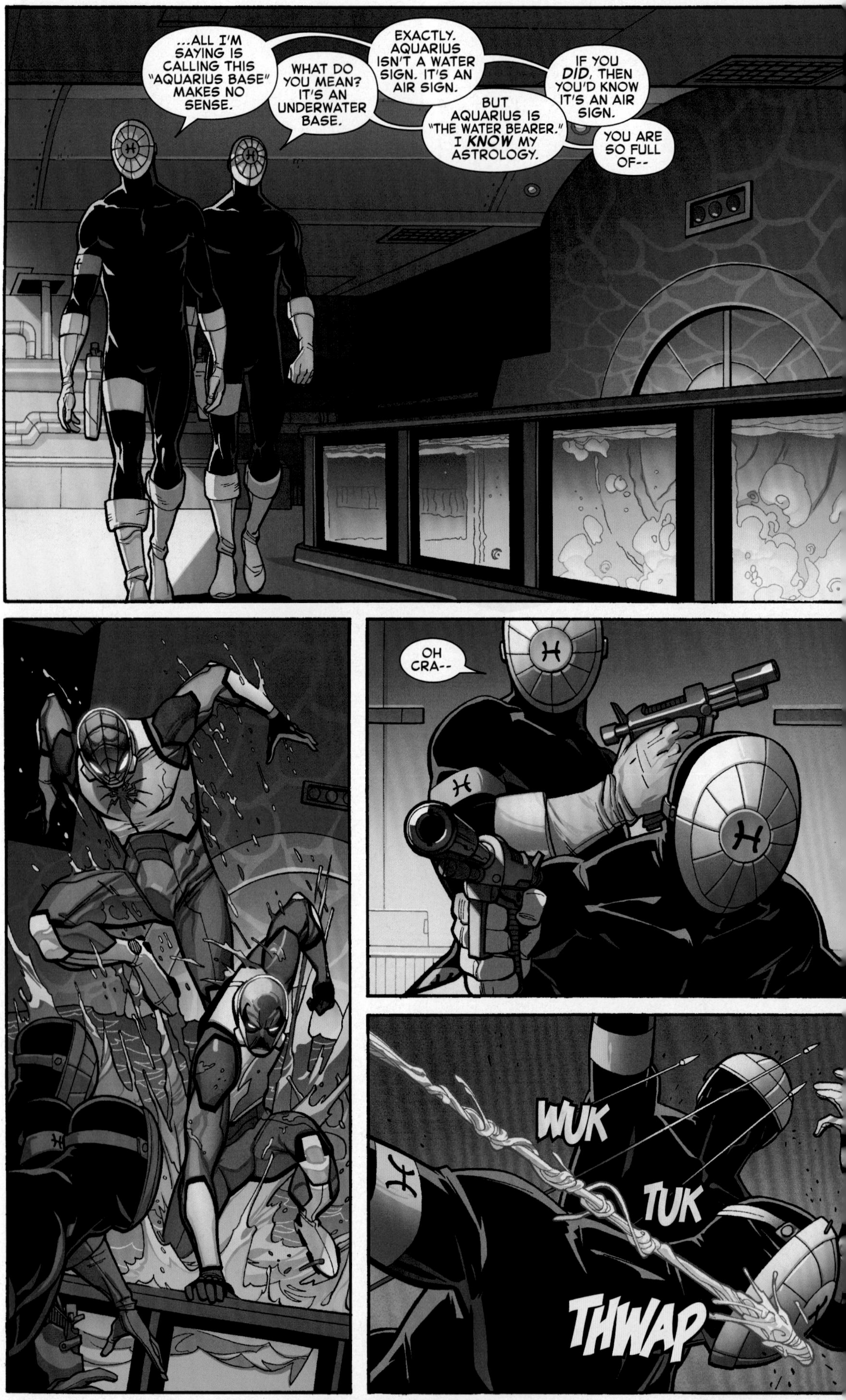

...ALL I'M SAYING IS CALLING THIS "AQUARIUS BASE" MAKES NO SENSE.
WHAT DO YOU MEAN? IT'S AN UNDERWATER BASE.
EXACTLY. AQUARIUS ISN'T A WATER SIGN. IT'S AN AIR SIGN.
BUT AQUARIUS IS "THE WATER BEARER." I *KNOW* MY ASTROLOGY.
IF YOU *DID*, THEN YOU'D KNOW IT'S AN AIR SIGN.
YOU ARE SO FULL OF--
OH CRA--
WUK
TUK
THWAP

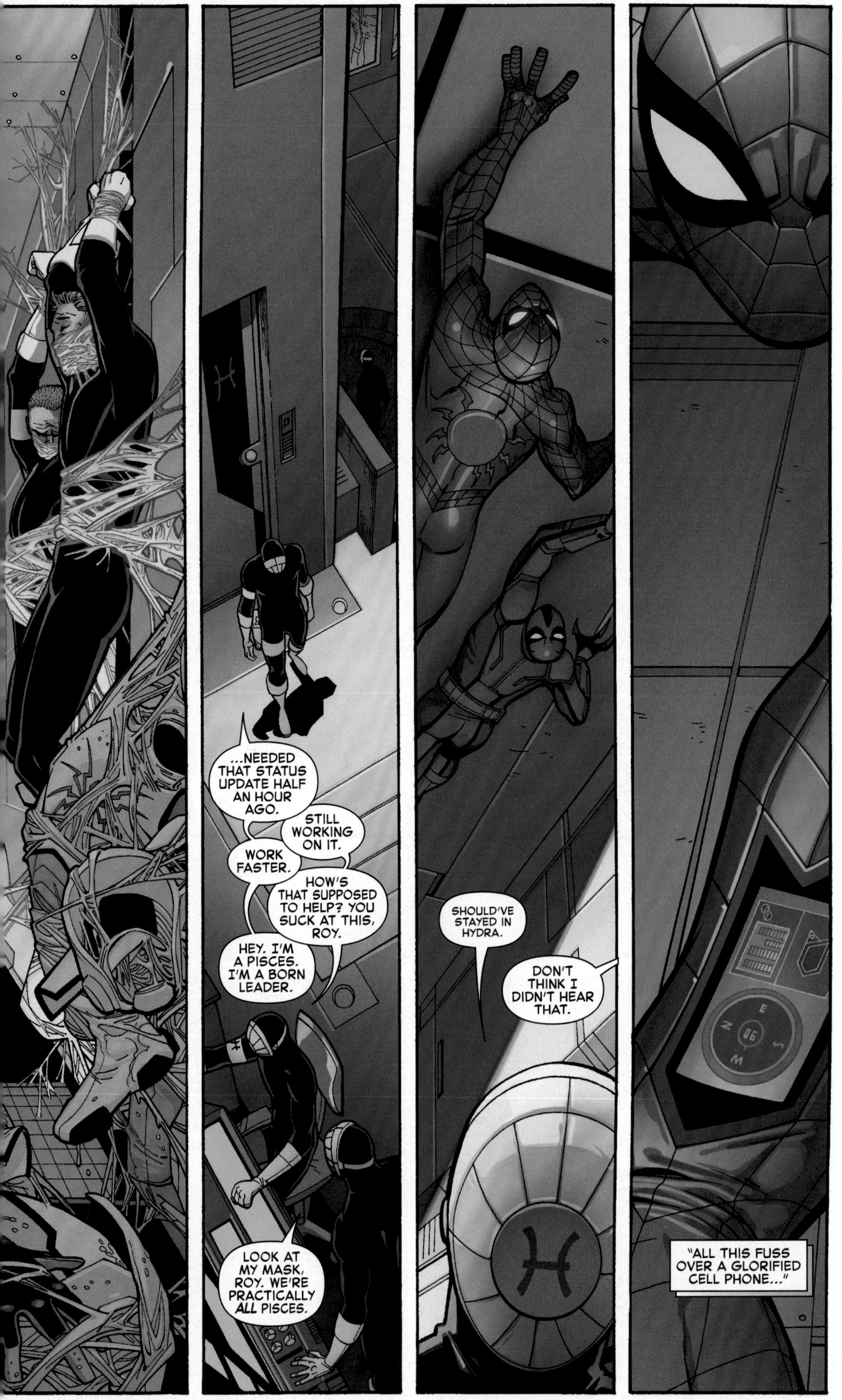
...NEEDED THAT STATUS UPDATE HALF AN HOUR AGO.
STILL WORKING ON IT.
WORK FASTER.
HOW'S THAT SUPPOSED TO HELP? YOU SUCK AT THIS, ROY.
HEY. I'M A PISCES. I'M A BORN LEADER.
LOOK AT MY MASK, ROY. WE'RE PRACTICALLY *ALL* PISCES.
SHOULD'VE STAYED IN HYDRA.
DON'T THINK I DIDN'T HEAR THAT.
"ALL THIS FUSS OVER A GLORIFIED CELL PHONE..."

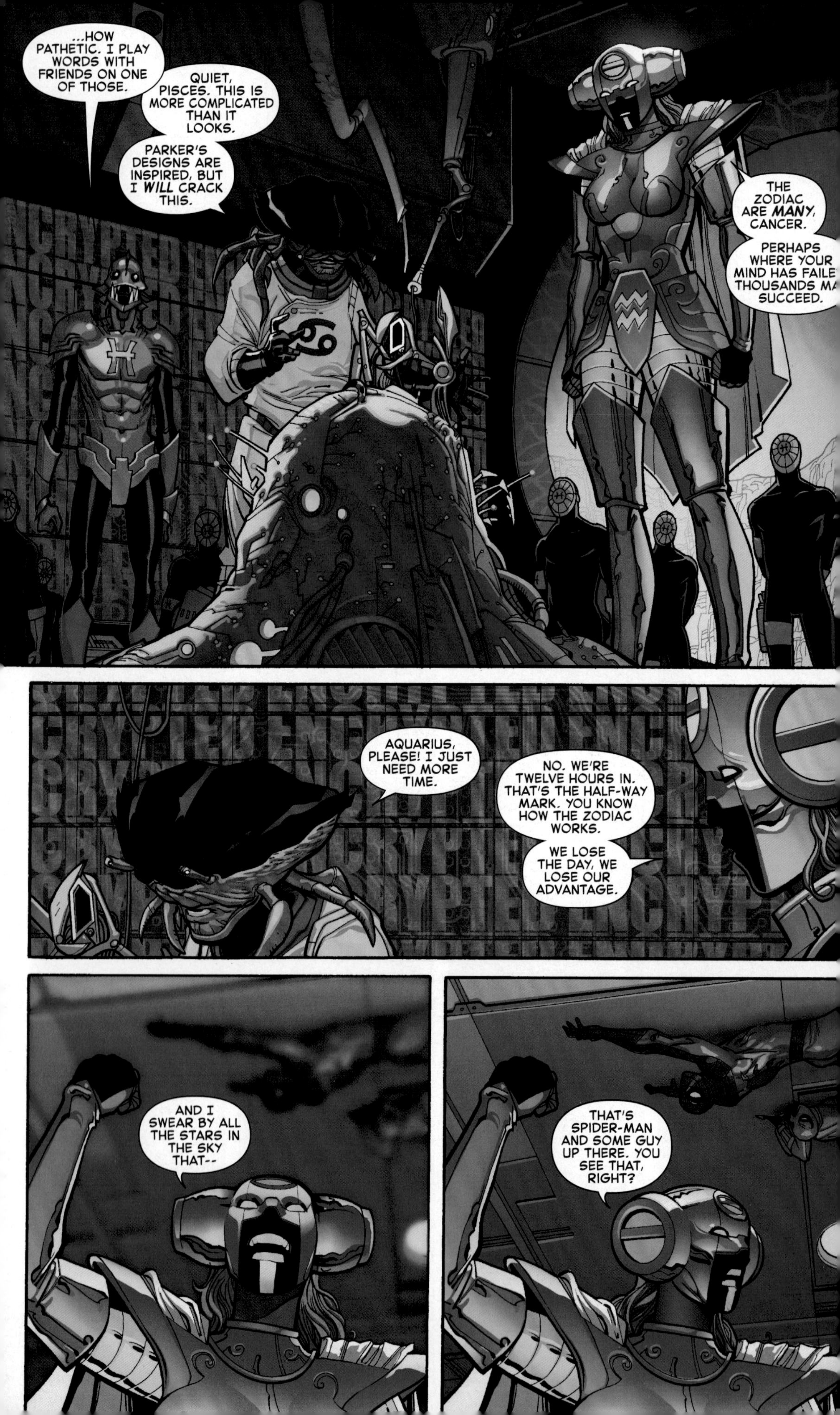
...HOW PATHETIC. I PLAY WORDS WITH FRIENDS ON ONE OF THOSE.
QUIET, PISCES. THIS IS MORE COMPLICATED THAN IT LOOKS.
PARKER'S DESIGNS ARE INSPIRED, BUT I *WILL* CRACK THIS.
THE ZODIAC ARE *MANY*, CANCER.
PERHAPS WHERE YOUR MIND HAS FAILE THOUSANDS MA SUCCEED.
AQUARIUS, PLEASE! I JUST NEED MORE TIME.
NO. WE'RE TWELVE HOURS IN. THAT'S THE HALF-WAY MARK. YOU KNOW HOW THE ZODIAC WORKS.
WE LOSE THE DAY, WE LOSE OUR ADVANTAGE.
AND I SWEAR BY ALL THE STARS IN THE SKY THAT--
THAT'S SPIDER-MAN AND SOME GUY UP THERE. YOU SEE THAT, RIGHT?

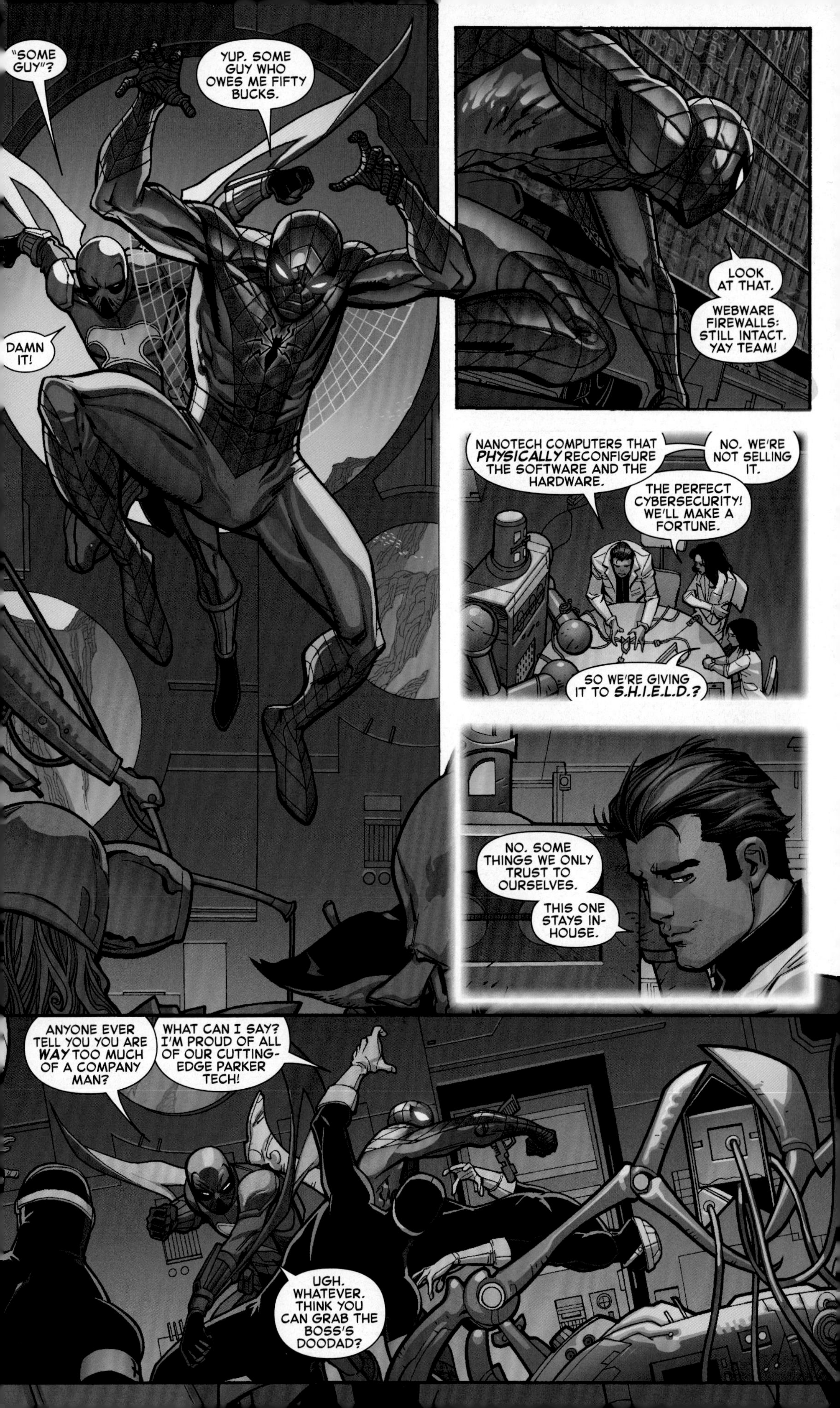
"SOME GUY"?
YUP. SOME GUY WHO OWES ME FIFTY BUCKS.
DAMN IT!
LOOK AT THAT.
WEBWARE FIREWALLS: STILL INTACT. YAY TEAM!
NANOTECH COMPUTERS THAT PHYSICALLY RECONFIGURE THE SOFTWARE AND THE HARDWARE.
THE PERFECT CYBERSECURITY! WE'LL MAKE A FORTUNE.
NO. WE'RE NOT SELLING IT.
SO WE'RE GIVING IT TO S.H.I.E.L.D.?
NO. SOME THINGS WE ONLY TRUST TO OURSELVES.
THIS ONE STAYS IN-HOUSE.
ANYONE EVER TELL YOU YOU ARE WAY TOO MUCH OF A COMPANY MAN?
WHAT CAN I SAY? I'M PROUD OF ALL OF OUR CUTTING-EDGE PARKER TECH!
UGH. WHATEVER. THINK YOU CAN GRAB THE BOSS'S DOODAD?

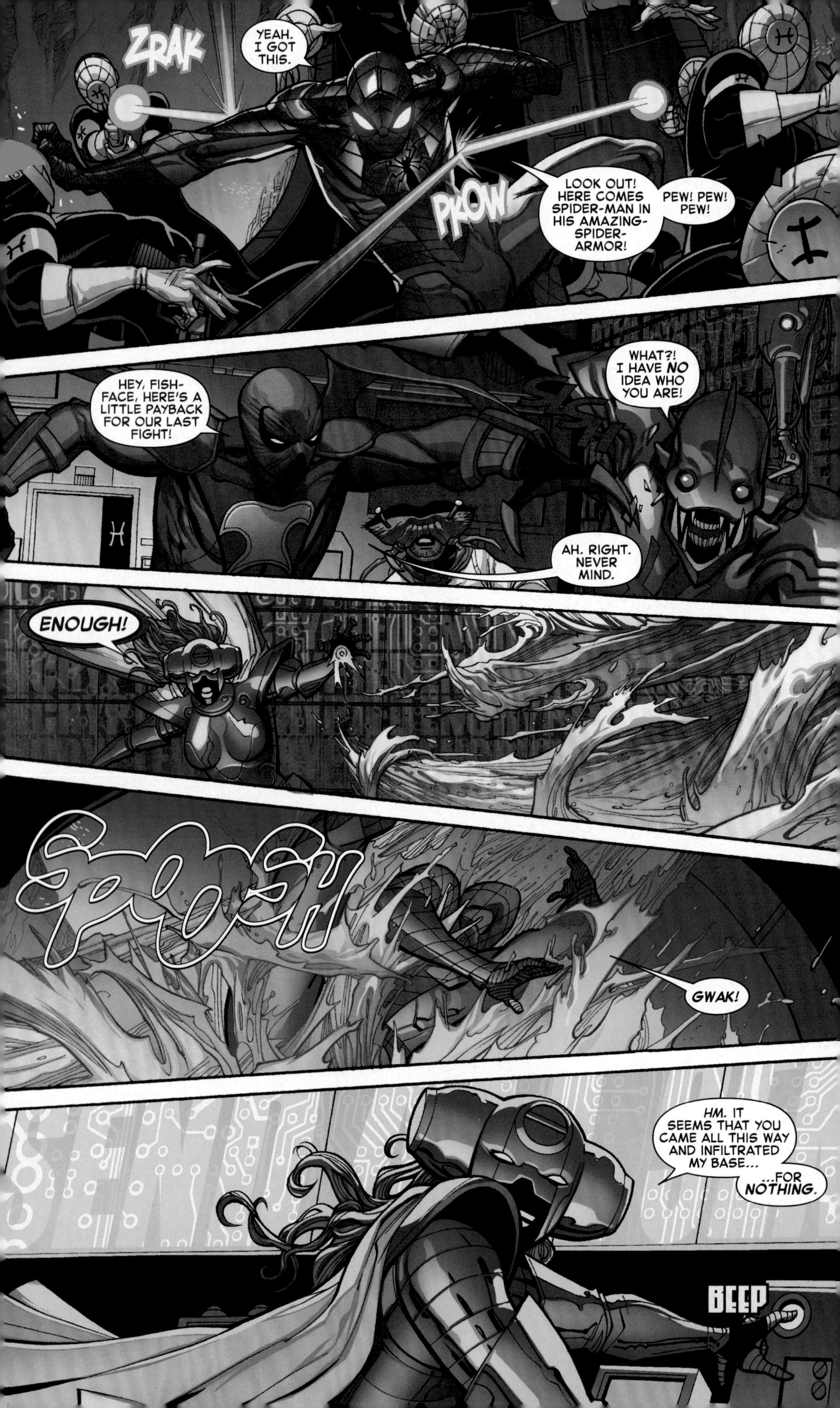
ZRAK
YEAH. I GOT THIS.
PKOW
LOOK OUT! HERE COMES SPIDER-MAN IN HIS AMAZING-SPIDER-ARMOR!
PEW! PEW! PEW!
HEY, FISH-FACE, HERE'S A LITTLE PAYBACK FOR OUR LAST FIGHT!
WHAT?! I HAVE NO IDEA WHO YOU ARE!
AH. RIGHT. NEVER MIND.
ENOUGH!
SPLOOSH
GWAK!
HM. IT SEEMS THAT YOU CAME ALL THIS WAY AND INFILTRATED MY BASE...
...FOR NOTHING.
BEEP

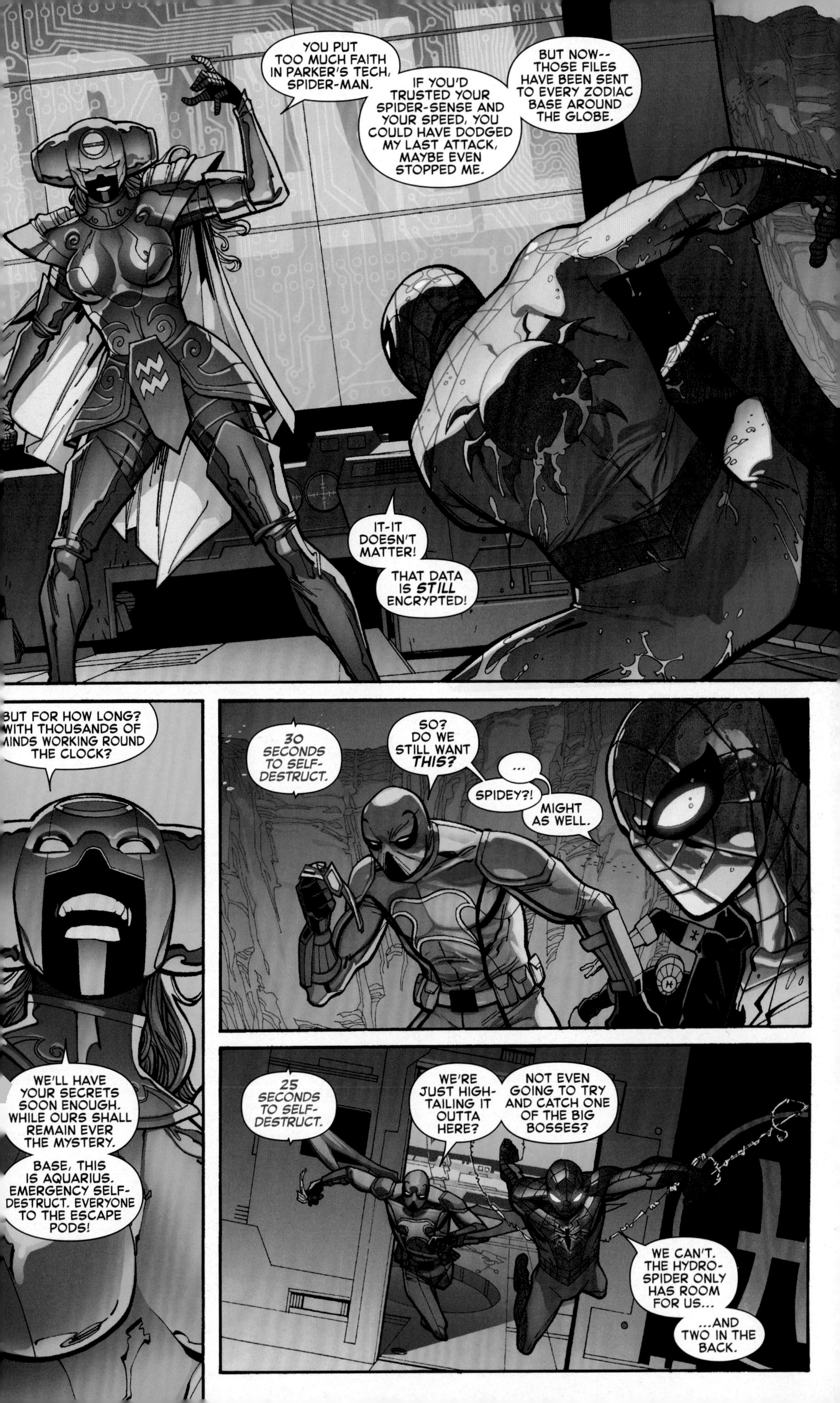
YOU PUT TOO MUCH FAITH IN PARKER'S TECH, SPIDER-MAN.
IF YOU'D TRUSTED YOUR SPIDER-SENSE AND YOUR SPEED, YOU COULD HAVE DODGED MY LAST ATTACK, MAYBE EVEN STOPPED ME.
BUT NOW-- THOSE FILES HAVE BEEN SENT TO EVERY ZODIAC BASE AROUND THE GLOBE.
IT-IT DOESN'T MATTER!
THAT DATA IS STILL ENCRYPTED!
BUT FOR HOW LONG? WITH THOUSANDS OF MINDS WORKING ROUND THE CLOCK?
WE'LL HAVE YOUR SECRETS SOON ENOUGH. WHILE OURS SHALL REMAIN EVER THE MYSTERY.
BASE, THIS IS AQUARIUS. EMERGENCY SELF-DESTRUCT. EVERYONE TO THE ESCAPE PODS!
30 SECONDS TO SELF-DESTRUCT.
SO? DO WE STILL WANT THIS?
...
SPIDEY?!
MIGHT AS WELL.
25 SECONDS TO SELF-DESTRUCT.
WE'RE JUST HIGH-TAILING IT OUTTA HERE?
NOT EVEN GOING TO TRY AND CATCH ONE OF THE BIG BOSSES?
WE CAN'T. THE HYDRO-SPIDER ONLY HAS ROOM FOR US...
...AND TWO IN THE BACK.

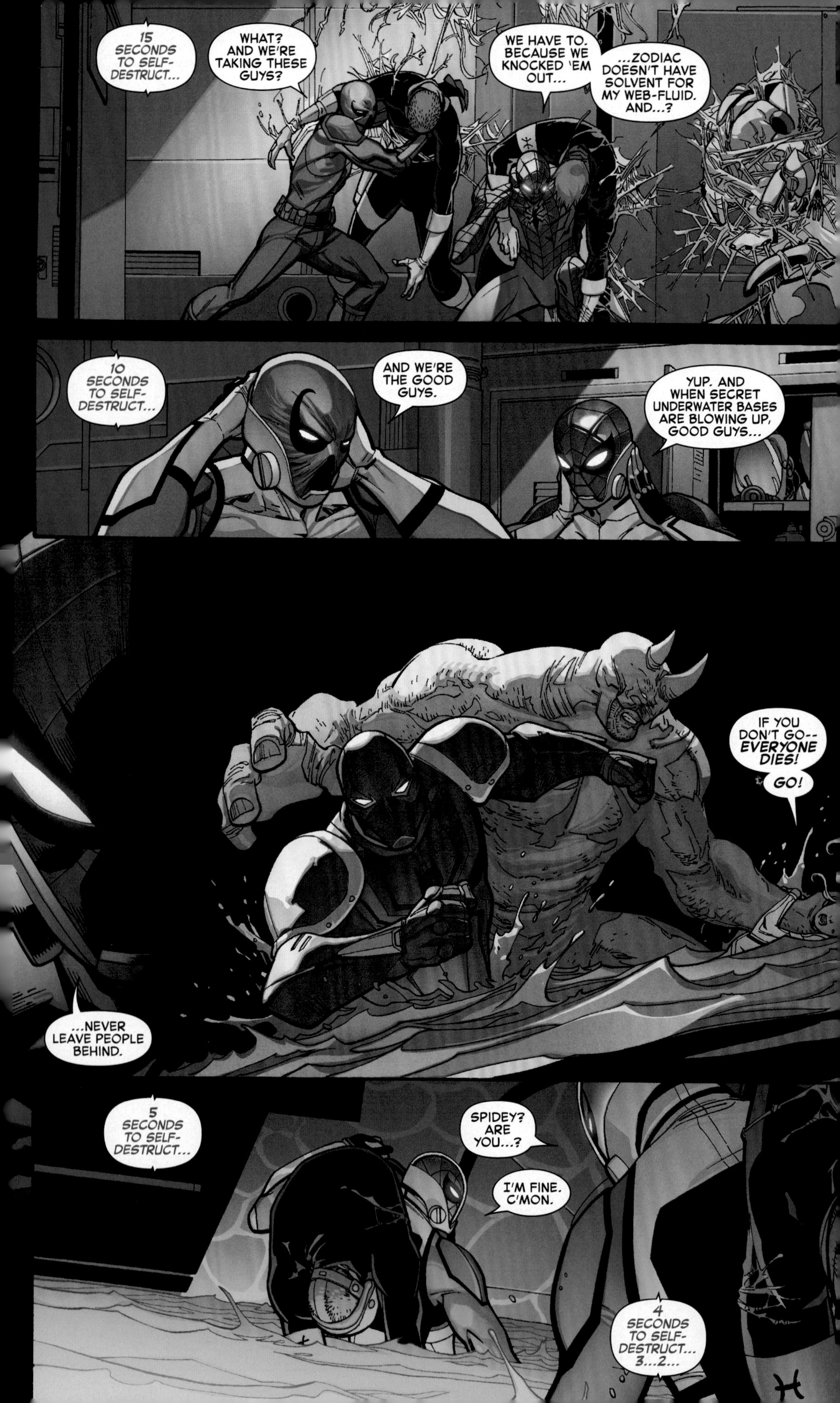
15 SECONDS TO SELF-DESTRUCT...
WHAT? AND WE'RE TAKING THESE GUYS?
WE HAVE TO. BECAUSE WE KNOCKED 'EM OUT...
...ZODIAC DOESN'T HAVE SOLVENT FOR MY WEB-FLUID. AND...?
10 SECONDS TO SELF-DESTRUCT...
AND WE'RE THE GOOD GUYS.
YUP. AND WHEN SECRET UNDERWATER BASES ARE BLOWING UP, GOOD GUYS...
...NEVER LEAVE PEOPLE BEHIND.
IF YOU DON'T GO-- EVERYONE DIES!
GO!
5 SECONDS TO SELF-DESTRUCT...
SPIDEY? ARE YOU...?
I'M FINE. C'MON.
4 SECONDS TO SELF-DESTRUCT... 3...2...

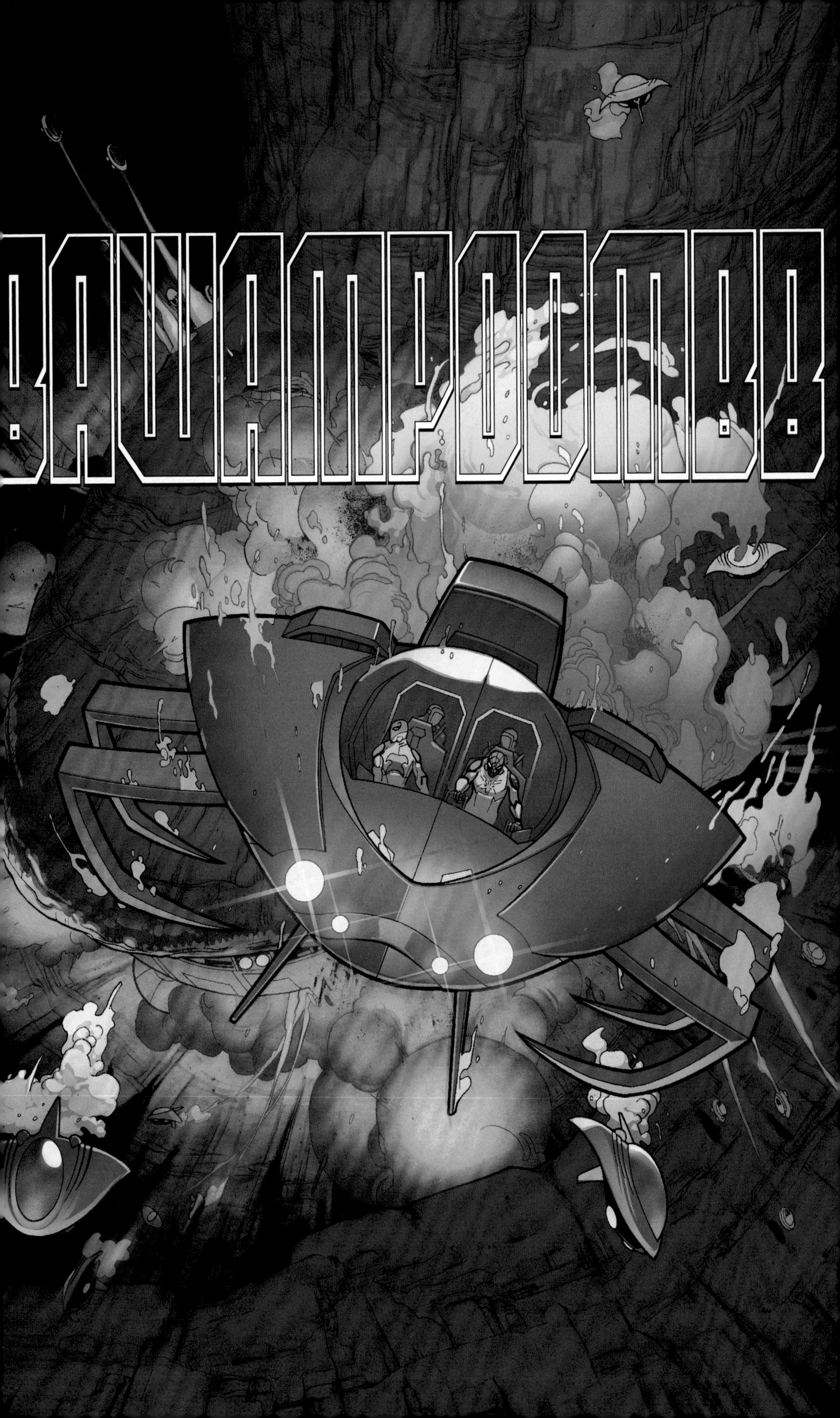

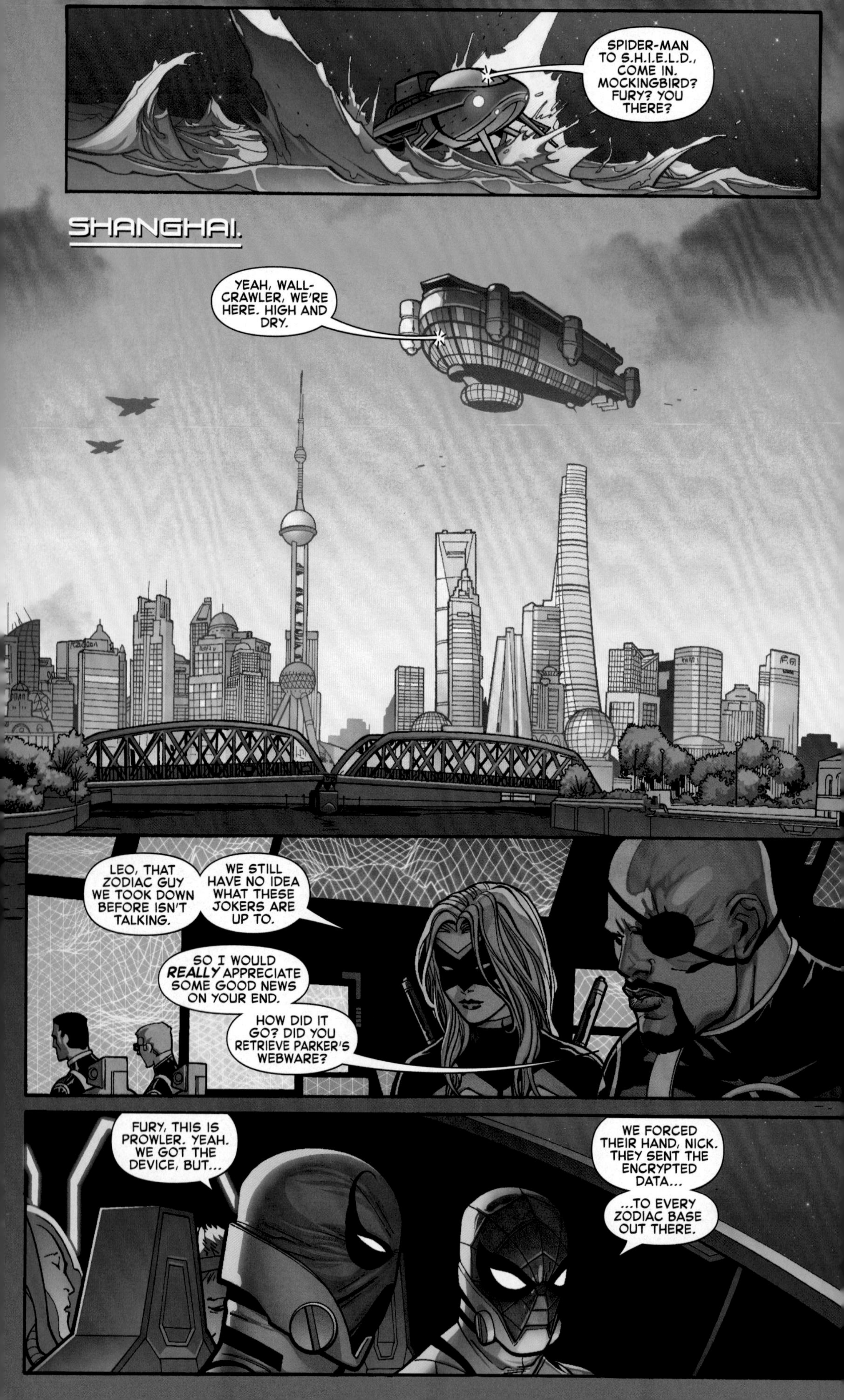
SPIDER-MAN TO S.H.I.E.L.D., COME IN. MOCKINGBIRD? FURY? YOU THERE?
SHANGHAI.
YEAH, WALL-CRAWLER, WE'RE HERE. HIGH AND DRY.
LEO, THAT ZODIAC GUY WE TOOK DOWN BEFORE ISN'T TALKING.
WE STILL HAVE NO IDEA WHAT THESE JOKERS ARE UP TO.
SO I WOULD REALLY APPRECIATE SOME GOOD NEWS ON YOUR END.
HOW DID IT GO? DID YOU RETRIEVE PARKER'S WEBWARE?
FURY, THIS IS PROWLER. YEAH. WE GOT THE DEVICE, BUT...
WE FORCED THEIR HAND, NICK. THEY SENT THE ENCRYPTED DATA...
...TO EVERY ZODIAC BASE OUT THERE.

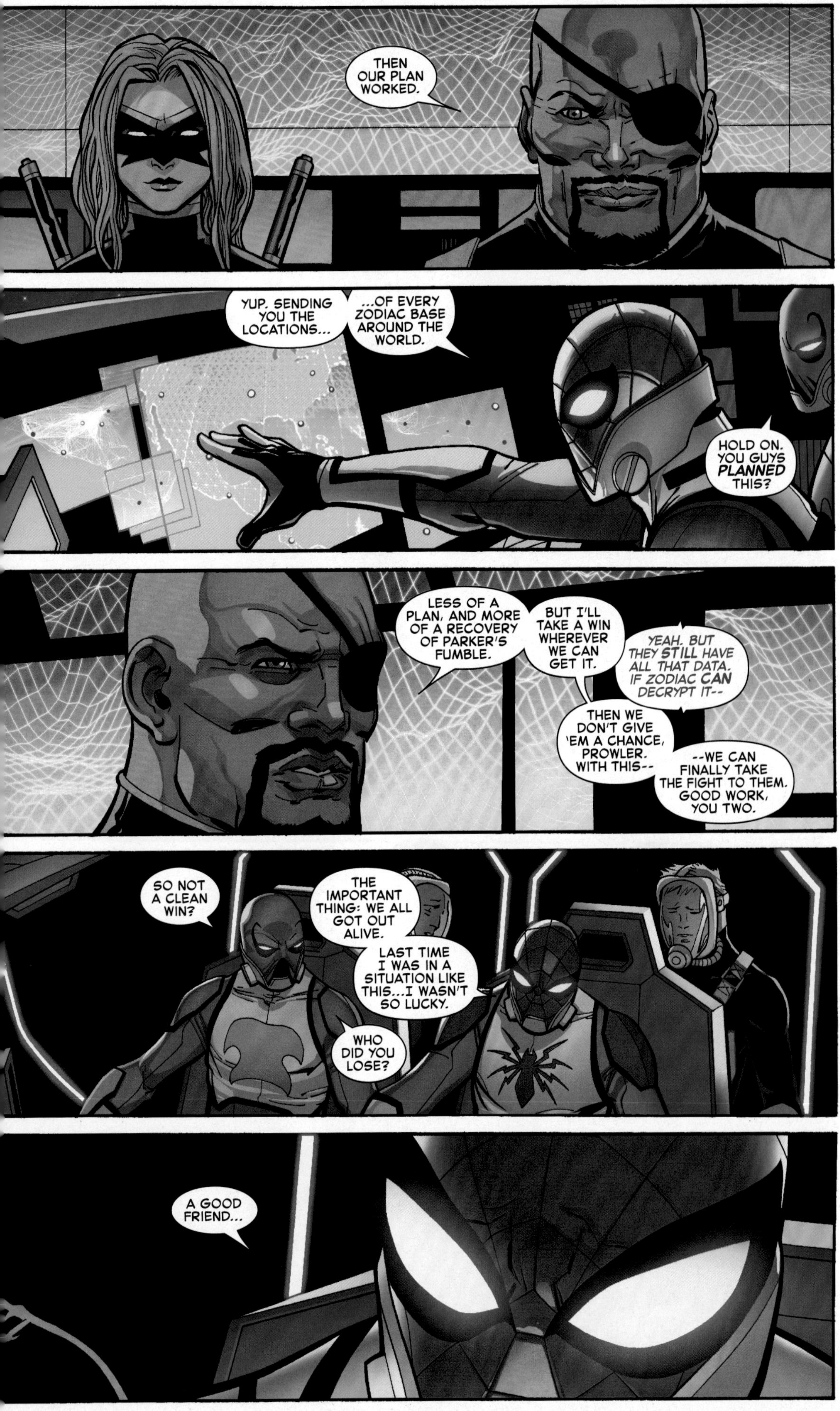
THEN OUR PLAN WORKED.
YUP. SENDING YOU THE LOCATIONS...
...OF EVERY ZODIAC BASE AROUND THE WORLD.
HOLD ON. YOU GUYS **PLANNED** THIS?
LESS OF A PLAN, AND MORE OF A RECOVERY OF PARKER'S FUMBLE.
BUT I'LL TAKE A WIN WHEREVER WE CAN GET IT.
*YEAH. BUT THEY **STILL** HAVE ALL THAT DATA. IF ZODIAC **CAN** DECRYPT IT--*
THEN WE DON'T GIVE 'EM A CHANCE, PROWLER. WITH THIS--
--WE CAN FINALLY TAKE THE FIGHT TO THEM. GOOD WORK, YOU TWO.
SO NOT A CLEAN WIN?
THE IMPORTANT THING: WE ALL GOT OUT ALIVE.
LAST TIME I WAS IN A SITUATION LIKE THIS...I WASN'T SO LUCKY.
WHO DID YOU LOSE?
A GOOD FRIEND...

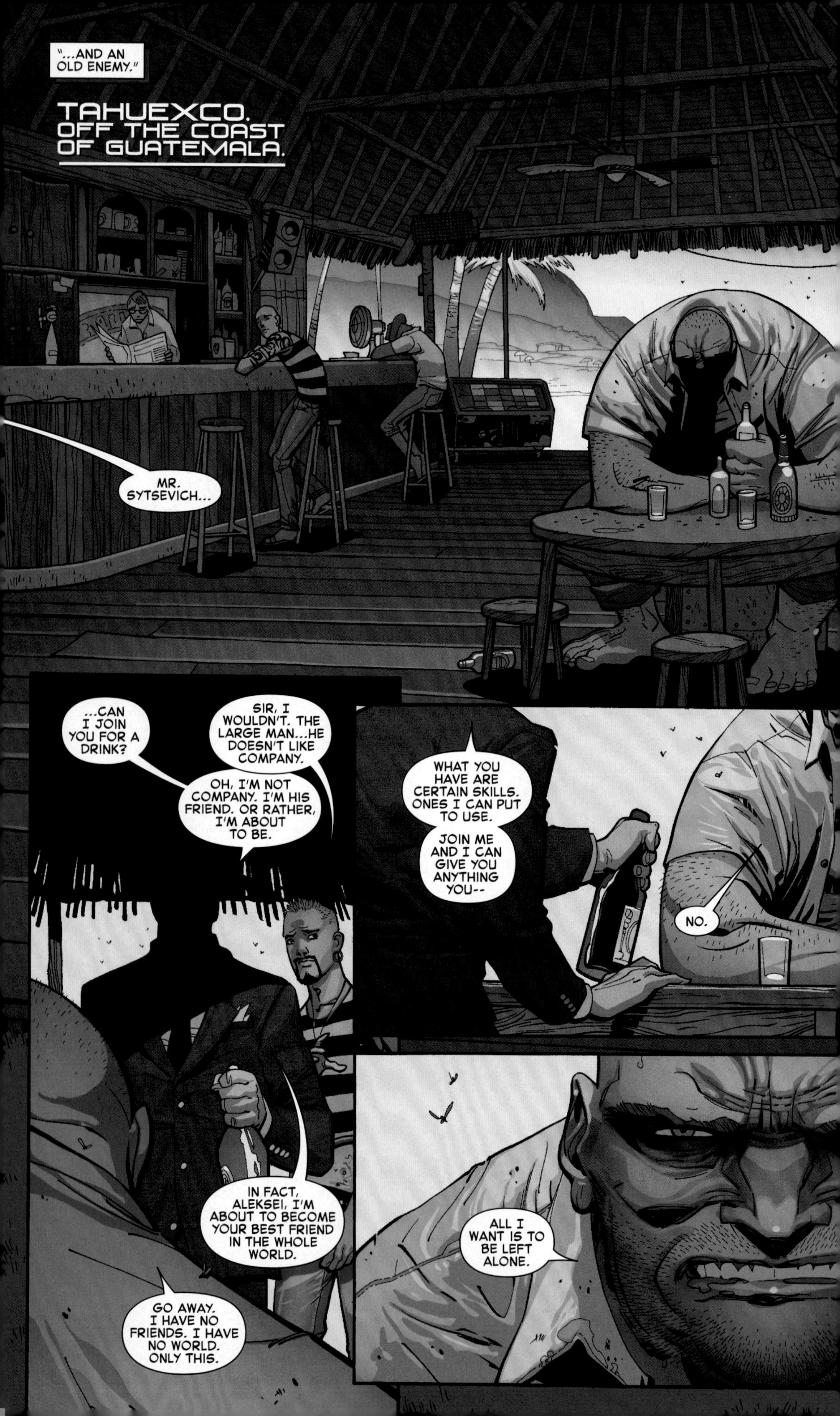
"...AND AN OLD ENEMY."
TAHUEXCO. OFF THE COAST OF GUATEMALA.
MR. SYTSEVICH...
...CAN I JOIN YOU FOR A DRINK?
SIR, I WOULDN'T. THE LARGE MAN...HE DOESN'T LIKE COMPANY.
OH, I'M NOT COMPANY. I'M HIS FRIEND. OR RATHER, I'M ABOUT TO BE.
IN FACT, ALEKSEI, I'M ABOUT TO BECOME YOUR BEST FRIEND IN THE WHOLE WORLD.
GO AWAY. I HAVE NO FRIENDS. I HAVE NO WORLD. ONLY THIS.
WHAT YOU HAVE ARE CERTAIN SKILLS. ONES I CAN PUT TO USE.
JOIN ME AND I CAN GIVE YOU ANYTHING YOU--
NO.
ALL I WANT IS TO BE LEFT ALONE.

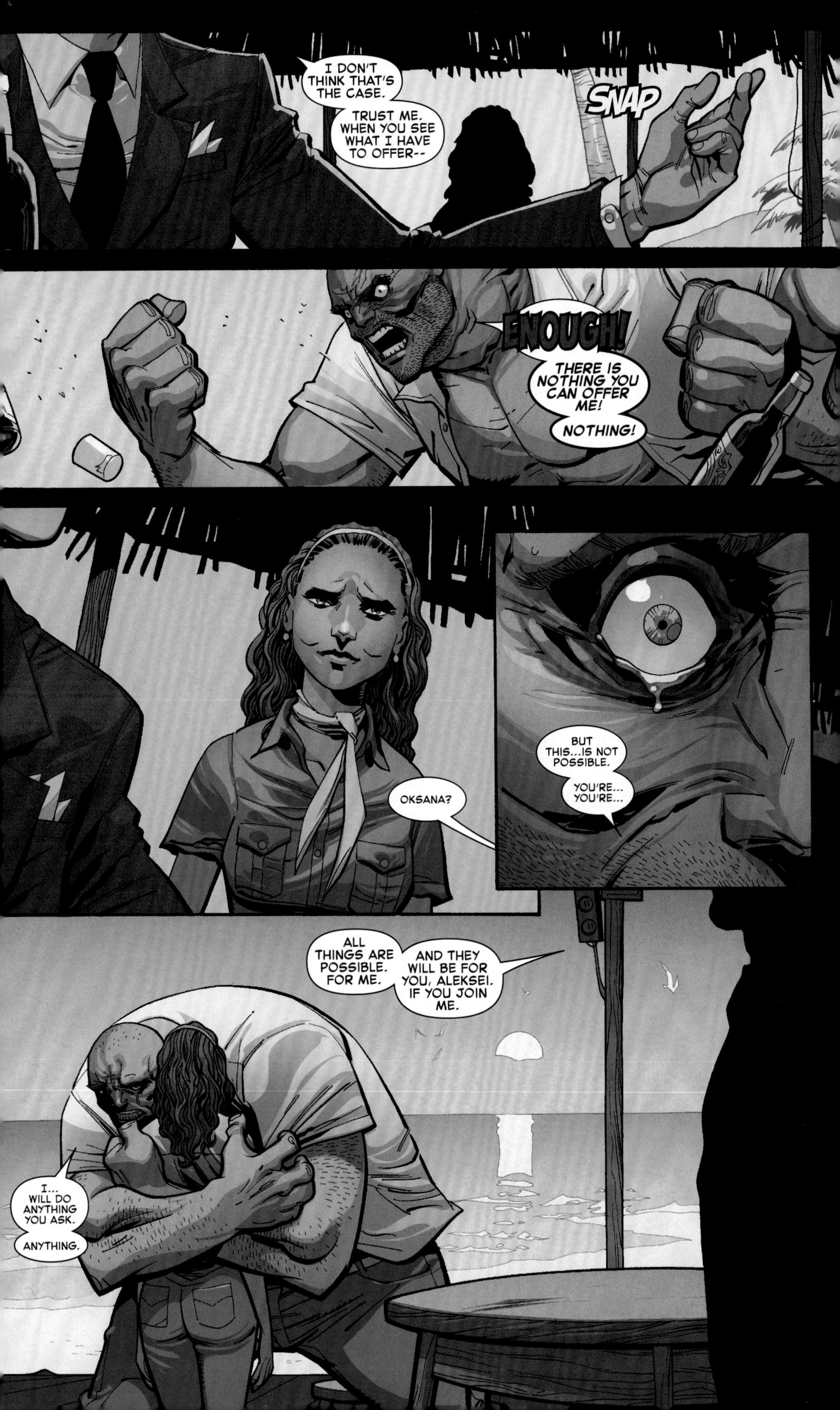

I DON'T THINK THAT'S THE CASE.
TRUST ME. WHEN YOU SEE WHAT I HAVE TO OFFER--
SNAP
ENOUGH!
THERE IS NOTHING YOU CAN OFFER ME!
NOTHING!
OKSANA?
BUT THIS...IS NOT POSSIBLE.
YOU'RE... YOU'RE...
ALL THINGS ARE POSSIBLE. FOR ME.
AND THEY WILL BE FOR YOU, ALEKSEI. IF YOU JOIN ME.
I... WILL DO ANYTHING YOU ASK.
ANYTHING.

3

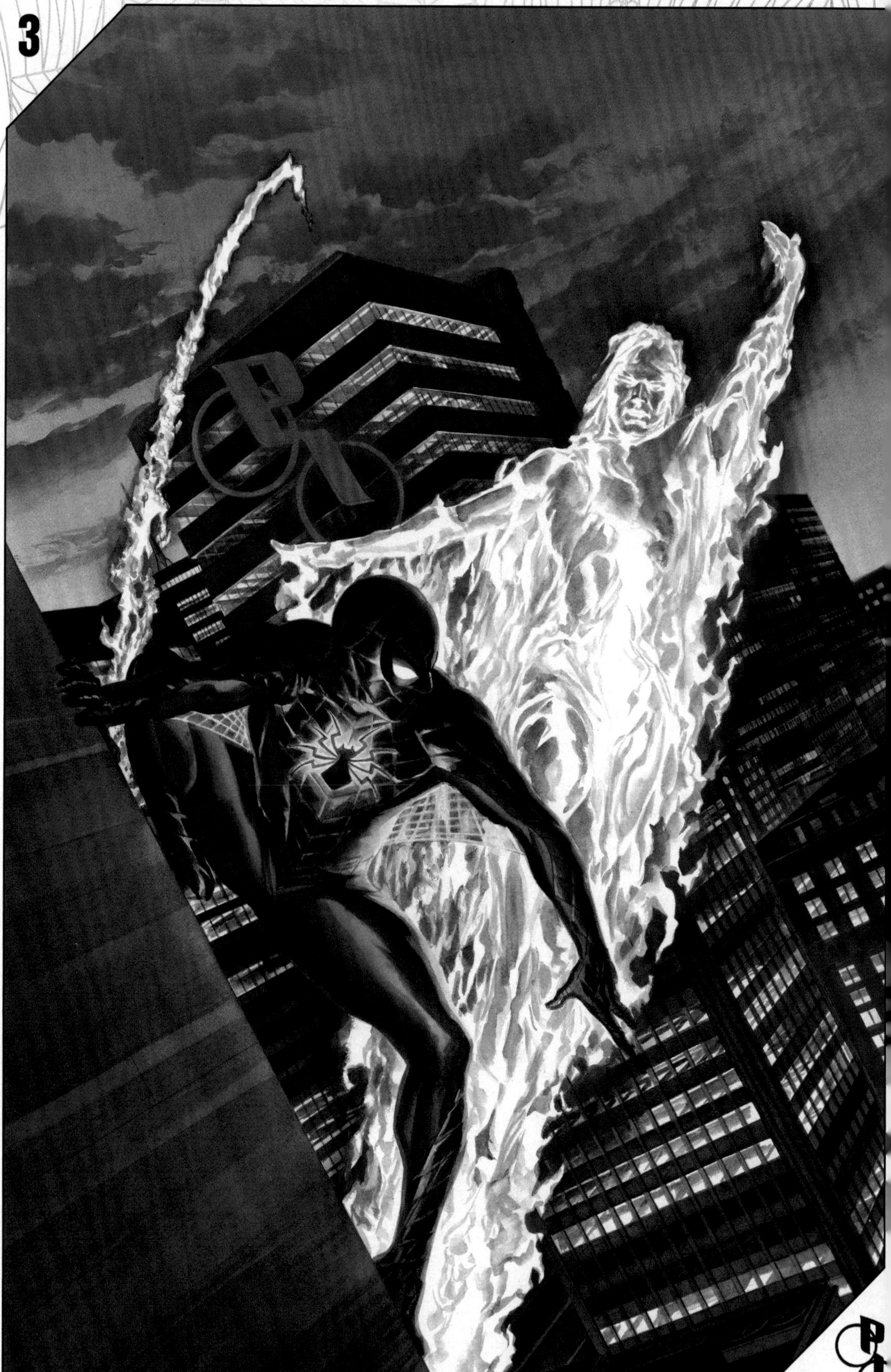

"FRIENDLY FIRE"

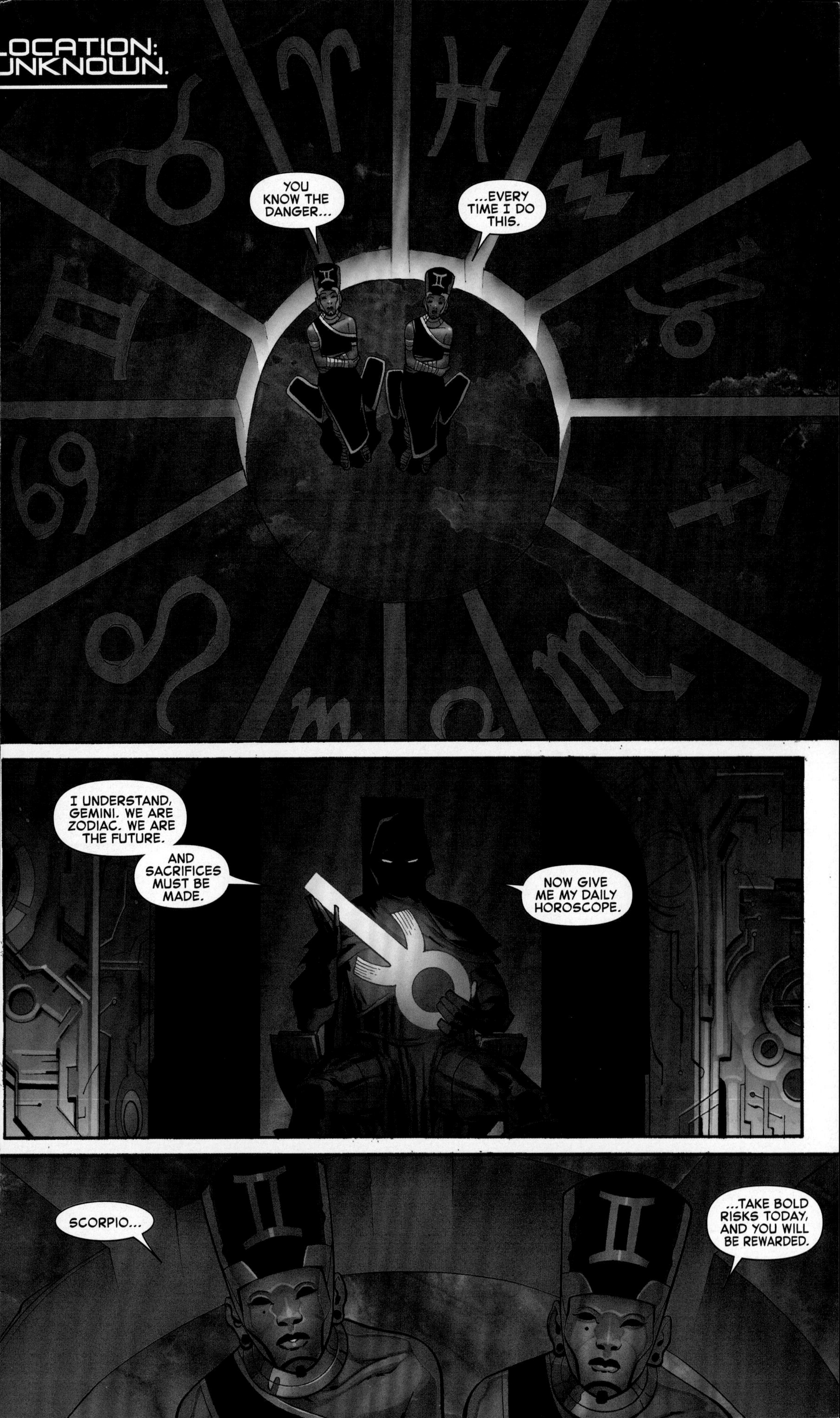
LOCATION: UNKNOWN.
YOU KNOW THE DANGER...
...EVERY TIME I DO THIS.
I UNDERSTAND, GEMINI. WE ARE ZODIAC. WE ARE THE FUTURE.
AND SACRIFICES MUST BE MADE.
NOW GIVE ME MY DAILY HOROSCOPE.
SCORPIO...
...TAKE BOLD RISKS TODAY, AND YOU WILL BE REWARDED.

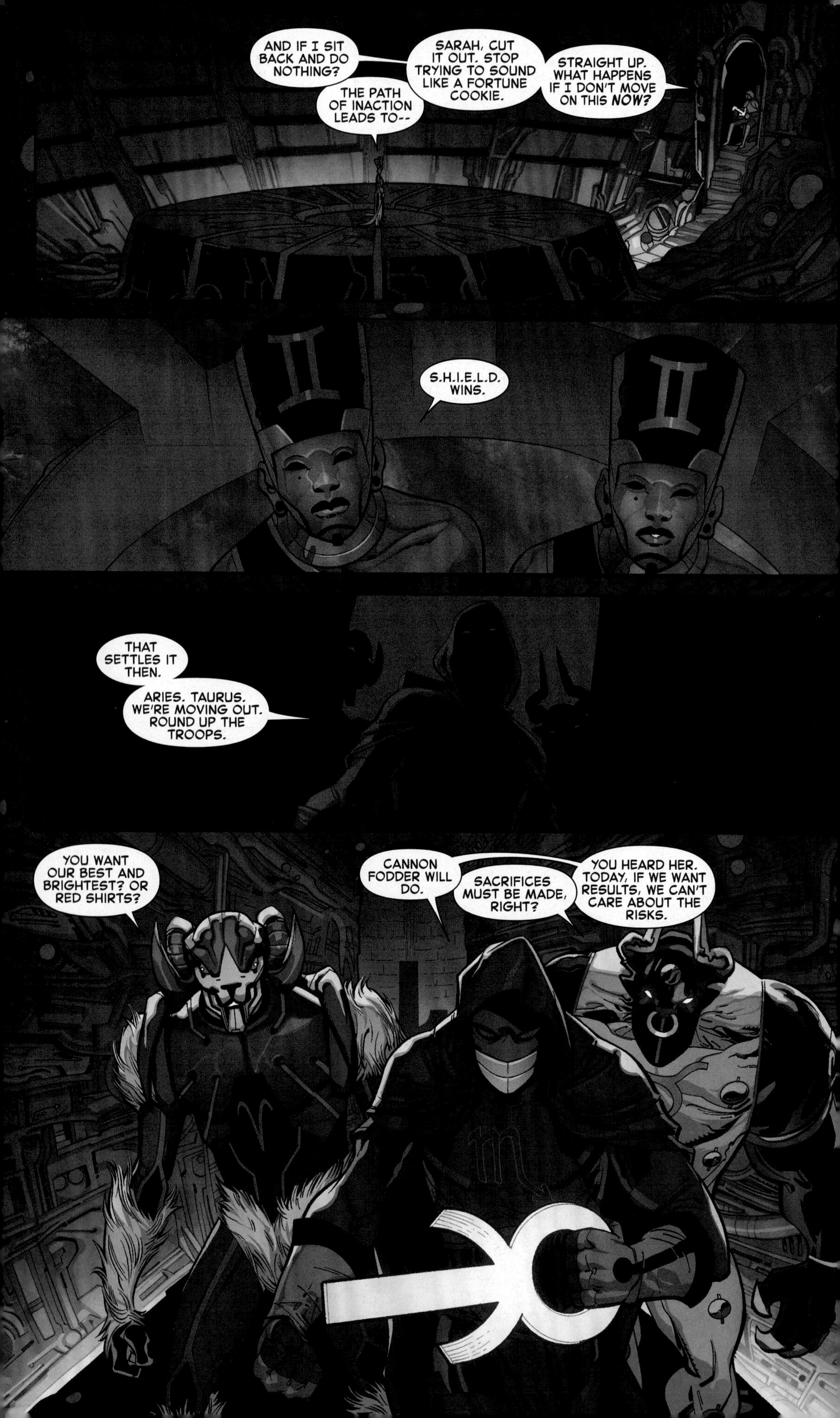

AND IF I SIT BACK AND DO NOTHING?
THE PATH OF INACTION LEADS TO--
SARAH, CUT IT OUT. STOP TRYING TO SOUND LIKE A FORTUNE COOKIE.
STRAIGHT UP. WHAT HAPPENS IF I DON'T MOVE ON THIS *NOW?*
S.H.I.E.L.D. WINS.
THAT SETTLES IT THEN.
ARIES. TAURUS. WE'RE MOVING OUT. ROUND UP THE TROOPS.
YOU WANT OUR BEST AND BRIGHTEST? OR RED SHIRTS?
CANNON FODDER WILL DO.
SACRIFICES MUST BE MADE, RIGHT?
YOU HEARD HER. TODAY, IF WE WANT RESULTS, WE CAN'T CARE ABOUT THE RISKS.

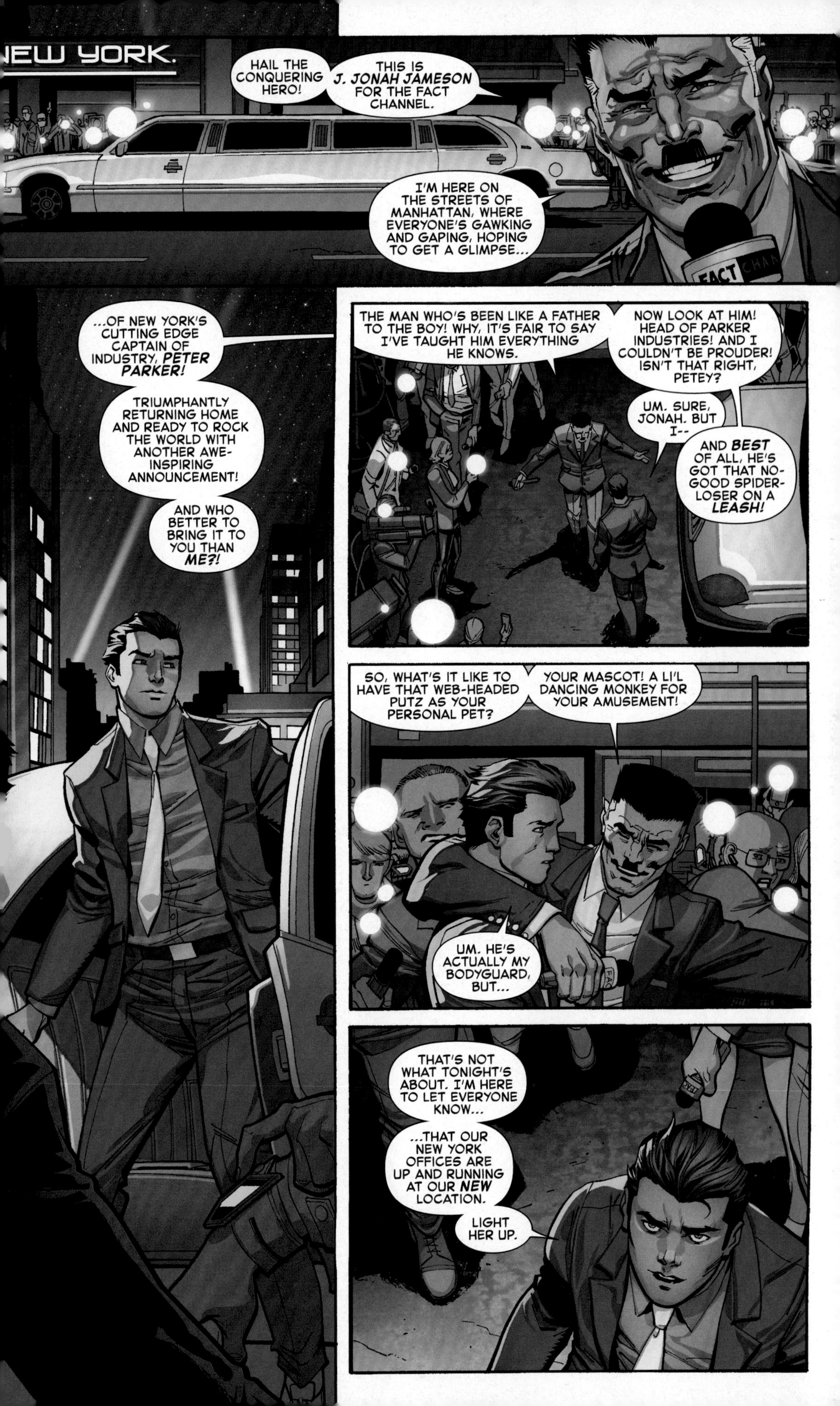
NEW YORK.
HAIL THE CONQUERING HERO!
THIS IS J. JONAH JAMESON FOR THE FACT CHANNEL.
I'M HERE ON THE STREETS OF MANHATTAN, WHERE EVERYONE'S GAWKING AND GAPING, HOPING TO GET A GLIMPSE...
FACT
...OF NEW YORK'S CUTTING EDGE CAPTAIN OF INDUSTRY, PETER PARKER!
TRIUMPHANTLY RETURNING HOME AND READY TO ROCK THE WORLD WITH ANOTHER AWE-INSPIRING ANNOUNCEMENT!
AND WHO BETTER TO BRING IT TO YOU THAN ME?!
THE MAN WHO'S BEEN LIKE A FATHER TO THE BOY! WHY, IT'S FAIR TO SAY I'VE TAUGHT HIM EVERYTHING HE KNOWS.
NOW LOOK AT HIM! HEAD OF PARKER INDUSTRIES! AND I COULDN'T BE PROUDER! ISN'T THAT RIGHT, PETEY?
UM. SURE, JONAH. BUT I--
AND BEST OF ALL, HE'S GOT THAT NO-GOOD SPIDER-LOSER ON A LEASH!
SO, WHAT'S IT LIKE TO HAVE THAT WEB-HEADED PUTZ AS YOUR PERSONAL PET?
YOUR MASCOT! A LI'L DANCING MONKEY FOR YOUR AMUSEMENT!
UM. HE'S ACTUALLY MY BODYGUARD, BUT...
THAT'S NOT WHAT TONIGHT'S ABOUT. I'M HERE TO LET EVERYONE KNOW...
...THAT OUR NEW YORK OFFICES ARE UP AND RUNNING AT OUR NEW LOCATION.
LIGHT HER UP.

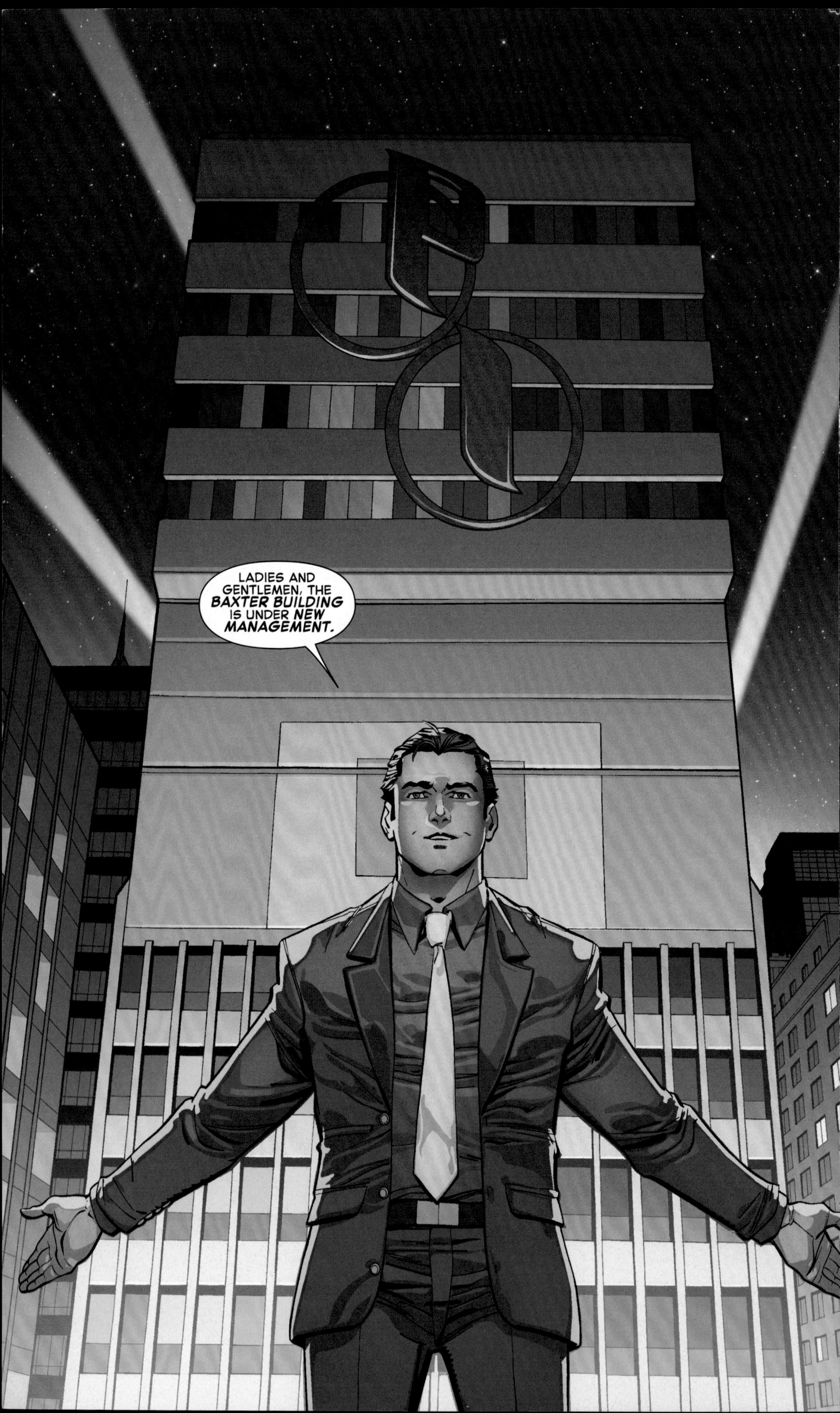
LADIES AND GENTLEMEN, THE BAXTER BUILDING IS UNDER NEW MANAGEMENT.

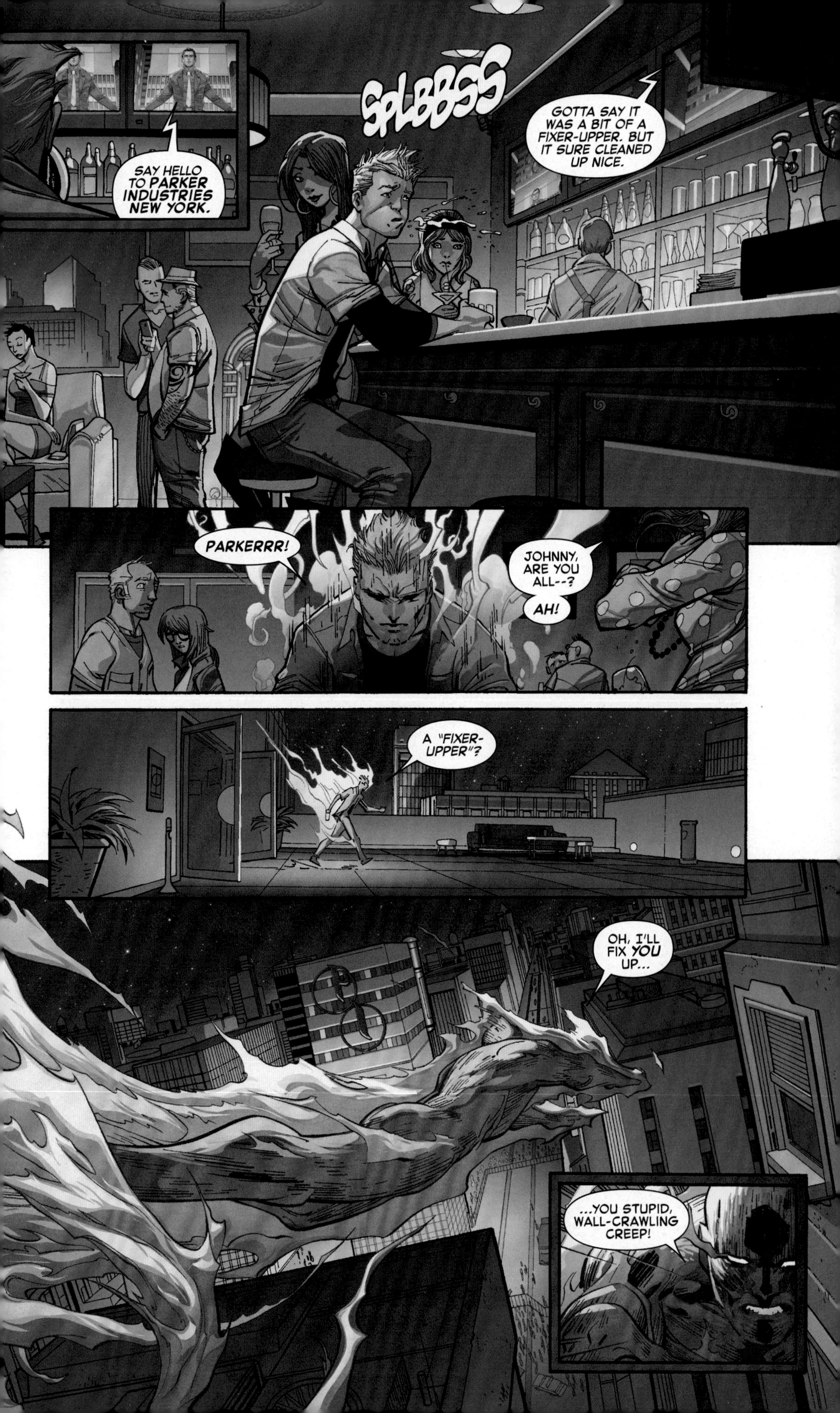
SAY HELLO TO PARKER INDUSTRIES NEW YORK.
SPLBBSS
GOTTA SAY IT WAS A BIT OF A FIXER-UPPER. BUT IT SURE CLEANED UP NICE.
PARKERRR!
JOHNNY, ARE YOU ALL--?
AH!
A "FIXER-UPPER"?
OH, I'LL FIX YOU UP...
...YOU STUPID, WALL-CRAWLING CREEP!

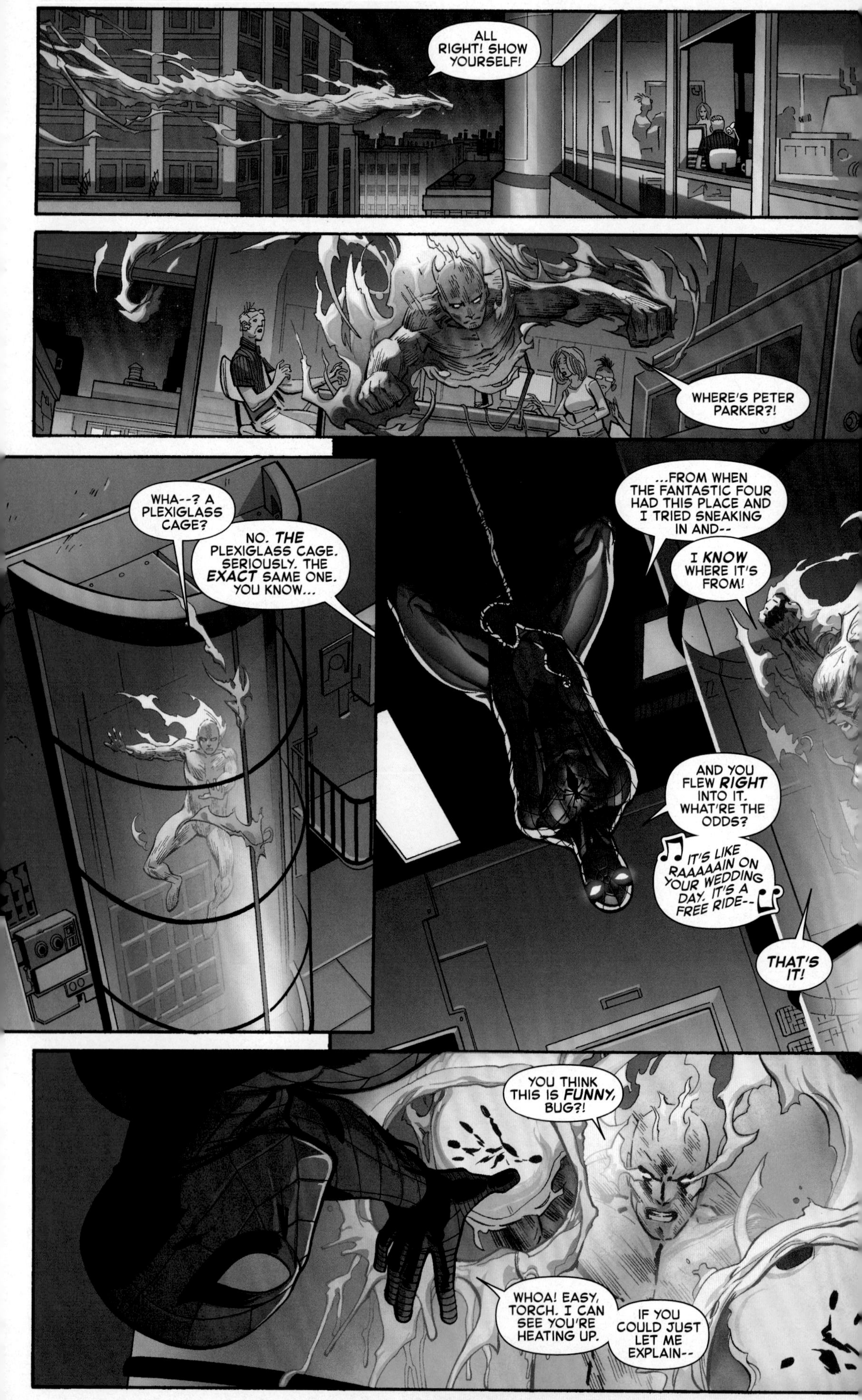
ALL RIGHT! SHOW YOURSELF!
WHERE'S PETER PARKER?!
WHA--? A PLEXIGLASS CAGE?
NO. *THE* PLEXIGLASS CAGE. SERIOUSLY. THE *EXACT* SAME ONE. YOU KNOW...
...FROM WHEN THE FANTASTIC FOUR HAD THIS PLACE AND I TRIED SNEAKING IN AND--
I *KNOW* WHERE IT'S FROM!
AND YOU FLEW *RIGHT* INTO IT. WHAT'RE THE ODDS?
IT'S LIKE RAAAAAIN ON YOUR WEDDING DAY. IT'S A FREE RIDE--
THAT'S IT!
YOU THINK THIS IS *FUNNY*, BUG?!
WHOA! EASY, TORCH. I CAN SEE YOU'RE HEATING UP.
IF YOU COULD JUST LET ME EXPLAIN--

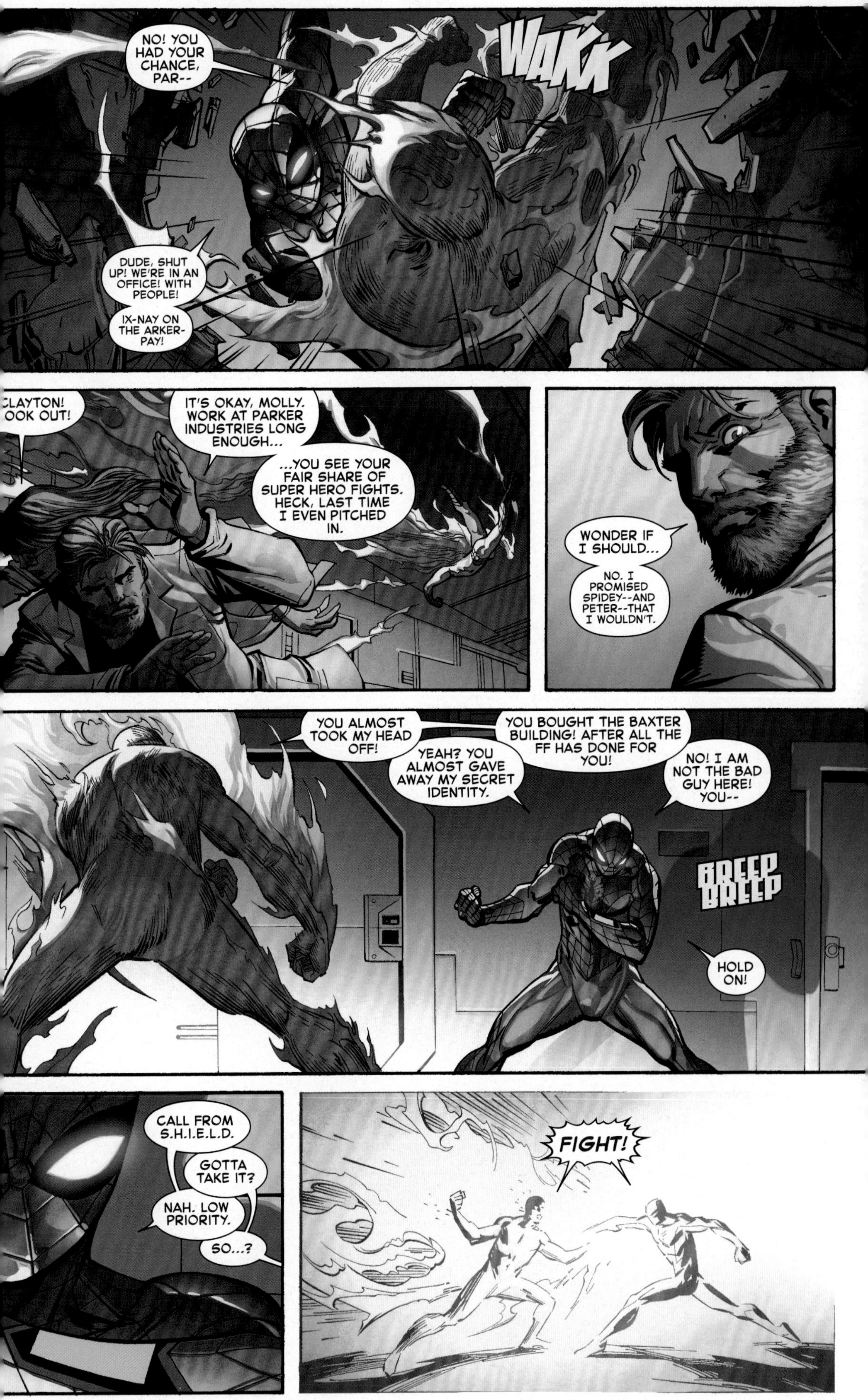
NO! YOU HAD YOUR CHANCE, PAR--
WAKK
DUDE, SHUT UP! WE'RE IN AN OFFICE! WITH PEOPLE!
IX-NAY ON THE ARKER-PAY!
CLAYTON! OOK OUT!
IT'S OKAY, MOLLY. WORK AT PARKER INDUSTRIES LONG ENOUGH...
...YOU SEE YOUR FAIR SHARE OF SUPER HERO FIGHTS. HECK, LAST TIME I EVEN PITCHED IN.
WONDER IF I SHOULD...
NO. I PROMISED SPIDEY--AND PETER--THAT I WOULDN'T.
YOU ALMOST TOOK MY HEAD OFF!
YEAH? YOU ALMOST GAVE AWAY MY SECRET IDENTITY.
YOU BOUGHT THE BAXTER BUILDING! AFTER ALL THE FF HAS DONE FOR YOU!
NO! I AM NOT THE BAD GUY HERE! YOU--
BREEP BREEP
HOLD ON!
CALL FROM S.H.I.E.L.D.
GOTTA TAKE IT?
NAH. LOW PRIORITY.
SO...?
FIGHT!

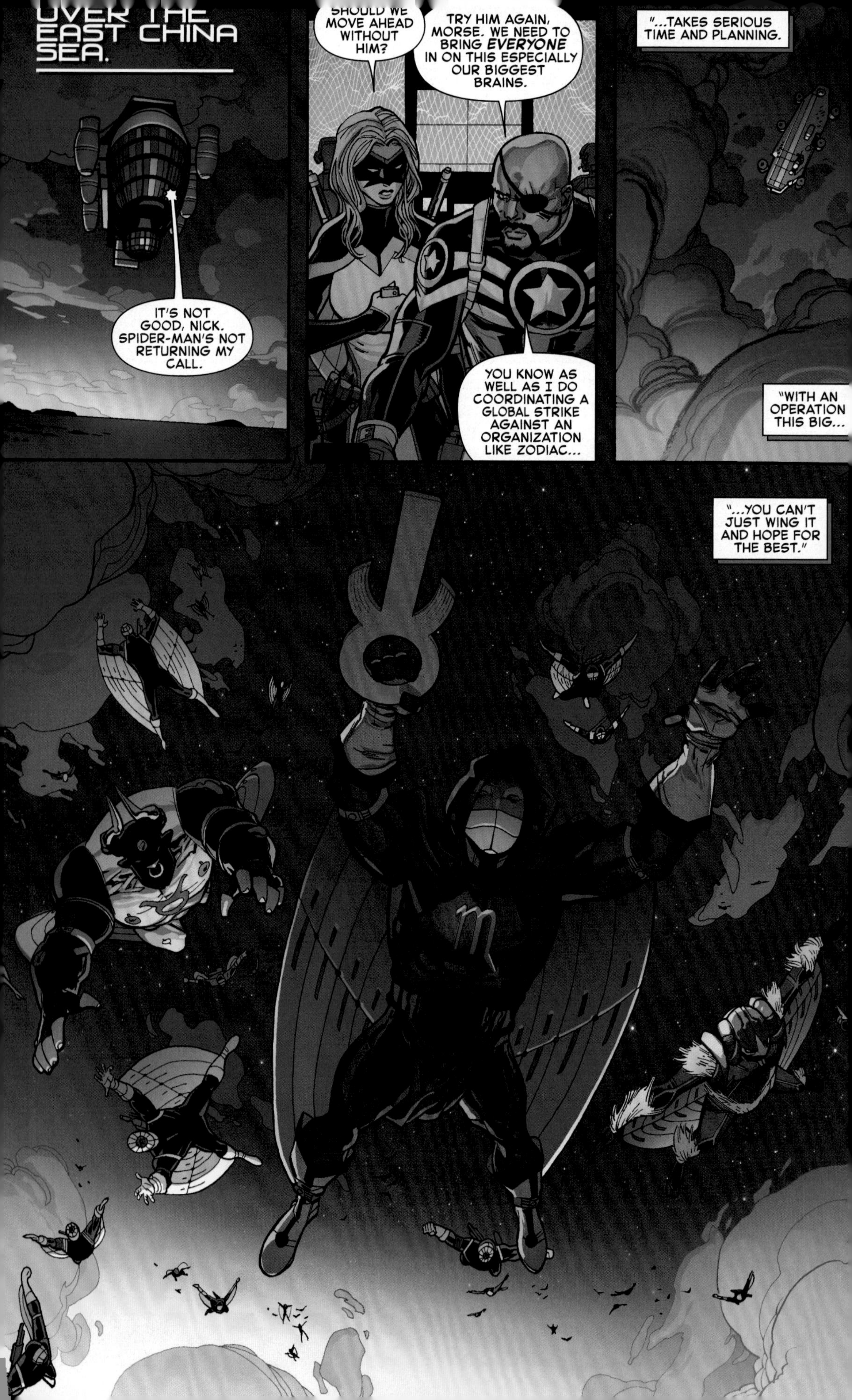
OVER THE EAST CHINA SEA.
IT'S NOT GOOD, NICK. SPIDER-MAN'S NOT RETURNING MY CALL.
SHOULD WE MOVE AHEAD WITHOUT HIM?
TRY HIM AGAIN, MORSE. WE NEED TO BRING EVERYONE IN ON THIS ESPECIALLY OUR BIGGEST BRAINS.
YOU KNOW AS WELL AS I DO COORDINATING A GLOBAL STRIKE AGAINST AN ORGANIZATION LIKE ZODIAC...
"...TAKES SERIOUS TIME AND PLANNING.
"WITH AN OPERATION THIS BIG...
"...YOU CAN'T JUST WING IT AND HOPE FOR THE BEST."

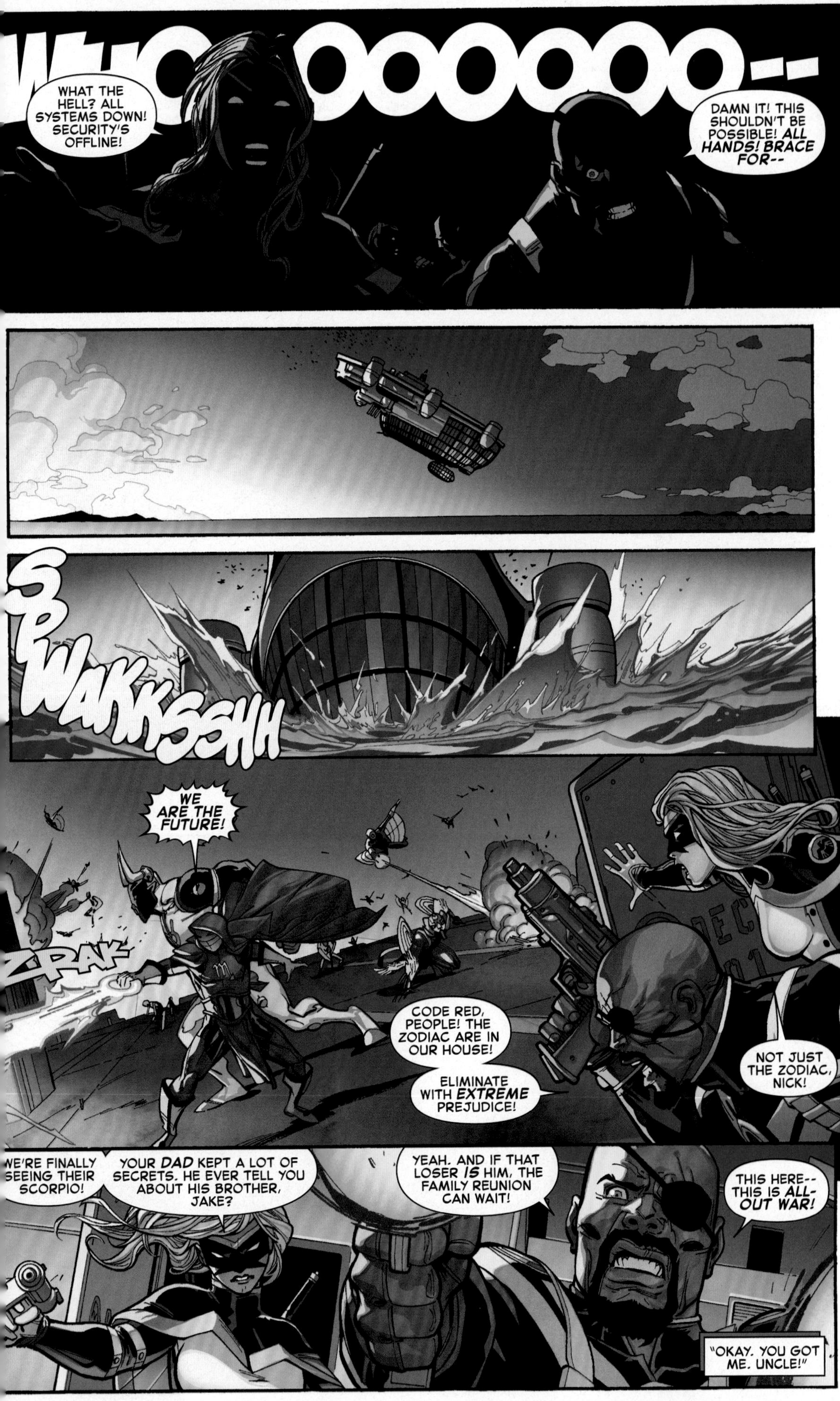
WHOOOOOOOOO--
WHAT THE HELL? ALL SYSTEMS DOWN! SECURITY'S OFFLINE!
DAMN IT! THIS SHOULDN'T BE POSSIBLE! ALL HANDS! BRACE FOR--
SPWAKKSSHH
WE ARE THE FUTURE!
ZRAK
CODE RED, PEOPLE! THE ZODIAC ARE IN OUR HOUSE!
ELIMINATE WITH EXTREME PREJUDICE!
NOT JUST THE ZODIAC, NICK!
WE'RE FINALLY SEEING THEIR SCORPIO!
YOUR DAD KEPT A LOT OF SECRETS. HE EVER TELL YOU ABOUT HIS BROTHER, JAKE?
YEAH. AND IF THAT LOSER IS HIM, THE FAMILY REUNION CAN WAIT!
THIS HERE-- THIS IS ALL-OUT WAR!
"OKAY. YOU GOT ME. UNCLE!"

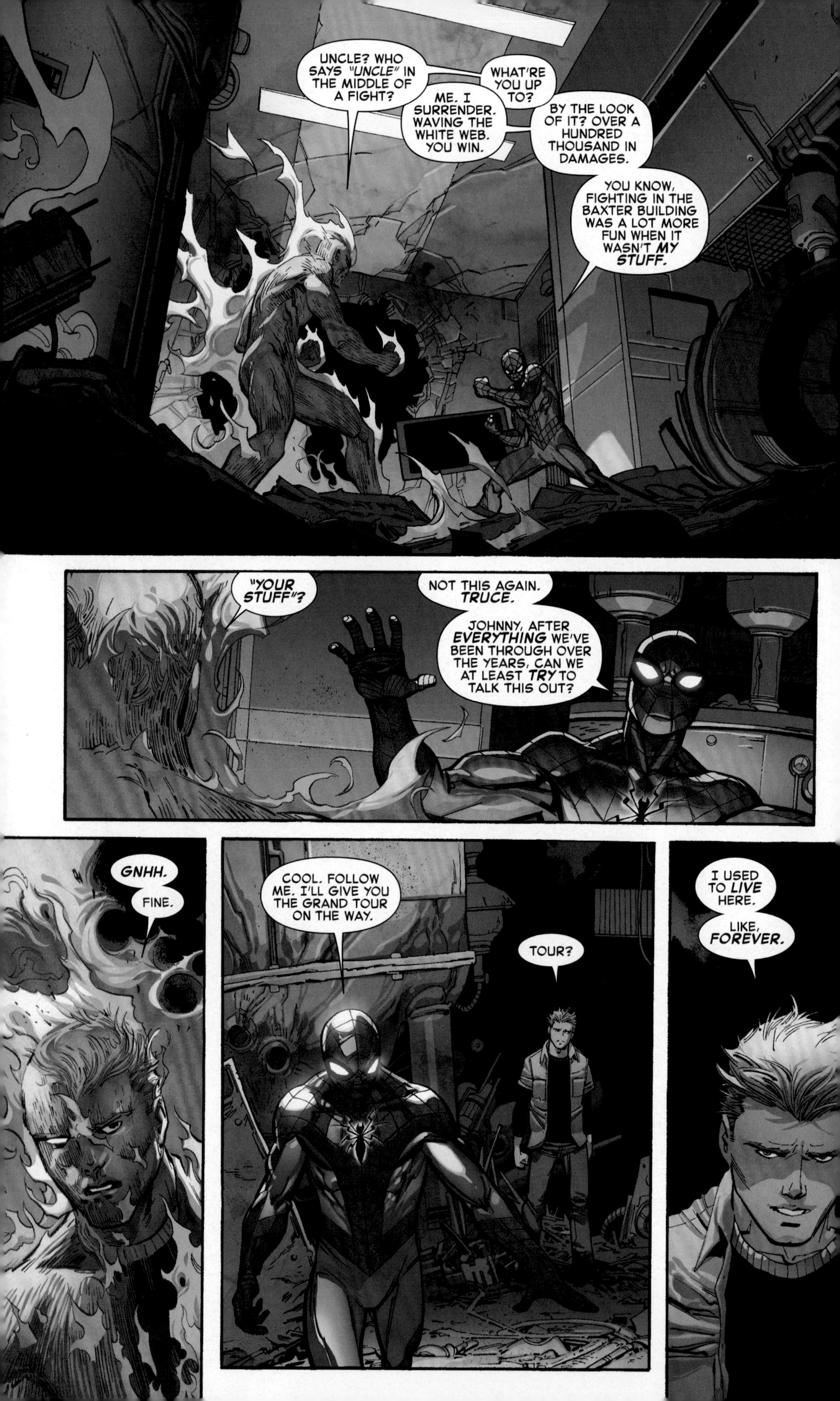
UNCLE? WHO SAYS "UNCLE" IN THE MIDDLE OF A FIGHT?
WHAT'RE YOU UP TO?
ME. I SURRENDER. WAVING THE WHITE WEB. YOU WIN.
BY THE LOOK OF IT? OVER A HUNDRED THOUSAND IN DAMAGES.
YOU KNOW, FIGHTING IN THE BAXTER BUILDING WAS A LOT MORE FUN WHEN IT WASN'T MY STUFF.
"YOUR STUFF"?
NOT THIS AGAIN. TRUCE.
JOHNNY, AFTER EVERYTHING WE'VE BEEN THROUGH OVER THE YEARS, CAN WE AT LEAST TRY TO TALK THIS OUT?
GNHH.
FINE.
COOL. FOLLOW ME. I'LL GIVE YOU THE GRAND TOUR ON THE WAY.
TOUR?
I USED TO LIVE HERE.
LIKE, FOREVER.

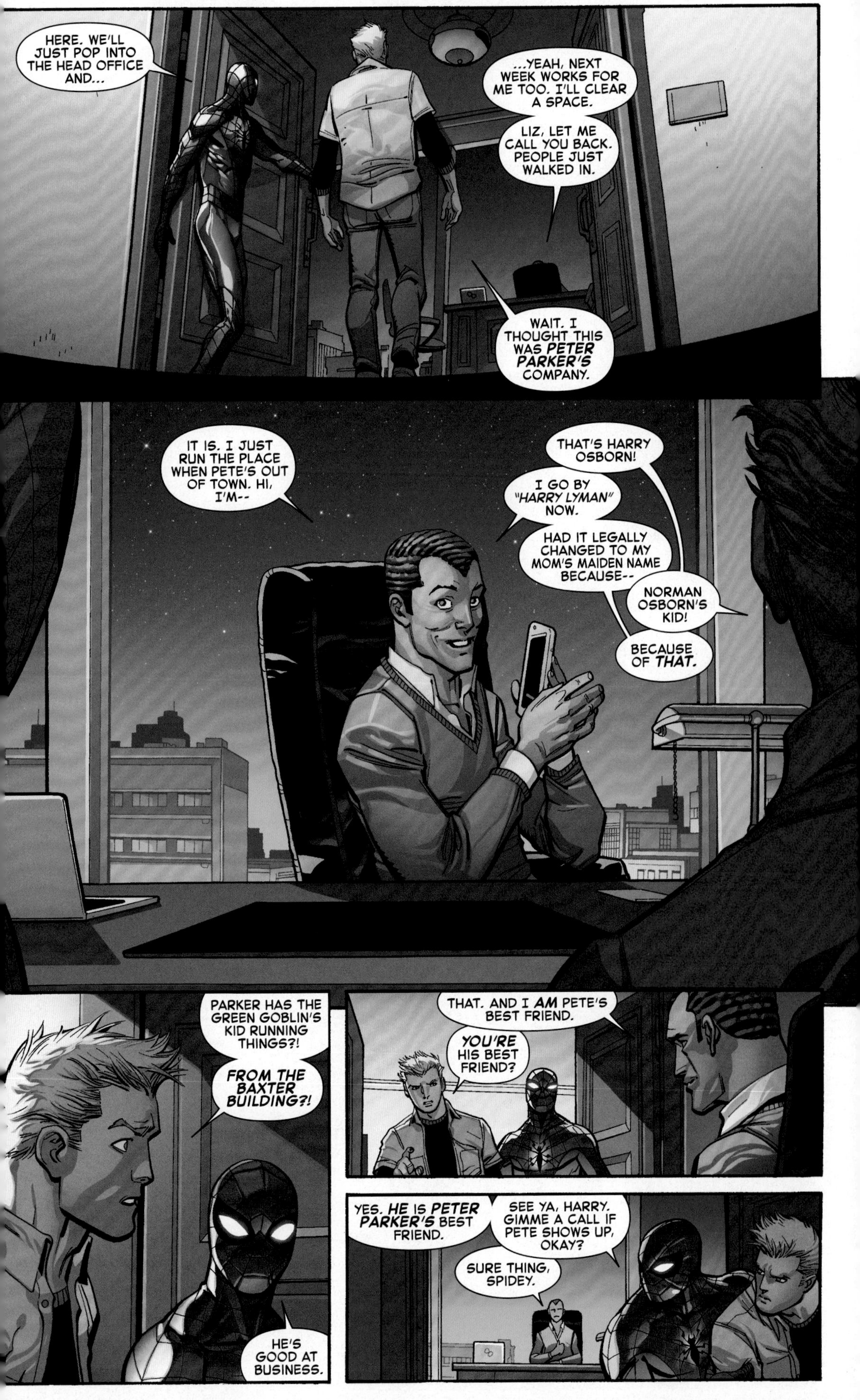
HERE. WE'LL JUST POP INTO THE HEAD OFFICE AND...
...YEAH, NEXT WEEK WORKS FOR ME TOO. I'LL CLEAR A SPACE.
LIZ, LET ME CALL YOU BACK. PEOPLE JUST WALKED IN.
WAIT. I THOUGHT THIS WAS *PETER PARKER'S* COMPANY.
IT IS. I JUST RUN THE PLACE WHEN PETE'S OUT OF TOWN. HI, I'M--
THAT'S HARRY OSBORN!
I GO BY *"HARRY LYMAN"* NOW.
HAD IT LEGALLY CHANGED TO MY MOM'S MAIDEN NAME BECAUSE--
NORMAN OSBORN'S KID!
BECAUSE OF *THAT.*
PARKER HAS THE GREEN GOBLIN'S KID RUNNING THINGS?!
FROM THE BAXTER BUILDING?!
HE'S GOOD AT BUSINESS.
THAT. AND I *AM* PETE'S BEST FRIEND.
YOU'RE HIS BEST FRIEND?
YES. *HE* IS *PETER PARKER'S* BEST FRIEND.
SEE YA, HARRY. GIMME A CALL IF PETE SHOWS UP, OKAY?
SURE THING, SPIDEY.

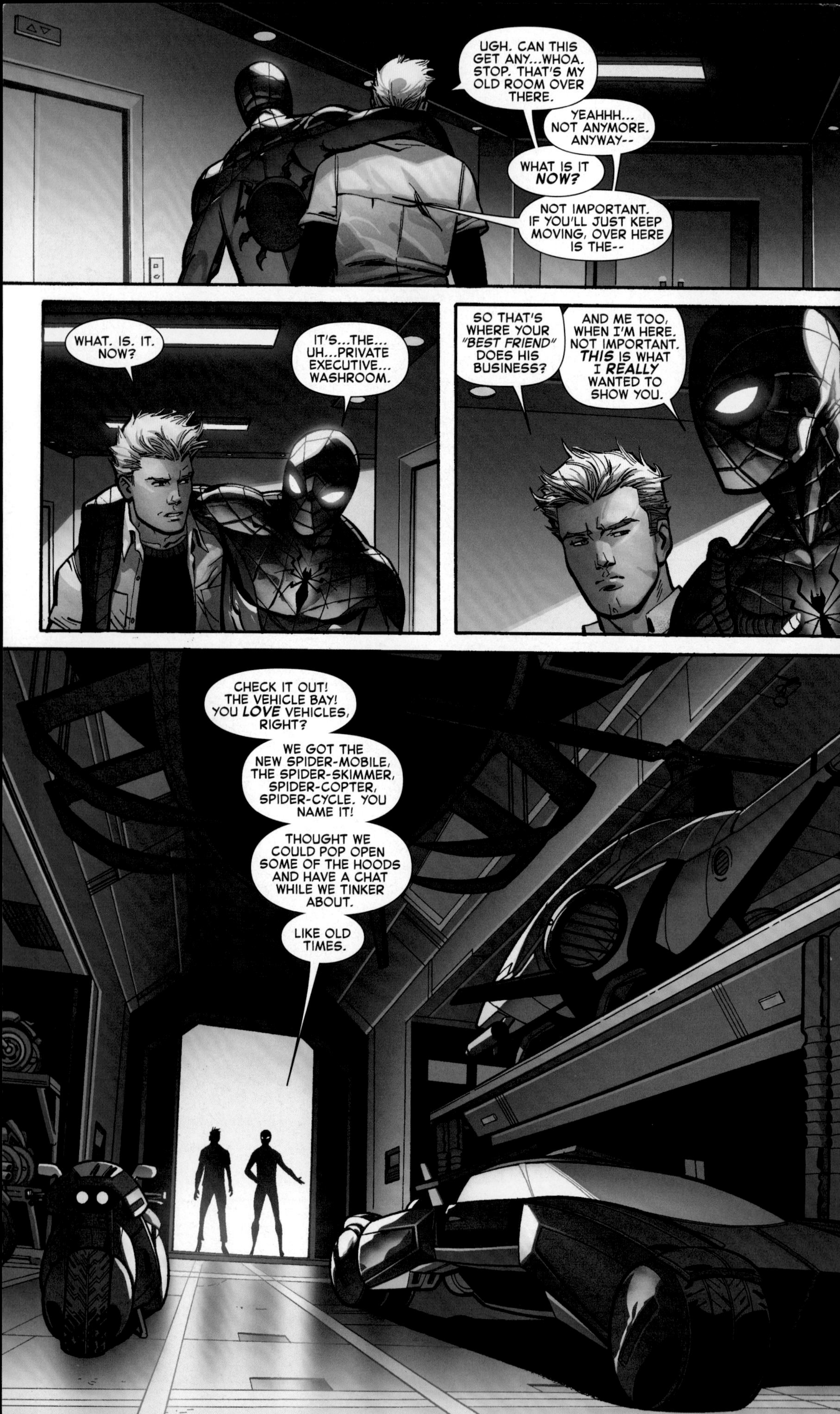
UGH. CAN THIS GET ANY...WHOA. STOP. THAT'S MY OLD ROOM OVER THERE.
YEAHHH... NOT ANYMORE. ANYWAY--
WHAT IS IT NOW?
NOT IMPORTANT. IF YOU'LL JUST KEEP MOVING, OVER HERE IS THE--
WHAT. IS. IT. NOW?
IT'S...THE... UH...PRIVATE EXECUTIVE... WASHROOM.
SO THAT'S WHERE YOUR "BEST FRIEND" DOES HIS BUSINESS?
AND ME TOO, WHEN I'M HERE. NOT IMPORTANT. THIS IS WHAT I REALLY WANTED TO SHOW YOU.
CHECK IT OUT! THE VEHICLE BAY! YOU LOVE VEHICLES, RIGHT?
WE GOT THE NEW SPIDER-MOBILE, THE SPIDER-SKIMMER, SPIDER-COPTER, SPIDER-CYCLE. YOU NAME IT!
THOUGHT WE COULD POP OPEN SOME OF THE HOODS AND HAVE A CHAT WHILE WE TINKER ABOUT.
LIKE OLD TIMES.

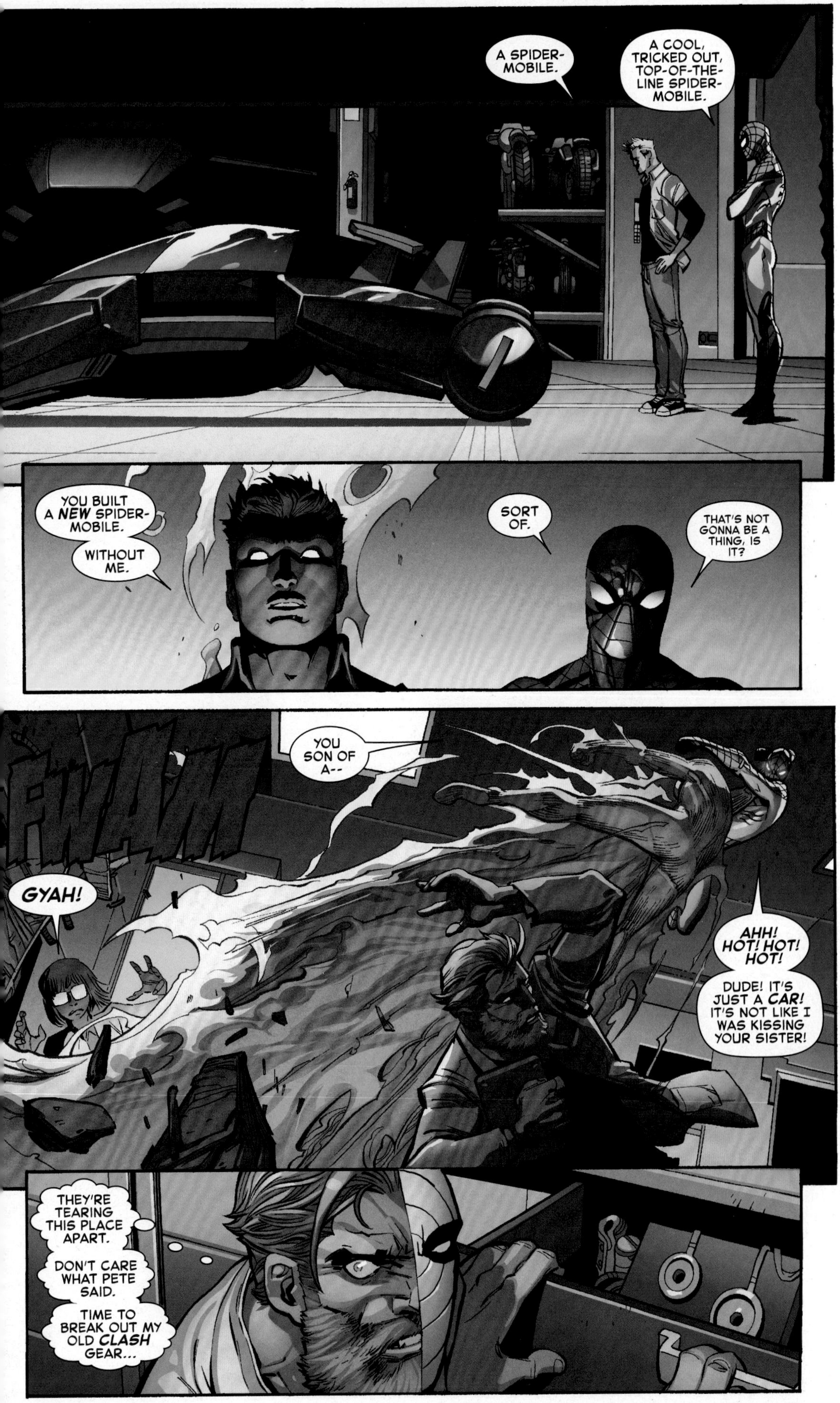
A SPIDER-MOBILE.
A COOL, TRICKED OUT, TOP-OF-THE-LINE SPIDER-MOBILE.
YOU BUILT A NEW SPIDER-MOBILE.
WITHOUT ME.
SORT OF.
THAT'S NOT GONNA BE A THING, IS IT?
FWAM
YOU SON OF A--
GYAH!
AHH! HOT! HOT! HOT!
DUDE! IT'S JUST A CAR! IT'S NOT LIKE I WAS KISSING YOUR SISTER!
THEY'RE TEARING THIS PLACE APART.
DON'T CARE WHAT PETE SAID.
TIME TO BREAK OUT MY OLD CLASH GEAR...

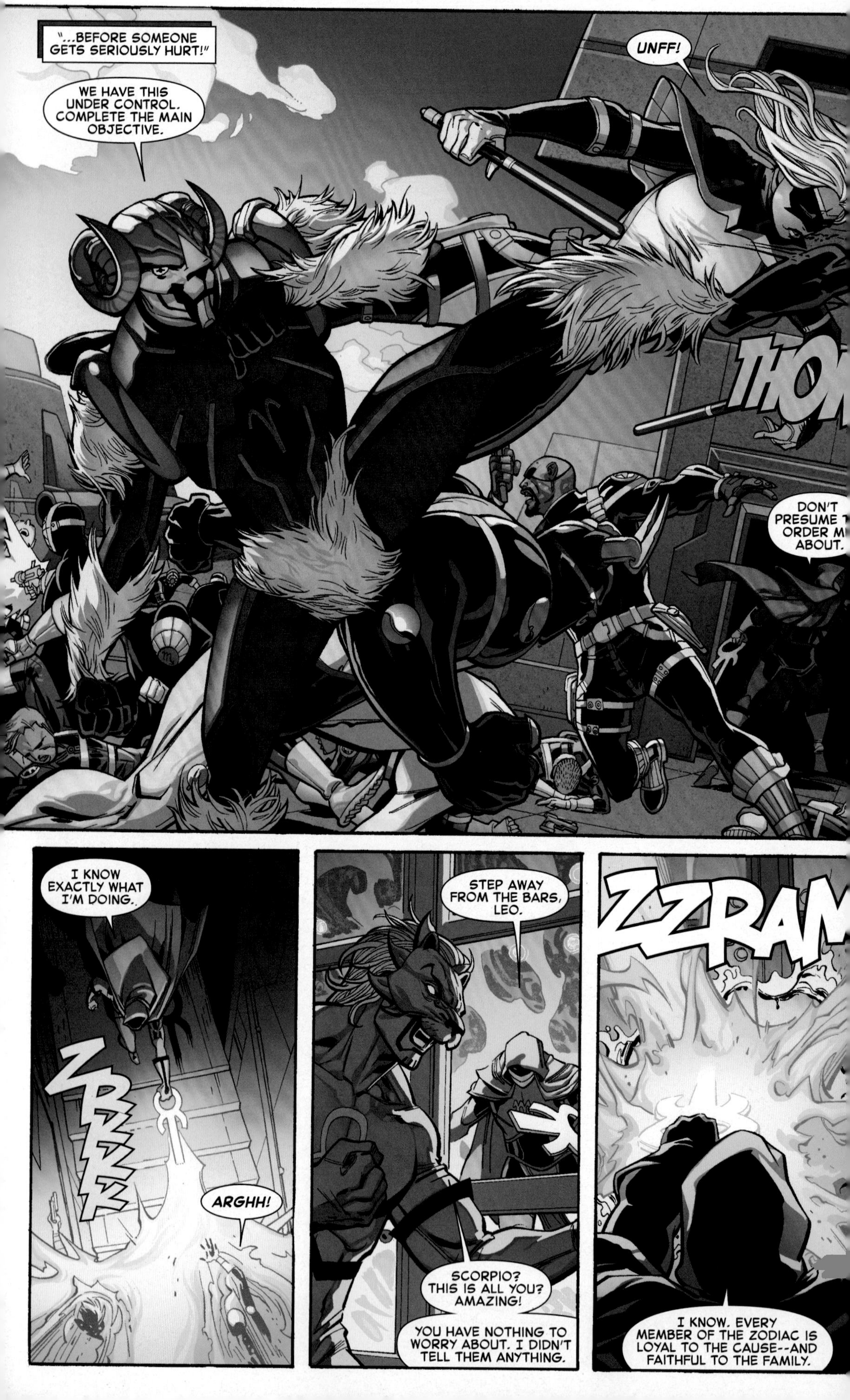
"...BEFORE SOMEONE GETS SERIOUSLY HURT!"
WE HAVE THIS UNDER CONTROL. COMPLETE THE MAIN OBJECTIVE.
UNFF!
THOM
DON'T PRESUME T ORDER M ABOUT.
I KNOW EXACTLY WHAT I'M DOING.
ZRRZZZ
ARGHH!
STEP AWAY FROM THE BARS, LEO.
SCORPIO? THIS IS ALL YOU? AMAZING!
YOU HAVE NOTHING TO WORRY ABOUT. I DIDN'T TELL THEM ANYTHING.
ZZRAM
I KNOW. EVERY MEMBER OF THE ZODIAC IS LOYAL TO THE CAUSE--AND FAITHFUL TO THE FAMILY.

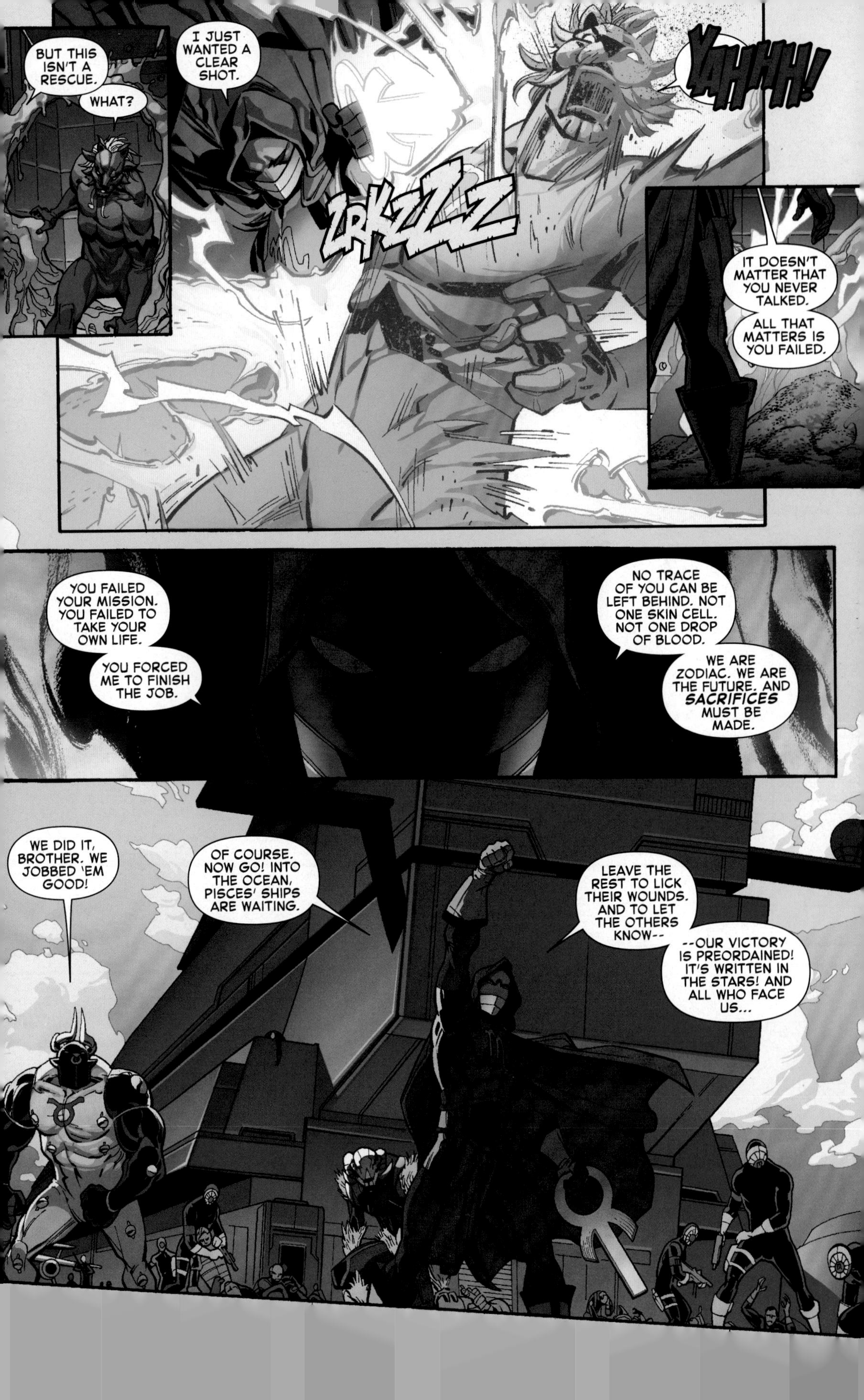

BUT THIS ISN'T A RESCUE.
WHAT?
I JUST WANTED A CLEAR SHOT.
YAHHHH!
ZRKZZZZ
IT DOESN'T MATTER THAT YOU NEVER TALKED.
ALL THAT MATTERS IS YOU FAILED.
YOU FAILED YOUR MISSION. YOU FAILED TO TAKE YOUR OWN LIFE.
YOU FORCED ME TO FINISH THE JOB.
NO TRACE OF YOU CAN BE LEFT BEHIND. NOT ONE SKIN CELL. NOT ONE DROP OF BLOOD.
WE ARE ZODIAC. WE ARE THE FUTURE. AND *SACRIFICES* MUST BE MADE.
WE DID IT, BROTHER. WE JOBBED 'EM GOOD!
OF COURSE. NOW GO! INTO THE OCEAN, PISCES' SHIPS ARE WAITING.
LEAVE THE REST TO LICK THEIR WOUNDS. AND TO LET THE OTHERS KNOW--
--OUR VICTORY IS PREORDAINED! IT'S WRITTEN IN THE STARS! AND ALL WHO FACE US...

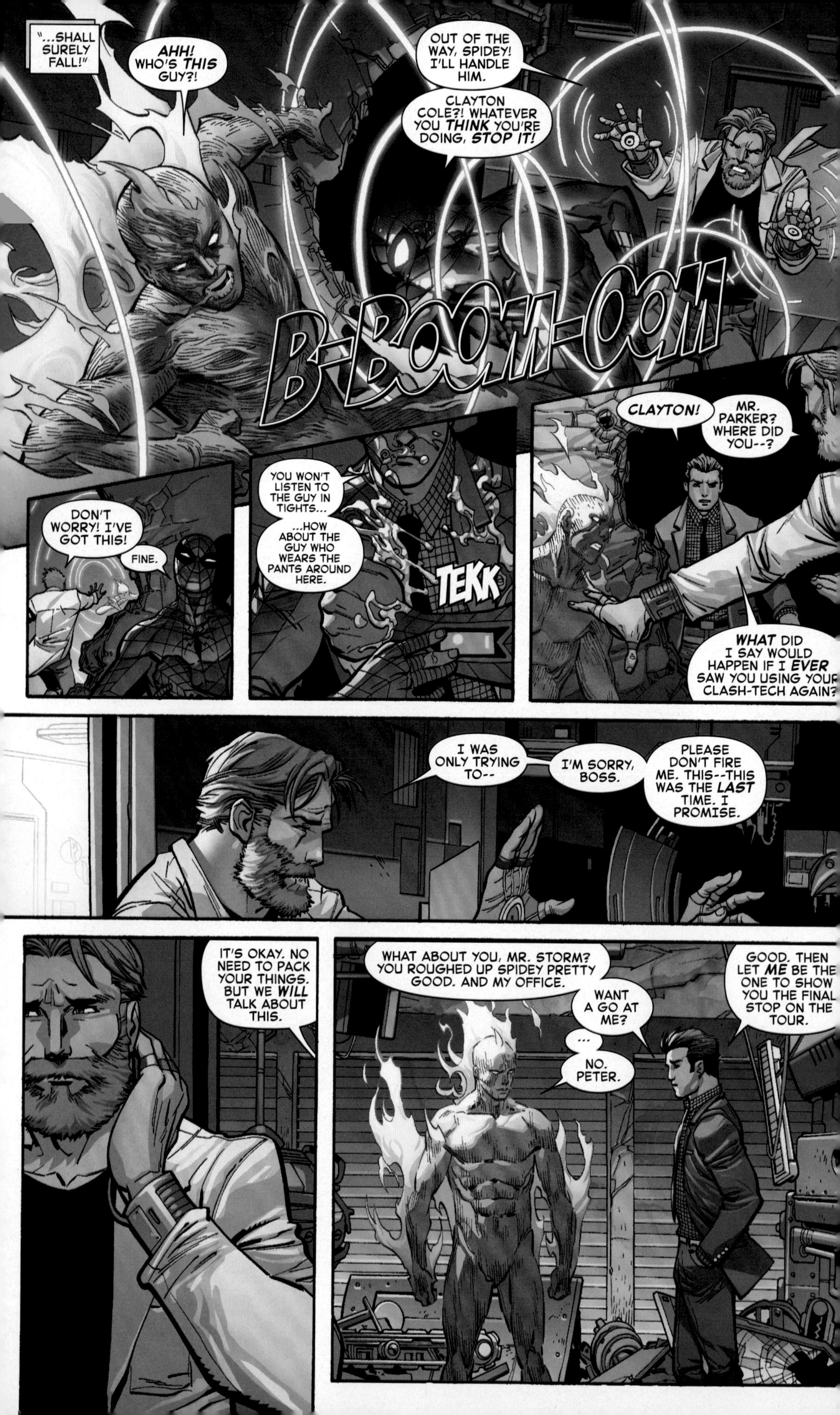
"...SHALL SURELY FALL!"
AHH! WHO'S THIS GUY?!
OUT OF THE WAY, SPIDEY! I'LL HANDLE HIM.
CLAYTON COLE?! WHATEVER YOU THINK YOU'RE DOING, STOP IT!
B-BOOM-OOM
DON'T WORRY! I'VE GOT THIS!
FINE.
YOU WON'T LISTEN TO THE GUY IN TIGHTS...
...HOW ABOUT THE GUY WHO WEARS THE PANTS AROUND HERE.
TEKK
CLAYTON!
MR. PARKER? WHERE DID YOU--?
WHAT DID I SAY WOULD HAPPEN IF I EVER SAW YOU USING YOUR CLASH-TECH AGAIN?
I WAS ONLY TRYING TO--
I'M SORRY, BOSS.
PLEASE DON'T FIRE ME. THIS--THIS WAS THE LAST TIME. I PROMISE.
IT'S OKAY. NO NEED TO PACK YOUR THINGS. BUT WE WILL TALK ABOUT THIS.
WHAT ABOUT YOU, MR. STORM? YOU ROUGHED UP SPIDEY PRETTY GOOD. AND MY OFFICE.
WANT A GO AT ME?
...
NO. PETER.
GOOD. THEN LET ME BE THE ONE TO SHOW YOU THE FINAL STOP ON THE TOUR.

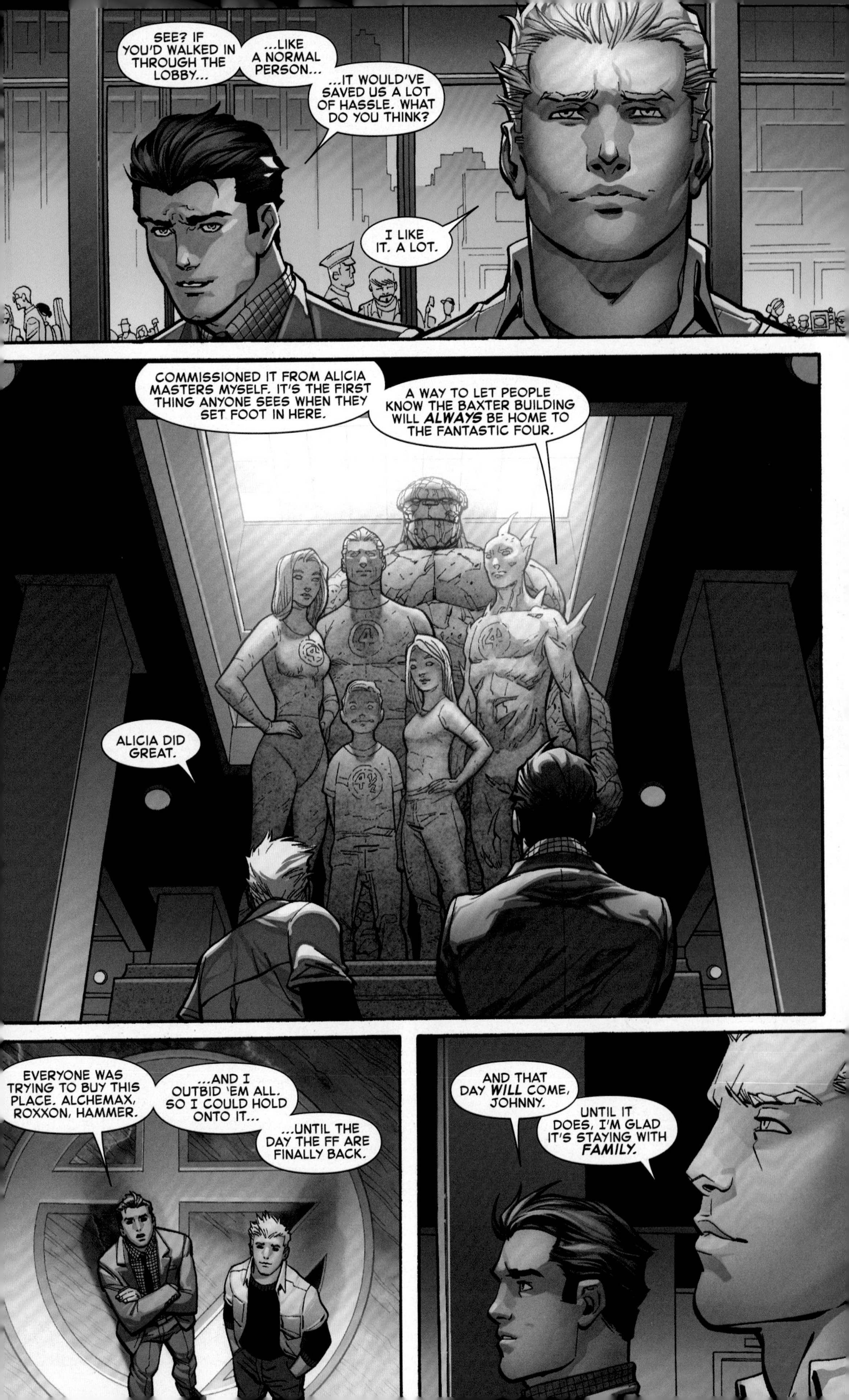
SEE? IF YOU'D WALKED IN THROUGH THE LOBBY...
...LIKE A NORMAL PERSON...
...IT WOULD'VE SAVED US A LOT OF HASSLE. WHAT DO YOU THINK?
I LIKE IT. A LOT.
COMMISSIONED IT FROM ALICIA MASTERS MYSELF. IT'S THE FIRST THING ANYONE SEES WHEN THEY SET FOOT IN HERE.
A WAY TO LET PEOPLE KNOW THE BAXTER BUILDING WILL ALWAYS BE HOME TO THE FANTASTIC FOUR.
ALICIA DID GREAT.
EVERYONE WAS TRYING TO BUY THIS PLACE. ALCHEMAX, ROXXON, HAMMER.
...AND I OUTBID 'EM ALL. SO I COULD HOLD ONTO IT...
...UNTIL THE DAY THE FF ARE FINALLY BACK.
AND THAT DAY WILL COME, JOHNNY.
UNTIL IT DOES, I'M GLAD IT'S STAYING WITH FAMILY.

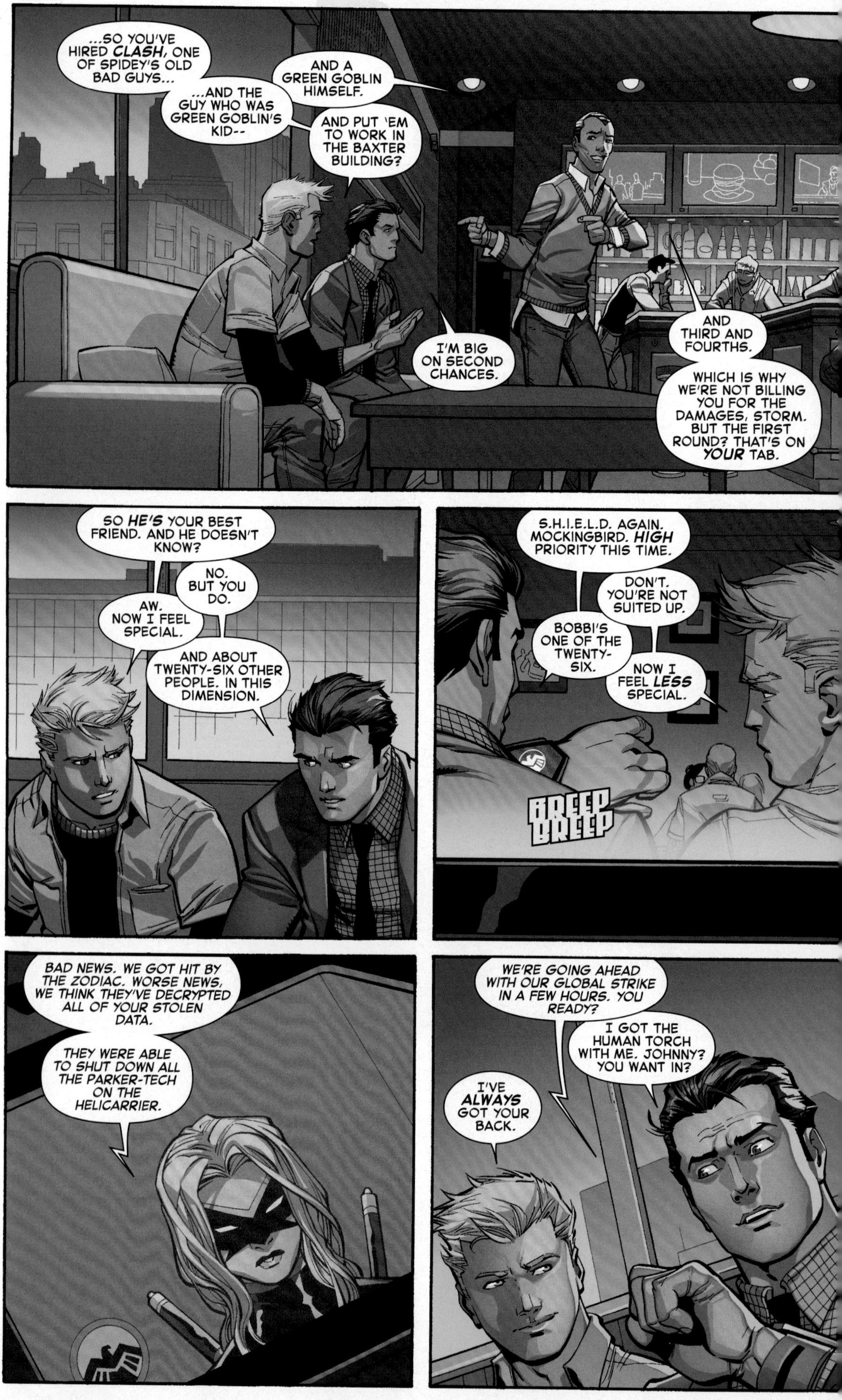
...SO YOU'VE HIRED CLASH, ONE OF SPIDEY'S OLD BAD GUYS...
...AND THE GUY WHO WAS GREEN GOBLIN'S KID--
AND A GREEN GOBLIN HIMSELF.
AND PUT 'EM TO WORK IN THE BAXTER BUILDING?
I'M BIG ON SECOND CHANCES.
AND THIRD AND FOURTHS.
WHICH IS WHY WE'RE NOT BILLING YOU FOR THE DAMAGES, STORM. BUT THE FIRST ROUND? THAT'S ON YOUR TAB.
SO HE'S YOUR BEST FRIEND. AND HE DOESN'T KNOW?
NO. BUT YOU DO.
AW. NOW I FEEL SPECIAL.
AND ABOUT TWENTY-SIX OTHER PEOPLE. IN THIS DIMENSION.
S.H.I.E.L.D. AGAIN. MOCKINGBIRD. HIGH PRIORITY THIS TIME.
DON'T. YOU'RE NOT SUITED UP.
BOBBI'S ONE OF THE TWENTY-SIX.
NOW I FEEL LESS SPECIAL.
BREEP BREEP
BAD NEWS. WE GOT HIT BY THE ZODIAC. WORSE NEWS, WE THINK THEY'VE DECRYPTED ALL OF YOUR STOLEN DATA.
THEY WERE ABLE TO SHUT DOWN ALL THE PARKER-TECH ON THE HELICARRIER.
WE'RE GOING AHEAD WITH OUR GLOBAL STRIKE IN A FEW HOURS. YOU READY?
I GOT THE HUMAN TORCH WITH ME. JOHNNY? YOU WANT IN?
I'VE ALWAYS GOT YOUR BACK.

ALL RIGHT, BOB. WE'LL BE SURE TO BE THERE FOR THE BIG GAME TOMORROW.

OOH! POKER?

BOWLING.

I'M OUT.

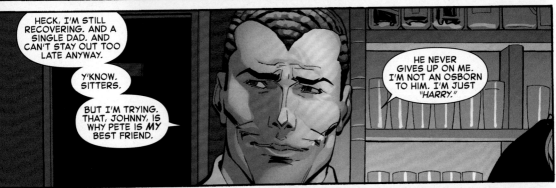

WELL, BIG MATCH AND ALL. WE PROBABLY SHOULDN'T BE DRINKING TONIGHT.

DO I EVER?

SAME. MINE AND PETER'S ARE NON-ALCOHOLIC.

HECK, I'M STILL RECOVERING. AND A SINGLE DAD. AND CAN'T STAY OUT TOO LATE ANYWAY.

Y'KNOW. SITTERS.

BUT I'M TRYING. THAT, JOHNNY, IS WHY PETE IS MY BEST FRIEND.

HE NEVER GIVES UP ON ME. I'M NOT AN OSBORN TO HIM. I'M JUST "HARRY."

NO. YOU'RE MORE THAN THAT TO PARKER. I CAN TELL.

YOU'RE FAMILY.

TO FAMILY.

CLINK

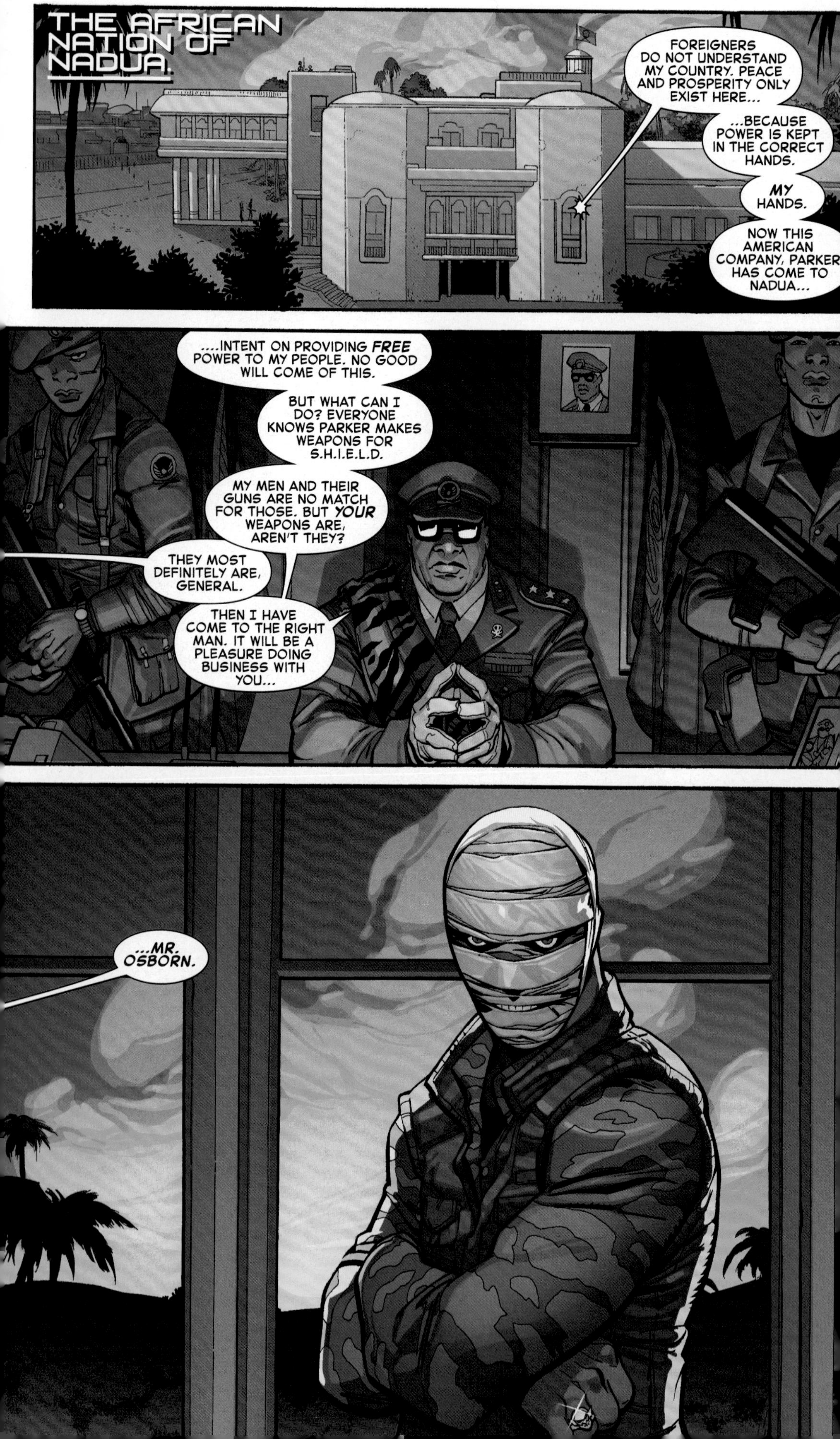

THE AFRICAN NATION OF NADUA.
FOREIGNERS DO NOT UNDERSTAND MY COUNTRY. PEACE AND PROSPERITY ONLY EXIST HERE...
...BECAUSE POWER IS KEPT IN THE CORRECT HANDS.
MY HANDS.
NOW THIS AMERICAN COMPANY, PARKER, HAS COME TO NADUA...
....INTENT ON PROVIDING FREE POWER TO MY PEOPLE. NO GOOD WILL COME OF THIS.
BUT WHAT CAN I DO? EVERYONE KNOWS PARKER MAKES WEAPONS FOR S.H.I.E.L.D.
MY MEN AND THEIR GUNS ARE NO MATCH FOR THOSE. BUT YOUR WEAPONS ARE, AREN'T THEY?
THEY MOST DEFINITELY ARE, GENERAL.
THEN I HAVE COME TO THE RIGHT MAN. IT WILL BE A PLEASURE DOING BUSINESS WITH YOU...
...MR. OSBORN.

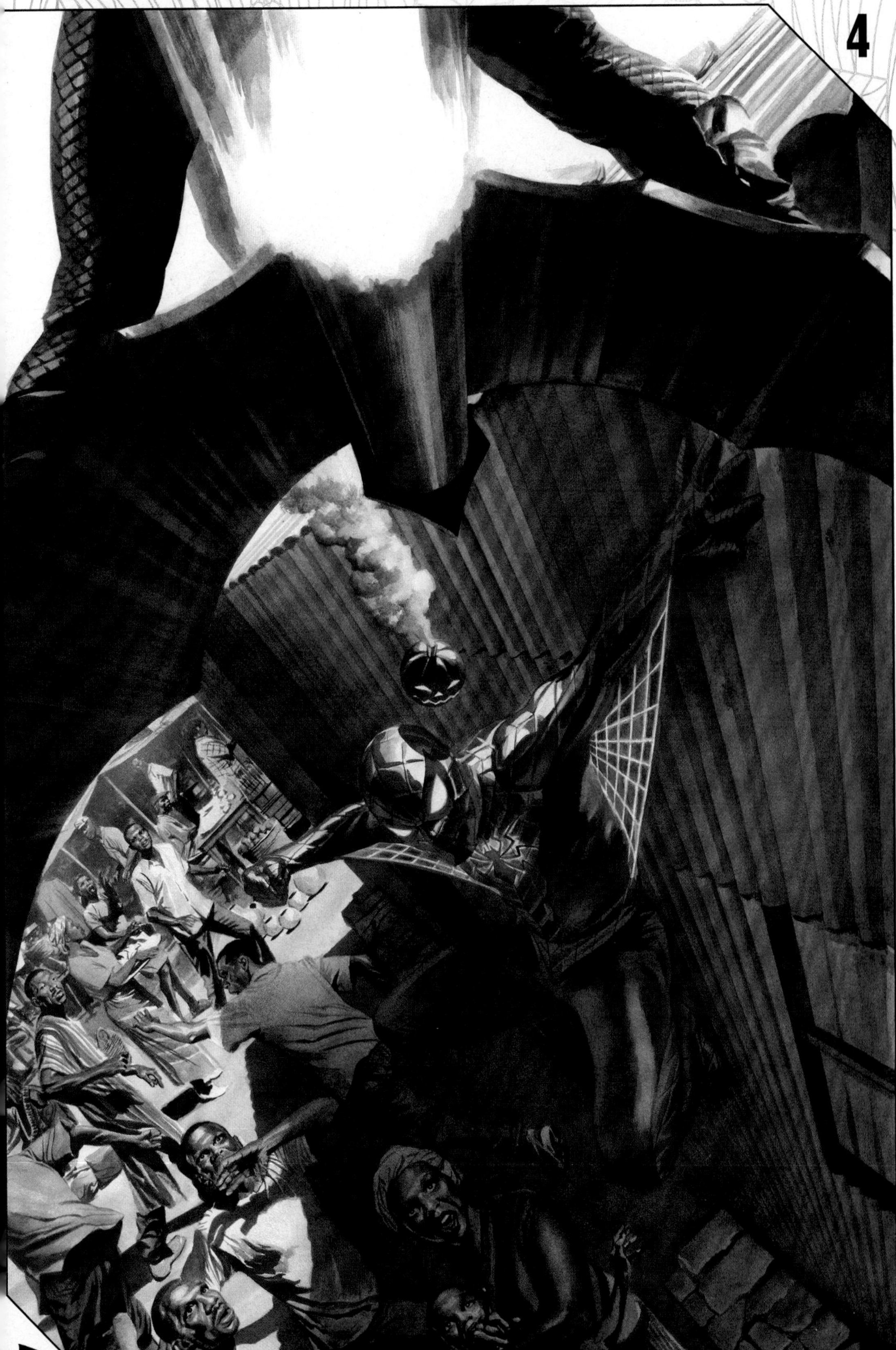

"HIGH PRIORITY"

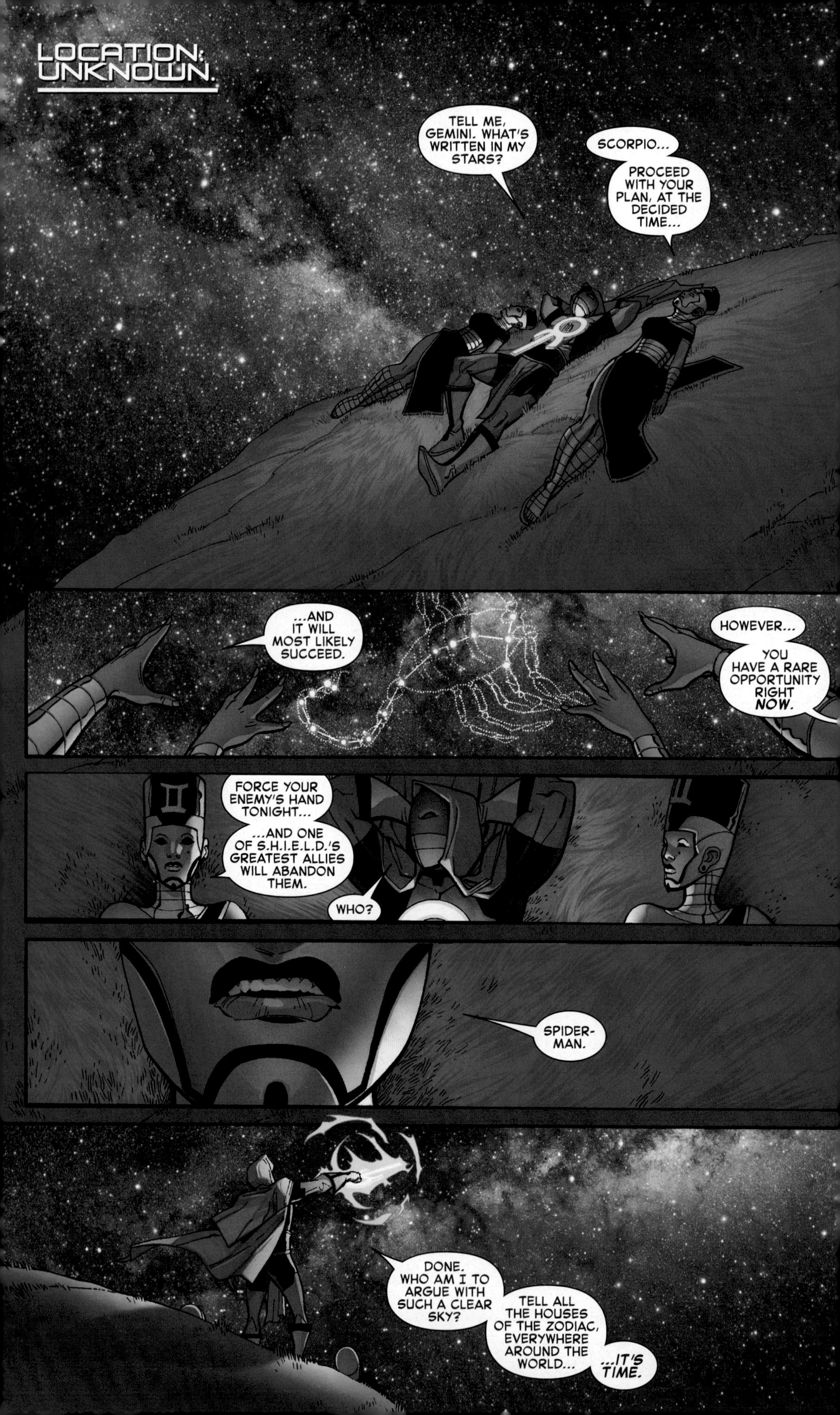
LOCATION: UNKNOWN.
TELL ME, GEMINI. WHAT'S WRITTEN IN MY STARS?
SCORPIO...
PROCEED WITH YOUR PLAN, AT THE DECIDED TIME...
...AND IT WILL MOST LIKELY SUCCEED.
HOWEVER...
YOU HAVE A RARE OPPORTUNITY RIGHT NOW.
FORCE YOUR ENEMY'S HAND TONIGHT...
...AND ONE OF S.H.I.E.L.D.'S GREATEST ALLIES WILL ABANDON THEM.
WHO?
SPIDER-MAN.
DONE. WHO AM I TO ARGUE WITH SUCH A CLEAR SKY?
TELL ALL THE HOUSES OF THE ZODIAC, EVERYWHERE AROUND THE WORLD...
...IT'S TIME.

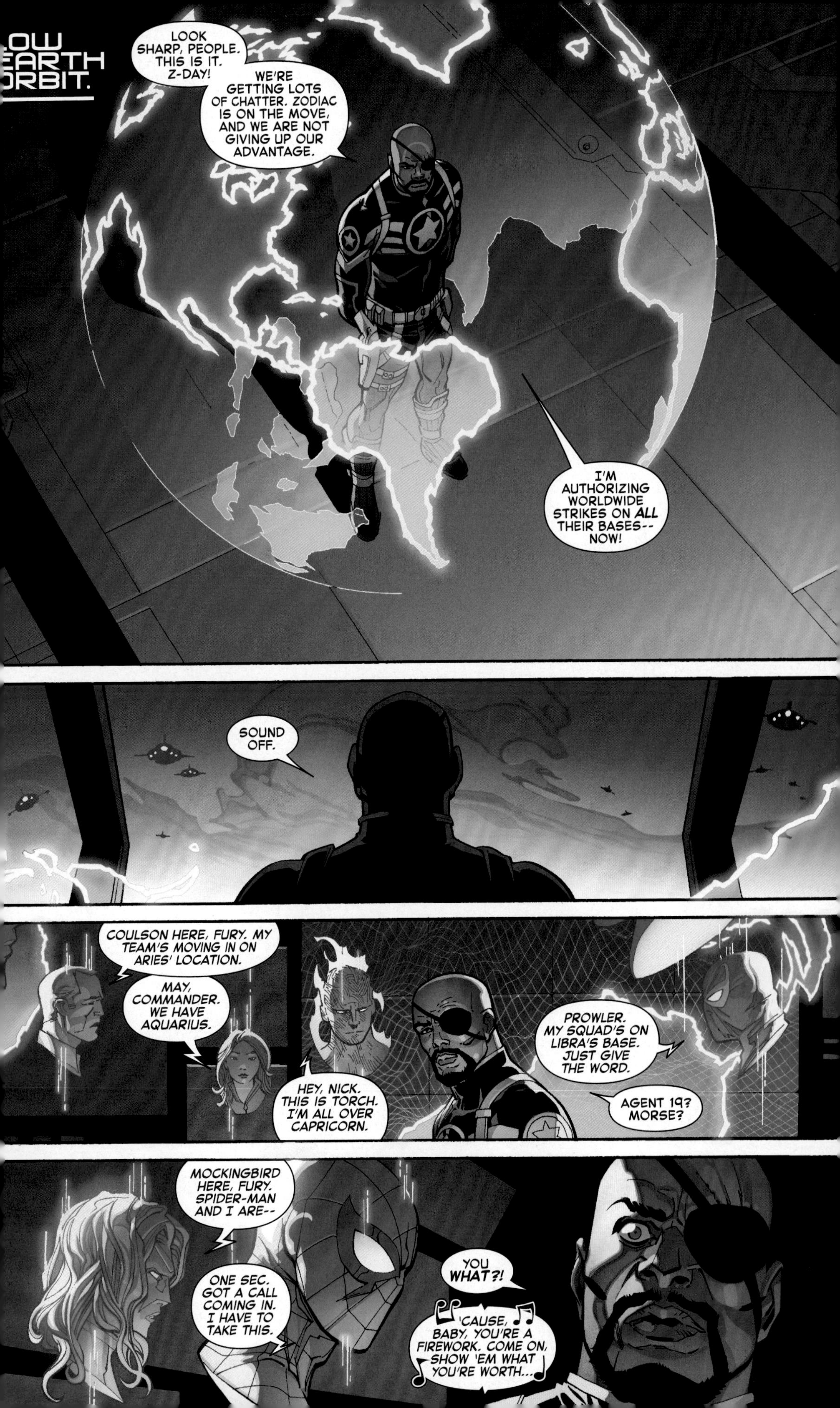
LOW EARTH ORBIT.
LOOK SHARP, PEOPLE. THIS IS IT. Z-DAY!
WE'RE GETTING LOTS OF CHATTER. ZODIAC IS ON THE MOVE, AND WE ARE NOT GIVING UP OUR ADVANTAGE.
I'M AUTHORIZING WORLDWIDE STRIKES ON ALL THEIR BASES--NOW!
SOUND OFF.
COULSON HERE, FURY. MY TEAM'S MOVING IN ON ARIES' LOCATION.
MAY, COMMANDER. WE HAVE AQUARIUS.
HEY, NICK. THIS IS TORCH. I'M ALL OVER CAPRICORN.
PROWLER. MY SQUAD'S ON LIBRA'S BASE. JUST GIVE THE WORD.
AGENT 19? MORSE?
MOCKINGBIRD HERE, FURY. SPIDER-MAN AND I ARE--
ONE SEC. GOT A CALL COMING IN. I HAVE TO TAKE THIS.
YOU WHAT?!
'CAUSE, BABY, YOU'RE A FIREWORK. COME ON, SHOW 'EM WHAT YOU'RE WORTH...

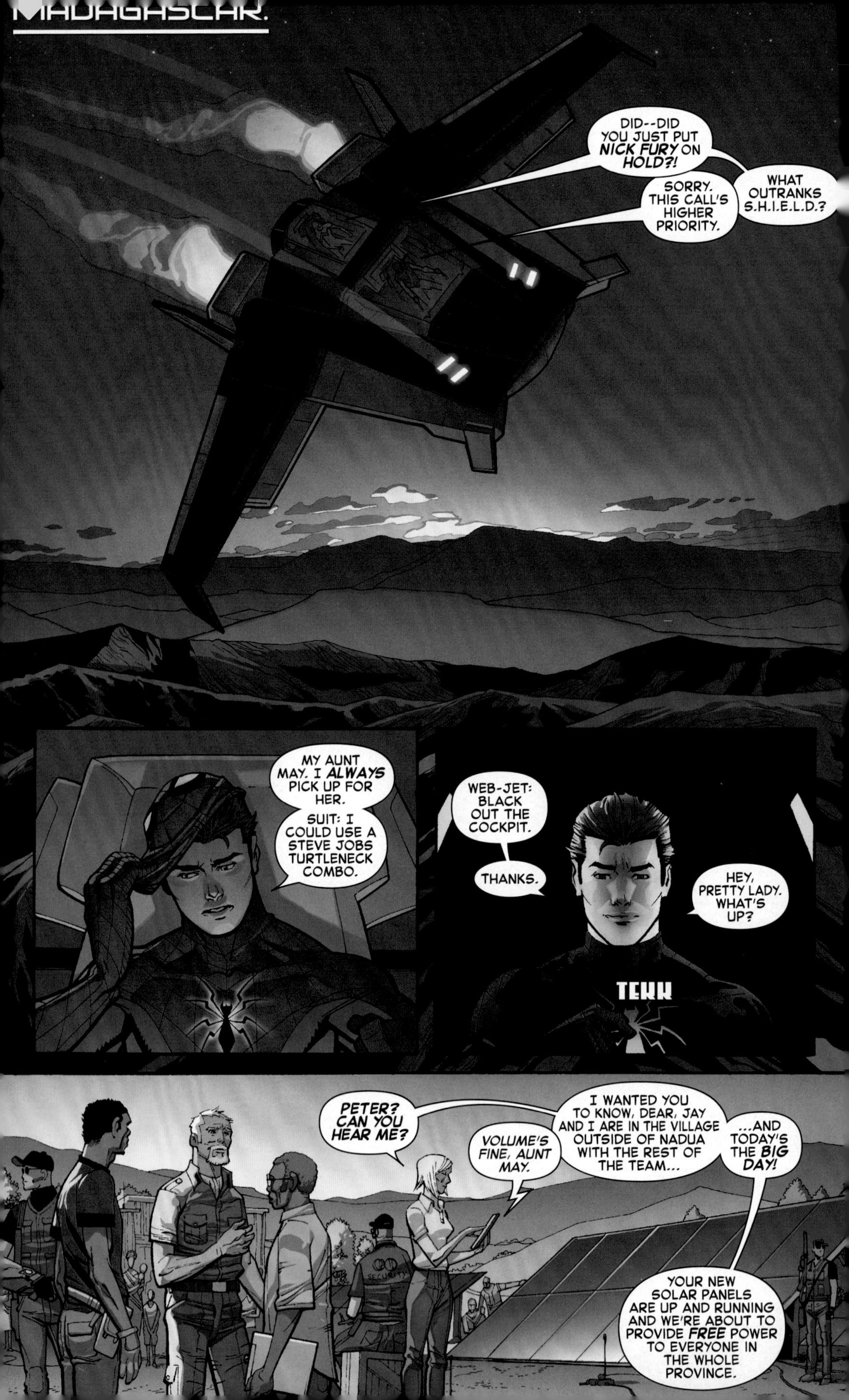
MADAGASCAR.
DID--DID YOU JUST PUT NICK FURY ON HOLD?!
SORRY. THIS CALL'S HIGHER PRIORITY.
WHAT OUTRANKS S.H.I.E.L.D.?
MY AUNT MAY. I ALWAYS PICK UP FOR HER.
SUIT: I COULD USE A STEVE JOBS TURTLENECK COMBO.
WEB-JET: BLACK OUT THE COCKPIT.
THANKS.
HEY, PRETTY LADY. WHAT'S UP?
TEKK
PETER? CAN YOU HEAR ME?
VOLUME'S FINE, AUNT MAY.
I WANTED YOU TO KNOW, DEAR, JAY AND I ARE IN THE VILLAGE OUTSIDE OF NADUA WITH THE REST OF THE TEAM...
...AND TODAY'S THE BIG DAY!
YOUR NEW SOLAR PANELS ARE UP AND RUNNING AND WE'RE ABOUT TO PROVIDE FREE POWER TO EVERYONE IN THE WHOLE PROVINCE.

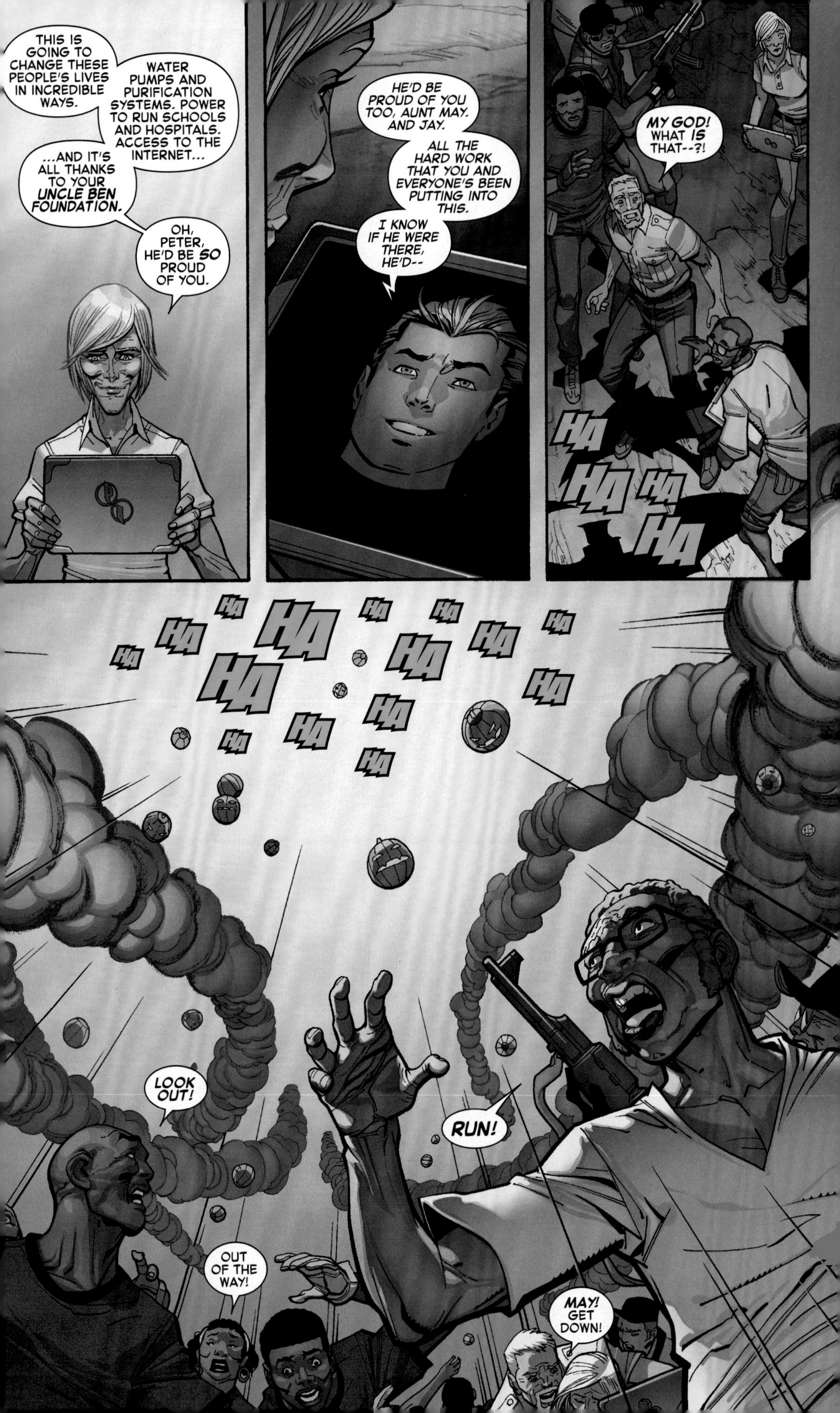

THIS IS GOING TO CHANGE THESE PEOPLE'S LIVES IN INCREDIBLE WAYS.
WATER PUMPS AND PURIFICATION SYSTEMS. POWER TO RUN SCHOOLS AND HOSPITALS. ACCESS TO THE INTERNET...
...AND IT'S ALL THANKS TO YOUR UNCLE BEN FOUNDATION.
OH, PETER, HE'D BE SO PROUD OF YOU.
HE'D BE PROUD OF YOU TOO, AUNT MAY. AND JAY.
ALL THE HARD WORK THAT YOU AND EVERYONE'S BEEN PUTTING INTO THIS.
I KNOW IF HE WERE THERE, HE'D--
MY GOD! WHAT IS THAT--?!
HA HA HA HA
HA HA HA HA HA HA HA HA HA HA HA HA HA HA
LOOK OUT!
RUN!
OUT OF THE WAY!
MAY! GET DOWN!

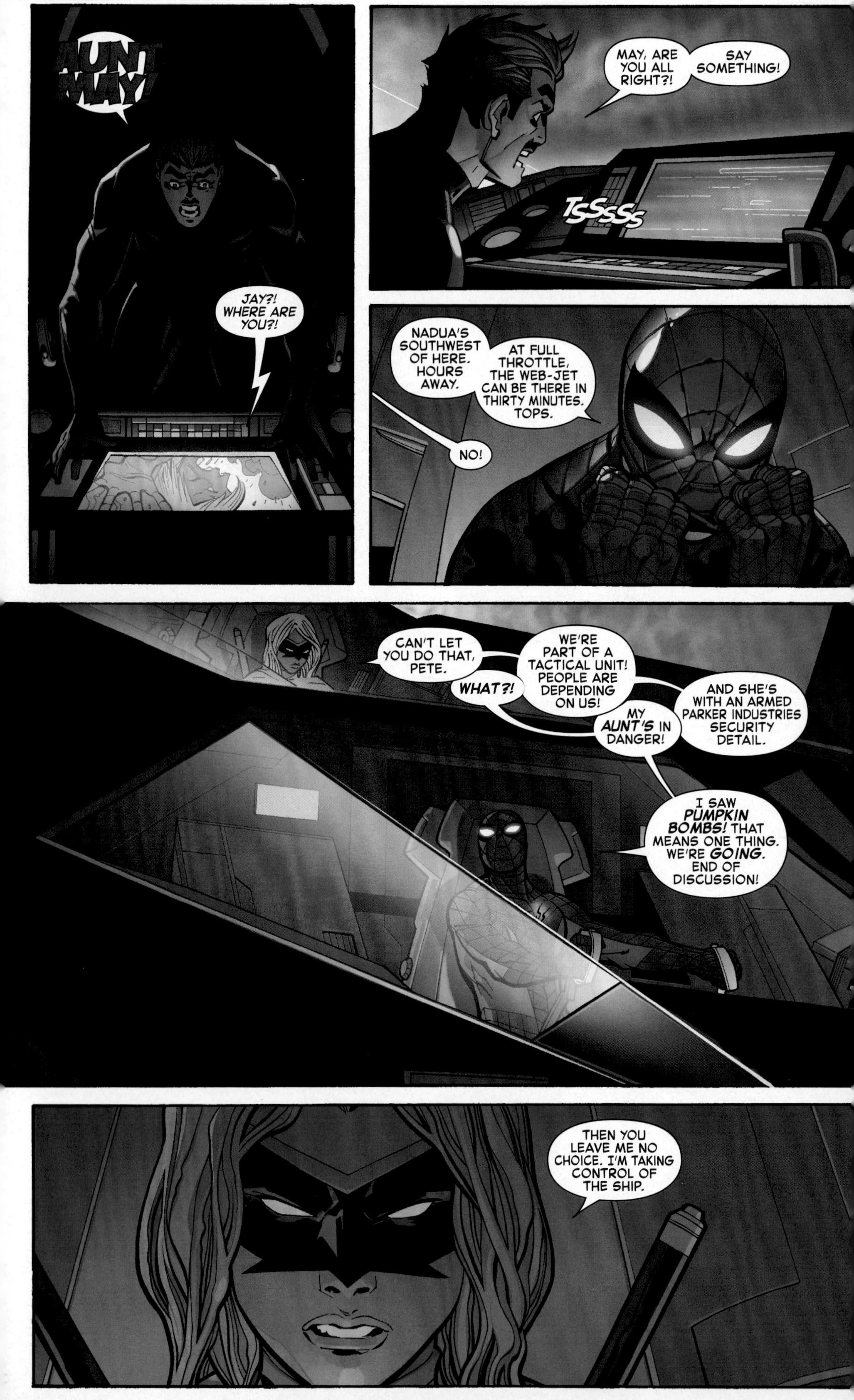
AUNT MAY!
JAY?! WHERE ARE YOU?!
MAY, ARE YOU ALL RIGHT?!
SAY SOMETHING!
TSSSSS
NADUA'S SOUTHWEST OF HERE. HOURS AWAY.
NO!
AT FULL THROTTLE, THE WEB-JET CAN BE THERE IN THIRTY MINUTES. TOPS.
CAN'T LET YOU DO THAT, PETE.
WHAT?!
WE'RE PART OF A TACTICAL UNIT! PEOPLE ARE DEPENDING ON US!
MY AUNT'S IN DANGER!
AND SHE'S WITH AN ARMED PARKER INDUSTRIES SECURITY DETAIL.
I SAW PUMPKIN BOMBS! THAT MEANS ONE THING. WE'RE GOING. END OF DISCUSSION!
THEN YOU LEAVE ME NO CHOICE. I'M TAKING CONTROL OF THE SHIP.

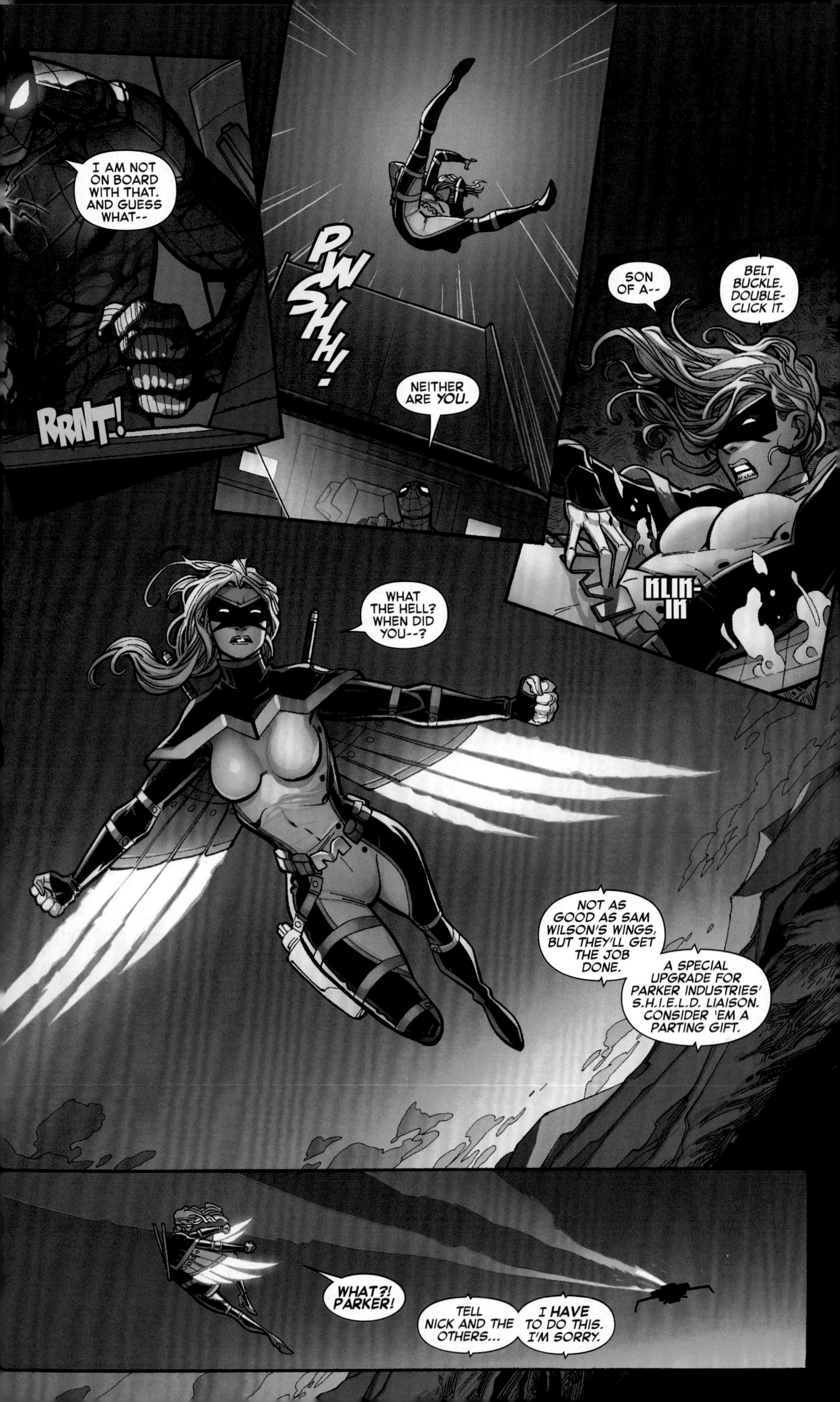

I AM NOT ON BOARD WITH THAT. AND GUESS WHAT--
RRNT!
PWSHH!
NEITHER ARE YOU.
SON OF A--
BELT BUCKLE. DOUBLE-CLICK IT.
KLIN-IK
WHAT THE HELL? WHEN DID YOU--?
NOT AS GOOD AS SAM WILSON'S WINGS, BUT THEY'LL GET THE JOB DONE.
A SPECIAL UPGRADE FOR PARKER INDUSTRIES' S.H.I.E.L.D. LIAISON. CONSIDER 'EM A PARTING GIFT.
WHAT?! PARKER!
TELL NICK AND THE OTHERS...
I HAVE TO DO THIS. I'M SORRY.

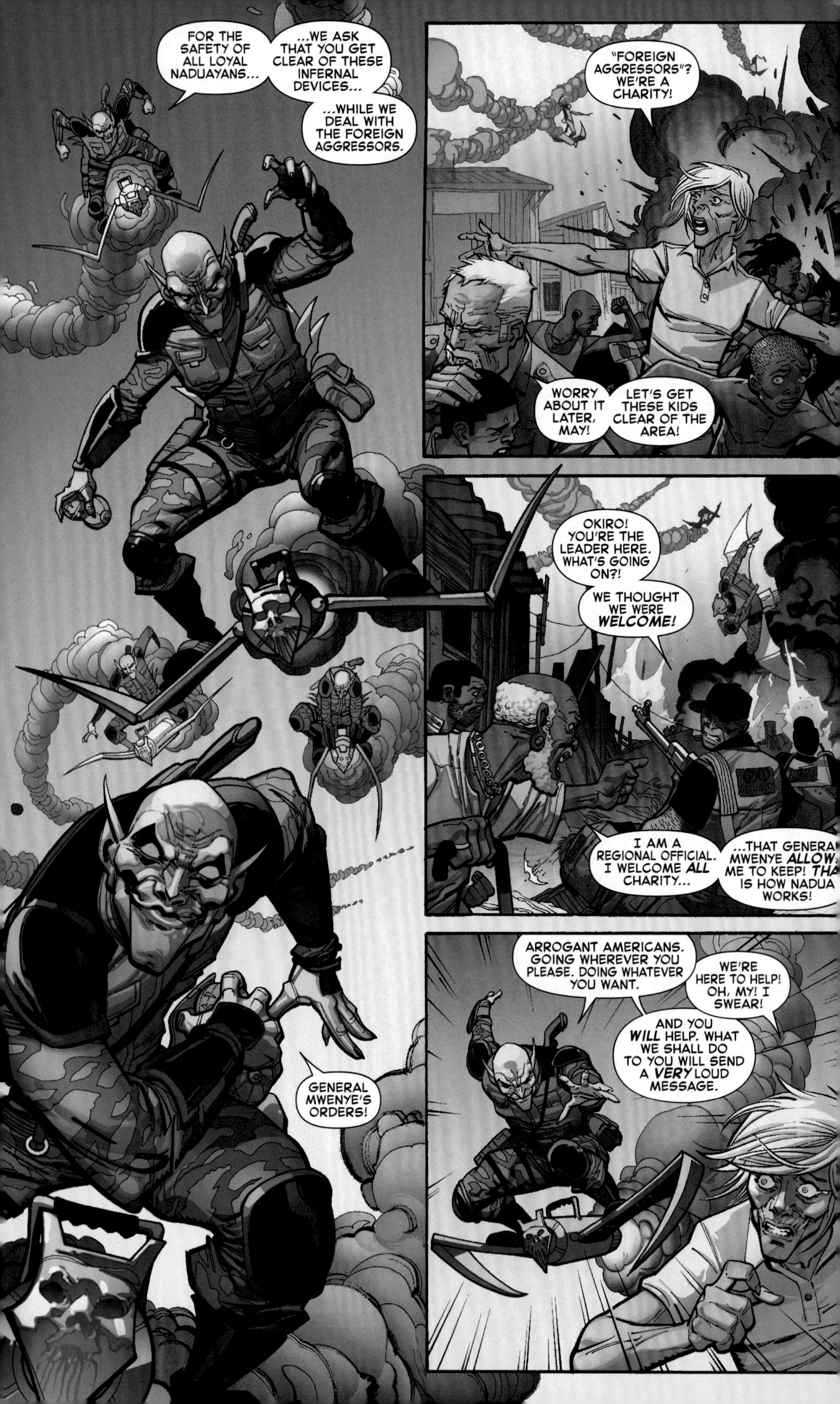
FOR THE SAFETY OF ALL LOYAL NADUAYANS...
...WE ASK THAT YOU GET CLEAR OF THESE INFERNAL DEVICES...
...WHILE WE DEAL WITH THE FOREIGN AGGRESSORS.
"FOREIGN AGGRESSORS"? WE'RE A CHARITY!
WORRY ABOUT IT LATER, MAY!
LET'S GET THESE KIDS CLEAR OF THE AREA!
OKIRO! YOU'RE THE LEADER HERE. WHAT'S GOING ON?!
WE THOUGHT WE WERE **WELCOME!**
I AM A REGIONAL OFFICIAL. I WELCOME **ALL** CHARITY...
...THAT GENERA MWENYE **ALLOW** ME TO KEEP! **THA** IS HOW NADUA WORKS!
GENERAL MWENYE'S ORDERS!
ARROGANT AMERICANS. GOING WHEREVER YOU PLEASE. DOING WHATEVER YOU WANT.
WE'RE HERE TO HELP! OH, MY! I SWEAR!
AND YOU **WILL** HELP. WHAT WE SHALL DO TO YOU WILL SEND A **VERY** LOUD MESSAGE.

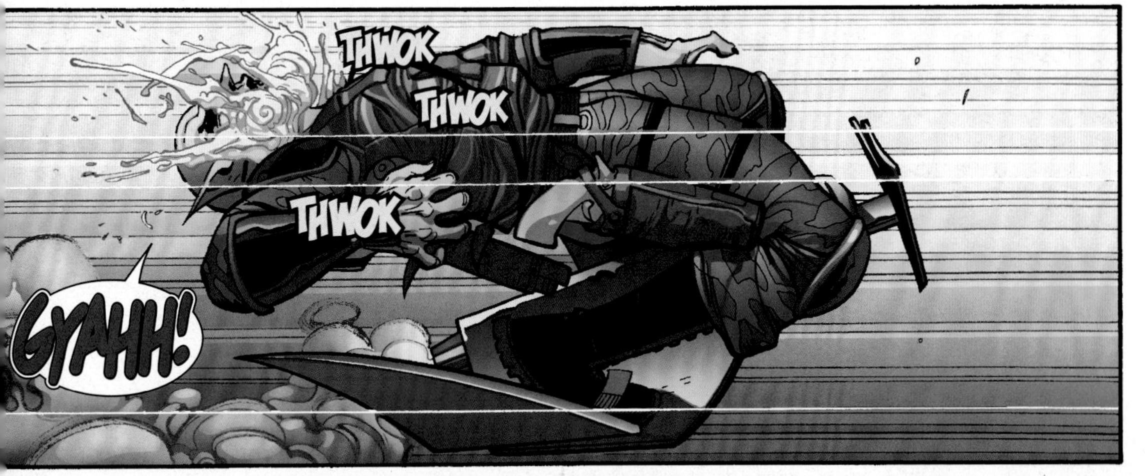
THWOK
THWOK
THWOK
GYAHH!

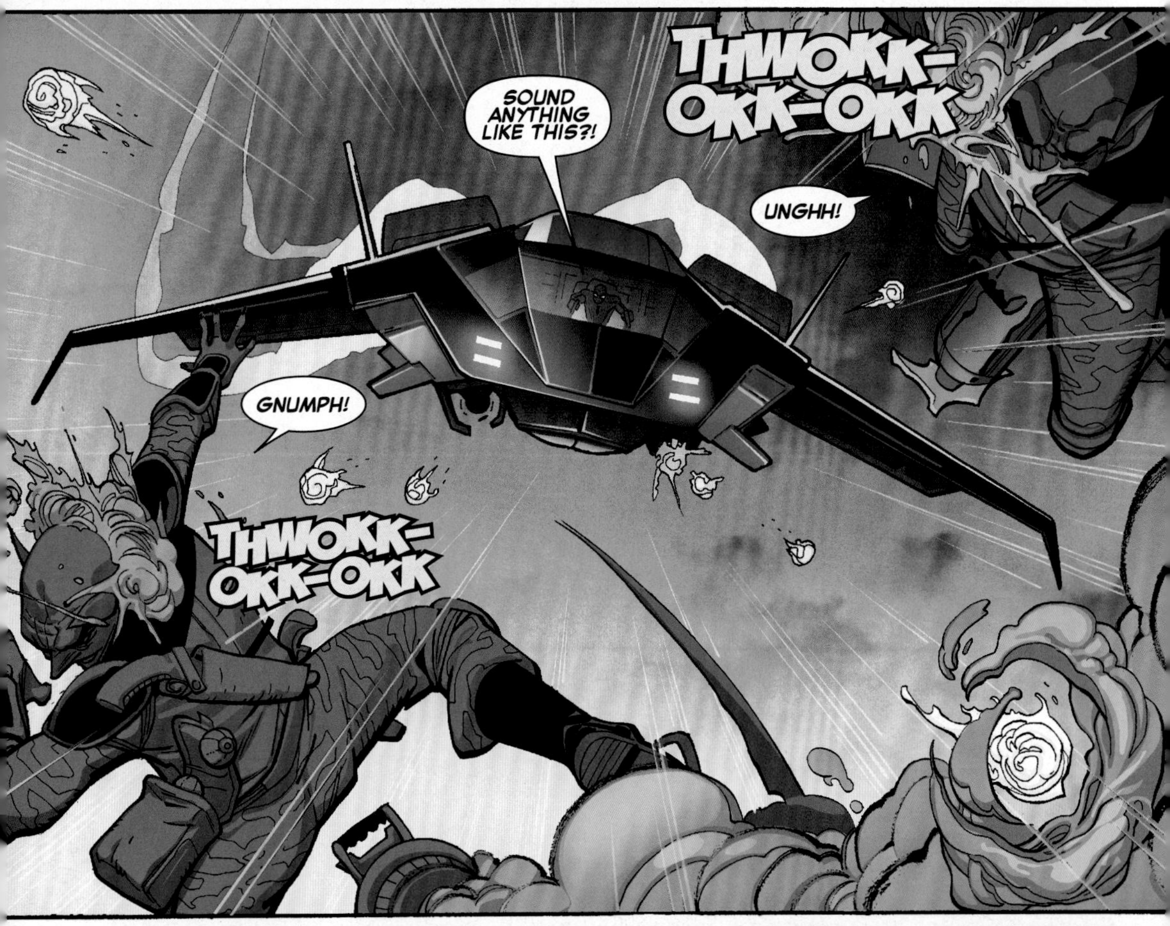
SOUND ANYTHING LIKE THIS?!
THWOKK-OKK-OKK
UNGHH!
GNUMPH!
THWOKK-OKK-OKK

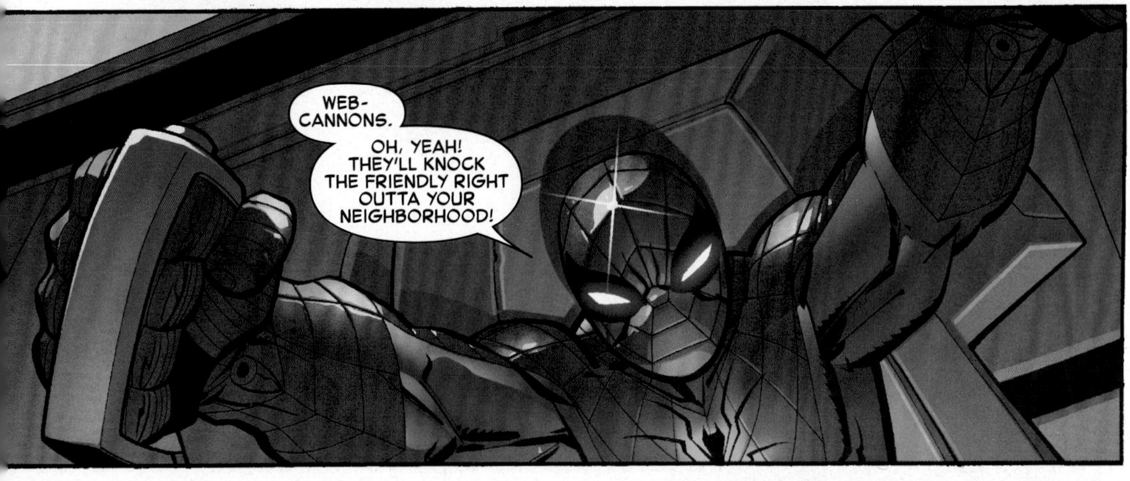
WEB-CANNONS.
OH, YEAH! THEY'LL KNOCK THE FRIENDLY RIGHT OUTTA YOUR NEIGHBORHOOD!

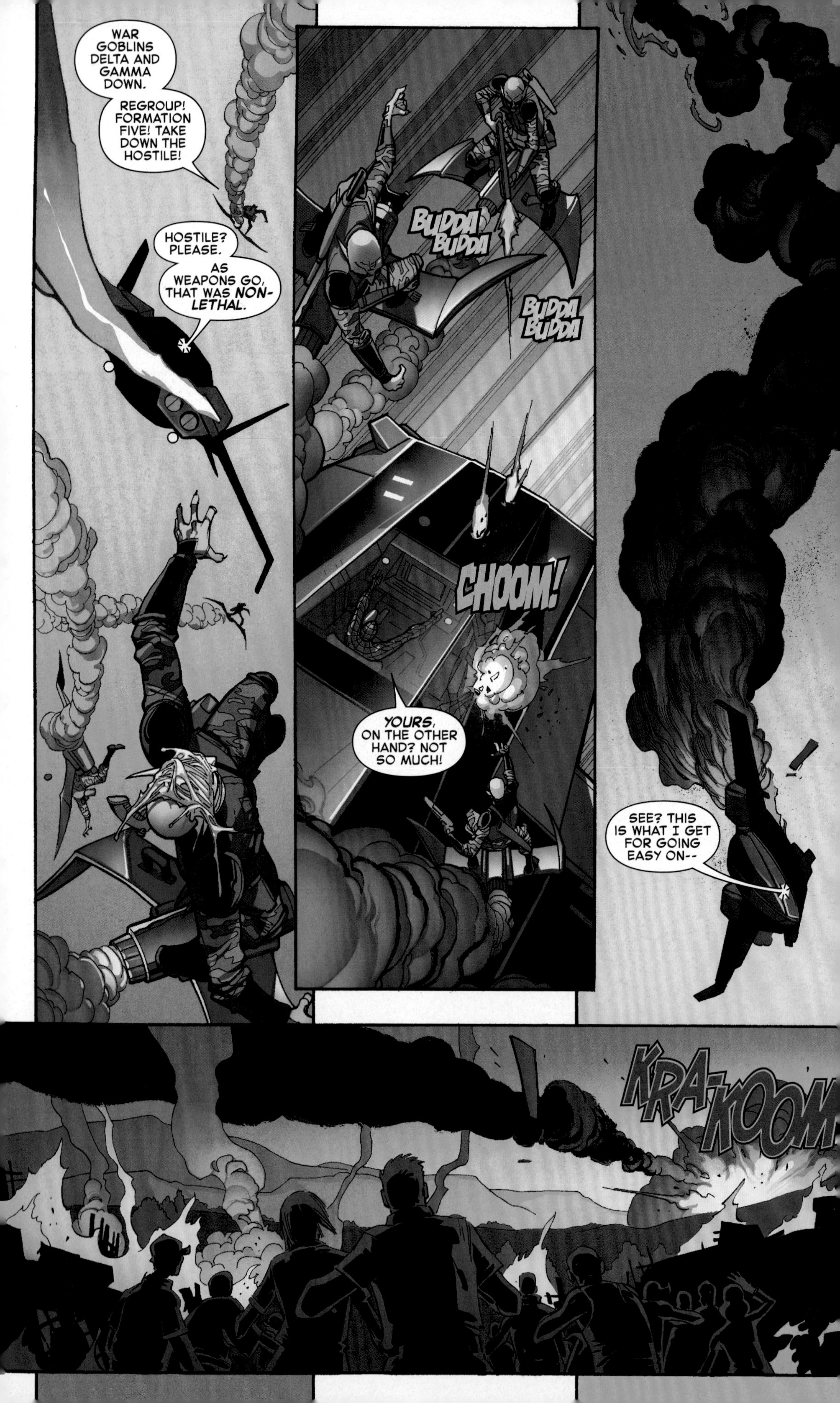

WAR GOBLINS DELTA AND GAMMA DOWN.
REGROUP! FORMATION FIVE! TAKE DOWN THE HOSTILE!
HOSTILE? PLEASE.
AS WEAPONS GO, THAT WAS NON-LETHAL.
BUDDA BUDDA
BUDDA BUDDA
CHOOM!
YOURS, ON THE OTHER HAND? NOT SO MUCH!
!
SEE? THIS IS WHAT I GET FOR GOING EASY ON--
KRA-KOOM

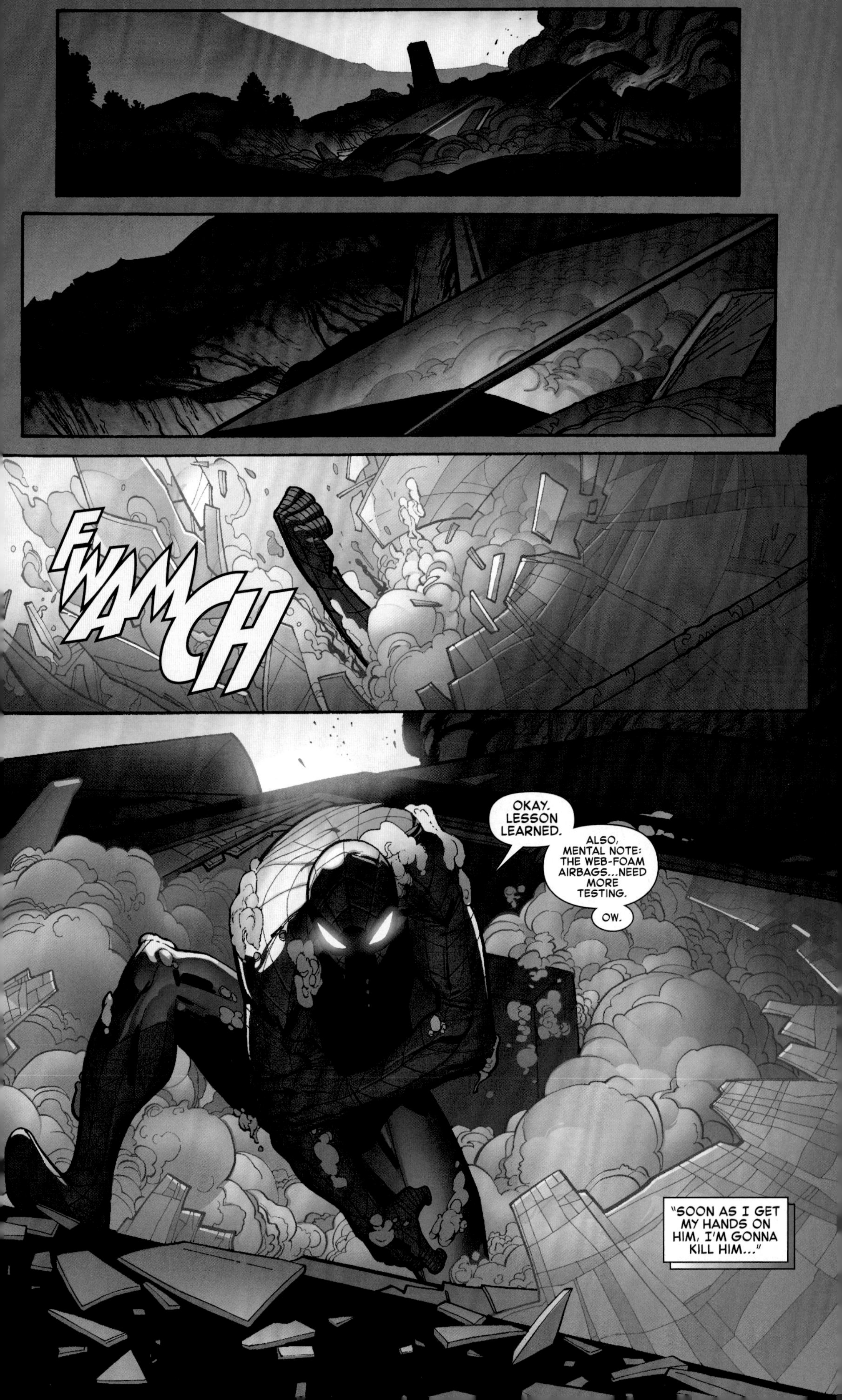
FWAMCH
OKAY. LESSON LEARNED.
ALSO, MENTAL NOTE: THE WEB-FOAM AIRBAGS...NEED MORE TESTING.
OW.
"SOON AS I GET MY HANDS ON HIM, I'M GONNA KILL HIM..."

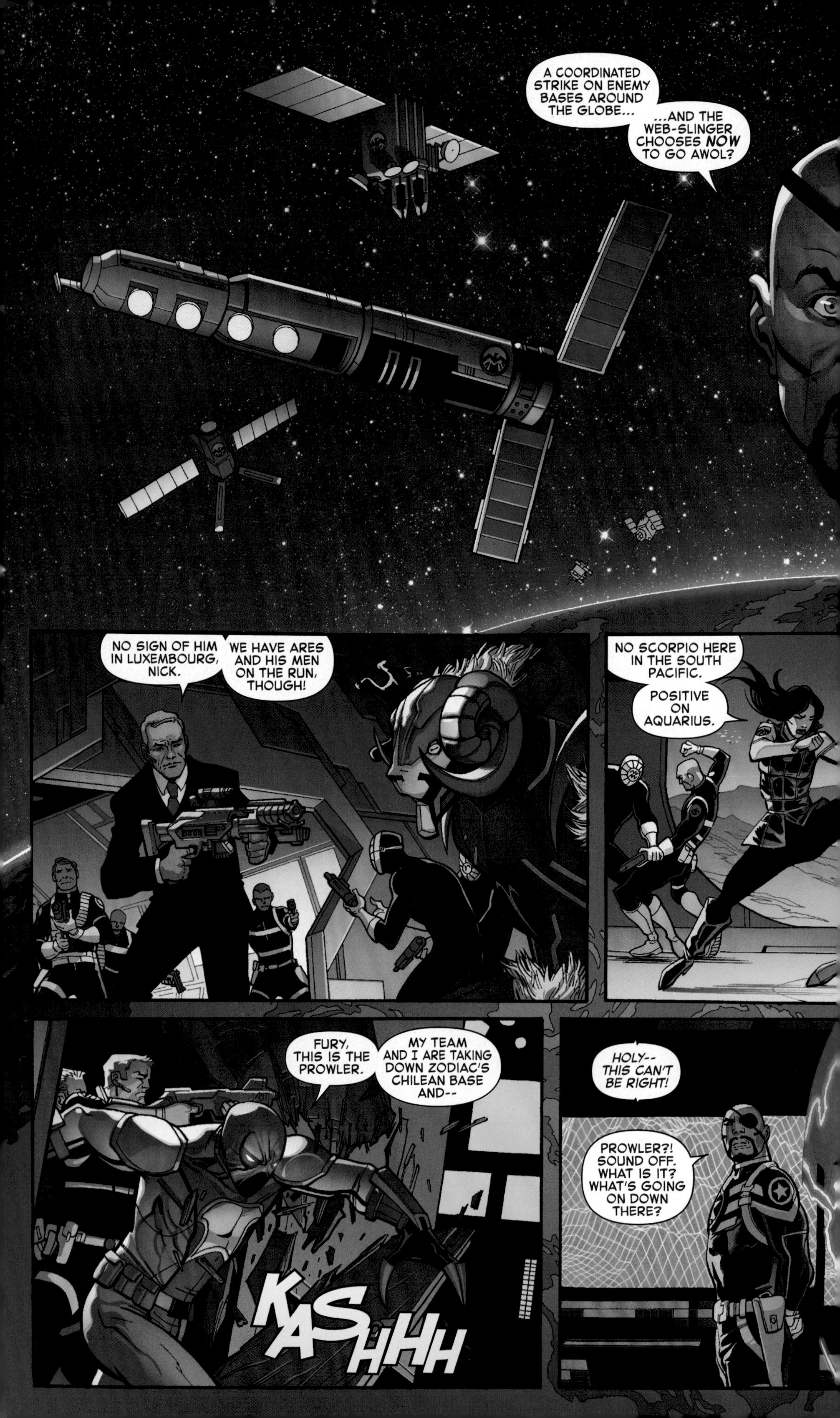
A COORDINATED STRIKE ON ENEMY BASES AROUND THE GLOBE...
...AND THE WEB-SLINGER CHOOSES *NOW* TO GO AWOL?
NO SIGN OF HIM IN LUXEMBOURG, NICK.
WE HAVE ARES AND HIS MEN ON THE RUN, THOUGH!
NO SCORPIO HERE IN THE SOUTH PACIFIC.
POSITIVE ON AQUARIUS.
FURY, THIS IS THE PROWLER.
MY TEAM AND I ARE TAKING DOWN ZODIAC'S CHILEAN BASE AND--
KASHHH
HOLY-- THIS CAN'T BE RIGHT!
PROWLER?! SOUND OFF. WHAT IS IT? WHAT'S GOING ON DOWN THERE?

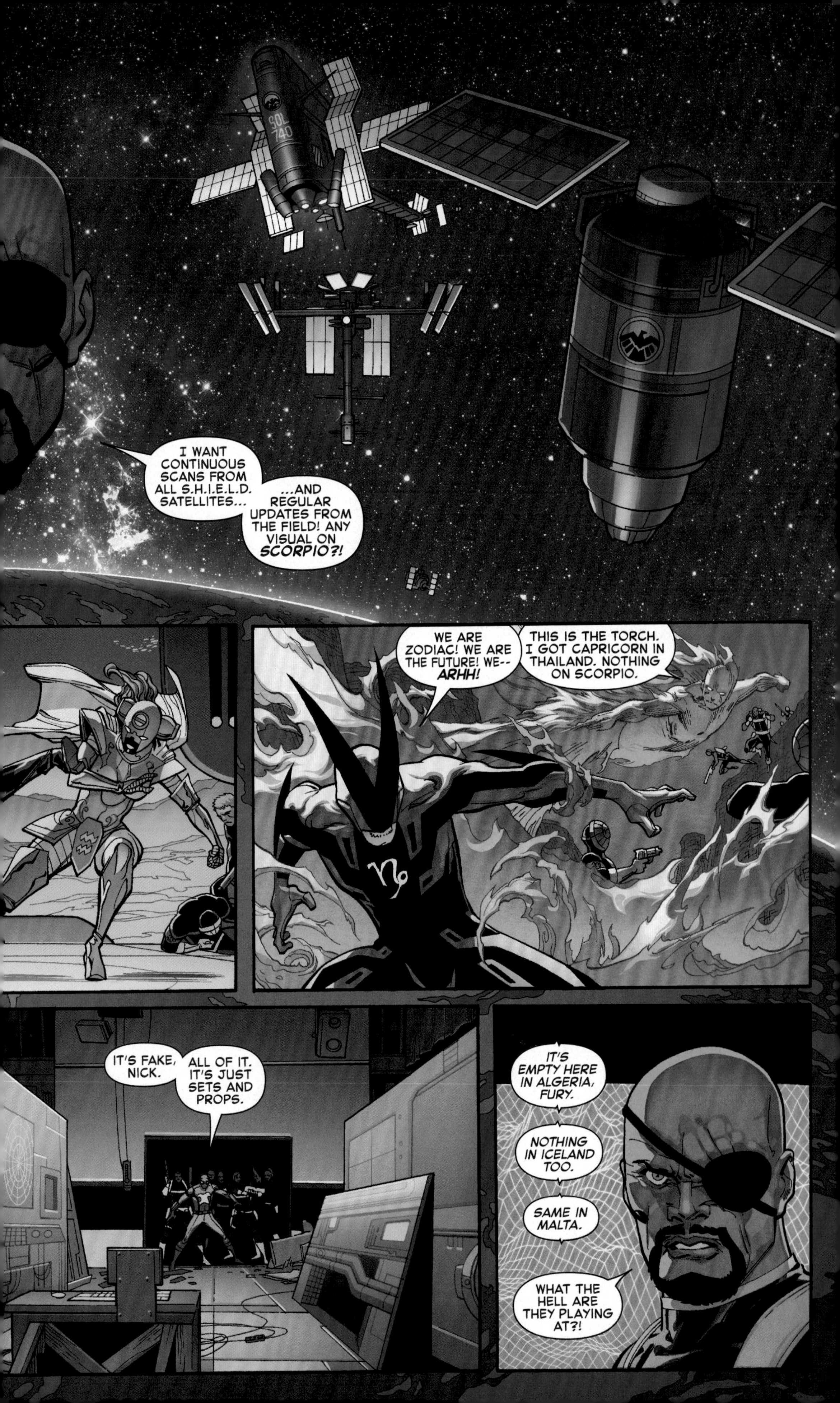

I WANT CONTINUOUS SCANS FROM ALL S.H.I.E.L.D. SATELLITES...
...AND REGULAR UPDATES FROM THE FIELD! ANY VISUAL ON SCORPIO?!
WE ARE ZODIAC! WE ARE THE FUTURE! WE-- ARHH!
THIS IS THE TORCH. I GOT CAPRICORN IN THAILAND. NOTHING ON SCORPIO.
IT'S FAKE, NICK.
ALL OF IT. IT'S JUST SETS AND PROPS.
IT'S EMPTY HERE IN ALGERIA, FURY.
NOTHING IN ICELAND TOO.
SAME IN MALTA.
WHAT THE HELL ARE THEY PLAYING AT?!

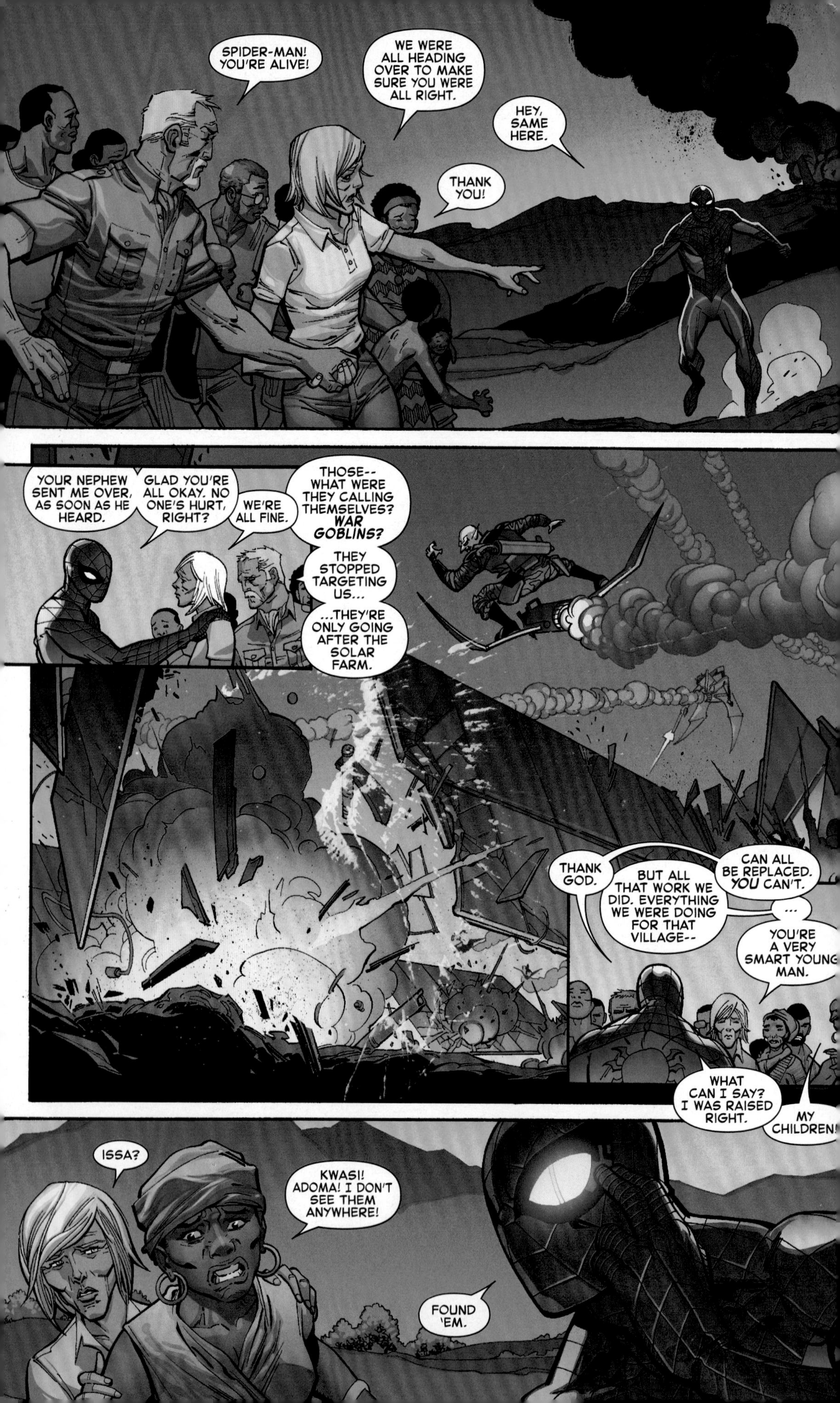
SPIDER-MAN! YOU'RE ALIVE!
WE WERE ALL HEADING OVER TO MAKE SURE YOU WERE ALL RIGHT.
HEY, SAME HERE.
THANK YOU!
YOUR NEPHEW SENT ME OVER, AS SOON AS HE HEARD.
GLAD YOU'RE ALL OKAY. NO ONE'S HURT, RIGHT?
WE'RE ALL FINE.
THOSE-- WHAT WERE THEY CALLING THEMSELVES? *WAR GOBLINS?*
THEY STOPPED TARGETING US...
...THEY'RE ONLY GOING AFTER THE SOLAR FARM.
THANK GOD.
BUT ALL THAT WORK WE DID. EVERYTHING WE WERE DOING FOR THAT VILLAGE--
CAN ALL BE REPLACED. *YOU* CAN'T.
...
YOU'RE A VERY SMART YOUNG MAN.
WHAT CAN I SAY? I WAS RAISED RIGHT.
MY CHILDREN!
ISSA?
KWASI! ADOMA! I DON'T SEE THEM ANYWHERE!
FOUND 'EM.

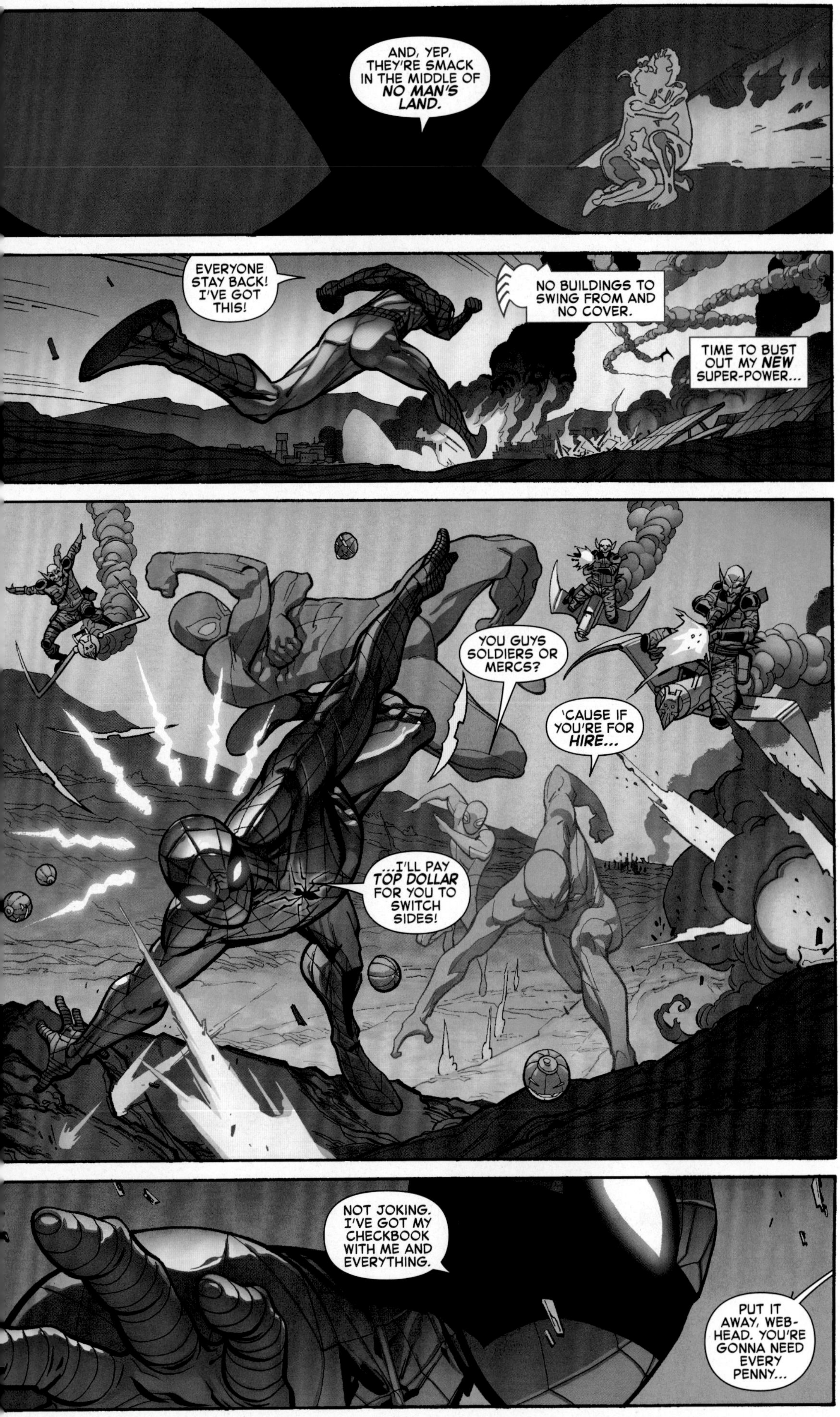
AND, YEP, THEY'RE SMACK IN THE MIDDLE OF NO MAN'S LAND.
EVERYONE STAY BACK! I'VE GOT THIS!
NO BUILDINGS TO SWING FROM AND NO COVER.
TIME TO BUST OUT MY NEW SUPER-POWER...
YOU GUYS SOLDIERS OR MERCS?
'CAUSE IF YOU'RE FOR HIRE...
...I'LL PAY TOP DOLLAR FOR YOU TO SWITCH SIDES!
NOT JOKING. I'VE GOT MY CHECKBOOK WITH ME AND EVERYTHING.
PUT IT AWAY, WEB-HEAD. YOU'RE GONNA NEED EVERY PENNY...

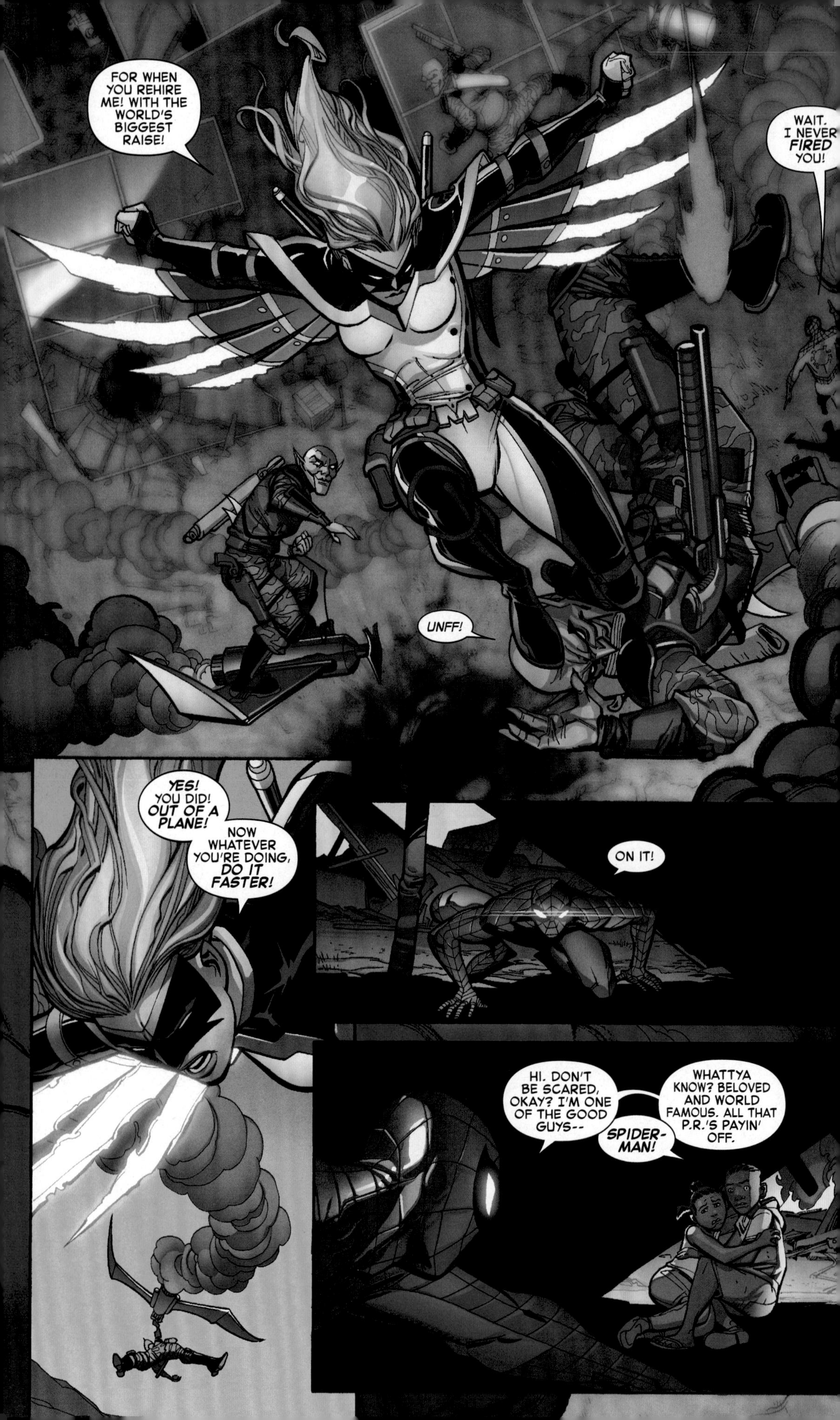
FOR WHEN YOU REHIRE ME! WITH THE WORLD'S BIGGEST RAISE!
WAIT. I NEVER FIRED YOU!
UNFF!
YES! YOU DID! OUT OF A PLANE!
NOW WHATEVER YOU'RE DOING, DO IT FASTER!
ON IT!
HI. DON'T BE SCARED, OKAY? I'M ONE OF THE GOOD GUYS--
SPIDER-MAN!
WHATTYA KNOW? BELOVED AND WORLD FAMOUS. ALL THAT P.R.'S PAYIN' OFF.

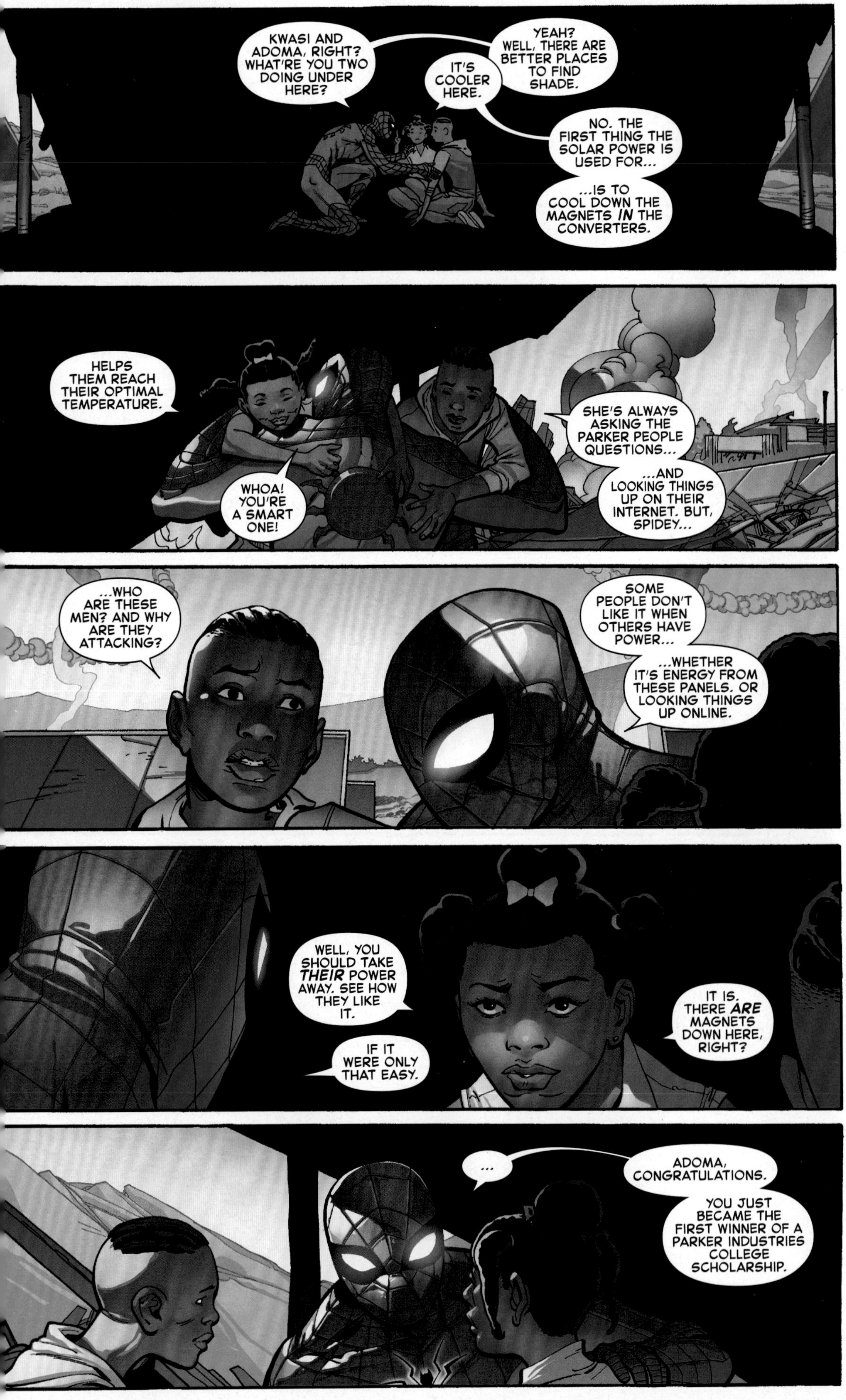
KWASI AND ADOMA, RIGHT? WHAT'RE YOU TWO DOING UNDER HERE?
IT'S COOLER HERE.
YEAH? WELL, THERE ARE BETTER PLACES TO FIND SHADE.
NO. THE FIRST THING THE SOLAR POWER IS USED FOR...
...IS TO COOL DOWN THE MAGNETS *IN* THE CONVERTERS.
HELPS THEM REACH THEIR OPTIMAL TEMPERATURE.
WHOA! YOU'RE A SMART ONE!
SHE'S ALWAYS ASKING THE PARKER PEOPLE QUESTIONS...
...AND LOOKING THINGS UP ON THEIR INTERNET. BUT, SPIDEY...
...WHO ARE THESE MEN? AND WHY ARE THEY ATTACKING?
SOME PEOPLE DON'T LIKE IT WHEN OTHERS HAVE POWER...
...WHETHER IT'S ENERGY FROM THESE PANELS. OR LOOKING THINGS UP ONLINE.
WELL, YOU SHOULD TAKE *THEIR* POWER AWAY. SEE HOW THEY LIKE IT.
IF IT WERE ONLY THAT EASY.
IT IS. THERE *ARE* MAGNETS DOWN HERE, RIGHT?
...
ADOMA, CONGRATULATIONS.
YOU JUST BECAME THE FIRST WINNER OF A PARKER INDUSTRIES COLLEGE SCHOLARSHIP.

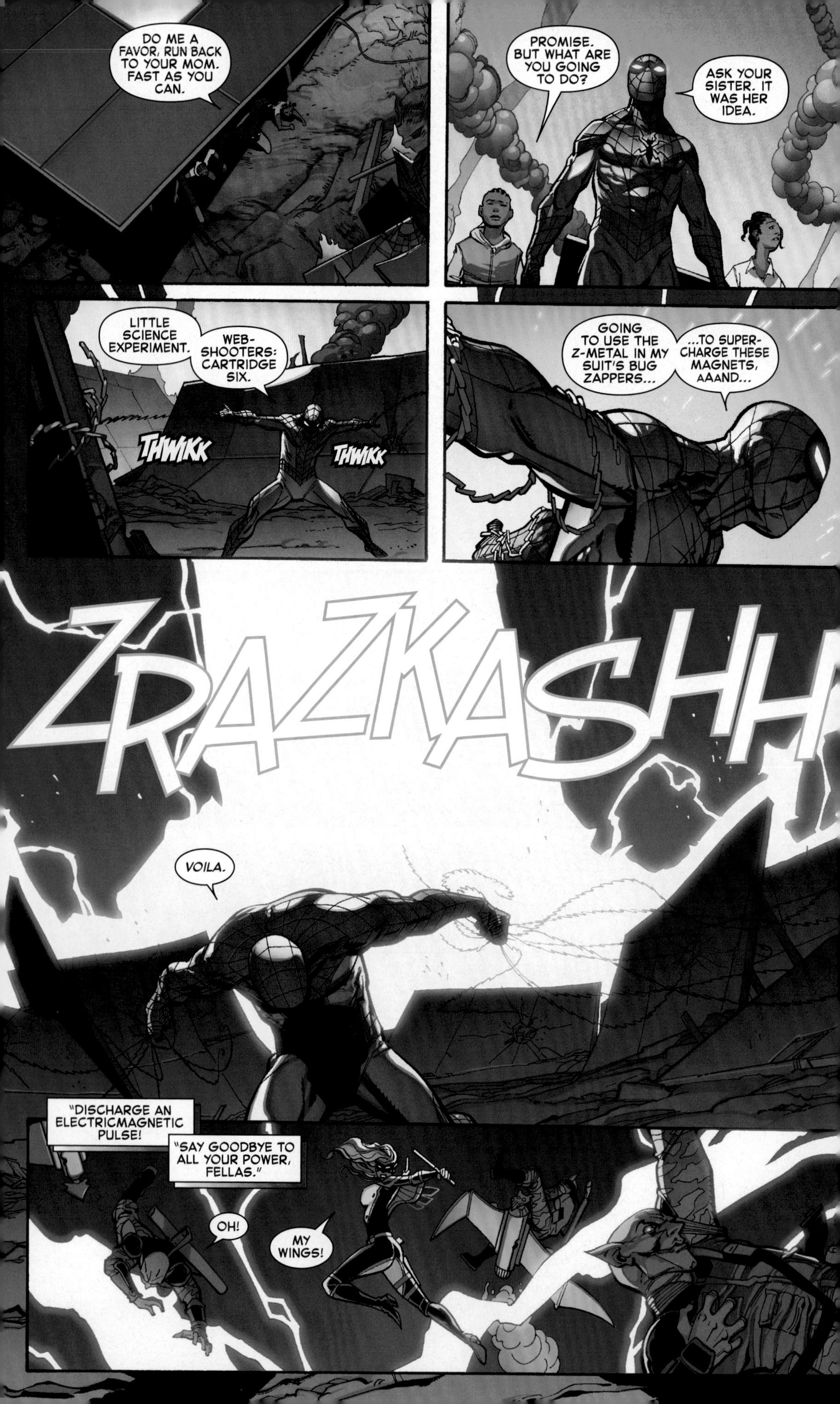
DO ME A FAVOR, RUN BACK TO YOUR MOM. FAST AS YOU CAN.
PROMISE. BUT WHAT ARE YOU GOING TO DO?
ASK YOUR SISTER. IT WAS HER IDEA.
LITTLE SCIENCE EXPERIMENT.
WEB-SHOOTERS: CARTRIDGE SIX.
THWIKK
THWIKK
GOING TO USE THE Z-METAL IN MY SUIT'S BUG ZAPPERS...
...TO SUPER-CHARGE THESE MAGNETS, AAAND...
ZRAZKASHH
VOILA.
"DISCHARGE AN ELECTRICMAGNETIC PULSE!
"SAY GOODBYE TO ALL YOUR POWER, FELLAS."
OH!
MY WINGS!

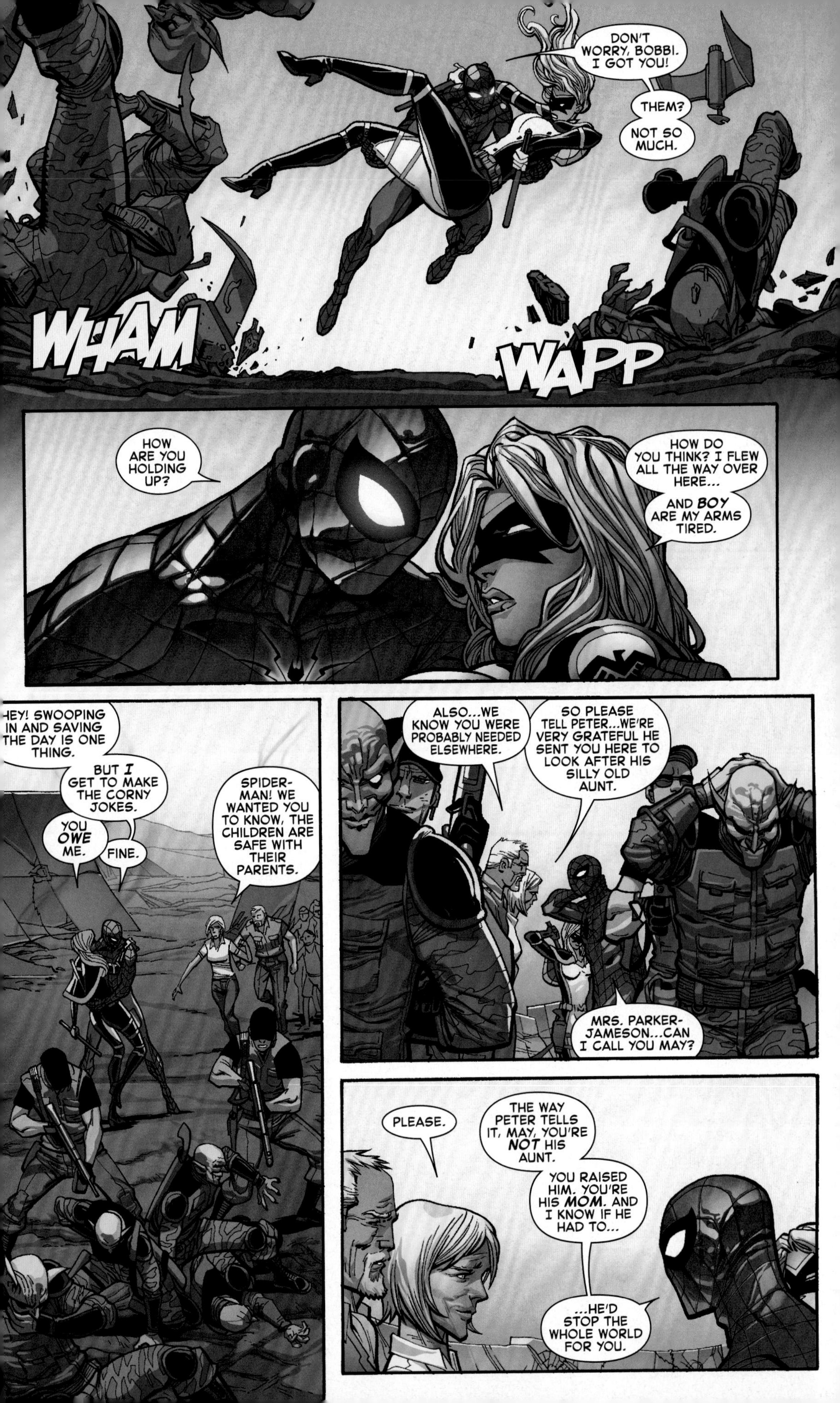
DON'T WORRY, BOBBI. I GOT YOU!
THEM?
NOT SO MUCH.
WHAM
WAPP
HOW ARE YOU HOLDING UP?
HOW DO YOU THINK? I FLEW ALL THE WAY OVER HERE...
AND BOY ARE MY ARMS TIRED.
HEY! SWOOPING IN AND SAVING THE DAY IS ONE THING.
BUT I GET TO MAKE THE CORNY JOKES.
YOU OWE ME.
FINE.
SPIDER-MAN! WE WANTED YOU TO KNOW, THE CHILDREN ARE SAFE WITH THEIR PARENTS.
ALSO...WE KNOW YOU WERE PROBABLY NEEDED ELSEWHERE.
SO PLEASE TELL PETER...WE'RE VERY GRATEFUL HE SENT YOU HERE TO LOOK AFTER HIS SILLY OLD AUNT.
MRS. PARKER-JAMESON...CAN I CALL YOU MAY?
PLEASE.
THE WAY PETER TELLS IT, MAY, YOU'RE NOT HIS AUNT.
YOU RAISED HIM. YOU'RE HIS MOM. AND I KNOW IF HE HAD TO...
...HE'D STOP THE WHOLE WORLD FOR YOU.

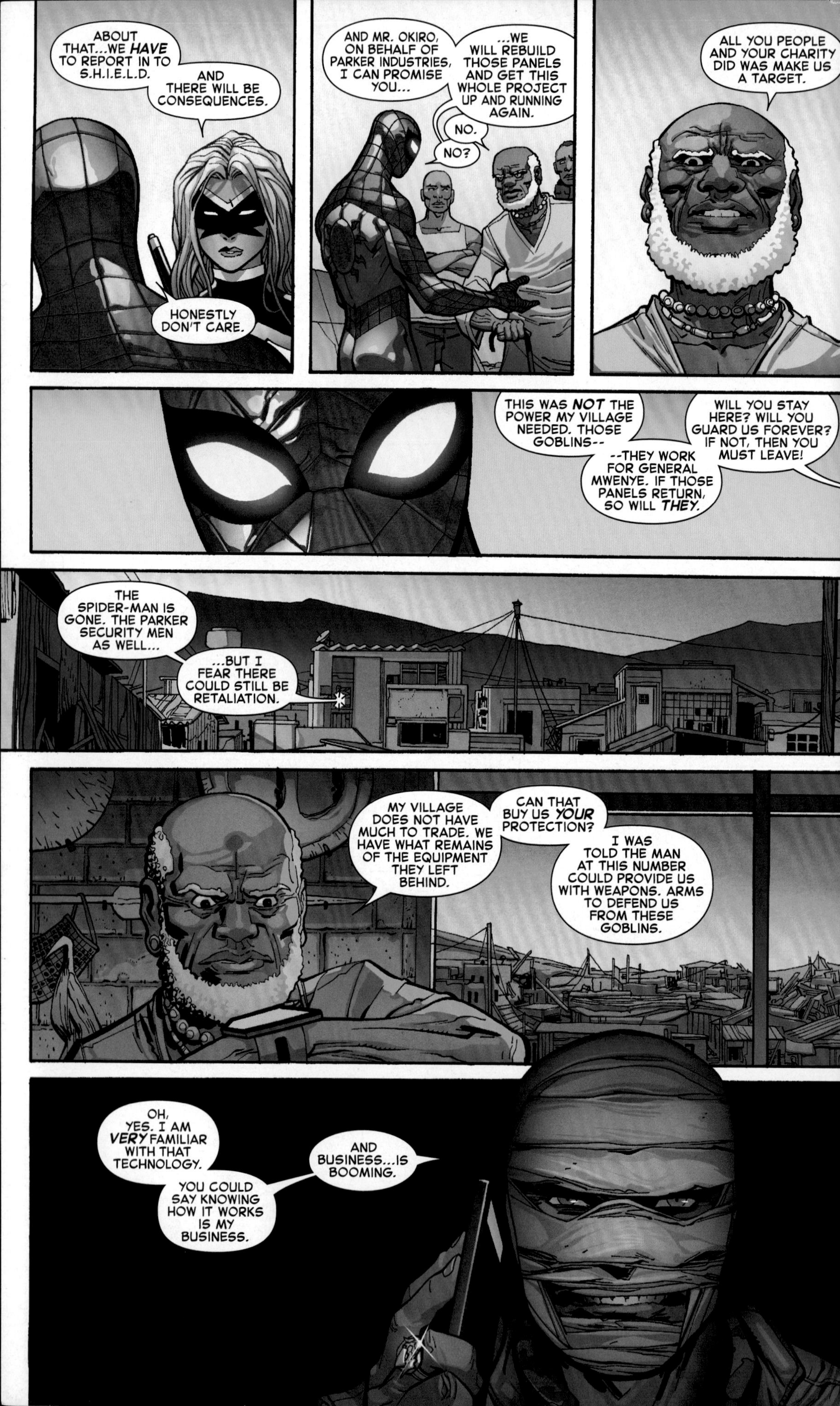
ABOUT THAT...WE HAVE TO REPORT IN TO S.H.I.E.L.D.
AND THERE WILL BE CONSEQUENCES.
HONESTLY DON'T CARE.
AND MR. OKIRO, ON BEHALF OF PARKER INDUSTRIES, I CAN PROMISE YOU...
...WE WILL REBUILD THOSE PANELS AND GET THIS WHOLE PROJECT UP AND RUNNING AGAIN.
NO.
NO?
ALL YOU PEOPLE AND YOUR CHARITY DID WAS MAKE US A TARGET.
THIS WAS NOT THE POWER MY VILLAGE NEEDED. THOSE GOBLINS--
--THEY WORK FOR GENERAL MWENYE. IF THOSE PANELS RETURN, SO WILL THEY.
WILL YOU STAY HERE? WILL YOU GUARD US FOREVER? IF NOT, THEN YOU MUST LEAVE!
THE SPIDER-MAN IS GONE. THE PARKER SECURITY MEN AS WELL...
...BUT I FEAR THERE COULD STILL BE RETALIATION.
MY VILLAGE DOES NOT HAVE MUCH TO TRADE. WE HAVE WHAT REMAINS OF THE EQUIPMENT THEY LEFT BEHIND.
CAN THAT BUY US YOUR PROTECTION?
I WAS TOLD THE MAN AT THIS NUMBER COULD PROVIDE US WITH WEAPONS. ARMS TO DEFEND US FROM THESE GOBLINS.
OH, YES. I AM VERY FAMILIAR WITH THAT TECHNOLOGY.
YOU COULD SAY KNOWING HOW IT WORKS IS MY BUSINESS.
AND BUSINESS...IS BOOMING.

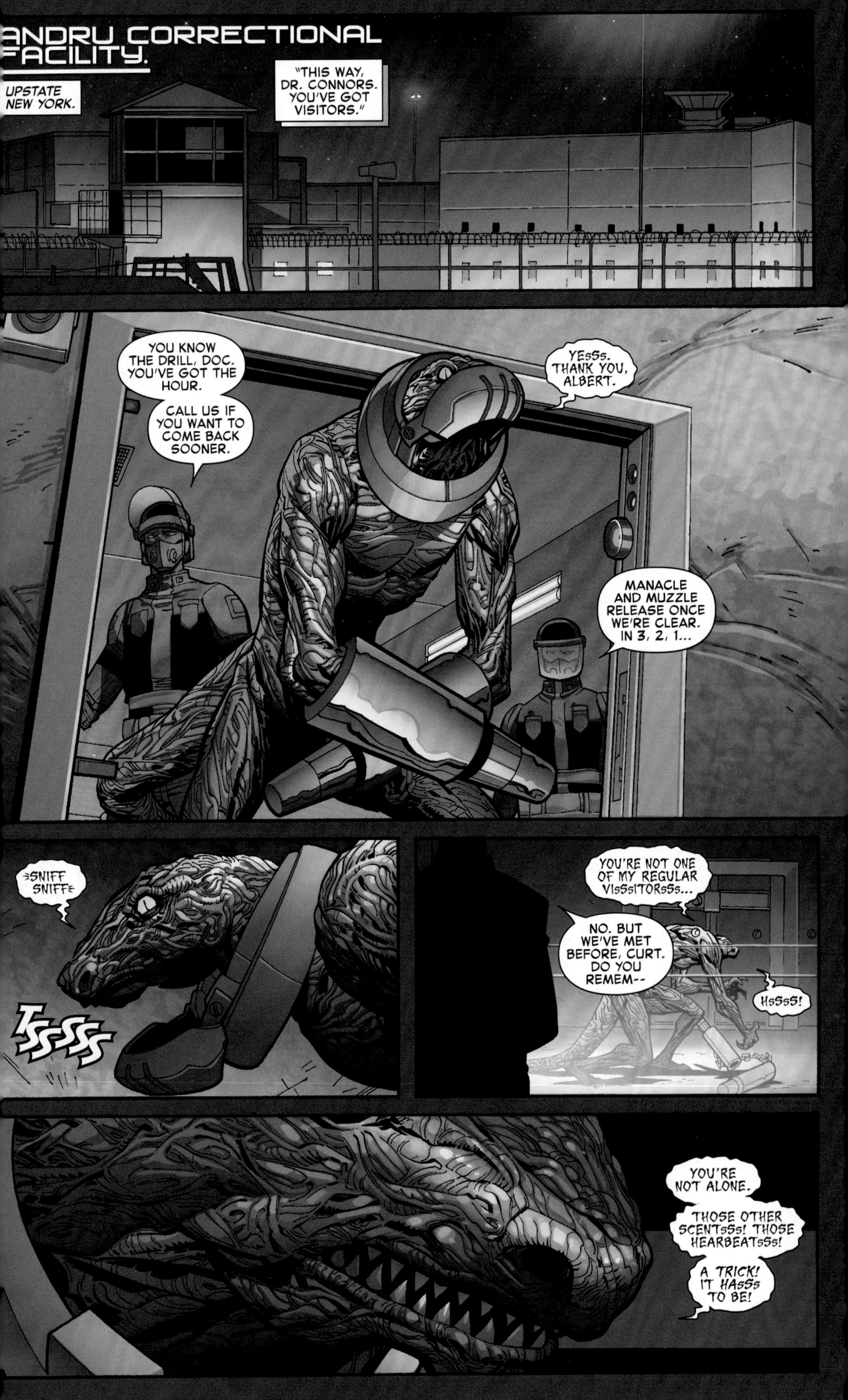
ANDRU CORRECTIONAL FACILITY.
UPSTATE NEW YORK.
"THIS WAY, DR. CONNORS. YOU'VE GOT VISITORS."
YOU KNOW THE DRILL, DOC. YOU'VE GOT THE HOUR.
CALL US IF YOU WANT TO COME BACK SOONER.
YEsSs. THANK YOU, ALBERT.
MANACLE AND MUZZLE RELEASE ONCE WE'RE CLEAR. IN 3, 2, 1...
SNIFF SNIFF
TSSSSS
YOU'RE NOT ONE OF MY REGULAR VIsSsITORsSs...
NO. BUT WE'VE MET BEFORE, CURT. DO YOU REMEM--
HsSsS!
YOU'RE NOT ALONE.
THOSE OTHER SCENTsSs! THOSE HEARBEATsSs!
A TRICK! IT HAsSs TO BE!

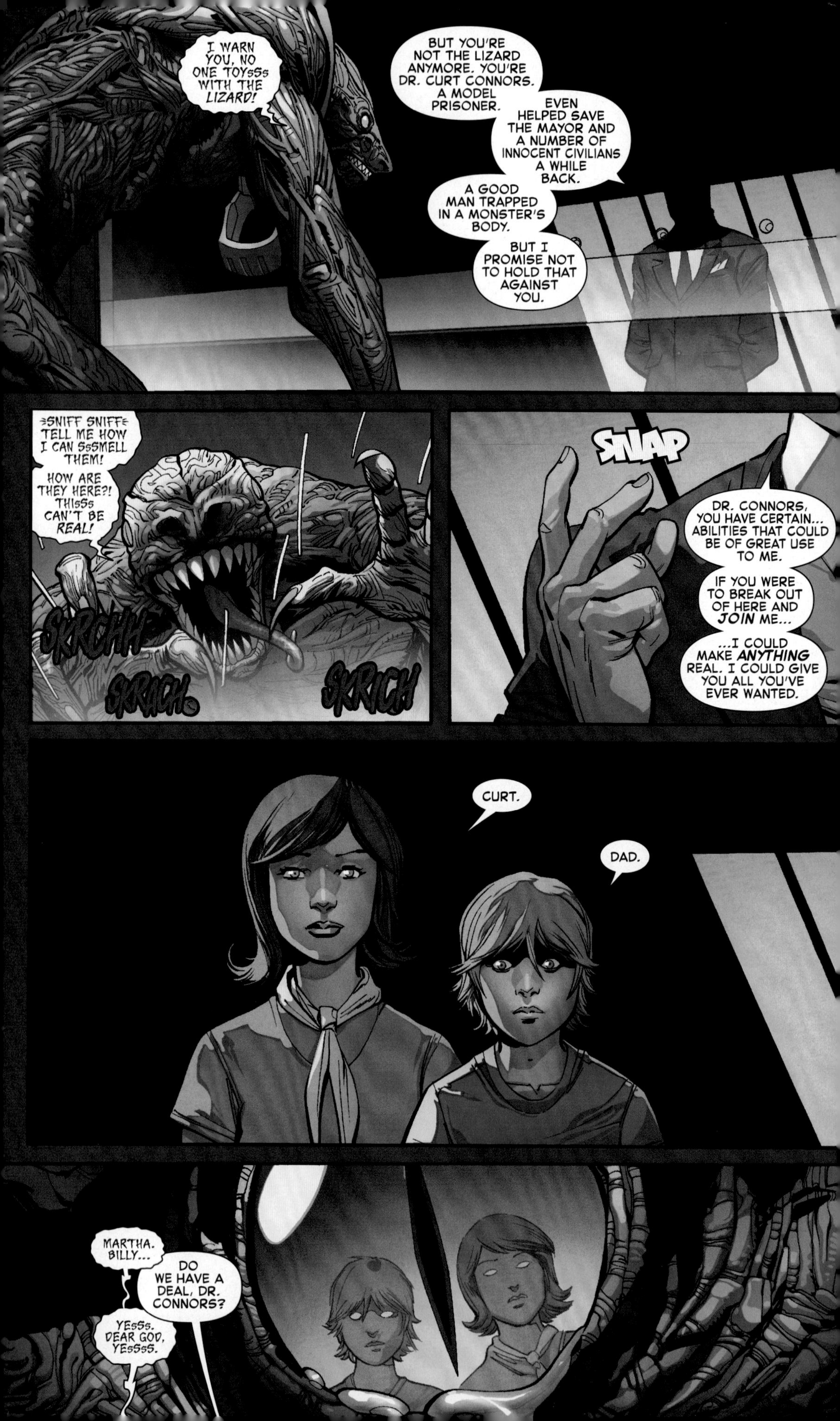
I WARN YOU, NO ONE TOYSsS WITH THE LIZARD!
BUT YOU'RE NOT THE LIZARD ANYMORE. YOU'RE DR. CURT CONNORS. A MODEL PRISONER.
EVEN HELPED SAVE THE MAYOR AND A NUMBER OF INNOCENT CIVILIANS A WHILE BACK.
A GOOD MAN TRAPPED IN A MONSTER'S BODY.
BUT I PROMISE NOT TO HOLD THAT AGAINST YOU.
SNIFF SNIFF
TELL ME HOW I CAN SsSMELL THEM!
HOW ARE THEY HERE?! THISSs CAN'T BE REAL!
SKRCHH
SKRACH
SKRICH
SNAP
DR. CONNORS, YOU HAVE CERTAIN... ABILITIES THAT COULD BE OF GREAT USE TO ME.
IF YOU WERE TO BREAK OUT OF HERE AND JOIN ME...
...I COULD MAKE ANYTHING REAL. I COULD GIVE YOU ALL YOU'VE EVER WANTED.
CURT.
DAD.
MARTHA. BILLY...
DO WE HAVE A DEAL, DR. CONNORS?
YESsS. DEAR GOD, YESSSS.

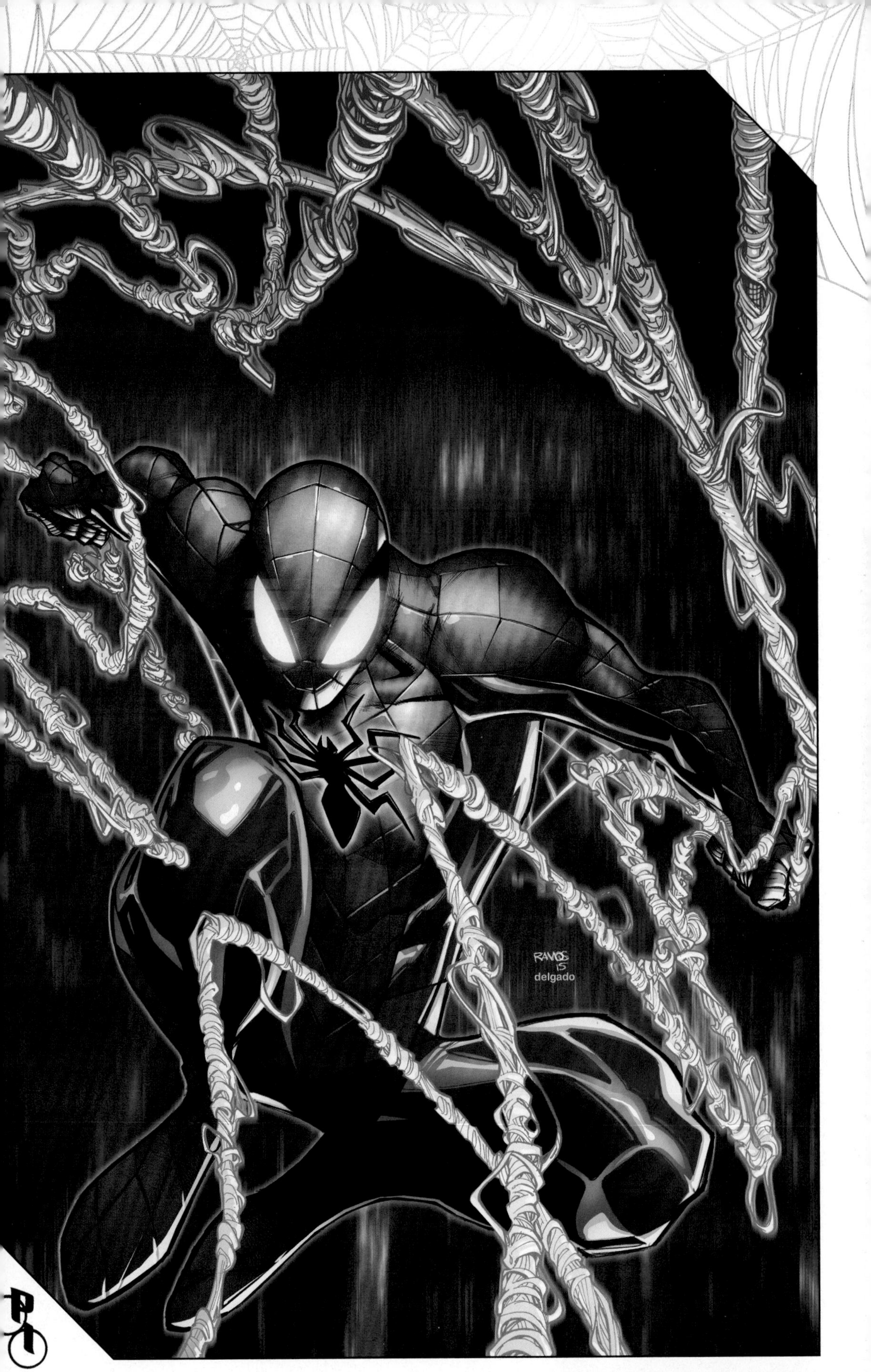
RAMOS
15
delgado

#1 VARIANT BY HUMBERTO RAMOS & EDGAR DELGADO

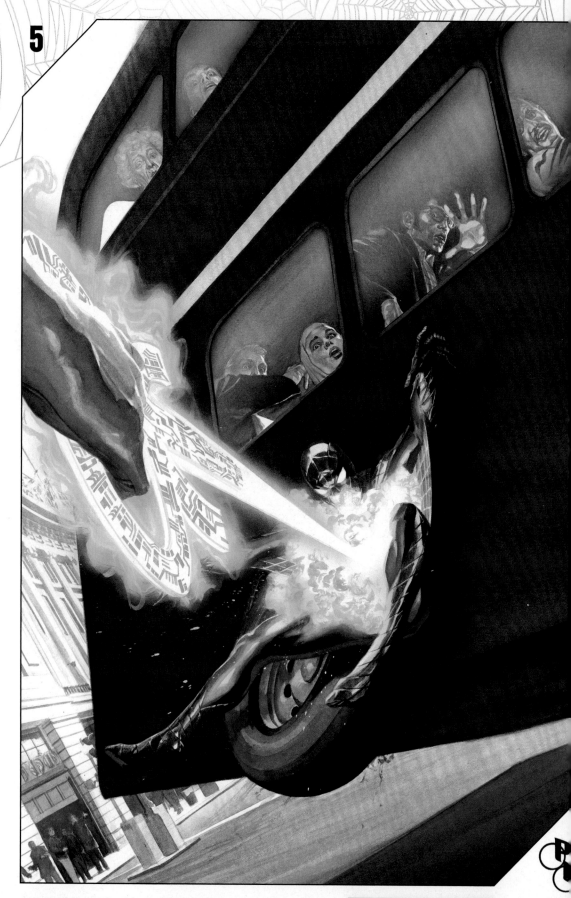

"SET IN STONE"

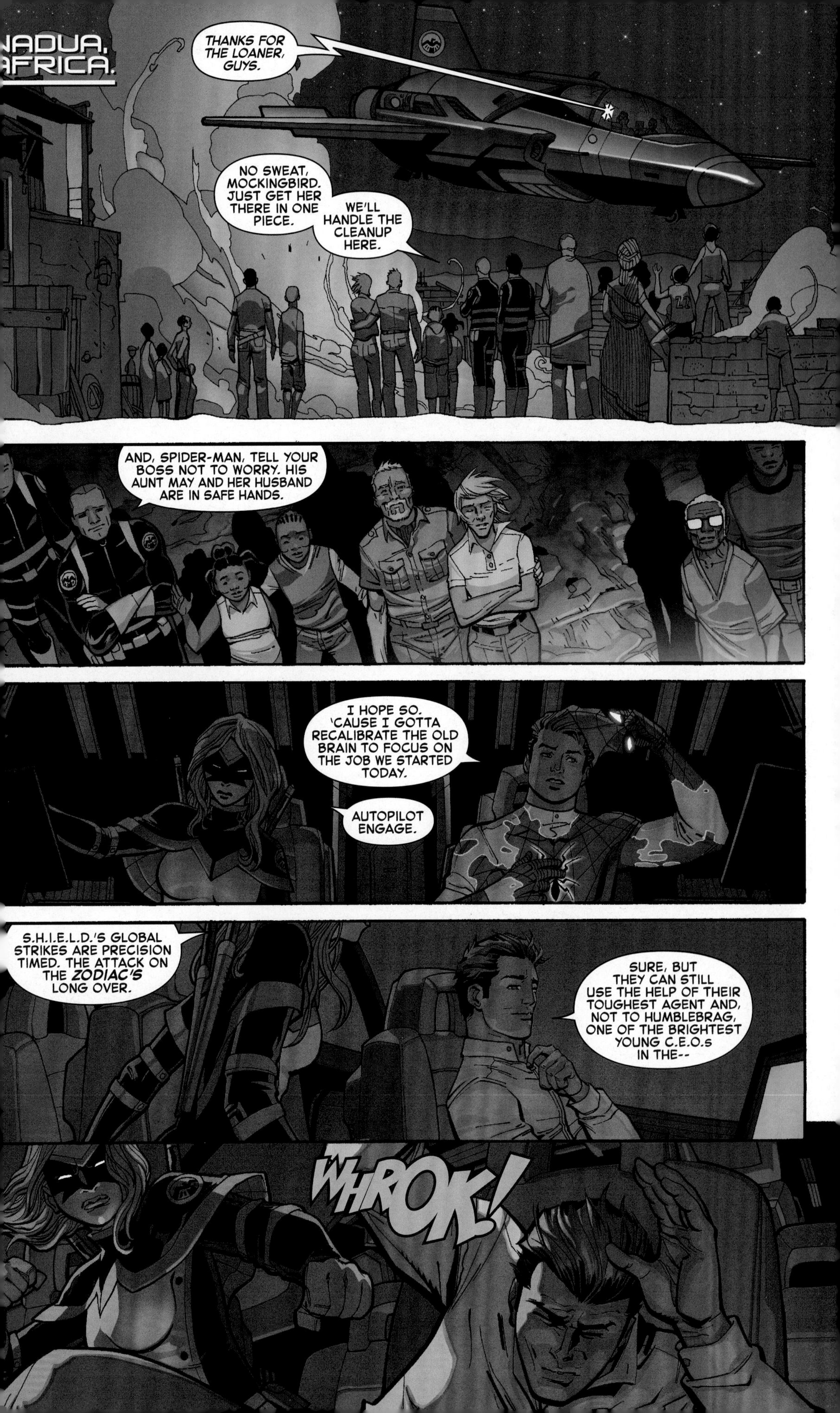
NADUA, AFRICA.
THANKS FOR THE LOANER, GUYS.
NO SWEAT, MOCKINGBIRD. JUST GET HER THERE IN ONE PIECE.
WE'LL HANDLE THE CLEANUP HERE.
AND, SPIDER-MAN, TELL YOUR BOSS NOT TO WORRY. HIS AUNT MAY AND HER HUSBAND ARE IN SAFE HANDS.
I HOPE SO. 'CAUSE I GOTTA RECALIBRATE THE OLD BRAIN TO FOCUS ON THE JOB WE STARTED TODAY.
AUTOPILOT ENGAGE.
S.H.I.E.L.D.'S GLOBAL STRIKES ARE PRECISION TIMED. THE ATTACK ON THE ZODIAC'S LONG OVER.
SURE, BUT THEY CAN STILL USE THE HELP OF THEIR TOUGHEST AGENT AND, NOT TO HUMBLEBRAG, ONE OF THE BRIGHTEST YOUNG C.E.O.s IN THE--
WHROK!

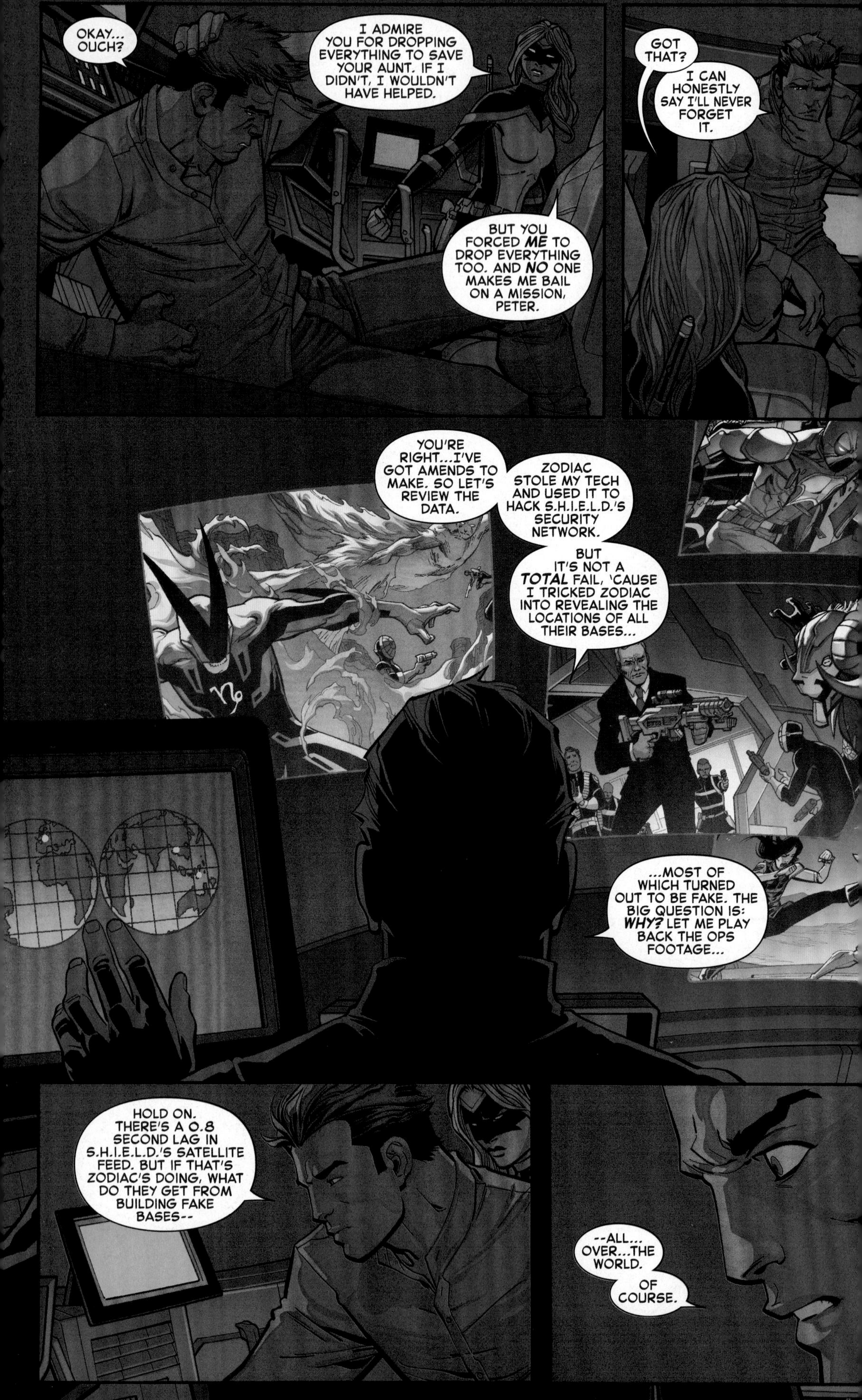
OKAY... OUCH?
I ADMIRE YOU FOR DROPPING EVERYTHING TO SAVE YOUR AUNT. IF I DIDN'T, I WOULDN'T HAVE HELPED.
BUT YOU FORCED *ME* TO DROP EVERYTHING TOO. AND *NO* ONE MAKES ME BAIL ON A MISSION, PETER.
GOT THAT?
I CAN HONESTLY SAY I'LL NEVER FORGET IT.
YOU'RE RIGHT...I'VE GOT AMENDS TO MAKE. SO LET'S REVIEW THE DATA.
ZODIAC STOLE MY TECH AND USED IT TO HACK S.H.I.E.L.D.'S SECURITY NETWORK.
BUT IT'S NOT A *TOTAL* FAIL, 'CAUSE I TRICKED ZODIAC INTO REVEALING THE LOCATIONS OF ALL THEIR BASES...
...MOST OF WHICH TURNED OUT TO BE FAKE. THE BIG QUESTION IS: *WHY?* LET ME PLAY BACK THE OPS FOOTAGE...
HOLD ON. THERE'S A 0.8 SECOND LAG IN S.H.I.E.L.D.'S SATELLITE FEED. BUT IF THAT'S ZODIAC'S DOING, WHAT DO THEY GET FROM BUILDING FAKE BASES--
--ALL... OVER...THE WORLD.
OF COURSE.

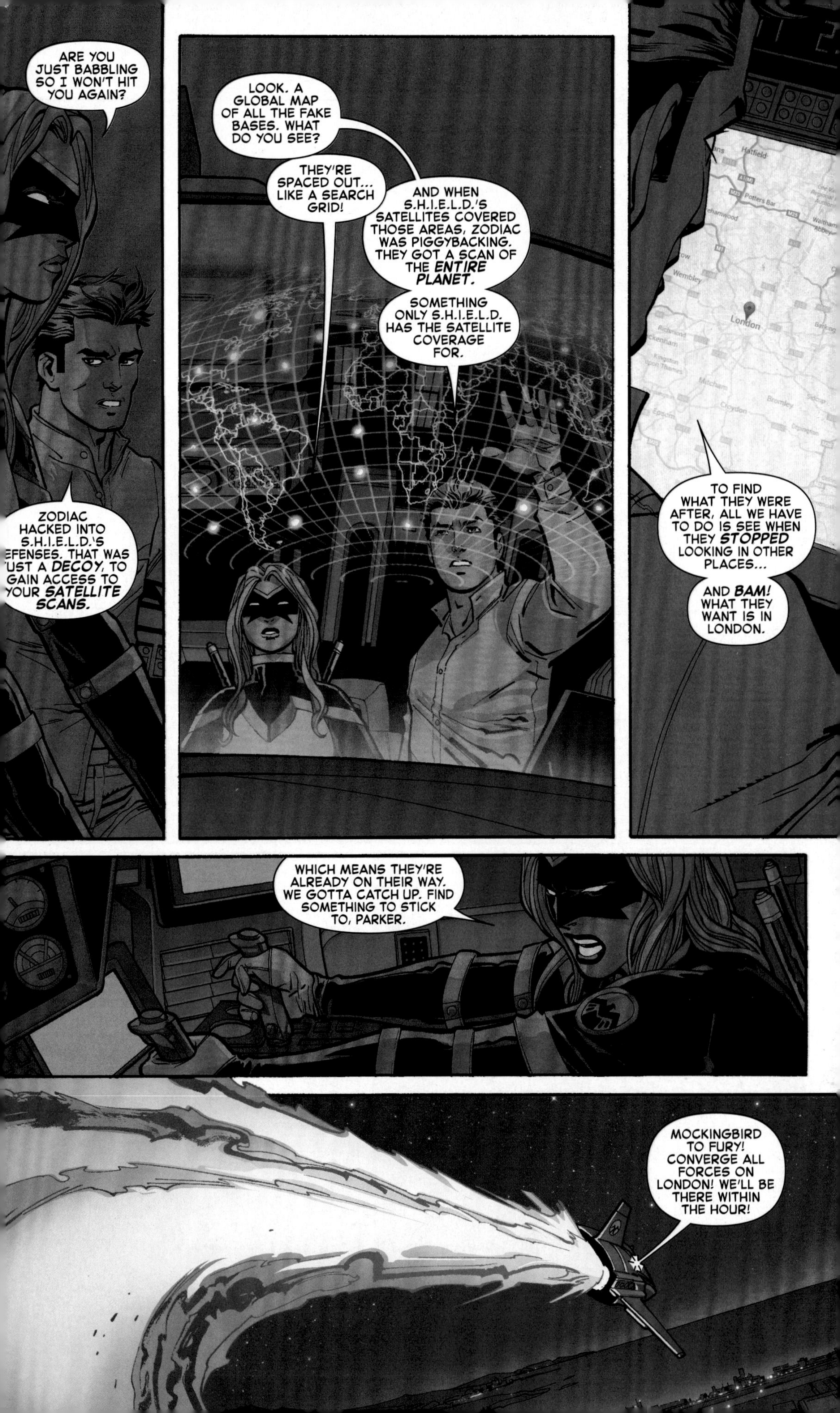

ARE YOU JUST BABBLING SO I WON'T HIT YOU AGAIN?
ZODIAC HACKED INTO S.H.I.E.L.D.'S EFENSES. THAT WAS UST A *DECOY,* TO GAIN ACCESS TO YOUR *SATELLITE SCANS.*
LOOK. A GLOBAL MAP OF ALL THE FAKE BASES. WHAT DO YOU SEE?
THEY'RE SPACED OUT... LIKE A SEARCH GRID!
AND WHEN S.H.I.E.L.D.'S SATELLITES COVERED THOSE AREAS, ZODIAC WAS PIGGYBACKING. THEY GOT A SCAN OF THE *ENTIRE PLANET.*
SOMETHING ONLY S.H.I.E.L.D. HAS THE SATELLITE COVERAGE FOR.
Hatfield
Potters Bar
Wembley
London
Richmond
Mitcham
Croydon
Bromley
TO FIND WHAT THEY WERE AFTER, ALL WE HAVE TO DO IS SEE WHEN THEY *STOPPED* LOOKING IN OTHER PLACES...
AND *BAM!* WHAT THEY WANT IS IN LONDON.
WHICH MEANS THEY'RE ALREADY ON THEIR WAY. WE GOTTA CATCH UP. FIND SOMETHING TO STICK TO, PARKER.
MOCKINGBIRD TO FURY! CONVERGE ALL FORCES ON LONDON! WE'LL BE THERE WITHIN THE HOUR!

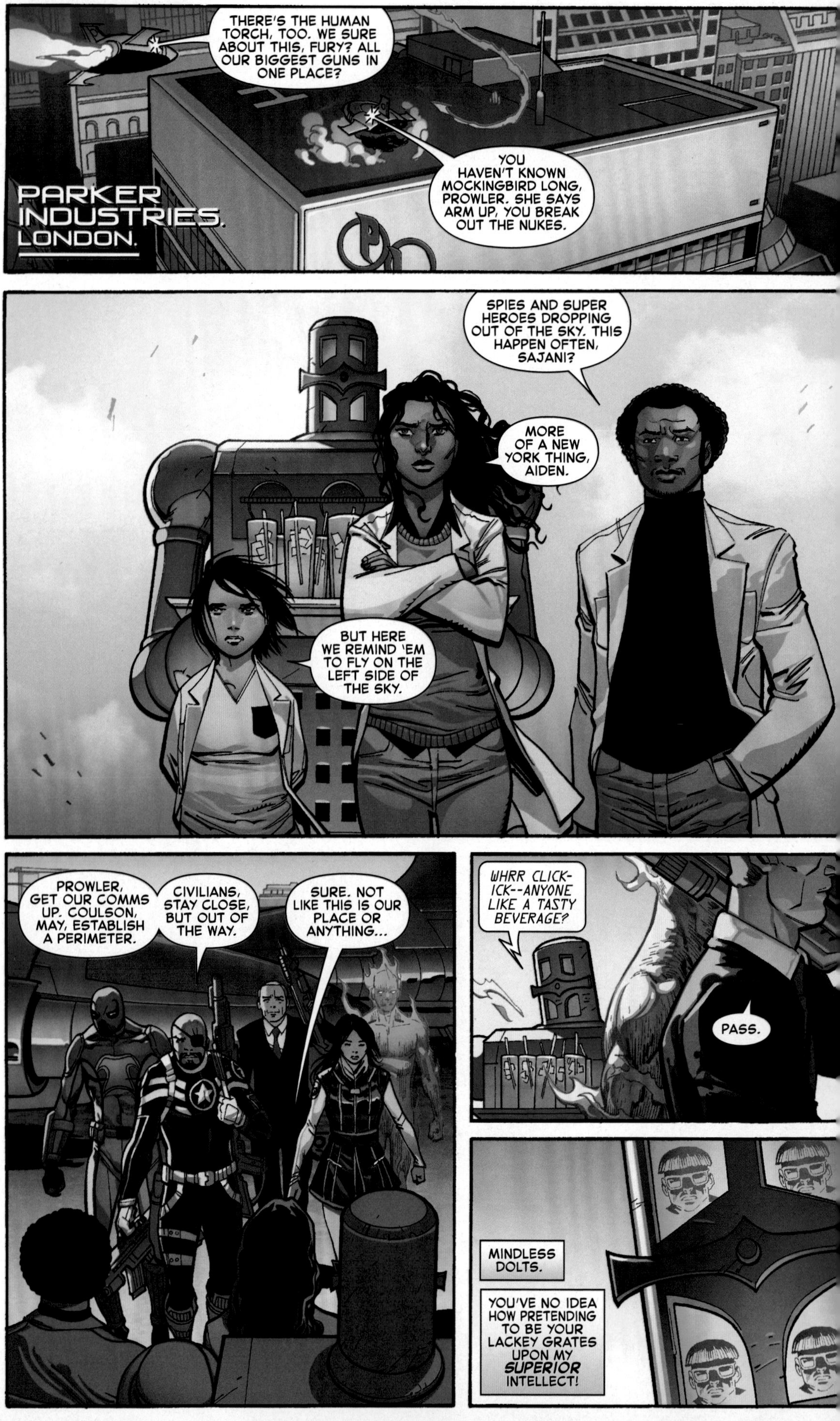
THERE'S THE HUMAN TORCH, TOO. WE SURE ABOUT THIS, FURY? ALL OUR BIGGEST GUNS IN ONE PLACE?
PARKER INDUSTRIES. LONDON.
YOU HAVEN'T KNOWN MOCKINGBIRD LONG, PROWLER. SHE SAYS ARM UP, YOU BREAK OUT THE NUKES.
SPIES AND SUPER HEROES DROPPING OUT OF THE SKY. THIS HAPPEN OFTEN, SAJANI?
MORE OF A NEW YORK THING, AIDEN.
BUT HERE WE REMIND 'EM TO FLY ON THE LEFT SIDE OF THE SKY.
PROWLER, GET OUR COMMS UP. COULSON, MAY, ESTABLISH A PERIMETER.
CIVILIANS, STAY CLOSE, BUT OUT OF THE WAY.
SURE. NOT LIKE THIS IS OUR PLACE OR ANYTHING...
WHRR CLICK-ICK--ANYONE LIKE A TASTY BEVERAGE?
PASS.
MINDLESS DOLTS.
YOU'VE NO IDEA HOW PRETENDING TO BE YOUR LACKEY GRATES UPON MY SUPERIOR INTELLECT!

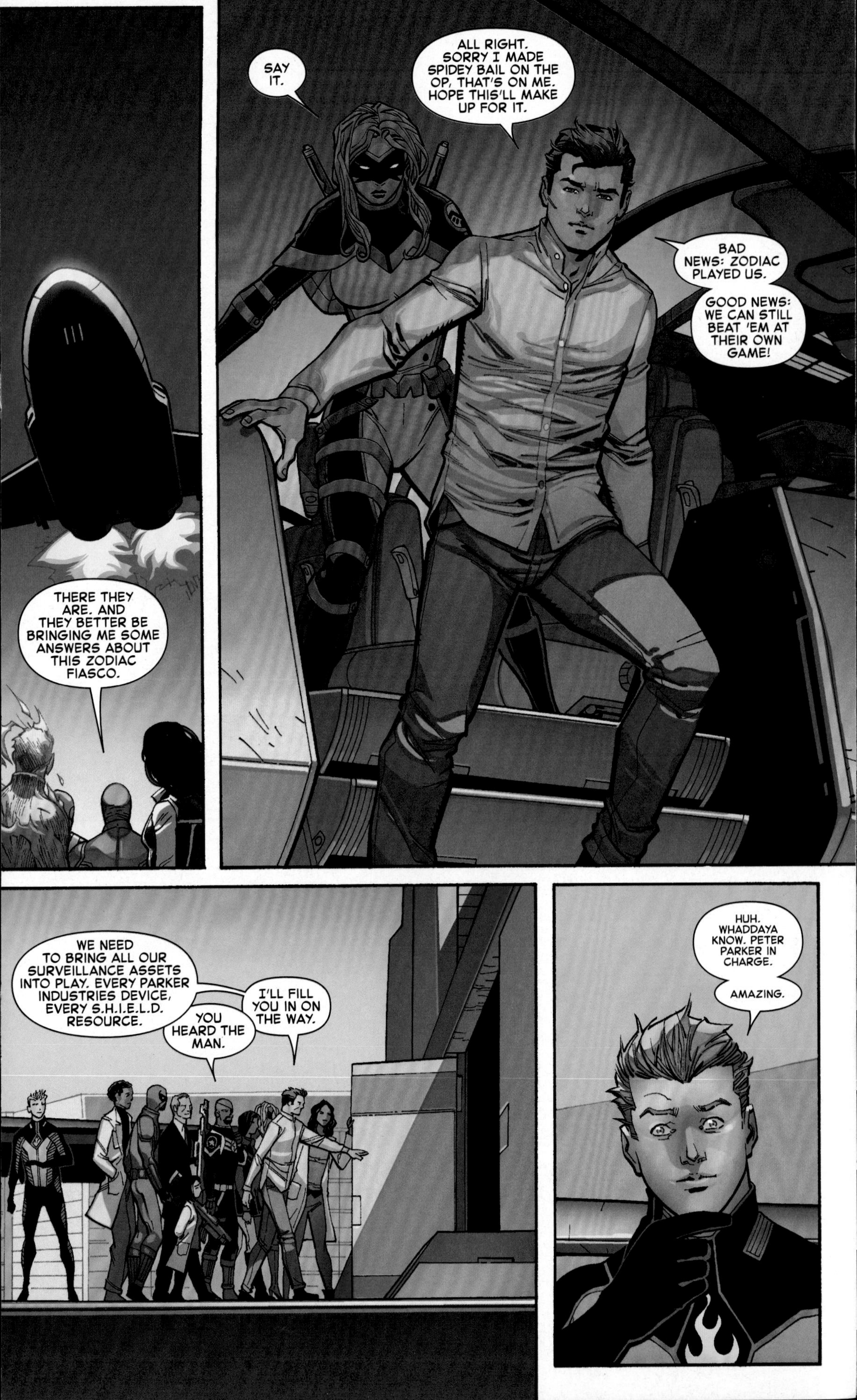
SAY IT.
ALL RIGHT. SORRY I MADE SPIDEY BAIL ON THE OP, THAT'S ON ME. HOPE THIS'LL MAKE UP FOR IT.
THERE THEY ARE. AND THEY BETTER BE BRINGING ME SOME ANSWERS ABOUT THIS ZODIAC FIASCO.
BAD NEWS: ZODIAC PLAYED US.
GOOD NEWS: WE CAN STILL BEAT 'EM AT THEIR OWN GAME!
WE NEED TO BRING ALL OUR SURVEILLANCE ASSETS INTO PLAY. EVERY PARKER INDUSTRIES DEVICE, EVERY S.H.I.E.L.D. RESOURCE.
YOU HEARD THE MAN.
I'LL FILL YOU IN ON THE WAY.
HUH. WHADDAYA KNOW. PETER PARKER IN CHARGE.
AMAZING.

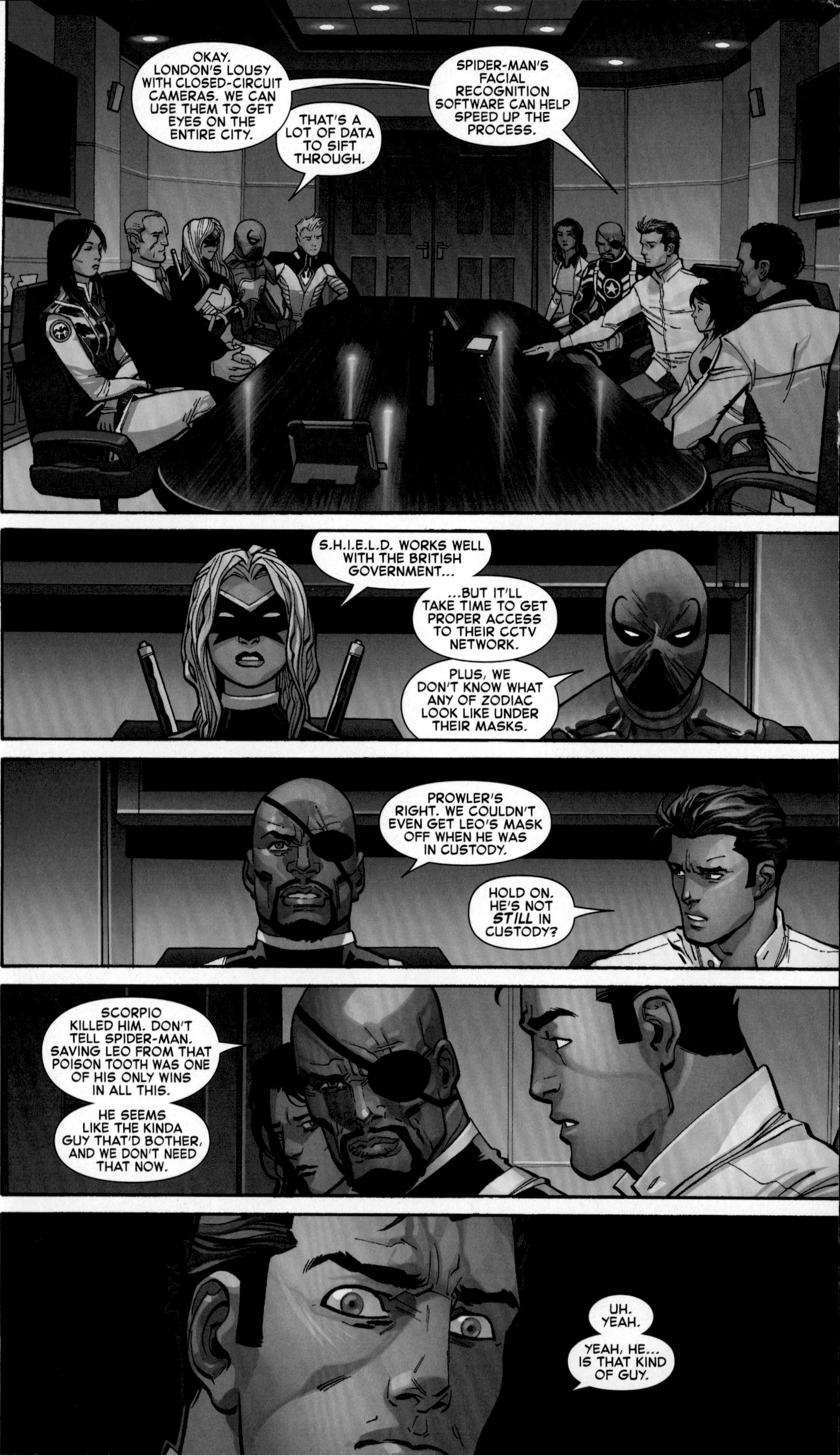
OKAY. LONDON'S LOUSY WITH CLOSED-CIRCUIT CAMERAS. WE CAN USE THEM TO GET EYES ON THE ENTIRE CITY.
THAT'S A LOT OF DATA TO SIFT THROUGH.
SPIDER-MAN'S FACIAL RECOGNITION SOFTWARE CAN HELP SPEED UP THE PROCESS.
S.H.I.E.L.D. WORKS WELL WITH THE BRITISH GOVERNMENT...
...BUT IT'LL TAKE TIME TO GET PROPER ACCESS TO THEIR CCTV NETWORK.
PLUS, WE DON'T KNOW WHAT ANY OF ZODIAC LOOK LIKE UNDER THEIR MASKS.
PROWLER'S RIGHT. WE COULDN'T EVEN GET LEO'S MASK OFF WHEN HE WAS IN CUSTODY.
HOLD ON. HE'S NOT *STILL* IN CUSTODY?
SCORPIO KILLED HIM. DON'T TELL SPIDER-MAN. SAVING LEO FROM THAT POISON TOOTH WAS ONE OF HIS ONLY WINS IN ALL THIS.
HE SEEMS LIKE THE KINDA GUY THAT'D BOTHER, AND WE DON'T NEED THAT NOW.
UH. YEAH.
YEAH, HE... IS THAT KIND OF GUY.

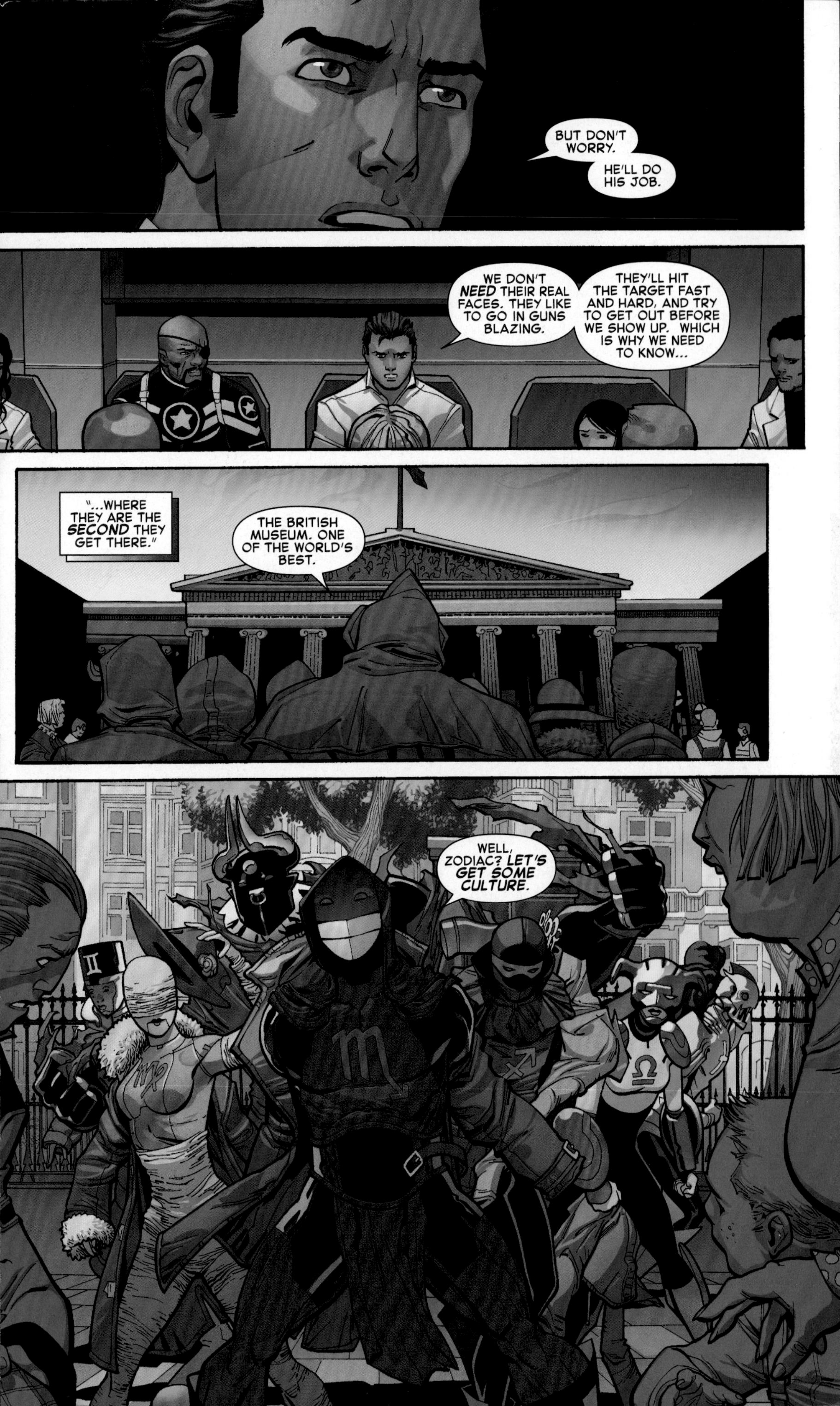
BUT DON'T WORRY.
HE'LL DO HIS JOB.
WE DON'T *NEED* THEIR REAL FACES. THEY LIKE TO GO IN GUNS BLAZING.
THEY'LL HIT THE TARGET FAST AND HARD, AND TRY TO GET OUT BEFORE WE SHOW UP. WHICH IS WHY WE NEED TO KNOW...
"...WHERE THEY ARE THE *SECOND* THEY GET THERE."
THE BRITISH MUSEUM. ONE OF THE WORLD'S BEST.
WELL, ZODIAC? *LET'S GET SOME CULTURE.*

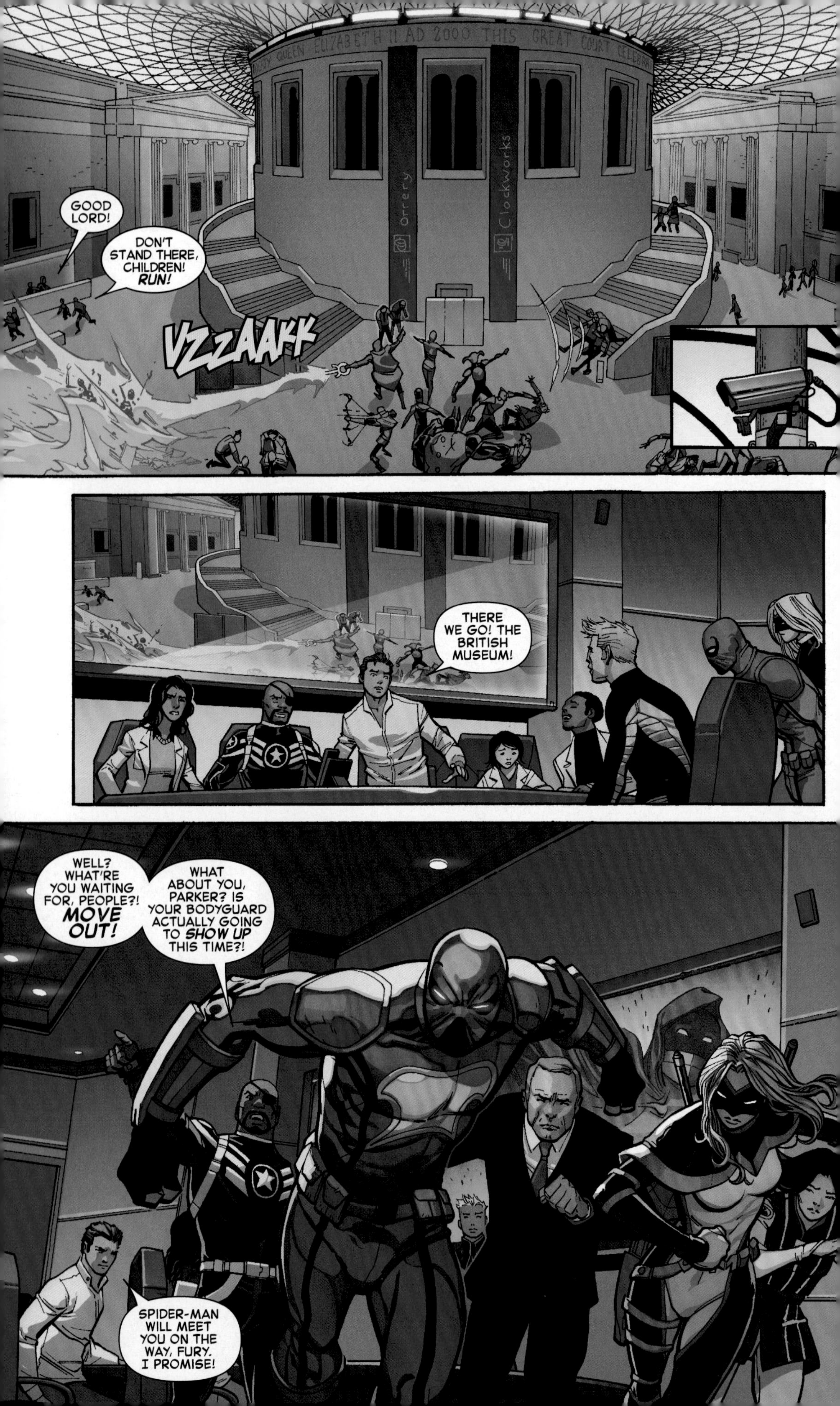

GOOD LORD!
DON'T STAND THERE, CHILDREN! RUN!
VZZAAKK
Orrery
Clockworks
THERE WE GO! THE BRITISH MUSEUM!
WELL? WHAT'RE YOU WAITING FOR, PEOPLE?! MOVE OUT!
WHAT ABOUT YOU, PARKER? IS YOUR BODYGUARD ACTUALLY GOING TO SHOW UP THIS TIME?!
SPIDER-MAN WILL MEET YOU ON THE WAY, FURY. I PROMISE!

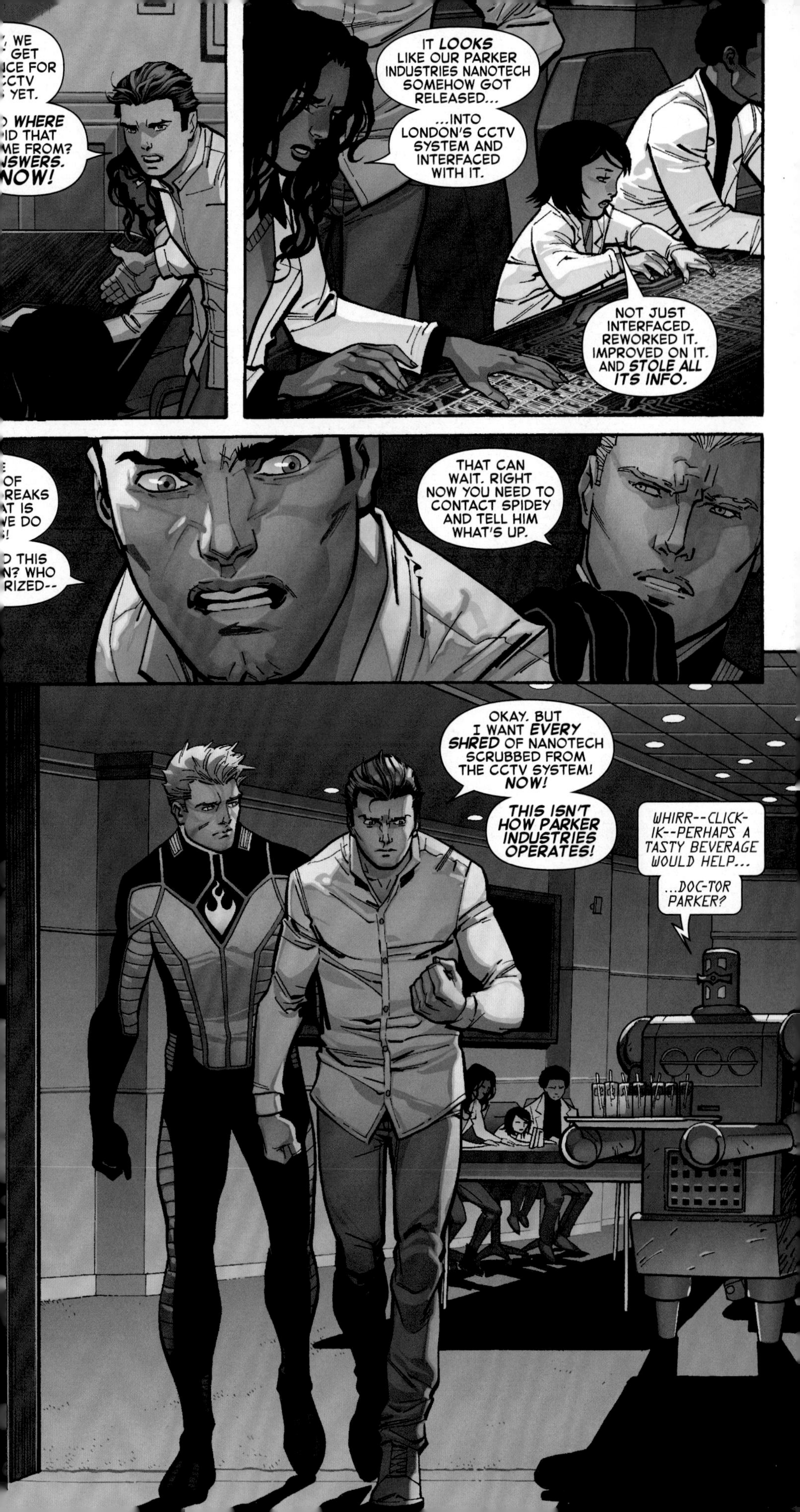

Z WE GET ICE FOR CCTV S YET.
D WHERE ID THAT ME FROM? NSWERS. NOW!
IT LOOKS LIKE OUR PARKER INDUSTRIES NANOTECH SOMEHOW GOT RELEASED...
...INTO LONDON'S CCTV SYSTEM AND INTERFACED WITH IT.
NOT JUST INTERFACED. REWORKED IT. IMPROVED ON IT. AND STOLE ALL ITS INFO.
E OF REAKS AT IS WE DO S!
D THIS N? WHO RIZED--
THAT CAN WAIT. RIGHT NOW YOU NEED TO CONTACT SPIDEY AND TELL HIM WHAT'S UP.
OKAY. BUT I WANT EVERY SHRED OF NANOTECH SCRUBBED FROM THE CCTV SYSTEM! NOW!
THIS ISN'T HOW PARKER INDUSTRIES OPERATES!
WHIRR--CLICK-IK--PERHAPS A TASTY BEVERAGE WOULD HELP...
...DOC-TOR PARKER?

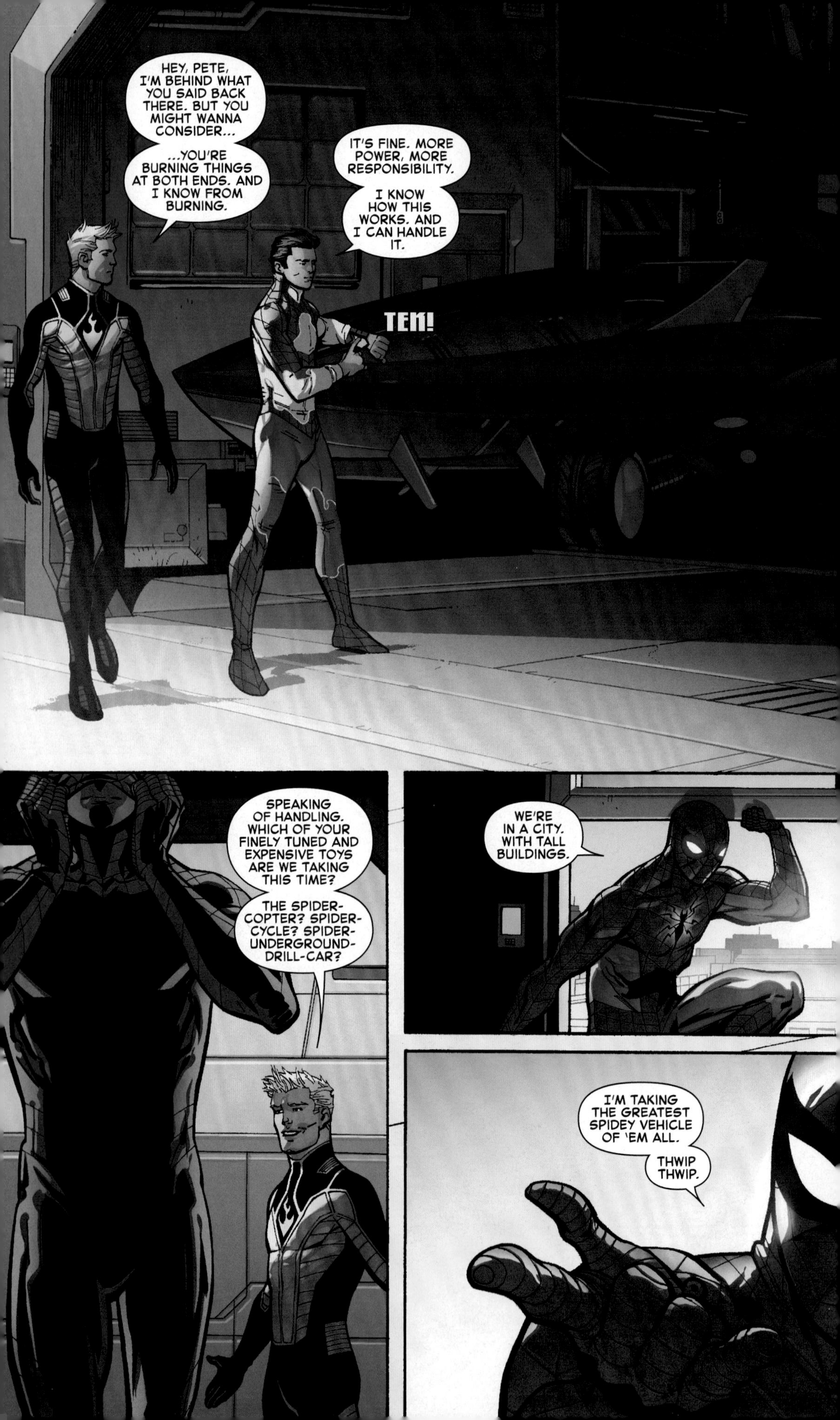
HEY, PETE, I'M BEHIND WHAT YOU SAID BACK THERE. BUT YOU MIGHT WANNA CONSIDER...
...YOU'RE BURNING THINGS AT BOTH ENDS. AND I KNOW FROM BURNING.
IT'S FINE. MORE POWER, MORE RESPONSIBILITY.
I KNOW HOW THIS WORKS. AND I CAN HANDLE IT.
TEH!
SPEAKING OF HANDLING. WHICH OF YOUR FINELY TUNED AND EXPENSIVE TOYS ARE WE TAKING THIS TIME?
THE SPIDER-COPTER? SPIDER-CYCLE? SPIDER-UNDERGROUND-DRILL-CAR?
WE'RE IN A CITY. WITH TALL BUILDINGS.
I'M TAKING THE GREATEST SPIDEY VEHICLE OF 'EM ALL.
THWIP THWIP.

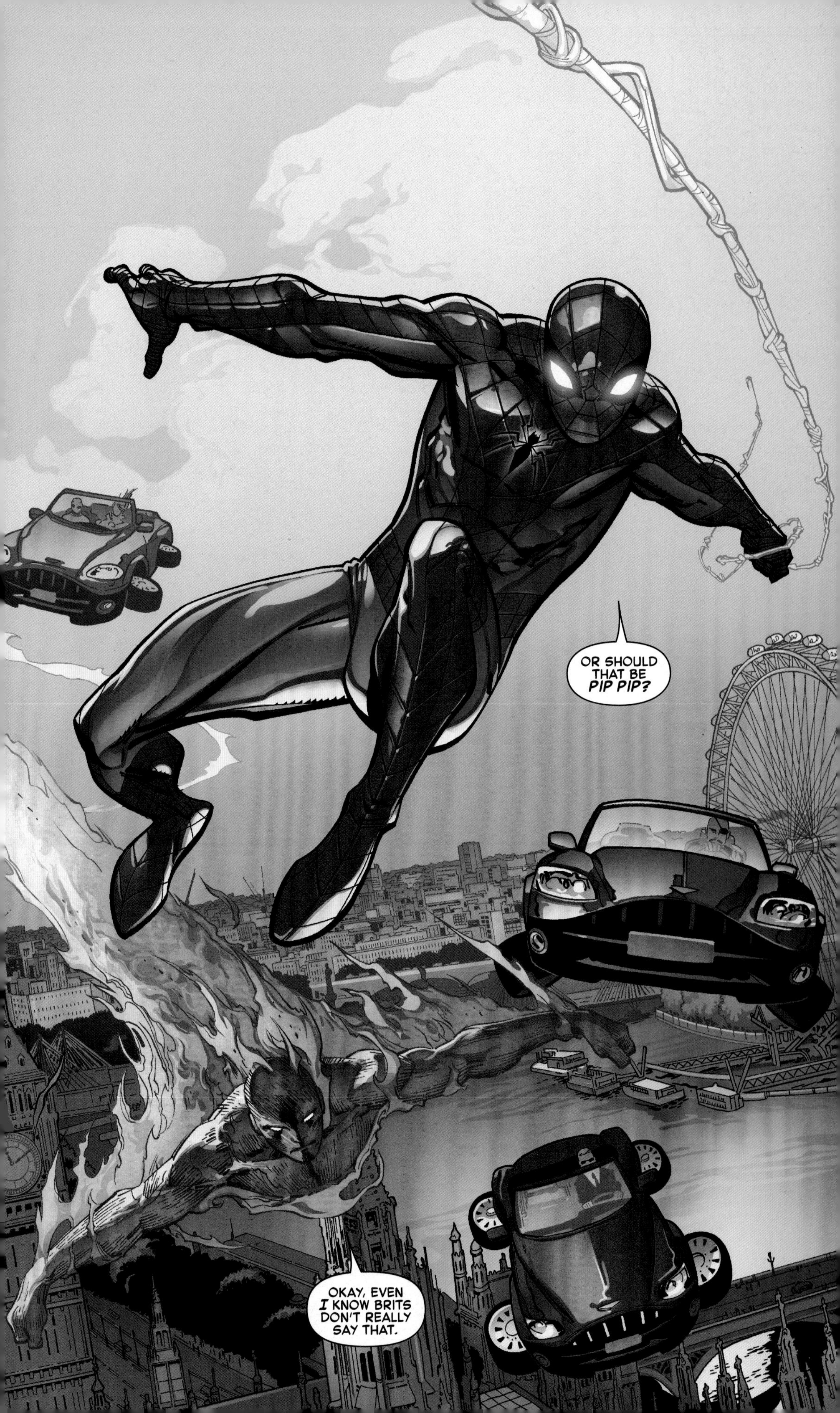
OR SHOULD THAT BE *PIP PIP?*
OKAY, EVEN *I* KNOW BRITS DON'T REALLY SAY THAT.

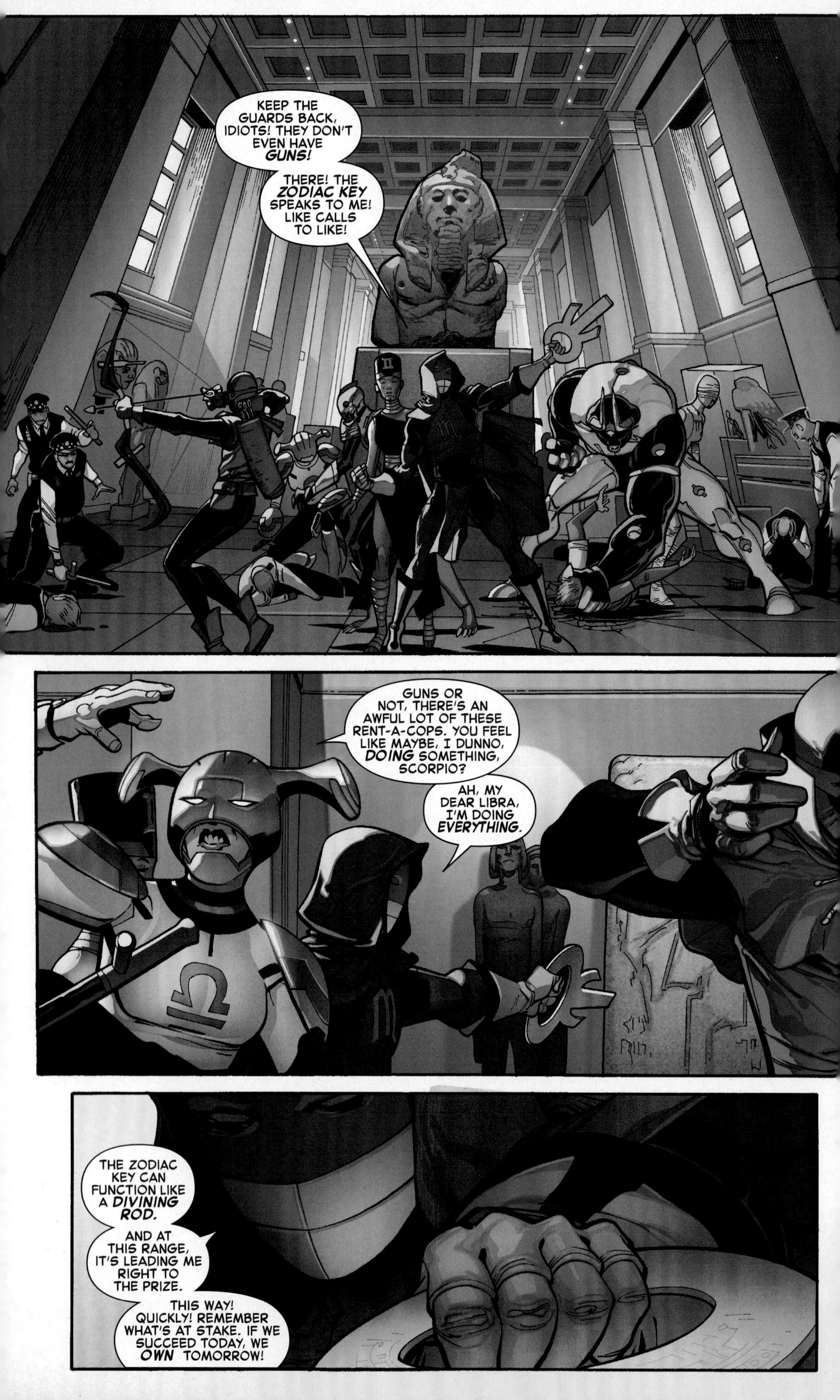
KEEP THE GUARDS BACK, IDIOTS! THEY DON'T EVEN HAVE GUNS!
THERE! THE ZODIAC KEY SPEAKS TO ME! LIKE CALLS TO LIKE!
GUNS OR NOT, THERE'S AN AWFUL LOT OF THESE RENT-A-COPS. YOU FEEL LIKE MAYBE, I DUNNO, DOING SOMETHING, SCORPIO?
AH, MY DEAR LIBRA, I'M DOING EVERYTHING.
THE ZODIAC KEY CAN FUNCTION LIKE A DIVINING ROD.
AND AT THIS RANGE, IT'S LEADING ME RIGHT TO THE PRIZE.
THIS WAY! QUICKLY! REMEMBER WHAT'S AT STAKE. IF WE SUCCEED TODAY, WE OWN TOMORROW!

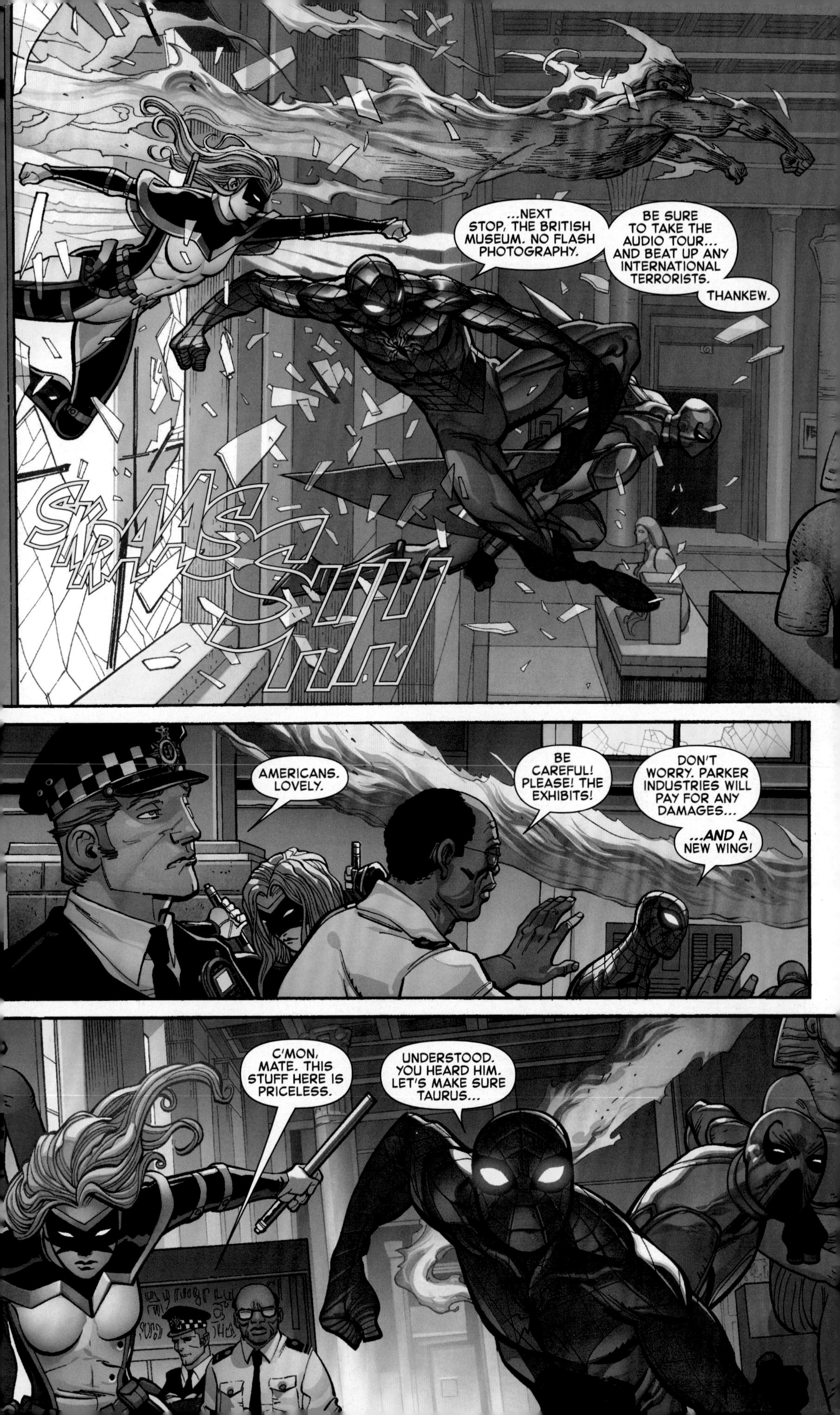
...NEXT STOP, THE BRITISH MUSEUM. NO FLASH PHOTOGRAPHY.
BE SURE TO TAKE THE AUDIO TOUR... AND BEAT UP ANY INTERNATIONAL TERRORISTS.
THANKEW.
SMASH
AMERICANS. LOVELY.
BE CAREFUL! PLEASE! THE EXHIBITS!
DON'T WORRY. PARKER INDUSTRIES WILL PAY FOR ANY DAMAGES...
...AND A NEW WING!
C'MON, MATE. THIS STUFF HERE IS PRICELESS.
UNDERSTOOD. YOU HEARD HIM. LET'S MAKE SURE TAURUS...

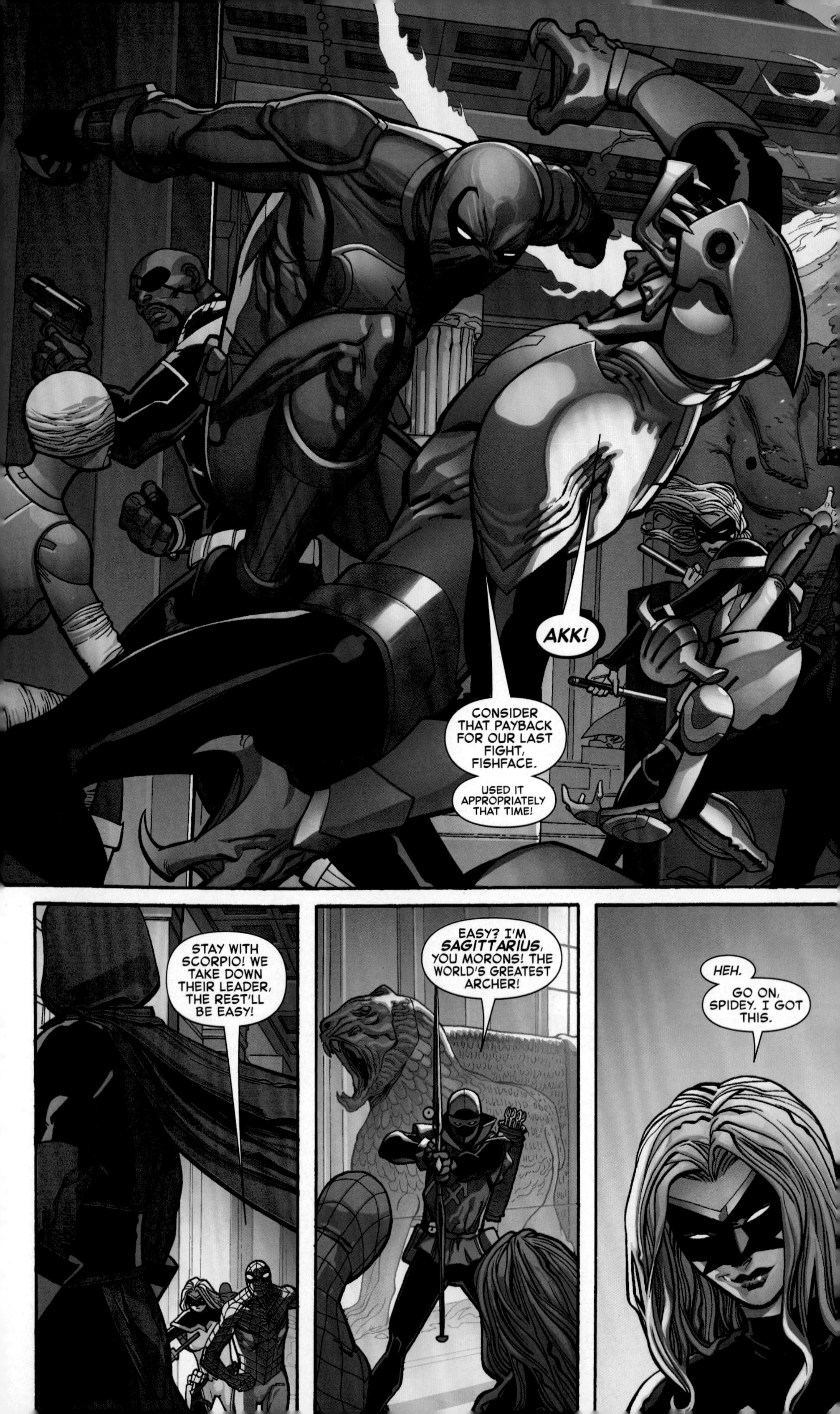
AKK!
CONSIDER THAT PAYBACK FOR OUR LAST FIGHT, FISHFACE.
USED IT APPROPRIATELY THAT TIME!
STAY WITH SCORPIO! WE TAKE DOWN THEIR LEADER, THE REST'LL BE EASY!
EASY? I'M SAGITTARIUS, YOU MORONS! THE WORLD'S GREATEST ARCHER!
HEH.
GO ON, SPIDEY. I GOT THIS.

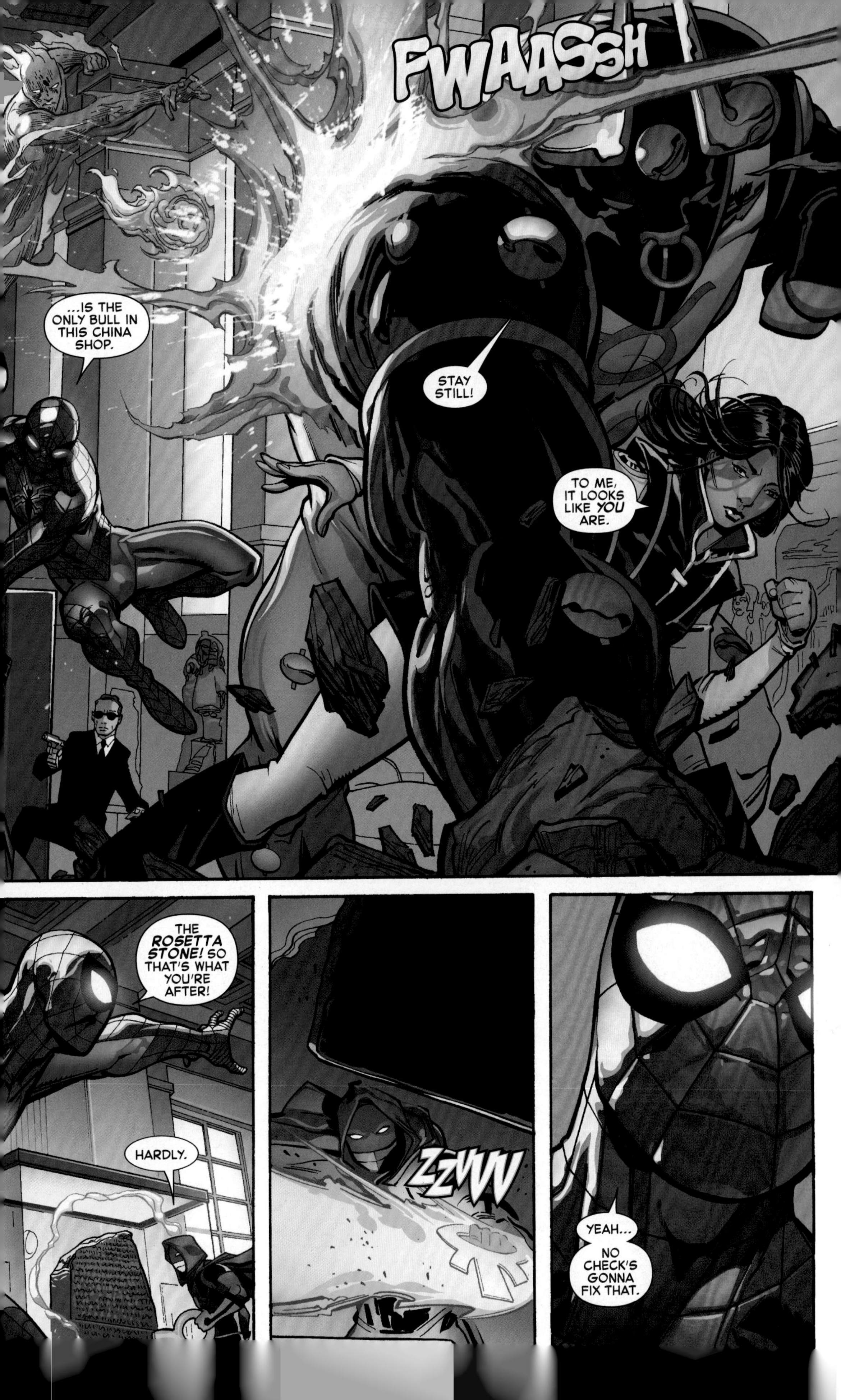
FWAASSH
...IS THE ONLY BULL IN THIS CHINA SHOP.
STAY STILL!
TO ME, IT LOOKS LIKE YOU ARE.
THE ROSETTA STONE! SO THAT'S WHAT YOU'RE AFTER!
HARDLY.
ZZVVVV
YEAH...
NO CHECK'S GONNA FIX THAT.

SEE, IT'S WHAT'S *INSIDE* THAT COUNTS.

MY PRIZE. NOTHING ELSE MATTERS.

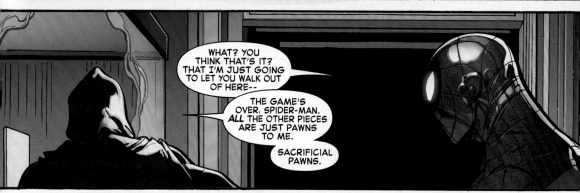

WHAT? YOU THINK THAT'S IT? THAT I'M JUST GOING TO LET YOU WALK OUT OF HERE--

THE GAME'S OVER, SPIDER-MAN. *ALL* THE OTHER PIECES ARE JUST PAWNS TO ME.

SACRIFICIAL PAWNS.

REMEMBER LEO?

SCORPIO! DON'T!

I WONDER, HOW MANY CAN YOU SAVE?

TAK

KRIK *KRIK* *KRIK* *KRIK* *KRIK* *KRIK*

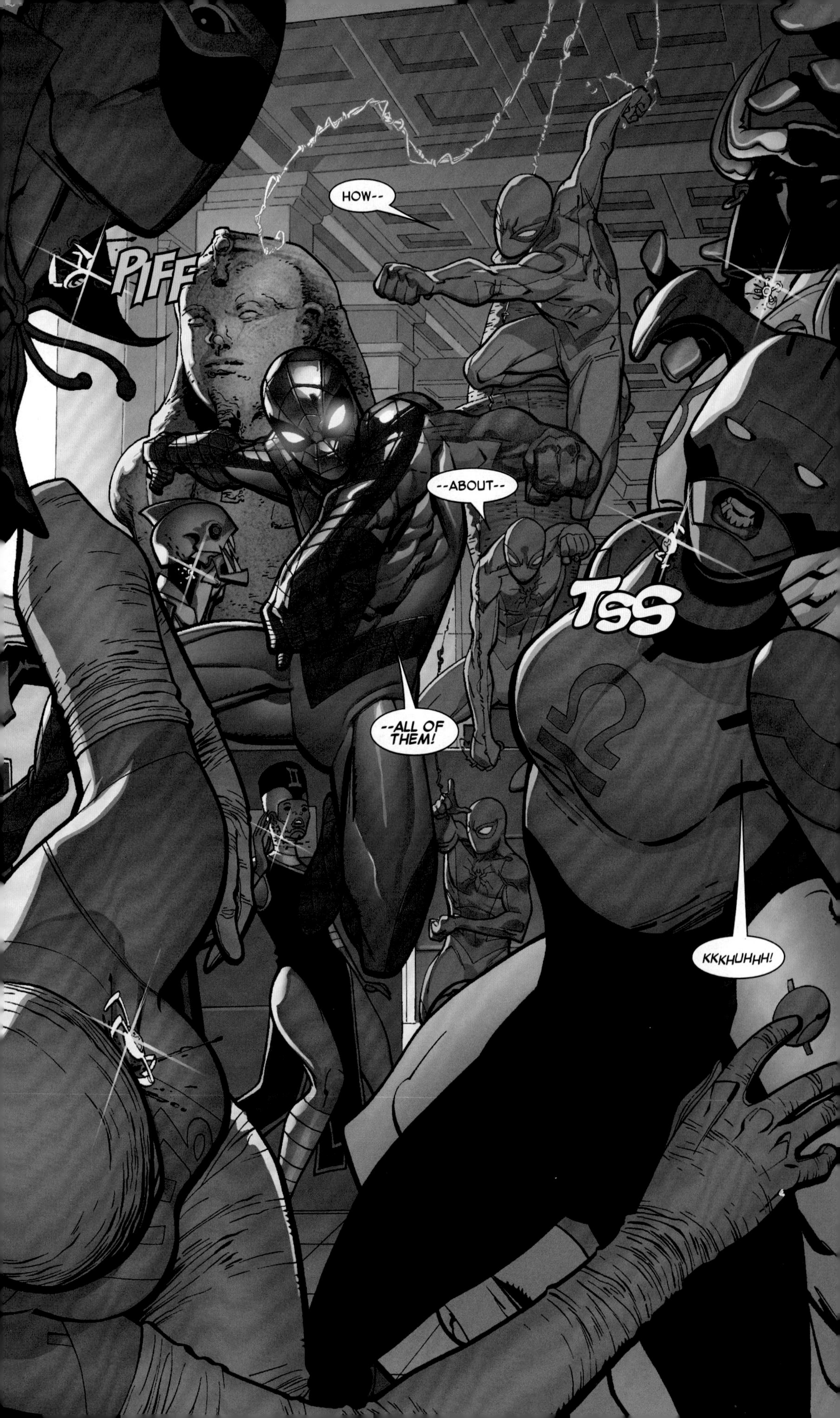
PIFF
HOW--
--ABOUT--
TSS
--ALL OF THEM!
KKKHUHHH!

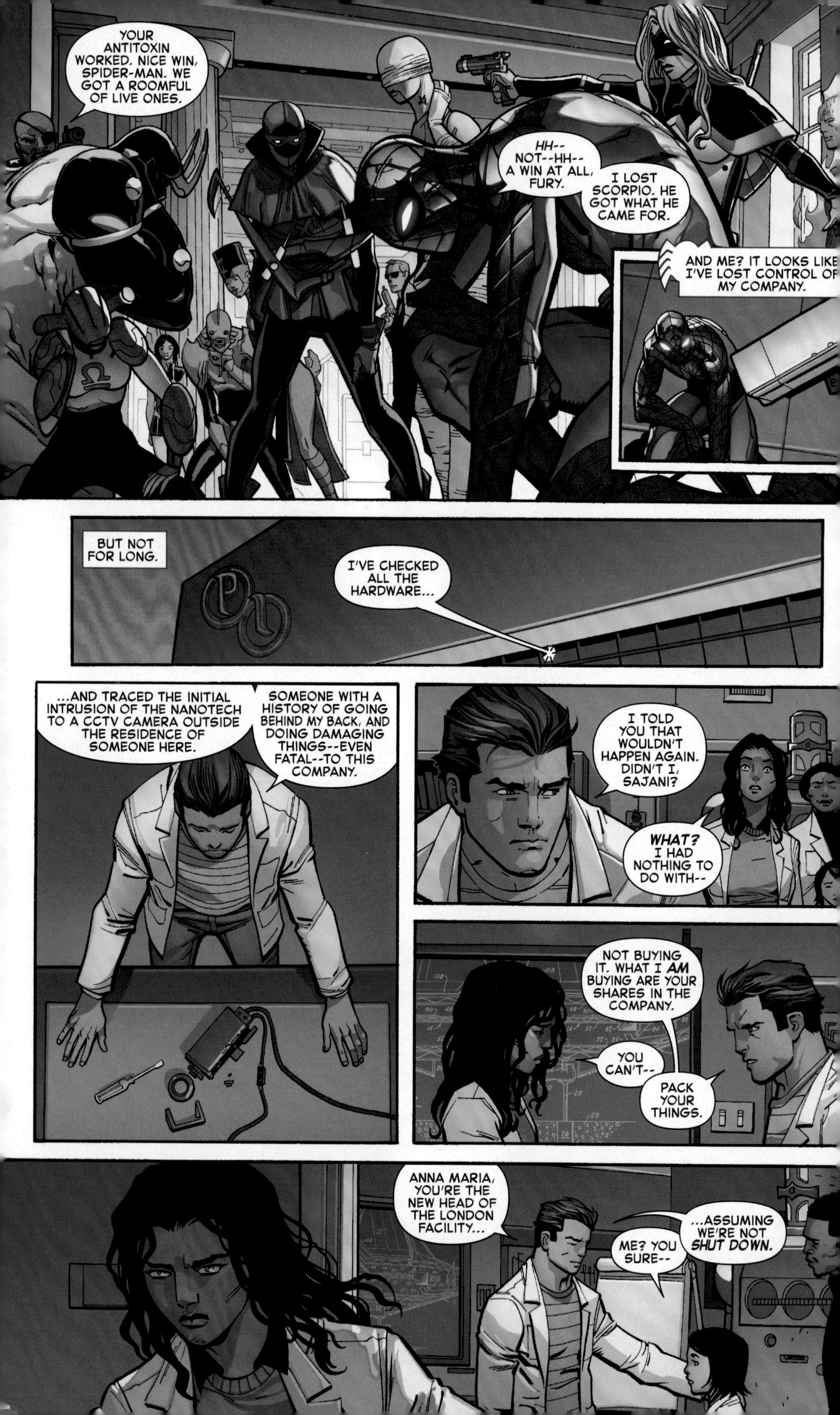
YOUR ANTITOXIN WORKED. NICE WIN, SPIDER-MAN. WE GOT A ROOMFUL OF LIVE ONES.
HH--NOT--HH--A WIN AT ALL, FURY.
I LOST SCORPIO. HE GOT WHAT HE CAME FOR.
AND ME? IT LOOKS LIKE I'VE LOST CONTROL OF MY COMPANY.
BUT NOT FOR LONG.
I'VE CHECKED ALL THE HARDWARE...
...AND TRACED THE INITIAL INTRUSION OF THE NANOTECH TO A CCTV CAMERA OUTSIDE THE RESIDENCE OF SOMEONE HERE.
SOMEONE WITH A HISTORY OF GOING BEHIND MY BACK, AND DOING DAMAGING THINGS--EVEN FATAL--TO THIS COMPANY.
I TOLD YOU THAT WOULDN'T HAPPEN AGAIN. DIDN'T I, SAJANI?
WHAT? I HAD NOTHING TO DO WITH--
NOT BUYING IT. WHAT I AM BUYING ARE YOUR SHARES IN THE COMPANY.
YOU CAN'T--
PACK YOUR THINGS.
ANNA MARIA, YOU'RE THE NEW HEAD OF THE LONDON FACILITY...
...ASSUMING WE'RE NOT SHUT DOWN.
ME? YOU SURE--

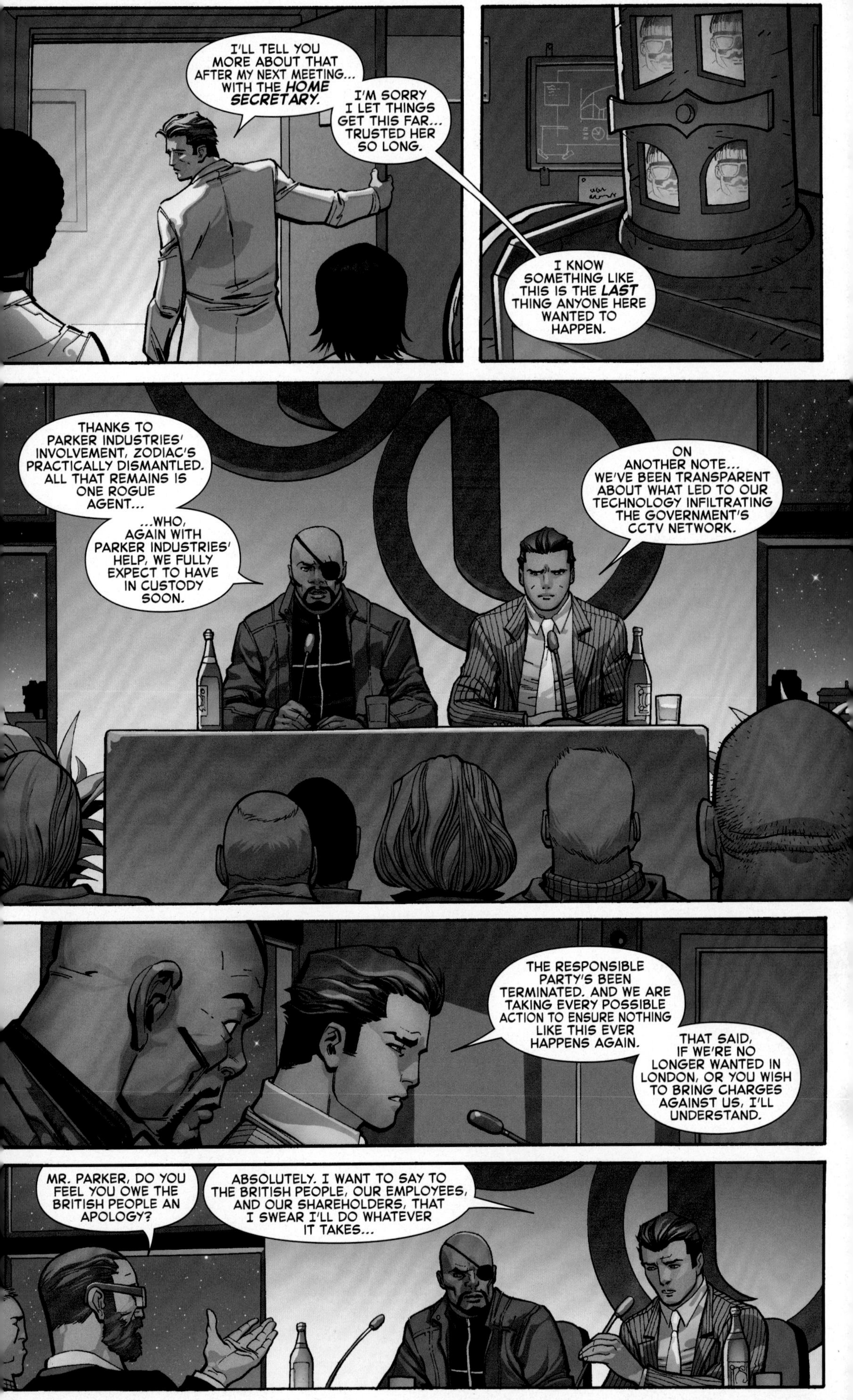
I'LL TELL YOU MORE ABOUT THAT AFTER MY NEXT MEETING... WITH THE HOME SECRETARY.
I'M SORRY I LET THINGS GET THIS FAR... TRUSTED HER SO LONG.
I KNOW SOMETHING LIKE THIS IS THE LAST THING ANYONE HERE WANTED TO HAPPEN.
THANKS TO PARKER INDUSTRIES' INVOLVEMENT, ZODIAC'S PRACTICALLY DISMANTLED. ALL THAT REMAINS IS ONE ROGUE AGENT...
...WHO, AGAIN WITH PARKER INDUSTRIES' HELP, WE FULLY EXPECT TO HAVE IN CUSTODY SOON.
ON ANOTHER NOTE... WE'VE BEEN TRANSPARENT ABOUT WHAT LED TO OUR TECHNOLOGY INFILTRATING THE GOVERNMENT'S CCTV NETWORK.
THE RESPONSIBLE PARTY'S BEEN TERMINATED. AND WE ARE TAKING EVERY POSSIBLE ACTION TO ENSURE NOTHING LIKE THIS EVER HAPPENS AGAIN.
THAT SAID, IF WE'RE NO LONGER WANTED IN LONDON, OR YOU WISH TO BRING CHARGES AGAINST US, I'LL UNDERSTAND.
MR. PARKER, DO YOU FEEL YOU OWE THE BRITISH PEOPLE AN APOLOGY?
ABSOLUTELY. I WANT TO SAY TO THE BRITISH PEOPLE, OUR EMPLOYEES, AND OUR SHAREHOLDERS, THAT I SWEAR I'LL DO WHATEVER IT TAKES...

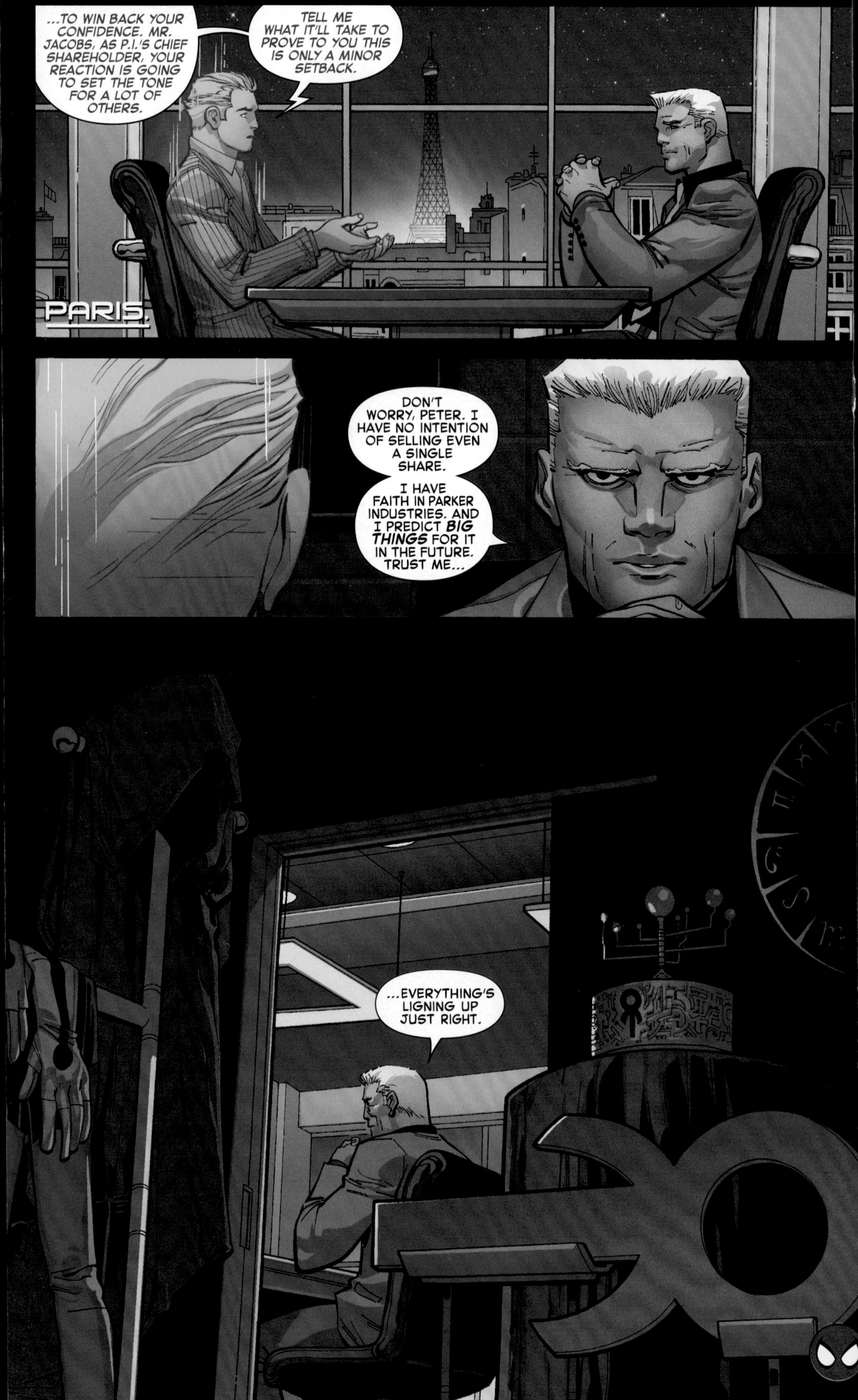
...TO WIN BACK YOUR CONFIDENCE. MR. JACOBS, AS P.I.'S CHIEF SHAREHOLDER, YOUR REACTION IS GOING TO SET THE TONE FOR A LOT OF OTHERS.
TELL ME WHAT IT'LL TAKE TO PROVE TO YOU THIS IS ONLY A MINOR SETBACK.
PARIS.
DON'T WORRY, PETER. I HAVE NO INTENTION OF SELLING EVEN A SINGLE SHARE.
I HAVE FAITH IN PARKER INDUSTRIES. AND I PREDICT *BIG THINGS* FOR IT IN THE FUTURE. TRUST ME...
...EVERYTHING'S LIGNING UP JUST RIGHT.

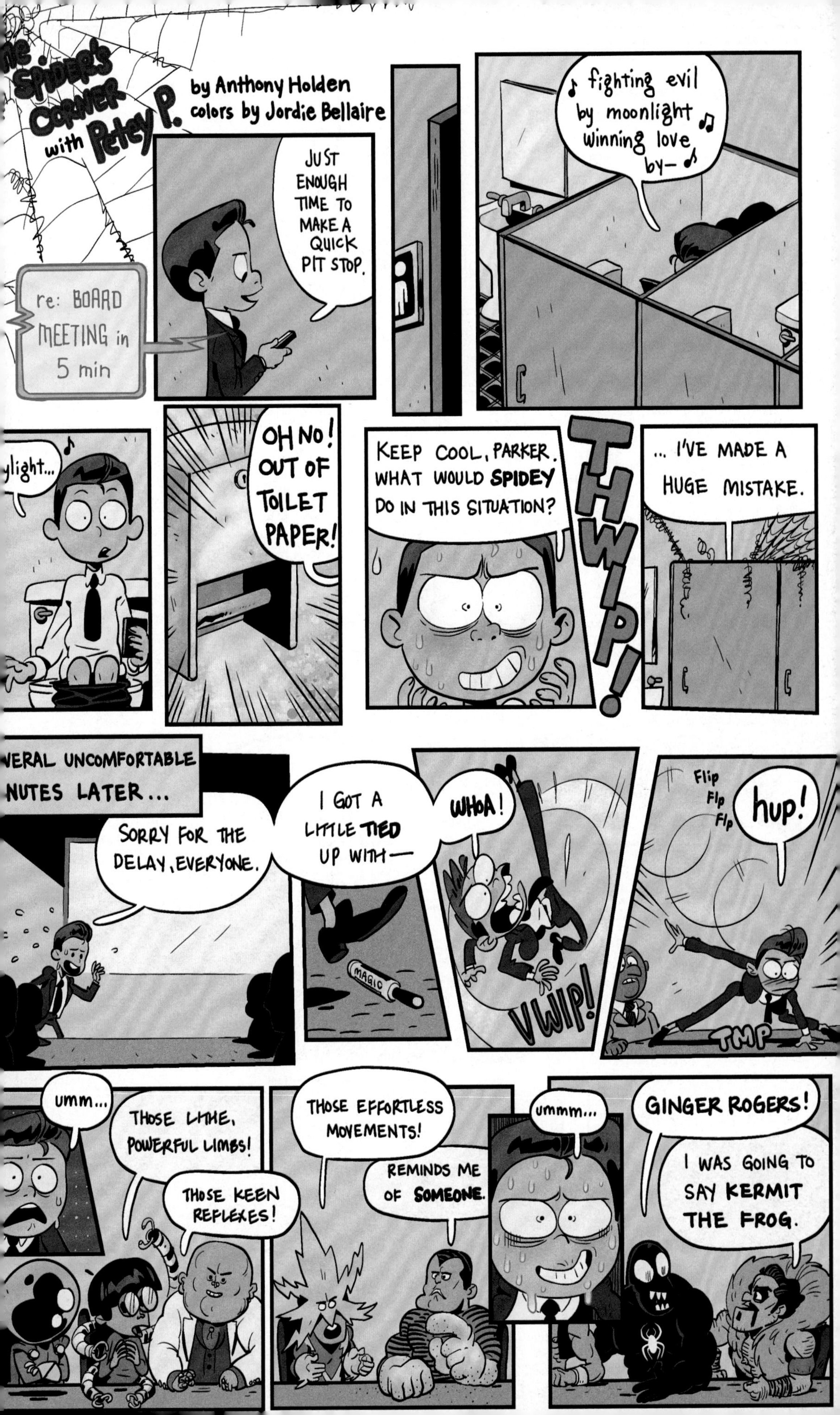

...he Spider's Corner with Petey P.
by Anthony Holden
colors by Jordie Bellaire
re: BOARD MEETING in 5 min
JUST ENOUGH TIME TO MAKE A QUICK PIT STOP.
♪ fighting evil by moonlight ♫ winning love by— ♪
...ylight... ♪
OH NO! OUT OF TOILET PAPER!
KEEP COOL, PARKER. WHAT WOULD SPIDEY DO IN THIS SITUATION?
THWIP!
... I'VE MADE A HUGE MISTAKE.
...VERAL UNCOMFORTABLE ...NUTES LATER...
SORRY FOR THE DELAY, EVERYONE.
I GOT A LITTLE TIED UP WITH—
MAGIC
WHOA!
VWIP!
Flip Flip Flip
hup!
TMP
umm...
THOSE LITHE, POWERFUL LIMBS!
THOSE KEEN REFLEXES!
THOSE EFFORTLESS MOVEMENTS!
REMINDS ME OF SOMEONE.
ummm...
GINGER ROGERS!
I WAS GOING TO SAY KERMIT THE FROG.

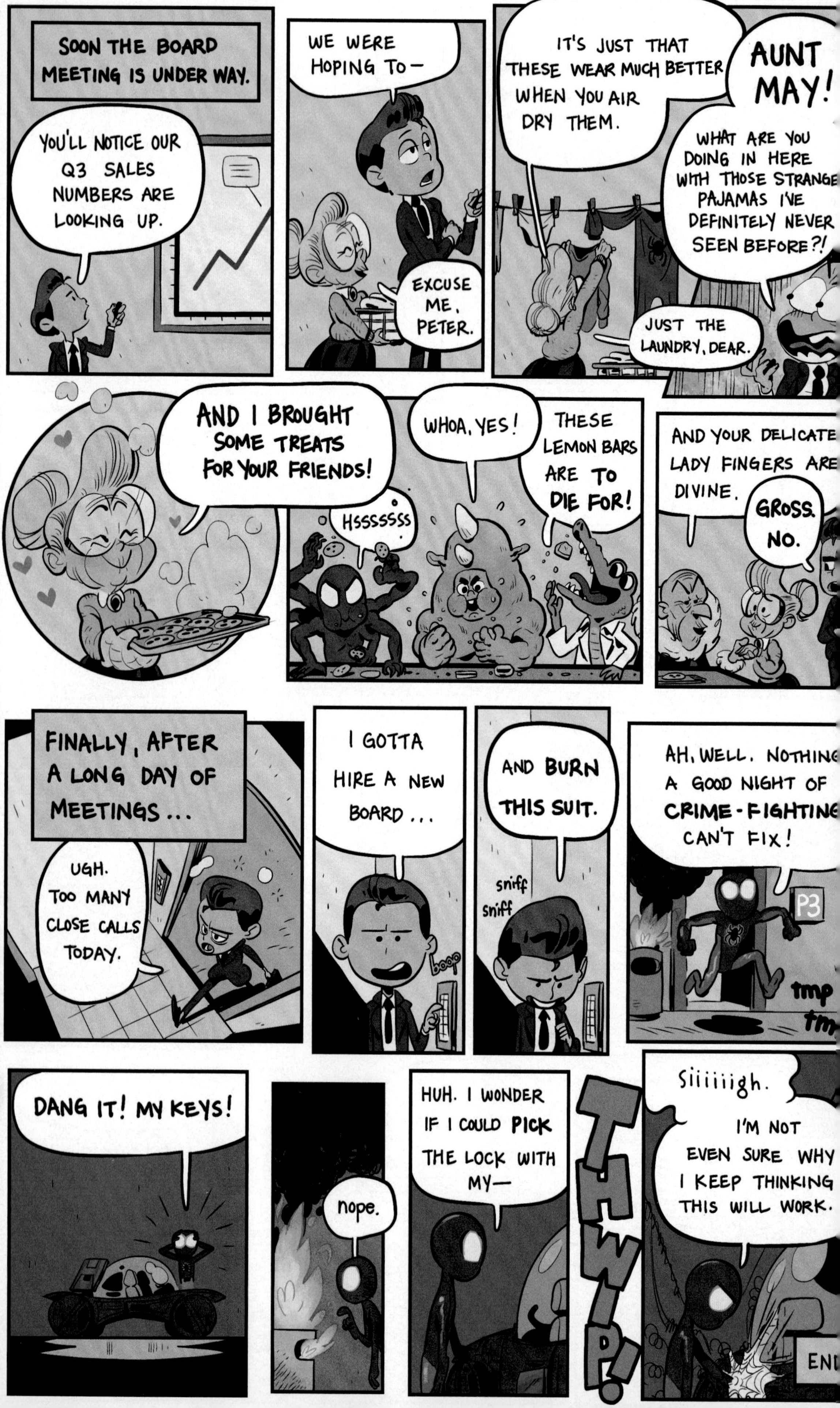
SOON THE BOARD MEETING IS UNDER WAY.
YOU'LL NOTICE OUR Q3 SALES NUMBERS ARE LOOKING UP.
WE WERE HOPING TO—
EXCUSE ME, PETER.
IT'S JUST THAT THESE WEAR MUCH BETTER WHEN YOU AIR DRY THEM.
AUNT MAY!
WHAT ARE YOU DOING IN HERE WITH THOSE STRANGE PAJAMAS I'VE DEFINITELY NEVER SEEN BEFORE?!
JUST THE LAUNDRY, DEAR.
AND I BROUGHT SOME TREATS FOR YOUR FRIENDS!
HSSSSSSS
WHOA, YES!
THESE LEMON BARS ARE TO DIE FOR!
AND YOUR DELICATE LADY FINGERS ARE DIVINE.
GROSS. NO.
FINALLY, AFTER A LONG DAY OF MEETINGS...
UGH. TOO MANY CLOSE CALLS TODAY.
I GOTTA HIRE A NEW BOARD...
boop
AND BURN THIS SUIT.
sniff
sniff
AH, WELL. NOTHING A GOOD NIGHT OF CRIME-FIGHTING CAN'T FIX!
P3
tmp
DANG IT! MY KEYS!
nope.
HUH. I WONDER IF I COULD PICK THE LOCK WITH MY—
THWIP!
Siiiiiigh.
I'M NOT EVEN SURE WHY I KEEP THINKING THIS WILL WORK.

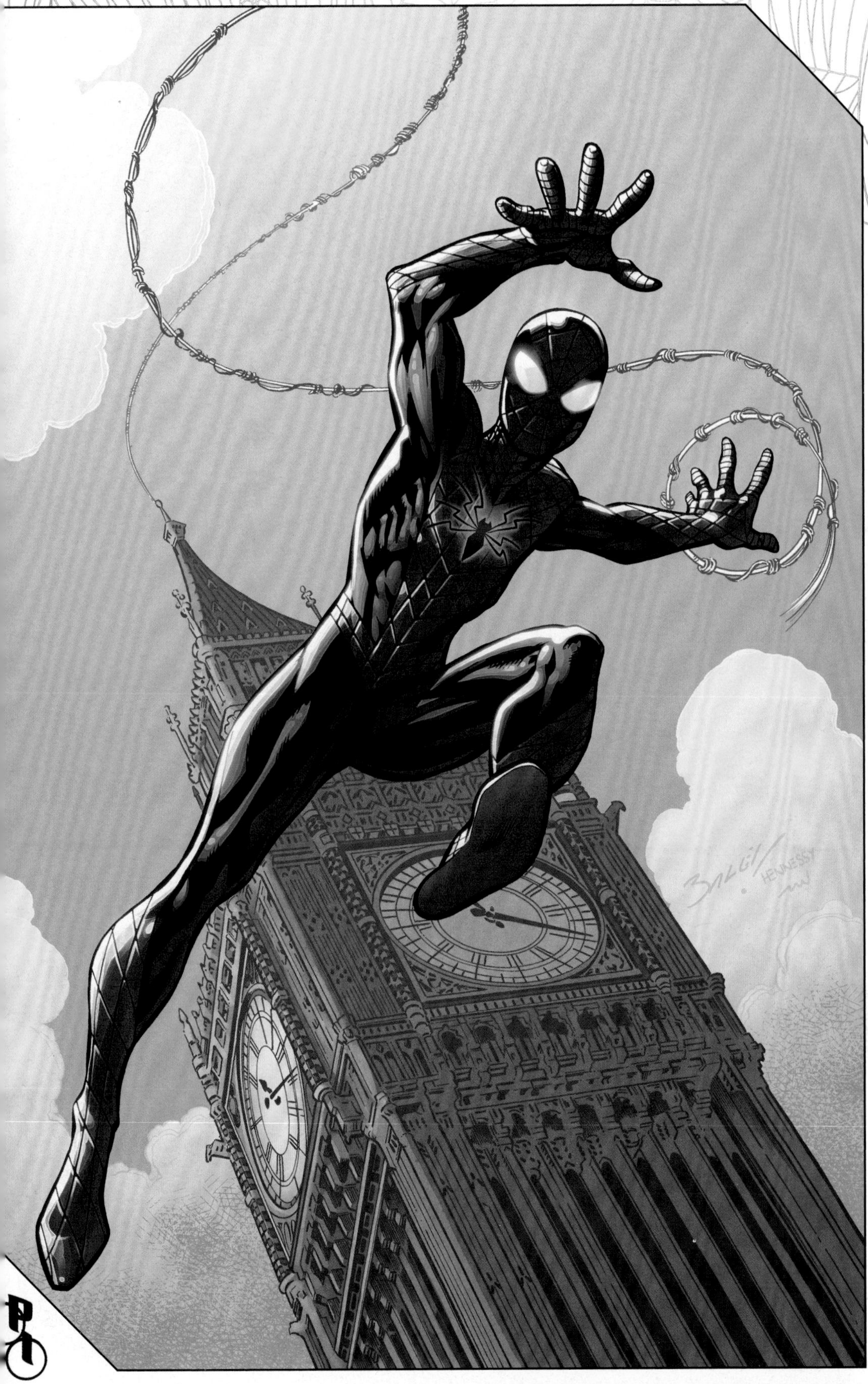

#1 VARIANT BY **MARK BAGLEY, ANDREW HENNESSY & NOLAN WOODARD**

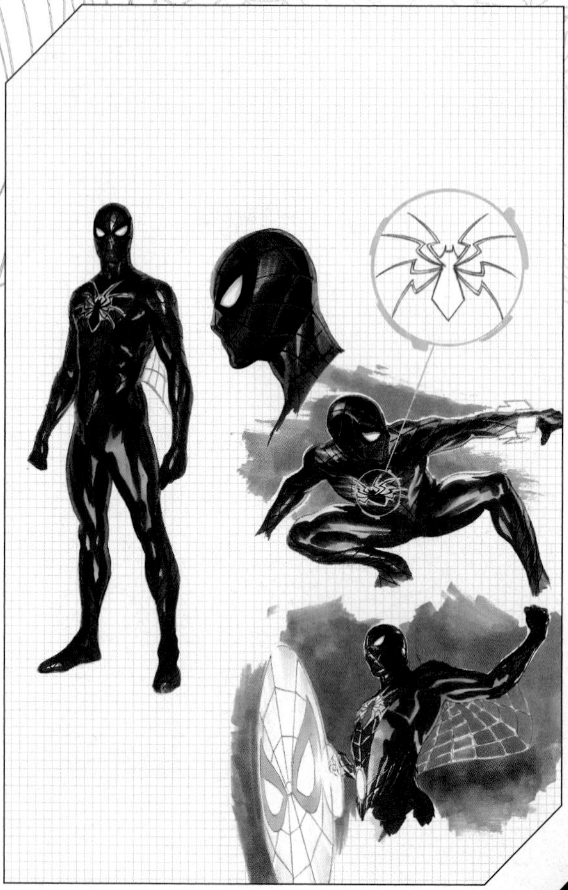

#1 DESIGN VARIANT BY **ALEX ROSS**

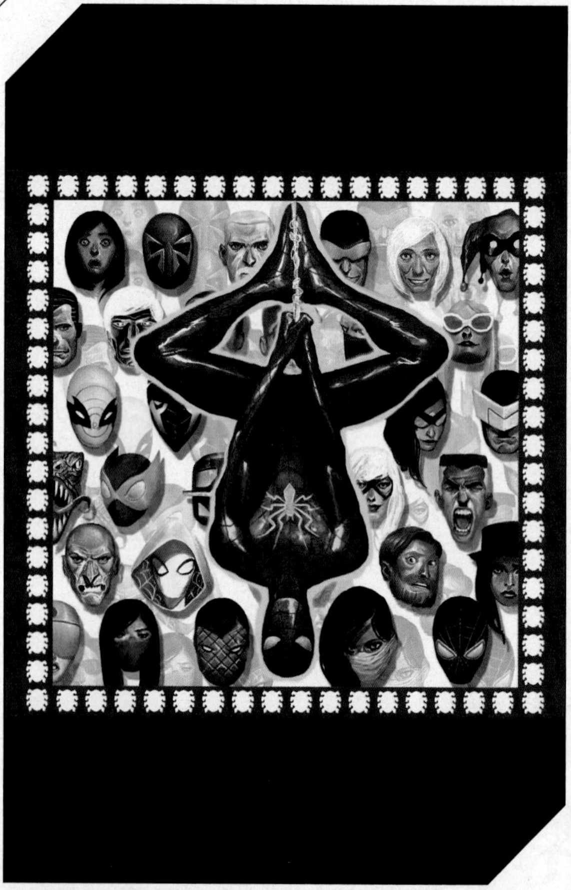

#1 HIP-HOP VARIANT BY **MIKE DEL MUNDO**

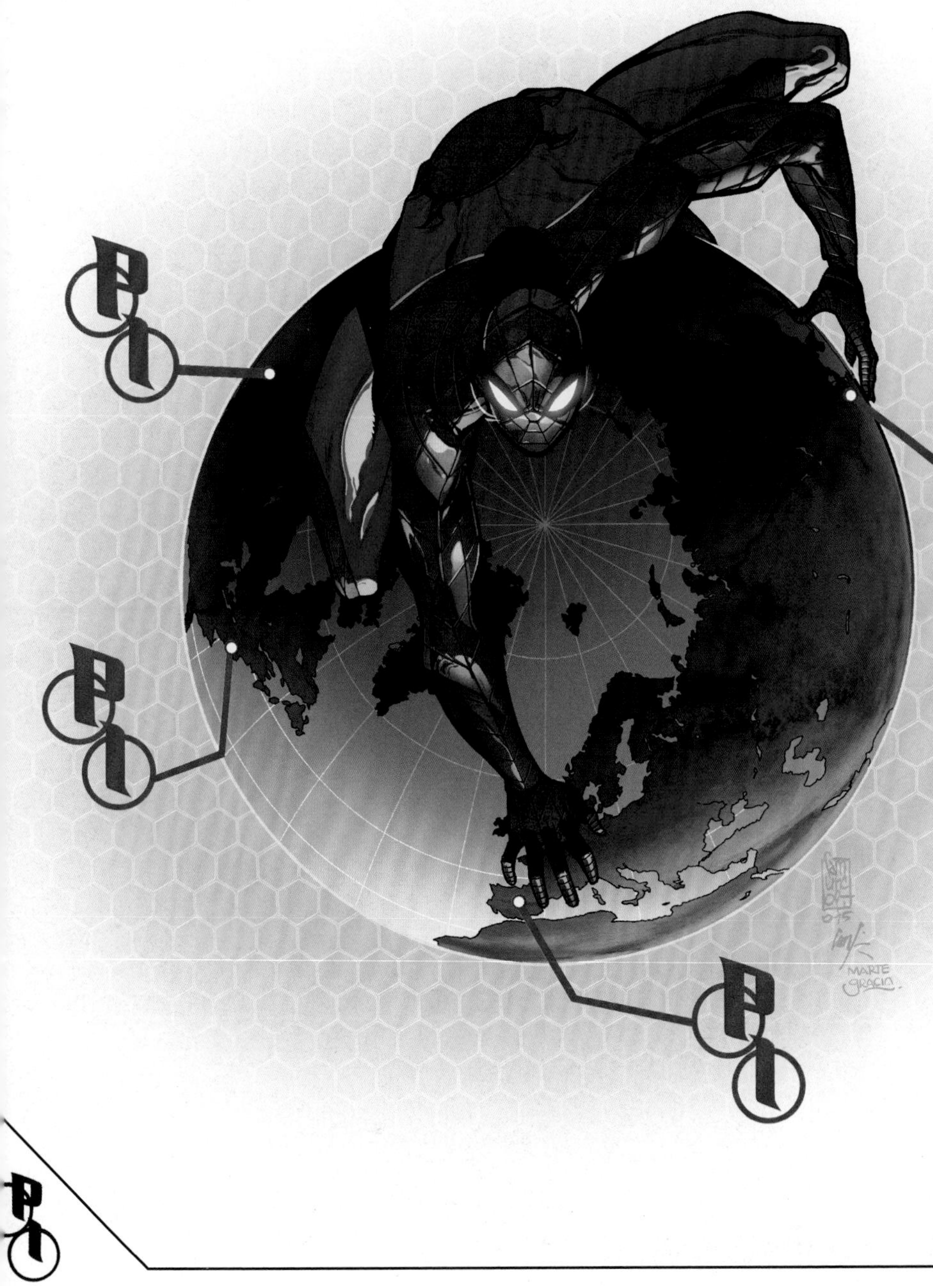

#2 VARIANT BY **GIUSEPPE CAMUNCOLI & MARTE GRACIA**

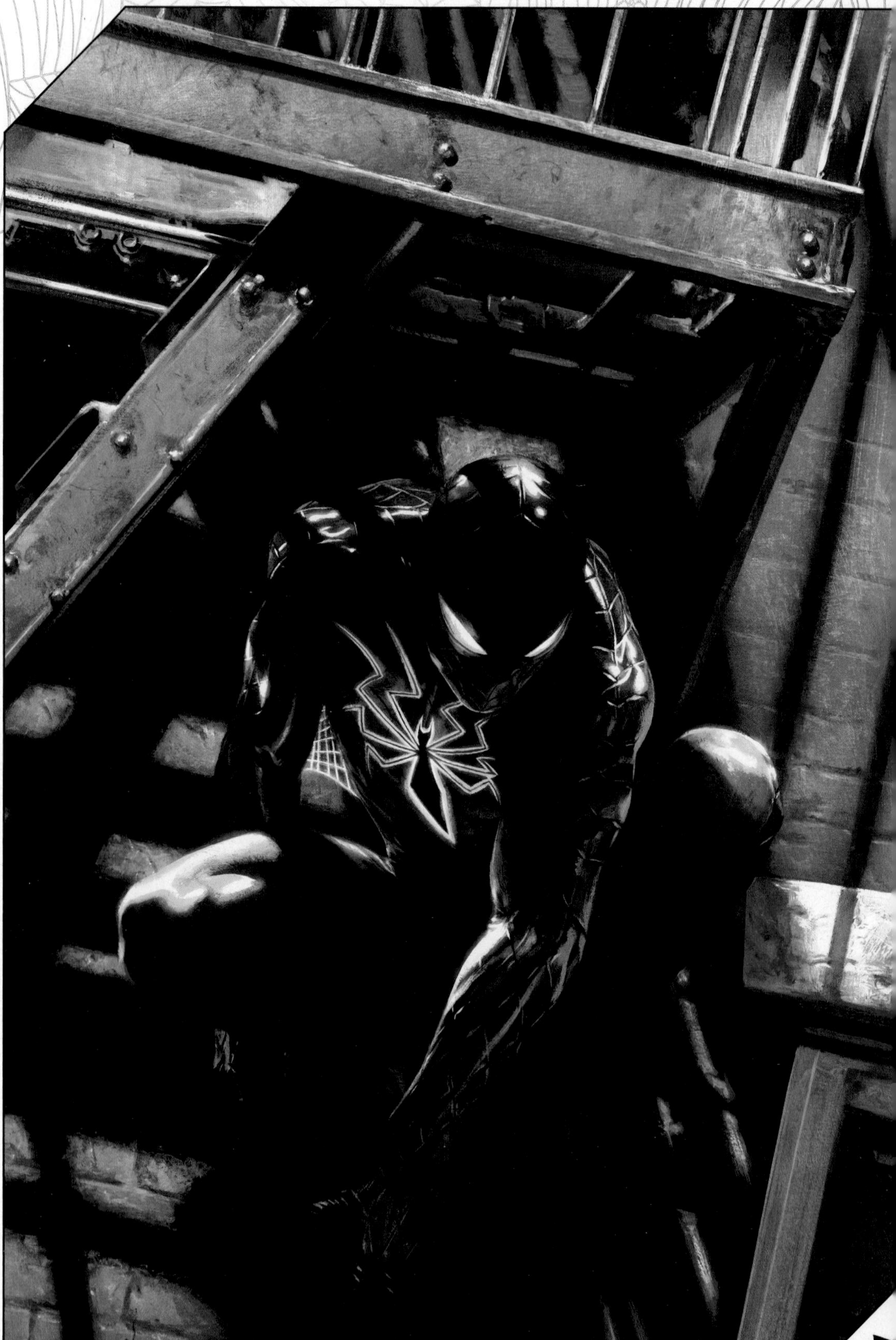

#3 VARIANT BY **GABRIELE DELL'OTTO**